VISIONARY COMPANY

Edinburgh Critical Studies in Modernist Culture
Series Editors: Tim Armstrong and Rebecca Beasley

Available

Modernism and Magic: Experiments with Spiritualism, Theosophy and the Occult
Leigh Wilson

Sonic Modernity: Representing Sound in Literature, Culture and the Arts
Sam Halliday

Modernism and the Frankfurt School
Tyrus Miller

Lesbian Modernism: Censorship, Sexuality and Genre Fiction
Elizabeth English

Modern Print Artefacts: Textual Materiality and Literary Value in British Print Culture, 1890–1930s
Patrick Collier

Cheap Modernism: Expanding Markets, Publishers' Series and the Avant-Garde
Lise Jaillant

Portable Modernisms: The Art of Travelling Light
Emily Ridge

Hieroglyphic Modernisms: Writing and New Media in the Twentieth Century
Jesse Schotter

Modernism, Fiction and Mathematics
Nina Engelhardt

Modernist Life Histories: Biological Theory and the Experimental Bildungsroman
Daniel Aureliano Newman

Modernism, Space and the City: Outsiders and Affect in Paris, Vienna, Berlin, and London
Andrew Thacker

Modernism Edited: Marianne Moore and the Dial *Magazine*
Victoria Bazin

Modernism and Time Machines
Charles Tung

Primordial Modernism: Animals, Ideas, transition (1927–1938)
Cathryn Setz

Modernism and Still Life: Artists, Writers, Dancers
Claudia Tobin

The Modernist Exoskeleton: Insects, War, Literary Form
Rachel Murray

Novel Sensations: Modernist Fiction and the Problem of Qualia
Jon Day

Hotel Modernity: Corporate Space in Literature and Film
Robbie Moore

The Modernist Anthropocene: Nonhuman Life and Planetary Change in James Joyce, Virginia Woolf and Djuna Barnes
Peter Adkins

Asbestos – The Last Modernist Object
Arthur Rose

Visionary Company: Hart Crane and Modernist Periodicals
Francesca Bratton

Forthcoming

Modernism and the Idea of Everyday Life
Leena Kore-Schröder

Modernism and Religion: Poetry and the Rise of Mysticism
Jamie Callison

Abstraction in Modernism and Modernity: Human and Inhuman
Jeff Wallace

Sexological Modernism: Queer Feminism and Sexual Science
Jana Funke

The Modernist Long Poem: Gnosticism, the First World War and the Sympathetic Imagination
Jamie Wood

Modernism, Material Culture and the First World War
Cedric Van Dijck

www.edinburghuniversitypress.com/series/ecsmc

VISIONARY COMPANY

Hart Crane and Modernist Periodicals

Francesca Bratton

EDINBURGH
University Press

Edinburgh University Press is one of the leading university presses in the UK. We publish academic books and journals in our selected subject areas across the humanities and social sciences, combining cutting-edge scholarship with high editorial and production values to produce academic works of lasting importance. For more information visit our website: edinburghuniversitypress.com

© Francesca Bratton 2022

Edinburgh University Press Ltd
The Tun – Holyrood Road
12(2f) Jackson's Entry
Edinburgh EH8 8PJ

Typeset in 10/12.5 Adobe Sabon by
IDSUK (DataConnection) Ltd

A CIP record for this book is available from the British Library

ISBN 978 1 4744 8151 9 (hardback)
ISBN 978 1 4744 8152 6 (paperback)
ISBN 978 1 4744 8153 3 (webready PDF)
ISBN 978 1 4744 8154 0 (epub)

The right of Francesca Bratton to be identified as the author of this work has been asserted in accordance with the Copyright, Designs and Patents Act 1988, and the Copyright and Related Rights Regulations 2003 (SI No. 2498).

CONTENTS

List of Tables	vi
Acknowledgements	vii
Series Editors' Preface	x
Abbreviations	xi
Dedication	xiv
Introduction	1
1 'Imagist in amber': Post-Decadent Poetry and Greenwich Village	17
2 'Are you Futuristic or are you not?': Adversarial Editing and European Avant-Gardes	56
3 'Champion mixed metaphors': Graduating to *The Dial* and *Poetry*	94
4 'A scattered chapter': Publishing *The Bridge*	128
5 'They have been lost': A Year in Mexico City	166
Epilogue: 'The Shelley of my age': Hart Crane's Afterlives	191
Appendices	201
1 An Overview of Crane's Periodical Publishers	202
2 Timeline of Crane's Periodical Publications	205
3 Timeline of Crane's Known Rejections	211
Bibliography	215
Index	242

TABLES

4.1 *The Bridge*, Section Outline 133
4.2 *The Bridge*, Overview of Periodical Publication 134

ACKNOWLEDGEMENTS

This book owes a great deal to my brilliant friends, colleagues and mentors. My sincere thanks goes to my PhD supervisor, Jason Harding. I am extremely grateful for his guidance and expertise, meticulous reading of drafts, and inspiring ideas and encouragement. I have benefited greatly from conversation with my doctoral examiners, Mark Ford and Stephen Regan, whose ideas have been vital in transforming this project from thesis to book. I am immensely grateful to Rebecca Beasley and Tim Armstrong, my series editors at EUP, who have brilliantly guided this project from proposal to final version. My thanks to my anonymous reviewers, and to the team at EUP for their care throughout the editing and publishing process: Jackie Jones, Susannah Butler, Fiona Conn, Ersev Ersoy, Caitlin Murphy and my copy-editor, Andrew Kirk.

A special thanks to Megan Girdwood for helping me over the line, reading numerous drafts and offering reassurance when I needed it most, and to Camilla Sutherland for many years of thinking and working through ideas together, shaping this project in countless ways. I thank Nicoletta Asciuto for her endless wisdom, vital conversation and our energising collaborative work, and Rick de Villiers for friendship and clear-eyed advice. I am grateful to Lucy Campbell, Jack Quin, Clare Moriarty, Fiona Mozley, Ellinor Mattson, Fraser Riddell, Tom Smith and Mika Vale for conversation, translations, hilarity and gardening tips – all of which have been invaluable. Thanks also to Kate Bone, Marc Botha, Kirsty Day, Ann-Marie Einhaus, Neilson MacKay, George Potts, Silvan Wittwer and Alex Peat for countless illuminating discussions.

ACKNOWLEDGEMENTS

I have had the huge privilege of wonderful teachers at UCL, Oxford and Durham. I am forever grateful to Alison Shell for her support and encouragement during my time at UCL and beyond, to Tara Stubbs who supervised my MSt dissertation, which sowed the seeds for this book, and to the late Michael O'Neill for discussion of this work as it progressed. This project has moved with me through several institutions and four countries, which has been at turns stimulating and challenging. I am grateful to all in the Department of English at Maynooth University and to new colleagues at Uppsala University. I have so appreciated the warm welcome, seminars and the Skrivjunta! Thanks to Rona Cran for passing on wonderful suggestions to include in my Epilogue, and to Rebecca Wright for her help with the *Broom* archive. The pandemic presented numerous difficulties during the final stages, and I am tremendously grateful to Jocelyn Wilk at Columbia University Special Collections and Philip Coleman for help in sourcing materials at the eleventh hour.

This research was made possible with doctoral funding from the AHRC and research funding from the Kluge Center at the Library of Congress, which hosted my 2013–14 AHRC International Placement Scheme award, providing me with an energising environment in which to work on this project, as well as lifelong friends. My thanks to the following archives and their incredible teams: Columbia University Library, Princeton University Library, Beinecke Rare Book and Manuscript Library, Case Western Reserve University, Kent State University Library, Ohio State University Library, the National Library of Ireland, University of Chicago Library, University of Virginia Library, University of Pennsylvania Library, the British Library, the Bodleian Library, Brotherton Library, Bibliothèque Kandinsky and the American Library in Paris.

A big thank you to Cormac O'Malley for his help with the O'Malley archive, discussion of Crane's time in Mexico and permission to include material from the Ernie O'Malley archive at NYU. Quotations from the Monroe and Zabel papers appear with the permission of the University of Chicago and quotations from the Denis Devlin papers appear with permission from the National Library of Ireland. I am grateful to Frederick Courtright at Counterpoint for permission to quote from Alfred Corn's 'The Bridge, Palm Sunday'. Every effort has been made to obtain permission to use unpublished material, but I would be grateful for any further information that might be included in future printings of this book.

Parts of this book have appeared in different forms. A version of Chapter 1 appeared as '"An Imagist in Amber": Hart Crane's Early Publications in Greenwich Village', *English*, 68.261 (2019), pp. 1–34; short segments from Chapter 4 appeared as 'Hart Crane "from this side": Edgell Rickword and *The Calendar of Modern Letters*', *PN Review*, 46.4 (2020), pp. 52–4; and sections from Chapter 2 were published as '"Knitting Needles and Poppycock": Hitherto

Unknown Prose Pieces by Hart Crane and Bibliographic Clarifications', *Notes & Queries*, 66.2 (2019), pp. 313–14.

To my dear friends Katherine Riedel, Hannah Gwatkin, Sarah Acton, Lorenz Hilfiker, Shashwat Ganguly, Rob Ellard, Becca Dean, Emily Oxley and Julian Northcote – I have so appreciated your support and I hope we can be together again soon. Thanks to my family: my brother, Christopher, my parents, Felicity and Alan James, and my grandparents, Richard and Dorcas Gould, for their phone calls, letters and sheer blind faith. I thank Hart for bringing me to Karl.

SERIES EDITORS' PREFACE

This series of monographs on selected topics in modernism is designed to reflect and extend the range of new work in modernist studies. The studies in the series aim for a breadth of scope and for an expanded sense of the canon of modernism, rather than focusing on individual authors. Literary texts will be considered in terms of contexts including recent cultural histories (modernism and magic; sonic modernity; media studies) and topics of theoretical interest (the everyday; postmodernism; the Frankfurt School); but the series will also re-consider more familiar routes into modernism (modernism and gender; sexuality; politics). The works published will be attentive to the various cultural, intellectual and historical contexts of British, American and European modernisms, and to interdisciplinary possibilities within modernism, including performance and the visual and plastic arts.

ABBREVIATIONS

The versions of 'For the Marriage of Faustus and Helen' are cited in the notes as follows: 'For the Marriage of Faustus and Helen' in *Secession* in September 1923 is referred to as 'Faustus I'. 'For the Marriage of Faustus and Helen' in *Secession* in the winter 1923–24 number is referred to as 'Faustus II'. 'Voyages' appeared in *The Little Review* in a different numbered sequence. To avoid confusion, I refer to the poems according to their *White Buildings* numerical titles, with the following clarification in footnotes: 'Voyages III' ['II' in *TLR*]. Where 'Voyages I' and 'Voyages IV' are cited in the notes according to their original publication titles ('Poster' and 'Voyages', respectively), I include the *White Buildings* sequence number: 'Poster' ['I']. All references to poems and prose are to periodical versions, unless stated otherwise.

Archival collections are abbreviated as follows:

Crane Collection	Hart Crane Collection, American Literature Collection, Beinecke Rare Book and Manuscript Library, Yale University
Crane Collection, Austin	Hart Crane Collection, Harry Ransom Centre, University of Texas at Austin
Crane family papers	Hart Crane and Family Papers, Special Collections and Archives, Kent State University

ABBREVIATIONS

Crane papers	Hart Crane Papers, Rare Book and Manuscript Library, Columbia University
Crane/Munson correspondence	Hart Crane Correspondence to Gorham Munson and George Bryan, Rare Books and Manuscript Library, Ohio State University
Devlin papers	Literary Papers of Denis Devlin, National Library of Ireland
Dial/Thayer papers	*Dial*/Scofield Thayer Papers, American Literature Collection, Beinecke Rare Book and Manuscript Library, Yale University
Josephson papers	Matthew Josephson Papers, Manuscripts Division, Department of Rare Books and Special Collections, Princeton University Library, Harvey S. Firestone Memorial Library
Loeb/*Broom* correspondence	*Broom* Correspondence of Harold Loeb, Manuscripts Division, Department of Rare Books and Special Collections, Princeton University Library, Harvey S. Firestone Memorial Library
Monroe papers	Harriet Monroe Papers, Special Collections and Research Center, University of Chicago Library
O'Malley papers	Ernie O'Malley Papers, Archives of Irish America, Tamiment Library, Elmer Holmes Bobst Library, New York University Libraries
Pound papers	Ezra Pound Papers, American Literature Collection, Beinecke Rare Book and Manuscript Library, Yale University
Virginia Quarterly papers	The Papers of *The Virginia Quarterly Review*, Special Collections, University of Virginia Library
Zabel papers	Morton Dauwen Zabel Papers, Special Collections and Research Center, University of Chicago
Zigrosser papers	Carl Zigrosser Papers, Kislak Center for Rare Books and Manuscripts, University of Pennsylvania

For my grandparents

There are no stars tonight
But those of memory.
Yet how much room for memory there is
In the loose girdle of soft rain.
									Hart Crane

INTRODUCTION

In early December 1924 Hart Crane sent a curt letter to the writer and editor Gorham Munson requesting that Munson 'take whatever decisions or formalities are necessary to "excommunicate" me from your literary circle'. The letter, which followed a fractious lunch meeting between the two friends, referred to a long-standing argument between Munson's own journal, *Secession*, and its stalking horse, *Broom*. But Crane's deep irritation with Munson (their relationship never fully recovered from Crane's missive) reveals his broader principles as a poet. 'I am not prepared to welcome threats', Crane wrote, 'from any quarters that I know of – which are based on assumptions of my literary ambitions in relation to one group, faction "opportunity," or another.'[1] *Secession* and *Broom* were both 'exile' journals – two magazines edited by Americans in Europe, following the relative strength of the post-war dollar.[2] Their argument roughly mapped on to the Paris–Dada split between André Breton (*Secession*) and Tristan Tzara (*Broom*) and the emergence of Surrealism.

Munson had wished to claim Crane as a '*Secessionist*'. This would secure Crane's affiliation with the magazine in Munson's ongoing conflict with the

---

[1] Crane to Gorham Munson, 8 December 1924, *O My Land, My Friends: The Selected Letters of Hart Crane*, ed. Langdon Hammer and Brom Weber (New York: Four Walls Eight Windows, 1997), p. 202.
[2] Malcolm Cowley, *Exile's Return: A Literary Odyssey of the 1920s* (London: Penguin, 1994), p. 133.

Broom editors and Crane's friends, Matthew Josephson and Malcolm Cowley, who had taken over the journal from its founder, Harold Loeb. Crane was wary of being seen 'in relation' to any particular aesthetic programme, both for the sake of the development of his own art and his reception in contemporary circles. Crane's letters to Munson show his keenness to resist group affiliation and his aversion to Munson's 'rigorous' aesthetic 'program'. As Crane told Munson shortly before his December letter severed their friendship, his poetry required 'a certain amount of "confusion" to bring [it] into form', which was, he wrote, in conflict with the 'program' Munson had designed for *Secession*.[3]

Crane appeared in a roll call of transatlantic periodicals that were crucial to the development and dissemination of various strands of literary modernism between his first publication in September 1916 and 27 April 1932, when Crane went overboard from the SS *Orizaba*, en route from Vera Cruz to New York.[4] During his sixteen-year career, Crane amassed 109 publications in 26 journals, and published two volumes of poetry, *White Buildings* (1926) and *The Bridge* (1930), with a third, *Key West*, in draft at the time of his death.[5] By excavating a wealth of little-studied material, I have identified forgotten works by Crane, including prose and poem variants found in periodicals. The most significant find of my research is a 1931 poem written in Mexico, 'Nopal', showing Crane's sincere engagement with the post-Mexican revolution muralists. I found the poem in the archive of Ernie O'Malley, an Irish Republican Army officer during the War of Independence and, later, writer and art collector. Even O'Malley had believed that his cache of Crane's poems from the period had been lost.[6]

Piecing together Hart Crane's life among the magazines, inhabiting a complex set of literary networks and artistic communities, maps out one swathe

---

[3] Crane to Munson, 5 December 1924, *O My Land*, pp. 200–2.
[4] Harold Hart Crone [sic], 'C33', *Bruno's Weekly*, 3.15 (23 September 1916), p. 1008. For an account of Crane's death and its aftermath, see John Unterecker, *Voyager: A Life of Hart Crane* (New York: Farrar, Straus and Giroux, 1969), pp. 742–61, and Peggy Baird Conklin (née Baird Cowley), 'The Last Days of Hart Crane', in Susan Jenkins Brown (ed.), *Robber Rocks: Letters and Memories of Hart Crane, 1923–1932* (Middletown, CT: Wesleyan University Press, 1969), pp. 147–73.
[5] See Appendix 1. This figure collects all publications, including reprints. Crane, *White Buildings* (New York: Boni and Liveright, 1926); *The Bridge* (New York: Horace Liveright, 1930). *Key West* was in its final stages but was not published as a collection. The *Key West* poems first appeared in *Collected Poems of Hart Crane*, ed. Waldo Frank (New York: Horace Liveright, 1933).
[6] Ernie O'Malley to Harriet Monroe, c. January 1925, box 23, folder 25, O'Malley papers. Previous bibliographies are Joseph Schwartz and Robert C. Schweik, *Hart Crane: A Descriptive Bibliography* (Pittsburgh, PA: University of Pittsburgh Press, 1972); H. D. Rowe, 'Hart Crane: A Bibliography', *Twentieth Century Literature*, 1.2 (1955), pp. 94–113.

of early twentieth-century literary culture, offering a portrait of the dynamic literary communities in which he was immersed.⁷ Lauren Berlant wrote that intimacy 'can be portable, unattached to a concrete space: a drive that creates spaces around it through practices'. These spaces, they wrote, are 'produced relationally'.⁸ Practices of writing, publishing and editing form literary networks, with communities creating professional and social spaces that exist beyond the 'concrete space' of a magazine office, salon or (in Crane's case) the peripatetic writer's desk in a bedroom over an undertaker's office in the Village, a steam ship cabin or a restaurant table in Paris. This book is, in some ways, an experiment in biography, simultaneously tracking one strand of a writer's life through the material expressions of their relationality: a form of literary intimacy that creates and tracks across geographical and social spaces.

Intimacy takes various forms, encompassing friendship, eroticism, collaboration, ease and understanding as much as friction, conflict and ambivalence. Crane's publishing career demonstrates his ongoing resistance to a particular group affiliation (with varying levels of success). By virtue of this aversion, he sits within a unique cross-section of early twentieth-century periodicals and artistic communities. What emerges from tracking his periodical networks is a shifting, transnational coterie poetics. He adopted post-Decadent and Symbolist poses and a coded, queer aesthetic through his early interest in Greenwich Village journals, before experimenting with Dada and Surrealist forms in the pages of *Broom*, *Secession* and *transition* in the 1920s. In the final years of his life, he attempted to graduate from avant-garde circles in the pages of *The Dial*, *Poetry*, *The New Republic* and *The Saturday Review*. Exploring Crane's relationships with literary magazines offers a vivid portrait of forgotten periodicals and their artistic communities. An analysis of Crane's poems in their original periodical contexts sheds new light on the ways in which modernist poetry fused material and aesthetic experimentation. Wedding textual and literary-critical approaches to Crane's poetry and his avant-garde milieu offers a fresh reading of his works. Reconstructing his reception history allows me to shed critical assumptions of his difficulty or 'unintelligibility'; his poetry has been variously described by even his most brilliant and sensitive critics as 'confounding', with his 'logic of metaphor' branded 'a dense thicket', 'misleadingly termed', 'illogical' and 'so snarled, so dense that one can despair of ever

---

⁷ I am thinking here of Caroline Levine, and her insistence that 'readers and writers, embodied and located in time and space, bring specific knowledge to any aesthetic object, activating and reshaping its meanings', from *Forms: Whole, Rhythm, Hierarchy, Network* (Princeton, NJ: Princeton University Press, 2015), p. 24.
⁸ Lauren Berlant, 'Intimacy: A Special Issue', *Critical Inquiry*, 24.2 (1998), pp. 281–8 (pp. 284–5).

comprehensively analysing its purpose and function', and testament to Crane's 'relentless desire' not to 'make easy peace with the reader'.[9]

While by no means truly global, but with communities clustered in the US, the UK, France, Germany, Italy, Austria and Mexico, Crane's periodical networks nonetheless show the transnational dynamics of early twentieth-century literature. Through its exploration of Crane's close engagement with periodical culture, this book offers a rich and detailed panorama of twentieth-century literary and artistic communities. Crane's publishing career introduced him to now forgotten post-Decadent bohemian magazines of 1910s Greenwich Village, Irish nationalist networks in the US and Mexico, Dada- and Surrealist-influenced expatriate publications in Paris, the major modernist magazines *The Criterion* in London and *The Dial* in New York, nationally distributed magazines *The New Republic* and *The Nation*, and, during his final year in Mexico City, muralists, writers, politicians and political radicals. This book explores the ways in which the material contexts of Crane's periodical publications enrich our understanding of his poetry and various literary movements within modernism, including post-Decadence, Imagism, Futurism and Surrealism. In doing so, I recreate a vibrant portrait of transnational early twentieth-century modernism, challenging post hoc disciplinary boundaries; what Jahan Ramazani calls the 'single-nation genealogies [that] remain surprisingly entrenched'.[10]

Periodicals can offer a useful cross-section of the literary field, relatively unencumbered by retrospectively applied hierarchies. This book builds on vital work in the study of material texts and, more narrowly, periodical studies. Broadly, this book adapts an understanding of the relationship between materiality and textual interpretation from George Bornstein, Jerome McGann and D. F. McKenzie.[11] As my approach explores the institutions within which Crane operated, I draw on foundational work in the field such as Lawrence Rainey's remarkable study of the production and transmission of literature in

---

[9] Max Eastman, 'The Cult of Unintelligibility', *Harper's Magazine*, 158.947 (1929), pp. 632–9; Harriet Monroe, 'A Discussion with Hart Crane', *Poetry*, 29.1 (1926), pp. 34–41 (p. 35); Brian Reed, 'Hart Crane's Victrola', *Modernism/Modernity*, 7.1 (2000), pp. 99–125 (p. 102); Lee Edelman, *Transmemberment of Song: Hart Crane's Anatomies* (Stanford, CA: Stanford University Press, 1987), p. 8, 14; Angela Beckett, 'The (Ill)ogic of Metaphor in Crane's *The Bridge*', *Textual Practice*, 21.1 (2011), pp. 57–80; Colm Tóibín, *New Ways to Kill Your Mother* (London: Viking, 2012), p. 246.

[10] Jahan Ramazani, *A Transnational Poetics* (Chicago: University of Chicago Press, 2009), p. 23.

[11] George Bornstein, *Material Modernism: The Politics of the Page* (Cambridge: Cambridge University Press, 2001); Jerome McGann, *The Textual Condition* (Princeton, NJ: Princeton University Press, 1991); D. F. McKenzie, *Bibliography and the Sociology of Texts* (Cambridge: Cambridge University Press, 1999).

Institutions of Modernism, Jayne Marek's consideration of marginalised figures in *Women Editing Modernism: "Little" Magazines and Literary History* and Jason Harding's study of intellectual exchange in *The Criterion: Cultural Politics and Periodical Networks in Inter-War Britain*.[12] Chris Mourant in *Katherine Mansfield and Periodical Culture* and Victoria Bazin in *Modernism Edited: Marianne Moore and* The Dial *Magazine* have usefully extended this work on material modernism to the author story.[13] I combine this approach with the conviction that a study in material history might form a biography written askance, building a perspective of a life from individual, scattered publications to the broader communities that surrounded these magazines. Melanie Micir's *The Passion Projects* offered me vital new ways to think about questions forged through literary objects and to theorise queer intimacy and the archive, which has incisively shaped the way I think of materiality and relationality in this book.[14]

My own approach is highly influenced by the transnational turn in literary and periodical studies, with Eric Bulson's *Little Magazine, World Form* offering thought-provoking models for exploring Crane's complex literary networks.[15] Jahan Ramazani's *A Transnational Poetics* has suggested novel ways to reconsider 'the cross-national mobility and migrancy of modern and contemporary poetry under the single-nation banner'.[16] Rebecca Beasley has explored the imperative question of 'nationalising the transnationalism of modernism itself', highlighting how a transnational project will 'inevitably reassert the national categories it aims to move beyond' and the 'certain national imperatives' that undercut modernist processes of (as Ramazani writes) translating 'their frequent geographic displacement and cultural alienation into a poetics

---

[12] Lawrence Rainey, *Institutions of Modernism: Literary Elites and Public Culture* (New Haven, CT: Yale University Press, 1998); Jayne Marek, *Women Editing Modernism: "Little" Magazines and Literary History* (Lexington, KY: University Press of Kentucky, 1995); Jason Harding, *The Criterion: Cultural Politics and Periodical Networks in Interwar Britain* (Oxford: Oxford University Press, 2002). Mark Morrison's *The Public Face of Modernism: Little Magazines, Audiences and Reception, 1905–1920* (Madison, WI: University of Wisconsin Press, 2001) has also been vital to my research, as has the field-defining work in Peter Brooker and Andrew Thacker (eds), *The Oxford Critical and Cultural History of Modernist Magazines, Volumes I–III* (Oxford: Oxford University Press, 2009–16).

[13] Chris Mourant, *Katherine Mansfield and Periodical Culture* (Edinburgh: Edinburgh University Press, 2019); Victoria Bazin, *Modernism Edited: Marianne Moore and* The Dial *Magazine* (Edinburgh: Edinburgh University Press, 2019).

[14] Melanie Mircir, *The Passion Projects: Modernist Women, Intimate Archives, Unfinished Lives* (Princeton, NJ: Princeton University Press, 2019).

[15] Eric Bulson, 'Little Exiled Magazines', in *Little Magazine, World Form* (New York: Columbia University Press, 2016).

[16] Ramazani, *A Transnational Poetics*, p. 23.

of bricolage and translocation, dissonance and defamiliarization'.[17] I use the term 'transnational' neutrally, and for two reasons. First, Crane's networks were not truly global, but located in the US, Mexico and across Europe. Secondly, the term 'transnational', as Randolph Bourne knew when he penned his famous 1916 essay 'Trans-national America', contains within it the fact of borders, as well as the complex histories of national and nationalist politics in the early twentieth century, and the potential for the transnational to reinscribe the national.[18] The term transnational retains a sense of dialogue between writers through magazines and travel, as well as the relative ease with which some writers – such as Crane, white, middle-class and funded by his Guggenheim in Mexico in 1931 and travelling on a US passport with a favourable exchange rate between dollar and peso – could move between spaces, even remaining in Mexico after a series of nights in jail (the result of public intoxication). This term allows me to retain, to adapt from Sara Ahmed's work, a sense of both the open and shut door, depending on which side one stands.[19]

This book aims to re-evaluate Crane's poetic development, to elucidate individual works and to re-examine themes within the body of criticism dealing with his poetry. To do so requires an integrated approach to close reading and bibliographic analysis. Franco Moretti's principle of 'distant reading', appraising larger patterns, is useful to hold in mind when mapping out the complex terrain of the transnational literary magazines of the period. This has been keenly demonstrated by Hoyt Long and Richard Jean So's crucial Global Literary Networks project, working with datasets that, as Eric Bulson puts it, have 'the power to reveal what words, magazines, texts, or authors were in vogue in any given month'.[20] As Bulson suggests, global magazine networks were less a concrete reality and more 'a fantasy about the structure of a world that modernists and avant-gardists alike wanted to see'. Bulson returns to 'some of the modernists and avant-gardists who tried to figure out how they could trace the contours of a network that somehow managed to elude them all', looking at visualisations of literary culture from the period.[21]

An integrated approach is useful here, one that is at once attuned to the broader patterns of dynamics within artistic communities (as mapped out

---

[17] Rebecca Beasley, 'Pound's New Criticism', *Textual Practice*, 24.4 (2010), pp. 649–68 (p. 650).
[18] Randolph S. Bourne, 'Trans-national America', *The Atlantic Monthly*, 118.1 (1916), pp. 86–97.
[19] Sara Ahmed, 'Slammed Doors', *Feminist Killjoys*, 17 March 2020, available at <https://feministkilljoys.com/2020/03/17/slammed-doors/> (accessed 27 July 2021).
[20] Franco Moretti, *Distant Reading* (London: Verso, 2013); Hoyt Long and Richard Jean So, 'Turbulent Flow: A Computational Model of World Literature', *Modern Language Quarterly*, 77.3 (2016), pp. 345–67; Bulson, *Little Magazine, World Form*, p. 35.
[21] Bulson, *Little Magazine, World Form*, p. 37.

through periodicals) and to the detail of aesthetic production and conversation. This book weds textual, material, bibliographic and literary-critical approaches, resisting the idea that bibliographic and textual analysis should be treated separately, with periodicals understood as containing discrete caches of information or sources of data with no connection to the literary and artistic works that they published. As Eric B. White writes, 'textual studies, literary-historical analysis and transnational cultural studies can form complementary matrices of meaning'. Building on White's project in *Transatlantic Avant-Gardes: Little Magazines and Localist Modernism*, and his suggestion that 'bibliographic codes . . . expose tangible intellectual contact between international and local avant-gardes',[22] here I show that it is often through a granular examination of shared aesthetic experiments and conversations that overarching patterns are able to come into focus. From the polyvocal, polyglot modernism of *The Pagan* which expressed the multilingual reality of 1910s Greenwich Village, to conversations on Dada and Surrealism in the pages of *1924*, based in Woodstock, NY, examining the transnational groups of writerly communities within which Crane developed his poetry shows in precise detail the 'globe-traversing influences, energies, and resistances that – far from being minor deviations from nation-based fundamentals – styled and shaped poetry in English from the modernist era to the present', as Ramazani writes in *A Transnational Poetics*.[23]

Crane operated within a shifting field of variously interconnected journals, jostling for territory in a dynamic literary marketplace.[24] The precise nature of, in Bourdieu's terms, the 'cultural capital' at stake for each journal was naturally different. For *Secession*, for instance, there was an avant-garde cachet in a highly restricted, specialised audience, with a print run of 500, airing the internal arguments of the coterie.[25] For *The Dial*, there was value in a broader appeal and a significantly higher readership (9,500 in 1922).[26] This necessitated the opposite approach to Munson's, as Scofield Thayer and James Sibley Watson Jr put it, avoiding the coterie debates that might turn *The Dial* into a 'specialist enterprise'.[27] Crane's unique trajectory through the literary field makes

---

[22] Eric B. White, *Transatlantic Avant-Gardes: Little Magazines and Localist Modernism* (Edinburgh: Edinburgh University Press, 2013), p. 14.
[23] Ramazani, *A Transnational Poetics*, p. 23.
[24] See Pierre Bourdieu, *The Field of Cultural Production* (Cambridge: Polity, 1996).
[25] Gorham Munson, *The Awakening Twenties: A Memory-History of A Literary Period* (Baton Rouge, LA: Louisiana State University Press, 1985), p. 167.
[26] Lawrence Rainey, *Revisiting "The Waste Land"* (New Haven, CT: Yale University Press, 2005), p. 91.
[27] Scofield Thayer and James Sibley Watson, 'Statement of Intent', box 9, folder 309, *Dial/Thayer papers*.

his engagement with these publications revealing not only of his own poetic development and reception, but of the field's wider machinations, showing the dynamics of cultural capital operating between the broader appeal of *The Dial* and the highly specialist, avant-garde 'exile' journals.

By exploring Crane's complex networks of influence and exchange, this book resists the temptation to assert the overarching cultural importance of one poet or group. Part of my work here, rather, is to uncover the beginnings of canon formations, alliances and arguments and exclusionary practices that were, retrospectively, the overture to New Critical approaches to literary studies. As Harold Bloom, John T. Irwin, Brom Weber, R. W. Butterfield, Brian M. Reed, Paul Giles and Niall Munro have shown, Crane's poetry is attentive to the language and formal movements of his antecedents (Whitman, Dickinson, Melville, Mallarmé, Rimbaud, Swinburne, Wilde, Poe – among others).[28] As well as his clear inheritances from previous generations of poets, writers and artists, Crane's poetry was energised by the aesthetic questions that coursed through debate and artistic experimentation in his contemporary periodical culture. His poetry can be seen afresh by considering, in McKenzie's terms, 'the sociology of texts' and their 'processes of transmission, including production and reception'.[29]

I am able to follow in the footsteps of Thomas E. Yingling, in his vital *Hart Crane and the Homosexual Text*, Lee Edelman in *Transmemberment of Song* and Catherine A. Davies's *Whitman's Queer Children*,[30] but, alongside Niall Munro in *Hart Crane's Queer Modernist Aesthetic*, I argue that as well as an identifiable historical genealogy, Crane's queer poetics can be seen to have been forged within contemporary writerly and artistic communities.[31] The risks of publishing queer literature were high, as the publishers of Chicago's *Friendship and Freedom* found out after just two issues, when Henry Gerber, the newsletter's editor and founder of the city's Society for

---

[28] Harold Bloom, *The Anatomy of Influence: Literature as a Way of Life* (New Haven, CT: Yale University Press, 2011); John T. Irwin, *Appollinaire [sic] Lived in Paris, I Live in Cleveland, Ohio: Hart Crane's Poetry* (Baltimore, MD: Johns Hopkins University Press, 2011); Brom Weber, *Hart Crane: A Biographical and Critical Study* (New York: Russell and Russell, 1970); R. W. Butterfield, *The Broken Arc: A Study of Hart Crane* (Edinburgh: Oliver and Boyd, 1969); Brian Reed, *Hart Crane: After his Lights* (Tuscaloosa, AL: University of Alabama Press, 2006); Paul Giles, *Hart Crane: The Contexts of 'The Bridge'* (Cambridge: Cambridge University Press, 1986); Niall Munro, *Hart Crane's Queer Modernist Aesthetic* (Basingstoke: Palgrave, 2015).

[29] McKenzie, *Bibliography and the Sociology of Texts*, pp. 12–13.

[30] Thomas E. Yingling, *Hart Crane and the Homosexual Text* (Chicago: University of Chicago Press, 1990); Edelman, *Transmemberment of Song*; Catherine A. Davies, *Whitman's Queer Children* (London: Bloomsbury Academic, 2012).

[31] Munro, *Hart Crane's Queer Modernist Aesthetic*, pp. 4, 14, 185.

Human Rights, was jailed for two days after printing the second number.[32] In London, a lonely hearts magazine founded by Alfred Barrett, *The Link: A Monthly Social Medium For Lonely People*, was investigated by the Metropolitan Police for publishing requests for those seeking, in the parlance of the adverts, 'correspondence with own sex'. Barrett was imprisoned for two years.[33] The codes of Crane's poems were, I suggest here, influenced by community attempts to navigate censorship. As well as his saturation in Whitman's erotic language, Crane adopted the post-Decadent, queer-coded tropes of Greenwich Village publications. The extent to which these codes were understood within his own writerly circles was made clear by poems 'after' Crane written by Edwin Seaver, the editor of *1924*, and his friend Malcolm Cowley, which playfully inhabit the erotic language Crane had established. As Kadji Amin, Amber Jamilla Musser and Roy Pérez write: 'Form informs queerness, and queerness is best understood as a series of relations to form.'[34] Crane's 'logic of metaphor' sprang, I argue, from his development of his queer poetics. Its fugitive movements are at once exhilarating experiments and necessary precautions against a censorious society.

Crane's relationships with periodical publishers, editors and artistic communities decisively shaped his poetry, but also show their marks in the reception of his oeuvre. The legacies of these immediate appraisals can, as I discuss, be seen to have determined the direction of later criticism in both productive and troubling ways. In his landmark study, *Janus-Faced Modernism*, Langdon Hammer sets out the overbearing importance of Allen Tate's criticism to Crane's reception, such that 'Crane scholars have always had to take it into account; but they typically do so in order to *extricate* Crane from Tate'.[35] My work builds on this idea, but argues that Crane's immediate reception was built within a broader network of critics and institutions that – Tate included – established a critical language for Crane that has continued to shape narratives of his life and work. I differ in that I view Tate's central criticism as logically unsound: the idea of 'confusion', 'failure', 'illogic', 'unintelligibility' that dogs Crane's poetry. Such complaints, voiced contemporaneously by Tate, Harriet Monroe, Yvor Winters and Max Eastman (among others), are founded on a category mistake: that logic is in any way the concern of poetry or, more specifically in Crane's case,

---

[32] Jim Kepner and Stephen O. Murray, 'Henry Gerber', in *Before Stonewall: Activists for Gay and Lesbian Rights in Context*, ed. Vern L. Bullough (Abingdon: Routledge, 2008), p. 27.
[33] See H. G. Cocks, *Classified: The Secret History of the Personal Column* (London: Random House, 2009).
[34] Kadji Amin, Amber Jamilla Musser and Roy Pérez, 'Queer Form: Aesthetics, Race, and the Violences of the Social', *ASAP/Journal*, 2.2 (2017), pp. 227–39 (p. 228).
[35] Langdon Hammer, *Hart Crane and Allen Tate: Janus-Faced Modernism* (Princeton, NJ: Princeton University Press, 1993), p. xiv.

metaphor.³⁶ Meanwhile, charges from Conrad Aiken and Marianne Moore that Crane's poetry 'lacked discipline' are interlinked with the period's culture of homophobia, whereby Crane's homosexuality is equated with a general 'decadence' of character and lack of discipline that reveals itself in his poetry.³⁷

Delving into Crane's periodical networks has prompted the development of striking new approaches to considering literary form. Seemingly practical aspects of literary work (labour) have surprising aesthetic dimensions.³⁸ I argue that periodical publishing can be understood as part of a poem's form, emphasising its collage or fragmentary construction. The fragmentary, non-linear publication of *The Bridge* is, then, understood as central its aesthetic form – with implications for similar long poems of the period.³⁹ This project develops theories on the role of editorial practice in creativity, including the concept of 'adversarial editing' (in the case of *Broom* and *Secession*) and creative-critical editing work (in the cases of Marianne Moore and Harriet Monroe). As Bulson cannily points out in his chapter on 'Little Exiled Magazines', '[i]nstead of fostering the idea of a unified international community located somewhere "out there," the exile magazine could also reinforce the distance between contributors, editors, and their audience'. Bulson relates this to the 'multiple sites for distribution' that 'generated a cultural field that made it impossible for everyone involved to get their coordinates right and figure out just where they fit in and with whom'.⁴⁰ Building on this, I suggest that transnationalism and the 'exile' position were used as much to reassert distance and difference, reinscribing antagonistic relationships, as they were to build fruitful points of contact. An exploration of 'alliances of style and sensibility'⁴¹ between writerly communities should, then, be considered alongside more antagonistic relationships; transnational magazines such as *Broom* and *Secession* developed their sense of editing principles through adversarial contact (and, in turn, Crane negotiated between their aesthetic positions in 'For the Marriage of Faustus and Helen'). This is understood

---

³⁶ Allen Tate, 'Hart Crane and the American Mind', *Poetry*, 40.4 (1932), pp. 210–16; Monroe, 'A Discussion', p. 35; Yvor Winters, 'The Progress of Hart Crane', review of Crane, *The Bridge* (1930), *Poetry*, 36.3 (1930), pp. 153–65; Max Eastman, 'Poets Talking to Themselves', *Harper's Magazine*, 163.977 (1931), pp. 563–74; Eastman, 'The Cult of Unintelligibility'.

³⁷ Conrad Aiken, 'Briefer Mention: *White Buildings*', review of Crane, *White Buildings* (1926), *The Dial*, 82.4 (1927), p. 432; Marianne Moore, 'The Art of Poetry No. 4', interview by Donald Hall, *The Paris Review*, 26 (summer–fall 1961), pp. 41–66.

³⁸ As Peter Riley shows in *Against Vocation: Whitman, Melville, Crane and the Labors of American Poetry* (Oxford: Oxford University Press, 2019).

³⁹ There is, of course, a basic generic difference between a collection such as *White Buildings*, assembled retrospectively, and a planned, single-volume long poem such as *The Bridge*.

⁴⁰ Bulson, *Little Magazine, World Form*, p. 153.

⁴¹ Ibid., p. 153.

here according to Chantal Mouffe's definition of 'agonism', whereby conflict is not so much a 'struggle between enemies' but between 'adversaries', suggesting mutual respect, whereby the adversary's existence 'is perceived as legitimate'.[42] As such, the concept of 'adversarial editing' is coined to convey and explain the aesthetic identity of certain little magazines formed as oppositional to other magazines, and to explain Crane's negotiations between surrealist forms and 'machine-age' ideas in his poetry.[43]

Alongside the idea of adversarial editing, I develop a theory of creative-critical editing work, centred on Moore's editing of Crane at *The Dial*. I understand Moore's famous edit of 'The Wine Menagerie', in contrast to existing scholarship, as a work of creative criticism that undercuts Crane's 'logic of metaphor'.[44] Moore's reduction cleaves more closely to her own belief in 'the connection between criticism and creation' than an attempt to have the poem succinctly express Crane's intentions.[45] The critical undercurrents of Moore's edit, published as 'Again' in *The Dial* in 1926, were made explicit in Harriet Monroe's letter exchange with Crane, published in *Poetry* in October of the same year.[46] These two interventions by established and authoritative editors established a critical language for dealing with (and often dismissing) Crane's poetry.

Chapter 1 explores the Midwesterner Crane's entry into the lively literary and artistic communities of New York's *quartier Latin*, Greenwich Village, which, in the late 1910s, teemed with bookshops, theatres, cheap restaurants, galleries, artists' studios, the headquarters of civil and political organisations, literary salons and magazine offices.[47] Here I reconstruct his immersion in contemporary literary culture, carefully reading and responding to contemporaneous literary debates from his first publications in Guido Bruno's *Bruno's Weekly* (1915–16), *Bruno's Bohemia* (1918), and Joseph Kling's *The Pagan* (1916–21), magazines virtually absent from contemporary periodical studies scholarship, yet vital to Crane's development and that of many other international writers

---

[42] Chantal Mouffe, *For a Left Populism* (London: Verso, 2019), p. 31.
[43] A common term, 'machine age' was used as early as 1915 in Paul L. Haviland, 'We are Living in the Age of the Machine', *291*, 1.7–8 (1915), p. 1.
[44] For alternative interpretations of the Crane/Moore incident, see John Emil Vincent, *Queer Lyrics: Difficulty and Closure in American Poetry* (Basingstoke: Palgrave, 2002); Bazin, *Modernism Edited*, pp. 107–39; Yingling, *Hart Crane and the Homosexual Text*, pp. 108–9; Hammer, *Janus-Faced Modernism*, p. 145; Munro, *Hart Crane's Queer Modernist Aesthetic*, pp. 133; 189; Warner Berthoff, *Hart Crane: A Reintroduction* (Minneapolis, MN: University of Minnesota Press, 1989), p. 33.
[45] Crane and Marianne Moore, 'Again', *The Dial*, 80.5 (1926), p. 370.
[46] Monroe, 'A Discussion', pp. 34–41.
[47] Guido Bruno, 'Bohemia Over There', *Bruno's Bohemia*, 1.1 (1918), p. 1; Bruno, 'Bohemia Over Here', *Bruno's Bohemia*, 1.1 (1918), p. 2.

of the period.⁴⁸ Through archival research, this chapter offers crucial bibliographic clarifications to Crane's publishing record at *The Pagan*, introducing readers to a previously unattributed critical review, 'Tragi-Comique'.⁴⁹ Here I trace Crane's assimilation of 'emergent and vestigial styles' (to borrow Langdon Hammer's useful phrase) to his early involvement with the complex literary networks of Greenwich Village.⁵⁰ The chapter builds on work by Lee Edelman, Niall Munro and Thomas Yingling in focusing on Crane's development of a queer aesthetic, but diverges from extant scholarship by locating this sensibility in Crane's involvement with the literary communities of Greenwich Village, arguing that his early exposure to these literary codes was formative to his later poetry. Adapting Bornstein's useful concept, commentary on Crane's poetry, too, never quite escaped the 'aura' of original publication. Patterns established in his immediate reception were reproduced in later criticism, and for Crane's contemporaneous reviewers who set the tone of his reception, he never quite escaped his association with the Decadent literary fashions of the Village.⁵¹

Crane distanced himself from the Village journals in 1919, marking an aesthetic shift from the sincere experiments in post-Decadence and Imagism that characterise his early verse. Crane moved towards a cosmopolitan, 'machine-age' aesthetic and, in 'For the Marriage of Faustus and Helen', began to experiment with material poetic forms in which publishing becomes part of a poem's formal structure – in this case, emphasising its triptych arrangement. Chapter 2 examines Crane's interactions with the complex, transnational avant-garde networks of post-war Paris, Berlin, Vienna and Rome in the early 1920s through the US journals (some of which were edited from continental Europe) *Broom* (1921–23), *Secession* (1922–24), *Gargoyle* (1921–22), *1924* (1924) and *S4N* (1919–25). Through the discussion of Crane's publishing networks, this chapter introduces readers to a new piece of prose by Crane (written under a pseudonym) and highlights a variant of a poem missed by his bibliographers.⁵² Here the concept of 'adversarial editing' is introduced to convey and explain the

---

⁴⁸ See Victoria Kingham, 'Commerce, Little Magazines and Modernity', PhD thesis, De Montfort University, 2009. Crane's biographers have noted his work for *The Cleveland Plain Dealer*, but his tasks appear to have been mainly administrative. See Unterecker, *Voyager*, pp. 118–19.
⁴⁹ Crane, 'Tragi-Comique', *The Pagan*, 2.12–3.1 (1918), pp. 54–6. Further details in Francesca Bratton, '"Knitting Needles and Poppycock": Hitherto Unknown Prose Pieces by Hart Crane and Bibliographic Clarifications', *Notes & Queries*, 66.2 (2019), pp. 313–14.
⁵⁰ Adopted from Hammer's brief sketch of the New Orleans-based *Double Dealer*, a '"Janus-faced" enterprise, mixing emergent and vestigial styles in instructive ways', *Janus-Faced Modernism*, p. 233, n. 2.
⁵¹ Bornstein, *Material Modernism*, p. 7.
⁵² 'Religious Gunman' [Hart Crane], 'Knitting Needles and Poppycock', *1924*, 4 (December 1924), pp. 136–9; Crane, 'Voyages', *1924*, 4 (December 1924), p. 119.

aesthetic identity of certain little magazines formed in agonistic (Mouffe) opposition to other publications. In these cases, disagreement and the deliberate pursuit of distance (both geographically and in terms of ideas) was key to the magazine's operation and to the exploration of ideas in their pages. Resituating Crane's work within these adversarial early 1920s publications reveals the debts the poems 'For the Marriage of Faustus and Helen' and 'Voyages' owe to Crane's negotiation of *Broom*'s Dadaist impulses and the proto-Surrealist experiments of *Secession*. John T. Irwin's *Hart Crane's Poetry* has usefully explored canonical influences on Crane's work, including the overlooked presence of figures such as D. H. Lawrence, Henry Adams and Matthew Arnold. In contrast to Irwin's focus on mythic and canonical intertextuality, and his argument that Crane's 'logic of metaphor' owed debts to Symbolism, this chapter argues that the 'logic' is directly engaged with contemporary developments in the European avant-garde.[53]

Chapter 3 advances a theory of creative-critical editing work, relating to Marianne Moore's editing of Crane at *The Dial* (1920–29) and Harriet Monroe's framing of his work at *Poetry* (1912–present), and I bring to light two pseudonymous reviews by Crane in *The Dial*.[54] I build on my contextualisation of Crane's poetry among post-Decadent and exile journals by foregrounding how the 'aura' of the Village affected his uneasy reception at *The Dial* and *Poetry* in the mid-1920s. Crane's restrained early submissions to *The Dial* and the wide acclaim for 'My Grandmother's Love Letters' as his first supposedly mature poem are considered a brief entente, lost as Crane's more recognisable style of associative, juxtaposed metaphor was met with consistent rejections. Crane's difficult relationship with *The Dial* is encapsulated in Moore's notorious and dramatic edit of 'The Wine Menagerie', which cut the poem from 49 to 18 lines – a series of moves showing, for Bazin, Moore's 'pleasures of compression'.[55] I see Moore's creative criticism, however, as undercutting Crane's 'logic of metaphor' in a fundamental misapprehension of the workings of his poetry. Building on Gordon Tapper's reading of Crane's representation of the body in 'The Wine Menagerie' in *The Machine that Sings: Modernism, Hart Crane and the Culture of the Body*, I argue that Moore saps Crane's poem of its erotic charge as she shifts the

---

[53] Irwin, *Hart Crane's Poetry*, p. 382.
[54] Crane, 'Briefer Mention: Romer Wilson, *The Grand Tour*', review of Romer Wilson, *The Grand Tour of Alphonse Marichaud* (1923), *The Dial*, 76.3 (1924), p. 198; Crane, 'Briefer Mention: Thomas Moult, *The Best Poems of 1922*', review of Thomas Moult, *The Best Poems of 1922* (1923), *The Dial*, 76.3 (1924), p. 200. Documented in Nicholas Joost and Alvin Sullivan, '*The Dial*': *Two Author Indexes: Anonymous and Pseudonymous Contributors; Contributors in Clipsheets* (Carbondale, IL: Southern Illinois University, 1971).
[55] Bazin, *Modernism Edited*, p. 110.

work's metaphors to consider artistic rather than bodily 'thresholds'.[56] Reading Moore's edit alongside Monroe's 'A Discussion with Hart Crane' (letters published alongside 'At Melville's Tomb' in which she insisted Crane provide an authorial explanation of his 'confused mixed metaphors'), I suggest that these interventions established a critical language for dealing with (and often dismissing) Crane's poetry.[57] Negative responses to Crane's poetry often gestured towards the 1926 'Discussion'. Crane's own understudied letter of defence, in which he effectively suggests that Monroe's appraisal of his poetry is rooted in a simple category mistake (that logic is not the concern of metaphor), is reclaimed as a vital deflection of Moore's and Monroe's critiques, one which he was forced to articulate in the real-time argumentative literary culture of periodicals.

The Bridge sees Crane's material experimentations find their fullest form. In Chapter 4 I explore the periodical contexts of *The Bridge*. This is the first sustained and critical examination of the complicated genesis and publication of Crane's long poem. Here I show that he deliberately split the poem into fragments published across seven different journals on both sides of the Atlantic. The form of *The Bridge* is seen as a fertile exchange with Crane's various periodical cultures, an experiment with the literary fragment and processes of reassembly. Like Niall Munro, I am sceptical of the usefulness of the epic classification in relation to the poem.[58] Crane's publishing practices, I argue, constitute an aesthetic programme for *The Bridge*: the poem finds its form through dissemination and reconstitution via little magazines, a deliberately 'scattered chapter' (to borrow one of Crane's own characteristically self-aware phrases).[59] Its rejection of linear, narrative progressive structure in favour of a collaged, Cubist repetition of fragmentary images and rhythms is contextualised not only in terms of its dissemination in multiple periodicals, but Crane's long-standing interest in collage and fragment forms.[60] The status of *The Bridge* as an incoherent if grand failure is excavated as a critical truism propagated in magazines (such as *Poetry*) by critics Allen Tate and Yvor Winters, and highly influential on subsequent criticism of the poem. Close attention to the poem's original

---

[56] Gordon Tapper, *The Machine that Sings: Modernism, Hart Crane, and the Culture of the Body* (Abingdon: Routledge, 2006).

[57] Monroe, 'A Discussion', p. 35.

[58] Munro, *Hart Crane's Queer Modernist Aesthetic*, p. 78. Daniel Gabriel understands *The Bridge* as 'lyric-epic dialogism'; see Gabriel, *Hart Crane and the Modernist Epic: Canon and Genre Formation in Crane, Pound, Eliot and Williams* (Basingstoke: Palgrave, 2007).

[59] Crane, 'At Melville's Tomb', *Poetry*, 29.1 (1926), p. 25.

[60] As noted in 1930 by Percy Hutchinson, 'Hart Crane's Cubistic Poetry in *The Bridge*', *The New York Times*, 27 April 1930, p. 2.

fragmentary publication history and its 'processes of transmission' (McKenzie) challenge the idea of the poem as an incoherent failure, instead providing a radical rereading of the poem as a collage or Cubist work eschewing linearity of narrative and extolling beauty through abruptly juxtaposed images and repeated rhythmic effects.

Chapter 5 reassesses Crane's final year, introducing a lost poem, 'Nopal', from his unrealised Mexican epic.[61] By examining Crane's publications from the late 1920s, *Key West*, and his literary networks in Mexico during his Guggenheim Fellowship, I am able to challenge the myth of the self-destructive poet in a year of creative drought.[62] In the last years of his life, Crane published in nationally distributed, mass-circulation magazines, featuring in *Vanity Fair* in 1929, with poems in these periodicals consolidating his reputation.[63] This chapter discusses Crane's attempts to raise his profile as a reviewer, and his increasing interest in writing on the visual arts, as demonstrated by his early essay on the photographer H. W. Minns, and a note in a brochure advertising an evening with David Siqueiros at Casino Español in February 1932, marking the closure of his exhibition with a talk by the painter, written following conversations with Ernie O'Malley, a leading Republican intellectual during the Irish revolution (1916–23).[64] Crane's friendship with O'Malley provides an unprecedented insight into his Mexico years and the literary and artistic networks between the Global South, the US and the Irish Republic.

The book concludes by moving from the communities of Crane's lifetime to explore the ghostly 'address of friendship' in poems to and about him.[65] Here I briefly consider elegies to Crane published in *Poetry* and examine the magazine's ongoing curation of his reception, including its publication of William Logan's essay 'On Reviewing Hart Crane' in October 2008.[66] The epilogue concludes with a critical examination of patterns in poems to Crane published elsewhere, and the profound influence of Crane on twentieth-century and contemporary poets (while his critical reputation has somewhat languished),

---

[61] Crane, 'Nopal', box 2, folder 59, O'Malley papers.
[62] As seen in articles including Beatrice Pire's '"If you could die": Hart Crane's "Accursed Share"', *European Journal of American Studies*, 13.2 (2018), pp. 1–11.
[63] Unsigned, 'Singers of the New Age: A Group of Distinguished Poets Who Have Found Fresh Material in the American Scene', *Vanity Fair*, 33.1 (1929), p. 89.
[64] Crane, 'A Note on H.W. Mimms [sic]', *The Little Review*, 7.3 (1920), p. 60; Crane, 'Note on the Paintings of David Siqueiros', *La Exposición Siqueiros* (Mexico City: Casino Español, 1931), unpaginated.
[65] Jacques Khalip, 'Cruising Among Ghosts: Hart Crane's Friends', *Arizona Quarterly: A Journal of American Literature, Culture, and Theory*, 64.2 (2008), pp. 65–93 (pp. 67, 87).
[66] William Logan, 'On Reviewing Hart Crane', *Poetry*, 193.1 (2008), pp. 53–9.

including Geoffrey Hill, Mark Ford, Eileen Myles and Adrienne Rich.[67] I see poems such as Hill's 'Improvisations for Hart Crane', Ford's 'The Death of Hart Crane', Myles's 'hart!' and Rich's 'The Night Has a Thousand Eyes' as forming a body of creative criticism that challenges the dominant critical narratives that surround Crane's poetry. I argue that these poems form, to different degrees, critical essays-in-verse on the poet and his legacy. In the opening lines of his 'Improvisations for Hart Crane', Hill passes astute and sardonic comment on standard critical debates on the poet: 'Super-ego crash-meshed idiot-savant', writes Hill, of the 'artiste of neon, traffic's orator', 'Slumming for rum and rumba, dumb Rimbaud'.[68] Crane's invigorating legacy is seen as alive and well in these varied poetic engagements with his work, which are read as implicit meditations on Crane's ill-founded reputation for difficulty and his association with grand 'failure'.

This book brings a new perspective to Crane's life and work, showing the influence of various constellations of writers and artists on his poetry. Noting Sean Latham and Robert Scoles' suggestion that periodicals be viewed as 'autonomous objects of study', I suggest viewing journals as thoroughly humane objects.[69] Their material form is representative of particular individuals and broader communities in a myriad of various forms, aesthetic programmes, locations, and degrees of social and geographical closeness and separation. They are, therefore, objects utterly enmeshed with the lives of those who edited, contributed to, printed and published them. It is my hope that exploring this aspect of Crane's poetic life will show his work anew, retaining all its strangeness and ambiguities, and the vibrant, dynamic communities in which he lived and wrote.

---

[67] Geoffrey Hill, 'Improvisations for Hart Crane', *Daedalus*, 133.4 (2004), pp. 99–101; Mark Ford, 'The Death of Hart Crane', in *Six Children* (London: Faber and Faber, 2011), pp. 18–19; Eileen Myles, 'hart!', *Harp and Altar*, 6 (spring 2009), available at <http://www.harpandaltar.com/interior.php?t=s&i=6&p=39&e=68> (accessed 17 March 2021); Adrienne Rich, 'The Night Has a Thousand Eyes', in *Midnight Salvage* (New York: Norton, 1999), pp. 43–50.

[68] Hill, 'Improvisations for Hart Crane', p. 99.

[69] Sean Latham and Robert Scoles, 'The Changing Profession: The Rise of Periodical Studies', *PMLA*, 121.2 (2006), pp. 517–31 (p. 518).

I

'IMAGIST IN AMBER': POST-DECADENT POETRY AND GREENWICH VILLAGE

> He proceeds from one mixed metaphor to another, image on image, and we almost allow him his way with us because he makes, together with a confusion of images, a perfect gaunt and stately music ... His work is effect, not cause.
>
> Genevieve Taggard[1]

In his 1921 *flâneur*'s guide to New York City, *Hints to Pilgrims*, the dramatist and essayist Charles S. Brooks briefly interrupts his rhapsodies over the city's 'restaurants and theatres ... bridges ... the shipping ... parks ... fifth avenue ... electric signs' with a sketch of its 'quartier Latin', Greenwich Village. Brooks's interlude revolves around a brief meeting with a 'not entirely famous' young poet at his lodgings 'just North of Greenwich Village' in the spring of 1919. The poet, whose 'verses', Brooks writes, are 'of the newer sort', was the 19-year-old Hart Crane, then living above the offices of Margaret Anderson and Jane Heap's *Little Review* (which Brooks chauvinistically dubs '*The Shriek*'), and whose career began in the pages of the Village's lively journals.[2]

---

[1] Genevieve Taggard, 'An Imagist in Amber', review of Crane, *White Buildings* (1926), *The New York Herald Tribune*, 29 May 1927, p. 4.
[2] Charles S. Brooks, *Hints to Pilgrims* (New Haven, CT: Yale University Press, 1921), pp. 12–13; Bruno, 'Bohemia Over Here', p. 2.

Crane appears beslippered on the staircase of his dark, decaying, 'tarnished' and 'frescoed' building which, for Brooks, recalls Thomas De Quincey's glamorously decrepit 'vast gothic halls'. With its roots in an 'earlier bohemia in the lower Manhattan of the 1890s', the Village's distinct brand of modernism in the late 1910s was steeped in references to past generations of artists and writers. As Stephen Rogers has noted, its aesthetic was given particular 'impetus' by the 'spirit of Decadence' fashionable in local literary circles, including the pages of Crane's first magazine publishers, *Bruno's Weekly* and *The Pagan*.[3] At once a Wildean, loquacious dandy, and terse defender of the 'newer' poetry, Crane is presented as the Greenwich Village archetype made flesh in Brooks's self-described 'memorandum' of the 'characters' of New York City.[4] 'Emergent and vestigial styles', to borrow Langdon Hammer's useful phrase, operate in Crane's poetry as 'opposing energies [that] contend and cooperate, working to undo traditional authority and to reconstruct it in new forms'.[5] Crane's early publications in the post-Decadent, bohemian journals of Greenwich Village illuminate what was most distinct about his poetics: both modern and antique, European and American, formally experimental and traditional. His engagement with periodicals and the processes of publishing and revision from those early days in Greenwich Village fundamentally shaped his poetic development. Building on seminal queer readings of Crane by Thomas Yingling and Niall Munro, this chapter recovers the queer literary communities in which Crane's work was first honed and disseminated.

The much-mythologised culture of the Village in the 1910s was, according to Crane's friend, the writer and editor Malcolm Cowley, a distinct mixture of 'radicalism and bohemianism'. Animated equally by these 'two currents' of arts and liberal politics, as Cowley writes in *Exile's Return*, 'socialism, free love, anarchism, syndicalism, free verse' were all 'lumped together [. . .] the Villagers might get their heads broken in Union Square by the police before appearing at the Liberal Club to recite Swinburne in bloody bandages'.[6] A 1925 map of 'Greenwich Village Today' printed in *The Quill* shows the area teeming with bookshops, theatres, galleries, artists' studios, magazine offices (such as those of Guido Bruno's *Bruno's Weekly* and Joseph Kling's *The Pagan*), literary salons

---

[3] Stephen Rogers, 'Village Voices', in Brooker and Thacker (eds), *The Oxford Critical and Cultural History of Modernist Magazines, Volume II: North America 1894–1960*, pp. 445–64 (p. 446).
[4] Brooks, *Hints to Pilgrims*, p. 93.
[5] Hammer, *Janus-Faced Modernism*, p. 233, n. 2, p. ix.
[6] Cowley, *Exile's Return*, p. 66.

(Mabel Dodge's famous rooms at 23 Fifth Avenue), and the headquarters of civil and political organisations, such as the American Civil Liberties Union.[7]

The Village's demographic is elided in Cowley's homogeneous account; by the turn of the century the area was home to a significant immigrant population and a high number of German, Polish, Italian and Russian speakers. Bruno and Kling were both Jewish immigrants, from Prague (then the capital of Bohemia) and Russia, respectively.[8] As Jahan Ramazani has argued, modernist 'poets, novelists, playwrights, and readers also confound the boundaries of national and regional community, forging alliances of style and sensibility across vast distances of geography, history, and culture'. Literary works published in Greenwich Village magazines in the 1910s exhibit the 'central modernist strategies' and crucial 'practices of displacement' identified by Ramazani: 'transnational collage, polyglossia, syncretic allusiveness'. The Village is perhaps a supreme example or test case of modernist transnationalism, with its lively periodicals providing organs for transnational exchange and the 'cross-cultural generation of meanings'.[9] Crane's first publishers, *Bruno's Weekly* and *The Pagan*, demonstrate keen and sustained interest in the aesthetic strategies identified by Ramazani, cutting across national and generational boundaries. Both journals show the persistence of an idea of translocalism – the international cultural exchange within their pages being stamped by an ebulliently local and characterful sense of Greenwich Village. The eclecticism, multilingual syncretism and combination of localism with a global outlook exhibited in these magazines informed the magpie-like assimilative practice crucial to the development of Crane's poetry. This is borne out by his straightforward borrowings of *fin-de-siècle* tropes and homages to Oscar Wilde, Aubrey Beardsley and Stéphane Mallarmé in his early poems, as well as a later interest in the experiments of the European avant-garde, as he incorporated 'machine-age' subjects and proto-Surrealist experiments in his poetry from the early 1920s. As Crane questions in his late poem 'The Broken Tower', 'My word I poured. But was it cognate [. . .]?', with a sense perhaps of the mature poet evaluating the common thread throughout his poetry: his attempt at a transnational polyglot modernism forged in the crucible of Greenwich Village magazines.[10]

---

[7] Robert Edwards, 'Greenwich Village Today', in Kelsey McKinney, 'In the Galleries: A Map of Greenwich Village from the *Greenwich Village Quill*', *Ransom Center Magazine*, available at <https://sites.utexas.edu/ransomcentermagazine/2012/01/05/in-the-galleries-a-map-of-greenwich-village-from-the-greenwich-village-quill/> (accessed 14 May 2018).

[8] Ira Rosenwaike, *Population History of New York* (Syracuse, NY: Syracuse University Press, 1972), pp. 93, 95.

[9] Ramazani, *A Transnational Poetics*, p. 28.

[10] Crane, 'The Broken Tower', in *The Complete Poems of Hart Crane: The Centennial Edition*, ed. Marc Simon (New York: Liveright, 2001), pp. 160–1.

By January 1920 Crane had severed ties with *The Pagan*: 'Well I hope Kling will be able to sell out for the price of dinner', he remarked in a letter to Gorham Munson. 'Most of all that he sells out, and rids his own arms, as well as the public's, of that fetid corpse ... The last issue is the worst ever, and I don't think there are lower levels to be reached.'[11] The contempt that Crane developed for Kling's 'Magazine for Eudaemonists', doubtless piqued by Kling's recent rejection of his poem 'To Portapovitch', bears traces of Crane's antisemitism.[12] Nevertheless, Crane's complete rejection of *The Pagan* is surprising, given that he appeared seventeen times in Kling's Village magazine within three years. This amounts to 20 per cent of Crane's total publications over his sixteen-year career, from 1916 until his early death in 1932. Crane's *Pagan* publications included ten poems, critical prose, reviews and short editorial segments, and additional appearances in both the 1918 and 1919 *Pagan* anthologies.[13] While this high number of appearances is partially explained by the fact that Crane was able to exercise greater selectivity when approaching prospective publishers later in his career, he did, at least initially, find that *The Pagan* represented his own aesthetic interests. Crane even helped to edit the journal from April 1918 to April 1919, where, alongside fellow assistant editor Munson, his duties included writing reviews and editorial notes to poems. Although unpaid, the role furnished Crane with reviewer passes to the Village's theatres and the city's concert halls, as witnessed by his survey of local theatre in the April–May 1918 number.[14] *The Pagan*, with what Munson described as its 'yellow book sympathies', was instrumental in ensconcing Crane in the Village's cultural life, establishing his reputation as a young poet on the New York literary scene and exerting a significant influence on his poetic development.[15]

In the early 1920s Crane's interests shifted decisively from the *fin-de-siècle* tropes of poems such as 'Echoes' and 'The Hive' published in *The Pagan* to the post-Symbolist, Surrealist-informed 'logic of metaphor', Crane's idiosyncratic theory of poetics. Crane's articulation of the 'logic' coincided with the appearance of 'machinery', 'planes', 'cinemas' and 'streetcars' in his poems of

---

[11] Crane to Munson, 28 January 1920, in *The Letters of Hart Crane 1916–1932*, ed. Brom Weber (New York: Hermitage House, 1952), p. 31.

[12] Crane mentions Joseph Kling's rejection of 'To Portapovitch' in a letter to Carl Zigrosser, editor of *The Modern School*: Crane to Zigrosser, n.d., c. late January 1919, box 9, folder 346, Zigrosser papers. *The Modern School* published the poem as 'To Potapovitch [*sic*] (de la Ballet Russe)', 6.3 (1919), p. 80. Kling was a frequent target of Crane's antisemitism. See Crane to George B. Bryan, 23 April 1918, *O My Land*, p. 14.

[13] Crane, 'Fear', in *A Pagan Anthology*, ed. Joseph Kling (New York: Pagan Publishing Company, 1918), p. 18; Crane, 'Forgetfulness', in *A Second Pagan Anthology*, ed. Joseph Kling (New York: Pagan Publishing Company, 1919), p. 17.

[14] Unterecker, *Voyager*, p. 108; Crane, 'Tragi-Comique', pp. 54–6.

[15] Munson, *The Awakening Twenties*, p. 72.

the 1920s. *The Pagan* was formative to the young poet's development, and an analysis of his relationship with this journal is crucial to understanding the rapid shifts in his poetic style in the late 1910s, by which time 'yellow book' affinities were passé; Alfred Kreymborg, for instance, derisively remarked that another Village publication, *Rogue*, was dominated by 'esthetes, satirists, dandies, poets'.[16] In a 1919 letter, Crane writes (with an eye to publication) to Carl Zigrosser, the editor of a New Jersey-based magazine *The Modern School*: 'when here before the war I resided in the village, but at last I have made the break, I really like my new location, out a ways, much better'.[17] Crane's 'break' was both geographical and aesthetic; indeed, the two were inextricable, and a move out of Greenwich Village coincided with Crane's sloughing off the imitative pose of his juvenilia.

Reading Crane's first publications in their Greenwich Village contexts reveals how these early poems were in dialogue with a particular brand of post-Decadent poetry. This style assimilated influences from the *fin de siècle* and contemporaneous experiments in Imagism – an aesthetic active, to varying degrees, in the first journals in which he published, *Bruno's Weekly*, *Bruno's Bohemia* and *The Pagan*. Unpicking these varied strands of influence illuminates Crane's rationale for excluding what he considered juvenilia published in *The Pagan* and *The Brunos* from his first collection, *White Buildings* (1926). The Village magazines allowed him a public forum for his early poetry, but also ensured a lingering association with a particular 'post-Decadent' aesthetic throughout his life's work. Crane's oeuvre was permeated by this Greenwich Village 'aura', to borrow George Bornstein's evocative application of a concept originally theorised by Walter Benjamin, which insists on the irreducible situatedness of a text within its 'original sites of incarnation'.[18] To focus on Crane's Greenwich Village 'aura' is simultaneously to draw out the complex queer and transnational development of his poetry, and to identify the ways in which his critical reception remained constrained by a (latently homophobic) miscategorisation of his poetry as undisciplined and Decadent.

Experiments in Decadence: *Bruno's Weekly* and *Bruno's Bohemia*

Before *The Pagan*, Crane briefly found a congenial organ for his poetry in *Bruno's Weekly*. As he would later tell an interviewer, in 1916 he submitted

---

[16] Alfred Kreymborg, *Troubadour* (New York: Sagamore Press, 1957), p. 171.
[17] Munson, *The Awakening Twenties*, p. 76; Cowley, *Exile's Return*, pp. 48–55; Crane to Zigrosser, c. late January 1919, 12 February 1919, box 9, folder 346, Zigrosser papers.
[18] Bornstein, *Material Modernism*, p. 7; Walter Benjamin, 'The Work of Art in the Age of Mechanical Reproduction', in *Illuminations*, ed. Hannah Arendt, trans Harry Zohn (London: Pimlico, 1999), pp. 211–44.

two pieces of 'adolescent juvenilia' to *Bruno's Weekly*, 'C33' and 'Carmen de Boheme', in a 'white hot fury'.[19] He later regretted this impulsive decision: Bruno, who lacked the usual mores of periodical publishing, printed 'Carmen' two years after its submission in a new journal, *Bruno's Bohemia*, 'devoted to Life, Love, Letters'.[20] Tellingly, Bruno credits the poem to 'Harold H. Crane', a pen name Crane discarded early in 1917, adopting instead 'Hart', his mother's maiden name.[21]

Bruno, the 'Barnum' and marketeer of Greenwich Village bohemia, published an array of short-lived, cheaply produced magazines from his 'garret on Washington Square'.[22] As Stephen Rogers has noted, Bruno's journals were given 'impetus' by 'the spirit of Decadence' fashionable in the Village.[23] The Village's brand of modernism, expressed in journals such as the *Brunos*, *The Pagan*, *The Quill* and *Rogue*, was built around 'form[s] of cultural exchange' with London and Paris of the 1890s.[24] *Bruno's Weekly* included 106 references to Oscar Wilde and sixteen drawings by Aubrey Beardsley in its run between July 1915 and December 1916.[25] Openly queer publications such as London's *The Link* and Chicago's *Friendship and Freedom* (both published in the 1920s) were suppressed, with their editors jailed. In such a repressive climate, Bruno's repeated nods to Wilde appear to work as a coded advertisement of a sexually liberal, even queer aesthetic, all the while avoiding the gaze of the censor. Bruno was keenly aware of the risks involved, after his publication of Alfred Kreymborg's *Edna, The Girl of the Street* resulted in a brief prison sentence for publishing 'obscene material'.[26]

Through *Bruno's Weekly*, Crane was exposed to excerpts from Frank Harris's biography of Wilde, Wilde's unpublished letters, his essay 'Impressions of America', and his sonnet in vindication of freedom, 'Quantum Mutata'. Crane's poem 'C33' appeared in a feature called 'Oscar Wilde: Poems in His Praise', which

---

[19] Interview with Crane quoted in Unterecker, *Voyager*, p. 107.
[20] Crane states in this interview that these poems were submitted together in 1916, as Weber notes in *Hart Crane*, p. 34.
[21] Advertisement for *Bruno's Bohemia*, 1.1 (1918), back pages.
[22] Rogers, 'Village Voices', p. 445; Guido Bruno, 'Frontispiece to Greenwich Village', *Greenwich Village*, 2.1 (23 June 1915).
[23] Rogers, 'Village Voices', p. 446.
[24] Ibid., p. 446.
[25] Data collected from Princeton's Blue Mountain Project, available at <http://bluemountain.princeton.edu> (accessed 29 April 2018); Rogers, 'Village Voices', p. 459.
[26] Bruno's imprisonment is documented by Joseph Kling in 'Why Complain', *The Pagan*, 1.10 (1917), p. 42. Kingham identifies the pseudonym 'Ben S.' as Kling's in 'Commerce, Little Magazines, and Modernity', p. 163.

significantly also carried a poem by Wilde's lover, Alfred Douglas.[27] Elsewhere, Bruno reprinted translations of Charles Baudelaire's 'The Stranger' ('L'Étranger') and 'The Windows' ('Les Fenêtres'), published an autograph manuscript of G. K. Chesterton's 'A Song of Gifts to God', aired discussions on Arthur Symons's literary criticism, and printed frivolous articles such as 'The Importance of Neckties: The History of the Cravat', taken from an 1829 manual.[28] Despite these preoccupations, the *Brunos* were not aesthetically reactionary. Rather, Bruno's journals were, as Rogers puts it, 'transitional': nineteenth-century reprints appeared alongside new poetry and prose – in both traditional and experimental forms – as well as a range of works in translation and reviews of European periodicals. This cross-cultural, cosmopolitan and assimilative approach enabled 'emerging modernist writers' to 'find an outlet for their work'.[29] Moreover, *Bruno's Weekly* emphasises the extent to which Greenwich Village modernism was strikingly transnational in its exchanges and borrowings, and simultaneously contemporary and infused with the spirit of the Nineties; this important generational nexus encapsulates the extent to which Crane, as he himself quipped in a letter, had 'a little toe-nail in the last century'.[30]

Bruno's Weekly and *The Pagan* (which was based at the New York Socialist Party headquarters)[31] reflected the distinct energies of bohemia, radicalism and inchoate modernism in their editorial practices, a style Munson described as somewhat chaotic, adding that 'whatever policy *The Pagan* had was only Kling's personal taste'. *The Pagan* was particularly interested in nineteenth-century literature, and Munson commented that Kling 'liked the Russian realists of 1900, the Yiddish humourists of the Café Royal, and the Continental and English aesthetes of the Yellow Book period'.[32] 'In the Village', wrote

---

[27] Frank Harris, 'Oscar Wilde', *Bruno's Weekly*, 3.1 (17 June 1916), pp. 780–1; Oscar Wilde, 'Hitherto Unpublished Letters by Oscar Wilde', *Bruno's Weekly*, 2.11 (11 March 1916), pp. 543–4; Wilde, 'Quantum Mutata', *Bruno's Weekly*, 2.18 (29 April 1916), p. 655; Wilde, 'Impressions of America', *Bruno's Weekly*, 2.21 (20 May 1916), pp. 724–6; Crane, 'C33', p. 1008; Harold Hart Crane, 'Carmen de Boheme', *Bruno's Bohemia*, 1.1 (1918), p. 2; Alfred Douglas, 'To Oscar Wilde', *Bruno's Weekly*, 3.15 (23 September 1916), p. 1009.

[28] Charles Baudelaire, 'The Stranger', *Bruno's Weekly*, 1.13 (14 October 1915), p. 115; Baudelaire, 'The Windows', *Bruno's Weekly*, 1.13 (14 October 1915), p. 26; G. K. Chesterton, 'A Song of Gifts to God', [MS reproduction], *Bruno's Weekly*, 2.9 (26 February 1916), p. 503; H. Le Blanc, 'The Importance of Neckties: The History of the Cravat', *Bruno's Weekly*, 2.11 (11 March 1916), p. 3; Le Blanc, *The Art of Tying the Cravat: Demonstrated in Sixteen Lessons Including Thirty Two Different Styles Forming A Pocket Manual* (New York: D. A. Forbes, 1829).

[29] Rogers, 'Village Voices', p. 446.

[30] Crane to Allen Tate, 16 May 1922, *O My Land*, p. 85.

[31] Weber, *Hart Crane*, p. 13.

[32] Munson, *The Awakening Twenties*, pp. 75–7.

Cowley, 'we read Conrad. We read Wilde and Shaw.'[33] The *Brunos*, meanwhile showed a persistent interest in Decadent literature, as well as contributions from Bruno's 'poeta laureatus of Greenwich Village', Alfred Kreymborg, Richard Aldington, H.D., F. S. Flint and fellow Imagists, war poetry and, significantly, an early poem by Marianne Moore, 'Holes bored in a workbag by the scissors'.[34] Comprehensive reviews of contemporary journals appeared in *Bruno's Weekly* covering literary and radical political magazines based in the US and Europe, including *Others*, *In Which*, *The Minaret*, *The Little Review*, *Poetry*, *The Egoist*, *Expression*, *Der Sturm*, *The Phoenix*, and regular mocking appraisals of *Contemporary Verse*. *Contemporary Verse* was, as Niall Munro has commented, the 'intellectual slum' to which Ezra Pound derisively suggested Crane might send his poetry, asserting that his contributions would complement its 'consummate milk pudding milieu'.[35] In addition, Bruno published Djuna Barnes's *Book of Repulsive Women* and several important Imagist texts in his 15¢ chapbook series, including Aldington's *The Imagists*, Kreymborg's *Mushrooms*, *To My Mother* and *Edna, The Girl of the Street* which, as mentioned above, got Bruno 'in-dutch [with] the Comstock gang again', in the words of a wry report from the pages of *The Pagan*.[36]

Bruno's marketing of Greenwich Village bohemia extended to using his magazines as vehicles to advertise paid tours of his 'garret' where visitors could watch 'bohemian' painters at work, while space was dedicated to advertisements for studio spaces for rent and publishing ventures, such as Egmont Arens's 'Handbook of Bohemia', *The Little Book of Greenwich Village* (also advertised in *The Pagan*), which documented the cultural activities of the quarter; Bruno's memoir *Adventures in American Bookshops*; and his *Fragments from Greenwich Village*, an anthology of his own contributions to one of his magazines.[37]

---

[33] Cowley, *Exile's Return*, p. 20.
[34] Guido Bruno, 'Books and Magazines of the Week', *Greenwich Village*, 2.2 (15 July 1915), p. 66; Richard Aldington, 'The Imagists', *Greenwich Village*, 2.2 (15 July 1915), pp. 54–7; Marianne Moore, 'Holes Bored in a Workbag by the Scissors', *Bruno's Weekly*, 3.17 (7 October 1916), p. 1137; H.D., 'Huntress', *Greenwich Village*, 2.2 (15 July 1915), p. 57; F. S. Flint, 'Springs', *Greenwich Village*, 2.2 (15 July 1915), p. 59.
[35] Guido Bruno, 'Books and Magazines of the Week', *Bruno's Weekly*, 1.22 (18 December 1915), pp. 298–9, and 1.15 (30 October 1915), p. 162; Munro, *Hart Crane's Queer Modernist Aesthetic*, p. 35; Pound to Crane, n.d., c. 1918, folder 310, box 8, Crane Collection.
[36] Djuna Barnes, *The Book of Repulsive Women: 8 Rhythms and 5 Drawings* (New York: Bruno's Chapbooks, 1915); Richard Aldington, *The Imagists* (New York: Bruno's Chapbooks Special Series, 1915); Alfred Kreymborg, *Mushrooms: 16 Rhythms* (New York: Bruno's Chapbooks, 1915); Kreymborg, *To My Mother: Ten Rhythms* (New York: Bruno's Chapbooks, 1915); Kling as 'Ben S', 'Why Complain', p. 42.
[37] Egmont Arens, *Little Book of Greenwich Village* (New York: Washington Square Book Shop, 1918); Guido Bruno, *Adventures in American Bookshops, Antique Stores and Auction Rooms* (Detroit: The Douglas Book Shop, 1922); Bruno, *Fragments from Greenwich Village* (New York: Guido Bruno, 1921).

As Eric B. White comments, Bruno 'identified his target market' as 'thousands of people . . . who are getting acquainted with our metropolis from the top of the bus'.[38] Bruno's journal *Greenwich Village* sold this atmosphere by highlighting its sexually liberal ethos on its frontispiece:

> GREENWICH VILLAGE! Refuge of saints condemned to life in the crude hard realistic world, your playground of sensation – thirsty women with a yellow streak and of men that mistake the desire to sow wild oats for artistic inclination. GREENWICH VILLAGE! Where genius starved and gave the world the best it had, where fortunes were squandered and fortunes made, where heavens of earthly bliss prevail and tortures of hell are suffered, where night and day cease to be the regulating element of the world, where new ideas are developed into systems that will be overthrown tomorrow and substituted by others that will not live any longer.[39]

Bruno's coded queer aesthetic was of profound importance to Crane's early poetic development. As George Chauncey has explored, Greenwich Village's emergence as a gay centre was inextricably linked to broader progressive impulses in its bohemian community, its tolerance for 'nonconformity (or "eccentricity")' as well as 'cheap rents and cheap restaurants'.[40] Crane, who was beginning to explore his homosexuality, appears to have been drawn to the sexual liberalism and freedom that Bruno's magazines advertised, in stark contrast to how he saw the Midwest of his childhood: 'Cleveland is a hellish place.'[41] He seems to have been particularly attracted to Bruno's tacit support of Wilde, indicated through the near-weekly attention his magazines paid to the writer. Bruno's loyalty to an ostensibly outmoded Wildean post-Decadent style can be read as an allegory, to borrow from Yingling's interpretation of Eve Kosofsky Sedgwick's ideas on sexuality and dichotomy: 'indeed, the allegory is so strongly and openly coded as often to make homosexuality the "open secret" of the text'.[42] Bruno's repeated allusions to Wilde function as just such an 'open secret'. Crane's fascination with this code is underlined by his submission of 'C33' to *Bruno's Weekly*, a poem that takes its title from Wilde's cell number in Reading Gaol, which Wilde adopted as his own nom de plume for the first publication of *The Ballad of Reading Gaol* in 1898.[43]

---

[38] White, and Bruno as quoted in White, *Transatlantic Avant-Gardes*, p. 23.
[39] Bruno, 'Frontispiece to Greenwich Village'.
[40] George Chauncey, *Gay New York: Gender, Urban Culture, and the Makings of the Gay Male World, 1890–1940* (New York: Basic Books, 1994), p. 229.
[41] Crane to Yvor Winters, 27 January 1927, *O My Land*, p. 315.
[42] Yingling, *Hart Crane and the Homosexual Text*, p. 231, n. 19.
[43] Oscar Wilde as 'C.3.3.', *The Ballad of Reading Gaol* (London: Leonard Smithers, 1898).

The 'conscious notion of bohemianism, popularized by Puccini's opera' created a 'taste for bohemian style among the bourgeoisie', and Bruno (born Curt Joseph Kisch near Prague to a German-speaking Jewish family) provided a 'simulacrum of Continental European Bohemia'.[44] Bruno's publishing ventures earned him a reputation as a 'sleazy … untalented hanger on', 'a petty and disreputable profiteer in poetry and publishing'.[45] This reputation was developed into Djuna Barnes's profoundly antisemitic caricature of the editor as Felix Volkbein in her 1936 novel, *Nightwood*.[46] Bruno was attacked on 23 January 1916 in 'one of Mr Munsey's Sunday paper[s]' for being a charlatan with 'a taste for bohemianism'.[47] As well as the distinct antisemitism, such views propounded the false assumption that Bruno's acumen in the literary marketplace somehow diminished his ability to publish high-quality content. This is erroneous, particularly in light of Bruno's discovery of Crane and his championing of early work by Moore, Munson, Cowley, Barnes and Aldington.

Crane had been exposed to Greenwich Village bohemian journals at Laukhuff's bookstore in Cleveland, Ohio, a haven for the young poet as his parents' marriage collapsed. C. A. and Grace Hart Crane divorced in December 1916, which coincided with Hart Crane's withdrawal from Cleveland's East High School. Shortly after Christmas, the young poet left the Midwest for New York City.[48] In sending 'C33' and 'Carmen de Boheme' to *Bruno's Weekly*, he assumed that Bruno would be sympathetic to their aesthetic. Bruno's decision to publish Crane's poems highlights his dual interest in *fin-de-siècle* and contemporary experiments in poetry. At the same time, their recontextualisation in Bruno's journals throws into relief their straightforward, naïve quality, with some of their content derivative of accepted styles recognisable to the magazines' readers. As Brom Weber has noted, Crane may have been prompted to

---

[44] Aside from his own self-mythologising fragmentary memoirs, there is little available information on Bruno, with the exception of a biography by his nephew, Arnold I. Kisch, *The Romantic Ghost of Greenwich Village: Guido Bruno in His Garret* (Oxford: Peter Lang, 1976). Rogers, 'Village Voices', p. 450.

[45] Andrew Field, *Djuna: The Life and Times of Djuna Barnes* (New York: G.P. Putnam's Sons, 1983), p. 14, as quoted in Rogers, 'Village Voices', p. 446; Christine Stansell, *American Moderns: Bohemian New York and the Creation of a New Century* (Princeton, NJ: Princeton University Press, 2009), p. 334.

[46] Djuna Barnes, *Nightwood* (New York: New Directions, 2006). See Lara Trabowitz's complex account of antisemitism in *Nightwood* in 'In Search of "the Jew" in Djuna Barnes's *Nightwood*: Jewishness, Antisemitism, Structure, and Style', *Modern Fiction Studies*, 51.2 (2005), pp. 311–34.

[47] Bruno, *Fragments from Greenwich Village*, p. 28.

[48] Unterecker, *Voyager*, pp. 47–51.

write 'C33' after reading an article serialised in *Bruno's Weekly* in January and February 1916, 'The Story of Oscar Wilde's Life and Experience in Reading Gaol' by "His Warder"'.[49] Bruno appears to have recognised the derivative qualities of 'C33' and 'Carmen de Boheme', choosing to insert the poems within prose features on Village culture rather than publishing them as discrete contributions, as was his usual practice.

As Deborah Longworth argues, a 'post-Decadent' aesthetic was popular in the Village. Rather than pure imitation of Decadence and aestheticism, this essentially involved 'parodic appropriation', a 'smart sophistication that spoke young and modern New York as much as it did *fin-de-siècle/fin du globe* of 1890s London'.[50] Crane's early poetry was by no means 'parodic', in contrast to later poems such as 'The Wine Menagerie' (which I discuss elsewhere in this chapter), a poem written in 1925 that deftly stitches together sincere and playful allusions to Baudelaire's 'Enivrez-Vous' and *Les Paradis artificiels* to create a text that sits somewhere between homage and pastiche. Hardly articulating 'young and modern New York', 'C33' by contrast appeared as a simple homage in the 'Oscar Wilde: Poems in his Praise' feature, while 'Carmen de Boheme' punctuated a double-page feature by the editor titled 'Bohemia Over Here; Bohemia Over There', on the relationship between wartime Prague, 'the ancient city of bohemian Kings', and Greenwich Village.[51]

Its author's name misspelled as 'Harold H. Crone', 'C33' appeared alongside four other poems: 'Ode to Oscar Wilde', 'Oscar Wilde', 'Impressions of Oscar Wilde' and 'To Oscar Wilde'.[52] Although Crane's poem is fairly straightforward in its emulation of Decadent ideas, and while he does not attempt the 'parodic' attitude identified by Longworth as popular in these Village journals, the poem is more agnostic about Wilde as a literary influence than its placement in this feature suggests. The periodical context of 'C33' as a 'poem in praise' of Wilde effaces a reading that would place it in dialogue with its influences. Despite Bruno's relatively enlightened attitude towards Wilde's homosexuality, printing 'C33' in this context as a simple 'homage' to Wilde buries the subtle anxieties that Crane expresses in the poem relating to his own sexuality in a censorious society.[53]

---

[49] Weber, *Hart Crane*, p. 34; Unsigned, 'The Story of Oscar Wilde's Life and Experience in Reading Gaol', *Bruno's Weekly*, 2.4 (22 January 1916), pp. 400–1.

[50] Deborah Longworth, 'The Avant-Garde in the Village: *Rogue*', in Brooker and Thacker (eds), *The Oxford Critical and Cultural History of Modernist Magazines, Volume II: North America 1894–1960*, pp. 465–82 (p. 468).

[51] Bruno, 'Bohemia Over There', p. 1; Bruno, 'Bohemia Over Here', p. 2.

[52] William Salisbury, John W. Draper, Hart Crane, Jubal Agmenon and Allan Norton, 'Oscar Wilde: Poems in His Praise', *Bruno's Weekly*, 3.15 (23 September 1916), p. 1008.

[53] Mariani believes that Crane's first homosexual affair was late in 1919. See *The Broken Tower: A Life of Hart Crane* (New York: Norton, 2000), pp. 60–1.

In the poem, 'He' stands as a cipher for the young poet in his meditation on Wilde's incarceration ('penitence, must needs bring pain') and, as Munro has suggested, the poem's title becomes 'a badge of male homosexual suffering, connecting Wilde and certain of Crane's readers'.[54] 'C33' makes several direct references to Wilde's *Salomé*:

> He has woven rose-vines
> About the empty heart of night,
> And vented his long mellowed wines
> Of dreaming on the desert white
> With searing sophistry.
> And he tented with far thruths [sic] he would form
> The transient bosoms from the thorny tree.
>
> O Materna! to enrich thy gold head
> And wavering shoulders with a new light shed
>
> From penitence, must needs bring pain,
> And with it song of minor, broken strain.
> But you who hear the lamp whisper thru night
> Can trace paths tear-wet, and forget all blight.[55]

Crane's poem echoes Wilde's distinctly scriptural imagery, drawing particularly on his allusions to the Song of Songs and *Salomé*'s orientalist tropes. 'C33' recalls a number of descriptions from *Salomé*, 'roses in the garden', Jokanaan's 'mouth ... redder than roses', 'my garland of roses', 'stains of blood are as lovely as rose petals', 'the vine-trees of Edom', 'What wine is that, the wine of God? From what vineyards is it gathered', 'get thee to the desert', 'from the desert where he fed on locusts and wild honey'.[56] Crane's lamp that whispers 'thru night' along with the poem's 'rose-vines' suggest an allusion to Beardsley's drawing 'The Mysterious Rose Garden' depicting the Annunciation, printed in the January 1895 number of *The Yellow Book*. The nude Mary and clothed Gabriel stand against a trellis of roses, with the angel holding a lamp which looms into the foreground.[57] 'Wine' is central to the Decadent imagery of *Salomé*, and Crane may have had this in mind with the phrase 'vented his long mellowed wines', which, while being a literal description of airing wine before it is drunk, also signifies breathing or speaking and recalls Salomé to

---

[54] Munro, *Hart Crane's Queer Modernist Aesthetic*, p. 26.
[55] Crane, 'C33', p. 1008.
[56] Oscar Wilde, *Salomé* (London: John Lane, 1907), pp. 21, 22, 50, 50, 22, 44, 20, 7.
[57] Aubrey Beardsley, 'The Mysterious Rose Garden', *The Yellow Book*, 4 (1895), p. 14.

Jokanaan: 'Thy voice is wine to me.'[58] Crane also suggests Wilde's 'bitter self contempt', which had been a dominant aspect of his 'Experience in Reading Gaol' article. In Crane's poem, the 'transient' imaginings of Wilde in his cell become a 'thorny tree', and the poem, at thirteen lines, takes the form of a frustrated sonnet, the love poem *par excellence*.[59]

In the pejorative phrase 'searing sophistry', Crane's poem eludes Bruno's editorial framing of it as a straightforward emulation of Wilde. 'The transient bosoms form the thorny tree' is deliberately difficult to enunciate; the sentence's over-patterning forces it into stutters, tripping over fricatives with the phonic similarities between 'form' and 'thorn', and the repeated 'th' of 'the thorny'. Here Crane gently parodies Wilde's own patterning in *Salomé*, built around similar sonic features: 'a crown of thorns which they have placed on thy forehead'.[60] Crane's line is also metrically complex: near iambic pentameter, with 'transient' a dactyl uncomfortably positioned after the initial first unstressed syllable ('The'), upsetting the anticipated rhythm. In the following stanza, 'head' and 'shed' are forced into an awkward, but obvious, rhyme with the syntax twisted to accommodate it: 'with a new light shed'.[61] Through this accumulation of awkward formal details, Crane burlesques Wilde's mannerist style; 'C33', with its exploratory queer poetics, is less of a 'poem in praise' than Bruno's placement in the feature suggests.

The publication of 'Carmen de Boheme' in *Bruno's Bohemia* further illuminates Crane's debt to Bruno's magazines in the formative stages of his poetic development, while also drawing attention to the aesthetic concerns of the journal. Crane's use of Georges Bizet's 1875 opera *Carmen* is analogous to the way that tropes from Puccini's *La Bohème* were absorbed into Greenwich Village literary culture as cultural touchstones – there was, for instance, a local tea room named after the opera.[62] Crane's poem sits between ekphrasis and a sketch of a Village social gathering. The voice of the poem is somewhat detached from the gathering, observing at a distance. Crane offers both a description of the opera-goers and their surroundings encoded according to contemporary tastes, while also containing moments from Bizet, such as the gypsy wagon 'wiggling' away in the last stanza:

> Finale leaves in silence to replume
> Bent wings, and Carmen with her flaunts through the gloom
> Of whispering tapestry, brown with old fringe: —
> The winers leave too, and the small lamps twinge.

---

[58] Wilde, *Salomé*, p. 20.
[59] Unsigned, 'The Story of Oscar Wilde's Life and Experience in Reading Gaol', p. 400.
[60] Wilde, *Salomé*, p. 22.
[61] Crane, 'C33', p. 1008.
[62] Rogers, 'Village Voices', p. 486.

> Morning and through the foggy city gate
> A gypsy wagon wiggles, striving straight.
> And some dream still of Carmen's mystic face, —
> Yellow, pallid, like ancient lace.[63]

The cultural markers of *Carmen* and the Greenwich Village party scene become blurred in a way that mirrors the magpie-like cultural borrowing of the Village's 'bohemia', a transnational assimilation that was a key feature of Bruno's magazines.

In 'Carmen de Boheme' the young Crane self-consciously constructs a fashionably bohemian gathering at the opera, with details drawn from articles in Bruno's magazines that romanticised the Village's literary and social scene. Such self-mythogising articles and reviews included 'Greenwich Village: the Romance of one Night', 'In Our Village: Djuna's Exhibit' (which described 'the American Beardsley's' exhibition 'on the walls of Bruno's garret', where Bruno also held poetry readings), and 'Greenwich Village in Modern Fiction', a serial feature which emphasised the Village as a literary centre.[64] Bruno wrote in a feature titled 'Bohemia Everywhere':

> The public in general seems to think that this term [bohemia] applies to every man who wears long hair and a flowing black necktie, indulges in the absorption of alcoholic liquids, smokes cigarettes and has rather lax views about the relations between men and women, and then, in his leisure hours, he perhaps paints or writes poetry.[65]

Crane, writing from Cleveland, figures the poem's narrator as an observer of this Village crowd in its opening lines:

> Sinuously winding through the room
> On smokey tongues of sweetened cigarettes, —
> Plaintive yet proud the cello tones resume
> The andante of smooth hopes and lost regrets.[66]

---

[63] Crane, 'Carmen de Boheme', p. 2.
[64] Guido Bruno, 'Greenwich Village: The Romance of One Night', *Bruno's Weekly*, 1.13 (14 October 1915), p. 127; Bruno, 'In Our Village: Djuna's Exhibit', *Bruno's Weekly*, 1.14 (21 October 1915), pp. 142–3; Bruno, 'Greenwich Village in Modern Fiction', *Bruno's Weekly*, 1.16 (6 November 1915), p. 169; Bruno, advertisement for poetry reading, *Greenwich Village*, 2.1 (23 June 1915), p. 41.
[65] Guido Bruno, 'Bohemia Everywhere', *Bruno's Bohemia*, 1.1 (1918), p. 3.
[66] Crane, 'Carmen de Boheme', p. 2.

The 'absinthe sipping women' with their 'sweetened cigarettes', 'yellow [. . .] lace', 'bright peacocks' and 'wine hot lips' gesture towards the codes of Greenwich Village 'bohemia' described in Bruno's article published alongside the poem.[67]

With the music of *Carmen* 'sinuously winding through the room', the mixture of 'vestigial and emergent' poetic styles in 'Carmen de Boheme' seems to recall T. S. Eliot's 'The Love Song of J. Alfred Prufrock' (Crane once described a 'gallon of sherry' as 'smooth as Prufrock'), published in Harriet Monroe's Chicago-based *Poetry* magazine in June 1915.[68] The particular details of Crane's poem, however, once again borrow tropes associated with Wilde and Beardsley: 'Bright peacocks drink[ing] from flame pots' recalls the 'white peacocks' from *Salomé* and Beardsley's cover design for the play, and the accompanying illustration, *A Peacock Skirt*.[69] In his description of Carmen, Crane seems to allude to a poem by Wilde published in *Bruno's Weekly* in April 1916, 'La Mer', which contains Gothic descriptions of 'yellow' and 'ravelled lace'. Carmen appears in the final lines of Crane's poem with cadaverous 'yellow' skin like 'ancient lace'.[70] Carmen's death at the hands of the jealous José in Bizet's opera is alluded to in stanzas 4–5 in Crane's poem with the 'sweep, —a shattering', and '[d]isquieting', 'barbarous fantasy', 'the pulse in the ears' and the final pun on 'Morning'.[71] The overall effect of this multitude of collaged allusions is disorienting, with Crane not yet in control of the associative and allusive forms that characterise his later works. In both 'C33' and 'Carmen', Crane appears to be situating himself as an apprentice to a carefully selected group of poets, reworking tropes from Greenwich Village journals and fragments of *fin-de-siècle* poetry.

The importance of this initial, imitative stage is made manifest in 'The Wine Menagerie', a 1925 poem that knowingly presents a profusion of collaged images borrowed from Baudelaire and exemplifies Crane's 'logic of metaphor'. Crane outlined the concept of the 'logic' in a 1925 essay (only published posthumously), 'General Aims and Theories', but he first used this phrase publicly in a 1926 letter to Harriet Monroe after she requested a gloss of the 'champion mixed metaphors' in 'At Melville's Tomb', a poem Crane had submitted to *Poetry*.[72] Crane's 'logic' relies on juxtaposed images and metonymy (he called

---

[67] Ibid.
[68] Crane to Munson, 12 October 1922, *Letters*, p. 102; T. S. Eliot, 'The Love Song of J. Alfred Prufrock', *Poetry*, 6.3 (1915), pp. 130–5 (p. 130).
[69] Crane, 'Carmen de Boheme', p. 2; Wilde, *Salomé*, p. 58; Beardsley, *The Peacock Skirt*, in Wilde, *Salomé*, p. 2.
[70] Oscar Wilde, 'La Mer', *Bruno's Weekly*, 2.14 (1 April 1916), p. 3.
[71] Crane, 'Carmen de Boheme', p. 2.
[72] Monroe, 'A Discussion', pp. 34–41; Crane, 'General Aims and Theories', in *The Complete Poems and Selected Letters of Hart Crane*, ed. Langdon Hammer (New York: Library of America, 2006), pp. 160–4.

it his 'condensed metaphorical habit'), a resistance to paraphrase in favour of a paratactic approach:

> I may very possibly be more interested in the so-called illogical impingements of the connotations of words on the consciousness (and their combinations and interplay in metaphor on this basis) than I am interested in the preservation of their logically rigid significations at the cost of limiting my subject matter and perceptions involved in the poem.[73]

As Weber has discussed, this poetic theory drew on I. A. Richards's essay 'A Background for Contemporary Poetry', published in *The Criterion* in July 1925.[74] Well aware that he was entering into a larger debate within periodical networks, Crane added to Monroe: 'this argument over the dynamics of metaphor promises as active a future as has been evinced in the past'.[75] Crane's collaged metaphors and his use of allusion are underpinned by an interest in different types of fragmentary forms; both the 'logic of metaphor' and allusive fragments work through processes of association, either gesturing towards the 'connotations of words on the consciousness', or the original text from which the allusive fragment has been taken.

'The Wine Menagerie' marries this associative use of metaphor with a complex use of allusion, but directed to a different end than Crane's early apprentice poetry. The poem interrogates its own sources, Baudelaire's 'Enivrez-Vous' and *Les Paradis artificiels*, redirecting an overbearing influence into pastiche. In 'The Wine Menagerie', Crane moves from one associative – and metonymic – description to another. For instance, 'the forceps of the smile that takes her', which describes the flirting poet forcing a bartender to smile, morphs into the serpent's 'skin' as a 'facsimile of time'.[76] Crane's interest in these collaged forms stemmed from the Imagist preference for the juxtaposition of, to borrow Pound's phrase, individual 'instance[s] of time'.

This Imagist imperative became an increasingly important feature of Crane's later poetry, exemplified in a line from the 1926 poem 'Passage': 'And had I walked / The dozen particular decimals of time?'[77] Later poems such as 'The Wine Menagerie' build on Crane's interweaving of *fin-de-siècle* allusions in early poems such as 'C33' and 'Carmen de Boheme', but rather than imitation or

---

[73] Monroe, 'A Discussion', p. 36.
[74] Weber, *Hart Crane*, p. 272; I. A. Richards, 'A Background for Contemporary Poetry', *The Criterion*, 3.12 (1925), pp. 511–28.
[75] Monroe, 'A Discussion', p. 36.
[76] Crane, 'The Wine Menagerie', *Complete Poems*, pp. 23–4 (p. 23).
[77] Ezra Pound, 'A Few Don'ts by an Imagiste', *Poetry*, 1.6 (1913), pp. 200–6; Crane, 'Passage', *The Calendar of Modern Letters*, 3.2 (1926), pp. 106–7 (p. 106).

emulation, Crane is in control of his material. In 'Carmen de Boheme', while he is still testing these assimilative techniques, the rapid juxtaposition of metaphor is present only embryonically. Assessing Crane's early poems in their original periodical context in Bruno's journals shows the extent to which they were composed of reworkings from Greenwich Village 'bohemian' tropes and fragments of *fin-de-siècle* poetry, while highlighting how his later consolidation and mastery of these techniques and his queer aesthetic in his mature works owed a debt to this early, productive period.

THE *PAGAN*: IMAGISM, SYMBOLISM AND ASSIMILATION

While Crane's appearances in Bruno's journals were the result of one impulsive submission, *The Pagan* provided him with a platform for honing his assimilative poetic style from 1916 to 1919 and published his first reviews. Joseph Kling, the magazine's editor, wrote in 1917 that he wanted to 'print good stories, poems, plays, drawings etc.' with the aim, common to Village publications, of keeping at bay the 'repressive social and religious codes' that he deemed 'destructive to happiness'.[78] Kling's magazine had a small print run of 500, according to Munson, and his editing approach was consistently non-programmatic, without clear affiliation to any particular group.[79] However, as Kingham has shown, the journal was politically radical, with editorials contrasting 'the fashionable socialism of New York's "Bohemia"' with 'the working life of the Jewish east-side immigrant'.[80]

Like most Village journals, *The Pagan* took a firm anti-war stance after April 1917 and closely followed trade union politics and the activities of the Wobblies, the nickname of the international labour union, the Industrial Workers of the World, founded in Chicago in 1905.[81] Its tastes in the visual arts predominantly reflected those of the 1913 Armory Show.[82] This 'International Exhibition of Modern Art' aimed to showcase, for the first time, 'the works of the European Moderns' alongside those of US artists.[83] Written contributions to *The Pagan*, as Crane's poems demonstrate, are marked by their mixture of *fin-de-siècle* and contemporary influences. Kling had a distinctive

---

[78] Joseph Kling, 'In Answer to Numerous Questions', *The Pagan*, 2.5 (1917), front pages.
[79] In *Awakening Twenties*, p. 75, Munson notes that Kling 'claimed' to have a circulation of 2,000 in 1918. Munson suggests that 500 (the same run as *Secession*) is more likely.
[80] Kingham, 'Commerce, Little Magazines, and Modernity', p. 35.
[81] Joseph Kling, 'Paroles d'un Blesse', *The Pagan*, 1.7–8 (1916), p. 44.
[82] Artists who had visual artwork printed in *The Pagan* and who also appeared at the Armory Show were Henri Matisse, Edvard Munch, Rodin, George Bellows, Fernand Léger, A. Walkovitz, John Sloan, Paul Signac, Marguerite Zorach and George Luks.
[83] Arthur B. Davies, 'The Statement', in *Documents of the 1913 Armory Show: The Electrifying Moment of Modern Art's American Debut* (Tuscon, AZ: Hol Art Books, 2009), pp. 1–2 (p. 1).

sense of American modernism as a cosmopolitan and assimilative venture, and this is clear in his editing of the journal. These aspects became important for the editors of the 'exile' magazines and were formative for the young Crane. He even appears to have borrowed titles of poems that first appeared in *The Pagan*, such as 'Ave Maria' (by Kling), 'Lachrimae Christi' (by Louise G. Cann), and 'The Idiot' (by Eugene Jolas).[84]

The Pagan's title reflected the prevailing philosophies of Greenwich Village. As Cowley notes, one of the fashionable Village 'doctrines' was a nebulous concept of 'paganism' in which 'the body is a temple in which there is nothing unclean, a shrine to be adorned for the ritual of love'.[85] *The Masses*, 'a monthly magazine devoted to the interests of the working people', held 'Pagan Rout' balls to finance its publication, while a local restaurant, Strunsky's, advertised its 'Pagan' atmosphere.[86] These concepts were, at least in part, borrowed from Europe, and Kling's title was, presumably, also a nod to William Sharp's Sussex-based 1892 *Pagan Review*.[87] London literary tastes in the early 1910s had emphasised, as in John Middleton Murry's *Rhythm* for instance, a 'vitalist philosophy', drawing on Henri Bergson and the 'generative force of nature'.[88] Similarly, Vivien Locke Ellis's magazine *The Open Window* aimed to express 'the faun spirit, instinctive, unselfconscious'.[89]

In contrast to Bruno's journals, *The Pagan*'s interest in the *fin de siècle* was more overtly tempered by contemporary concerns as the magazine sought to define a distinctly American poetic mode (an aim that appealed to Crane throughout his career), one that reflected multilingual New York, where 'Manhattan's Lower East Side, two blocks away' from *The Pagan* offices, was home to '350,000 first and second generation Jewish immigrants from Eastern

---

[84] Joseph Kling, 'Ave Maria', *The Pagan*, 6.4–5 (1921), p. 30; Louise G. Cann, 'Lachrimae Christi', *The Pagan*, 4.6 (1919), pp. 36–7; Eugene Jolas, 'The Idiot', *The Pagan*, 4.1 (1919), p. 53; Crane's poems using these titles: 'Ave Maria', *The American Caravan: A Yearbook of American Literature*, 1 (September 1927), pp. 804–6; 'Lachrymae Christi', *The Fugitive*, 4.4 (1925), pp. 102–3; 'The Idiot' appeared in Jolas's own magazine, *transition*: 'El Idiota', *transition*, 9 (December 1927), p. 135.

[85] Cowley, *Exile's Return*, p. 60.

[86] Frontispiece, *The Masses*, 1.1 (1911); advertisement, *The Pagan*, 2.12–3.1 (1918), back pages.

[87] *The Pagan Review*, 1.1 (1892).

[88] See Peter Brooker, 'Harmony, Discord and Difference', in Brooker and Thacker (eds), *The Oxford Critical and Cultural History of Modernist Magazines, Volume I: Britain and Ireland, 1880–1955*, pp. 314–38.

[89] Dominic Hibberd, 'The New Poetry, Georgians and Others', in Brooker and Thacker (eds), *The Oxford Critical and Cultural History of Modernist Magazines, Volume I: Britain and Ireland, 1880–1955*, pp. 176–98 (p. 177).

Europe'.⁹⁰ Information on Kling is scarce but, like Bruno, it seems that he had emigrated to New York. His autobiographical poetic sequence 'Une Vie' suggests that he spent his childhood in Russia.⁹¹

Like Bruno's journals, *The Pagan* 'inhabit[ed] two worlds, America and old Europe'.⁹² Tellingly, in his letter to Kling published in the October 1916 number, Crane connects the 'new and distinct' presence of *The Pagan* in the 'American Renaissance of literature and art' to the journal's interest in 'the exoticism and richness of Wildes' [*sic*] poems'.⁹³ Kling's scope, however, went well beyond 1890s London. While Bruno took pains to review European periodicals, Kling also included a large proportion of works in translation, often, as Kingham notes, translating them himself.⁹⁴ References to 'old Europe' appeared more subtly than in Bruno's publications: a review of Mimi Aguglia's Italian-language performance of *Salomé* in New York shows a multilingual and intergenerational understanding of American modernism. Kling knowingly quotes lines that were also key to Beardsley's illustrations for the 1894 English edition by Elkin Mathews and John Lane, and quotes the Italian from Aguglia's performance: 'Voglio baciare la tua bocca / Iokanaan' ('I will kiss your mouth / Jokanaan'), enjoying the layers of translation from Wilde's original French to the Italian in his Anglophone journal.⁹⁵ Such allusions to the *fin de siècle* were assimilated with contributions from young, experimental poets such as Louis Zukofsky, Cowley, Munson, Eugene Jolas, Edward Nagle and a slightly older generation including Theodore Dreiser, Maxwell Bodenheim and many Europeans: Knut Hamsun, the Irish nationalist Padraic Colum (a friend of Crane's), Virgil Geddes and Fyodor Sologub, and grandees from 'old Europe' including Octave Mirbeau, Gabriele D'Annunzio and Arthur Schnitzler.

The Pagan's wide-ranging interests were an asset for the young poet experimenting with different voices, and the journal's assimilative aesthetic is well illustrated by Crane's contributions. A quick concordance using an anthology of nineteenth-century poetry is instructive when assessing Crane's use of stock *fin-de-siècle* tropes in *The Pagan* poems. A comparison with Lisa Rodensky's

---

⁹⁰ Kingham, 'Commerce, Little Magazines, and Modernity', p. 185.
⁹¹ Joseph Kling, 'Childhood–April–Russia', from 'Une Vie', *The Pagan*, 1.5 (1916), pp. 7–18 (p. 7).
⁹² Rogers, 'Village Voices', p. 464.
⁹³ Crane, 'To *The Pagan*', *The Pagan*, 1.6 (1916), p. 43; Kingham, 'Commerce, Little Magazines, and Modernity', pp. 159–63.
⁹⁴ Kingham, 'Commerce, Little Magazines, and Modernity', p. 160. Kling's advertisements for his first *Pagan Anthology* note that he translated a high proportion of contributions: 'Announcement No. 1', *The Pagan*, 2.10 (1918), back pages.
⁹⁵ Joseph Kling as 'Ben S', 'To My Brother Connoisseurs', *The Pagan*, 1.2 (1916), pp. 32–5 (p. 35); Wilde, *Salomé*, p. 25.

anthology, *Decadent Poetry from Wilde to Naidu*, reveals the extent of Crane's reliance on these images.[96] The anthology contains numerous examples of *fin-de-siècle* images that Crane used in his early poetry, including 34 of the moon, 47 of 'lips', 11 of 'honey', 42 of 'rose' and 6 of 'jewelled', while 'jade', 'gild', 'crimson', 'opal', 'fragile', 'marble', 'dance' and 'flare' all make frequent appearances. Crane's poetry in *The Pagan* evidences a tension between his attempts to use pared-down Imagist forms, and his use of tropes that had become synonymous with Decadent and *fin-de-siècle* poetry.

As Helen Carr has explored, Imagism was 'a disparate stormy group' that yet had 'many continuities':

> The Imagists, those 'verse revolutionaries' as Aldington dubbed them, sometimes portrayed themselves as sweeping away the debris of a moribund system and effecting a clean break with their predecessors. Yet for all their attacks on Victorianism they did not so much repudiate the past as create a new story about the traditions they had inherited.[97]

In contrast to the received history of Imagism – itself a product of its proponents' propaganda and myth-making – the magazines in which the varied poetic experiments of this diverse group appeared highlight the extent to which, rather than a total rupture with earlier poetic tradition, Imagism coalesced modern trends with those of the *fin de siècle*.

The assimilative aesthetic of the Village journals seems to have had a profound effect on the way Crane viewed poetic tradition at a moment when, as Munro writes, he was 'forming his aesthetic vocabulary'.[98] In 1923 Crane wrote to Munson: 'God DAMN this constant nostalgia for something always "new". This disdain for anything with the trace of the past in it!!'[99] Crane, following the examples of the 'post-Decadent' poetry in *Bruno's Weekly* and *The Pagan*, did not attempt to disguise his poetic inheritances: he flaunted them, sometimes in tension with one another, as in his descriptions in 'Cape Hatteras', a section from *The Bridge* which depicts a dogfight in which the skies are 'poetic citadels repeating to the stars', marked by the 'nasal whine' of the aeroplanes.[100] This blurring of machine-age violence and courtly Victoriana displays the links between Decadence and modernism analysed by David Weir,

---

[96] *Decadent Poetry from Wilde to Naidu*, ed. Lisa Rodensky (London: Penguin, 2006).
[97] Helen Carr, *The Verse Revolutionaries: Ezra Pound, H. D., and the Imagists* (London: Jonathan Cape, 2009), p. 3.
[98] Munro, *Hart Crane's Queer Modernist Aesthetic*, p. 30.
[99] Crane to Munson, 5 January 1923, *O My Land*, p. 11.
[100] Crane, 'Cape Hatteras', from *The Bridge, Complete Poems*, pp. 77–84 (pp. 77, 78).

whereby the former's combination of 'antiquarianism and antinaturalism' is seen as a forerunner of modernism's 'dehumanising hyperculturalism'.[101]

In the poem 'October–November' Crane combines a desire to portray 'instances in time' with a contradictory interest in, as Jean Moréas wrote in the 1886 'Symbolist Manifesto', 'depicting not the thing but the effect it produces'.[102] Genevieve Taggard pinpoints this fruitful tension in her review of Crane's first collection, *White Buildings*. Paraphrasing Moréas, she notes that Crane, the 'imagist in amber', builds his poems on a 'confusion of images', and that his work is 'effect, not cause' – that is to say, Crane is more interested in (as he wrote in 1925) 'the emotional dynamics' of the poem, and the reader's unpicking of the 'associational meanings'.[103] 'October–November' is almost a fabric of quotations from Mallarmé, despite its simple, Imagistic premise, detailing changes in light throughout the day:

> Indian-summer-sun
> With crimson feathers whips away the mists;
> Dives through the filter of trellises
> And gilds the silver on the blotched arbor seats.
>
> Now gold and purple scintillate
> On trees that seem dancing
> In delirium;
> Then the moon
> In a mad orange flare
> Floods the grape-hung night.[104]

Probably translating from the original French, Crane seems to have borrowed several descriptions from Mallarmé, such as 'so when I have sucked the gleam of grape-flesh', 'Among the dead leaves, at times when the forest flows / with gold and ashen tints', 'silvery mist glazing the willows', 'lashing the crimson space of naked gold' and 'memory laden [. . .] streams of purple redolence', all of which are all recalled in 'October–November'.[105] Crane's poem

---

[101] David Weir, *Decadence and the Making of Modernism* (Amherst, MA: University of Massachusetts Press, 1995) p. 16.
[102] Jean Moréas, 'The Symbolist Manifesto', in *Manifesto: A Century of Isms*, ed. and trans. Mary Ann Caws (Lincoln, NE: University of Nebraska Press, 2000), pp. 50–1.
[103] Taggard, 'An Imagist in Amber', p. 4; Crane, 'General Aims and Theories', p. 162.
[104] Crane, 'October–November', *The Pagan*, 1.7–8 (1916), p. 33.
[105] Stéphane Mallarmé, 'L'Après Midi d'un Faune' ('A Faun in the Afternoon'), in *Collected Poems and Other Verse*, trans. E. H. and A. M. Blackmore (Oxford: Oxford University Press, 2008), pp. 38–46 (p. 43), 'Le Nénuphar blanc' ('The White Water Lily'), ibid., p. 113; 'Hérodiade' ('Herodias'), ibid., pp. 193–7 (p. 193), 'Les Fenêtres' ('The Windows'), ibid., pp. 12–13.

is particularly in dialogue with Mallarmé's *Un coup de dés jamais n'abolira le hasard* (*A Dice Throw At Any Time Never Will Destroy Chance*), which contains an image of a 'solitary lost' and 'falling ... feather' ('plume solitaire éperdue') that 'on the invisible brow / scintillates' ('au front invisible / scintille'), in 'delirium' ('délire').[106] Crane's borrowings are somewhat jarring. The use of 'scintillate' falls too easily into its alternative, figurative meaning of compelling, sparkling intellectual brilliance, which is underlined by 'delirium', obscuring the simplicity of Crane's subject.

Crane's ostensibly simple study of changing light is confused by his 'filter' of mixed metaphors. Light 'dives' bird-like with 'crimson feathers', somehow transfigures and acquires the ability to 'gild' the 'blotched' (presumably mossy) 'arbor seats' with 'silver'. Meanwhile, the 'moon' in its 'mad orange flare' cannot help but echo Laforgue's 'pierrots lunaire' and his acidic barbs directed at poet 'dandies of the moon'. Crane returned to this image in two other early poems that dramatise and mock his attempts to write, with 'flesh of moons' in 'Modern Craft' (published in *The Pagan* in January 1918) and 'moons of spring' in 'Legende' (published in *The Modernist* in November 1919), a poem that turns on the poet's conviction that his 'vision will be erased'.[107]

In 'October–November', as in 'C33' and 'Carmen de Boheme', Crane's formal experiments still dictate the detail of his chosen metaphors. After the strict iambs of line two, the rhythm drops into an arrangement based on the sibilant qualities of words and phrases that are used, a little clumsily, to reflect the 'silver' and 'whip[ping]' of the light. 'Scintillate' and 'delirium' are chosen for the surface quality of their fluttering sound – as well as their allusions to Mallarmé. Rhythmically, this arrangement recalls Moréas's principle of 'ordered disorder'; 'scintillate' and 'delirium' are overly decorative in contrast to the aural simplicity of the iambic 'Now gold and purple' and 'On trees that seem' elsewhere in the stanza.[108] The 'seem' here is also important in tracing the development of Crane's verse, from favouring simile to confident metaphors: though the sun *'has'* these feather-like qualities, the trees merely *'seem'* to dance. Likewise, in 'Forgetfulness' (*The Pagan*, August–September 1918) Crane writes: 'Forgetfulness is *like*

---

[106] Stéphane Mallarmé, *Un coup de dés jamais n'abolira le hazard*, in *Collected Poems*, pp. 139–83. Given that these are near cognates ('scintille', 'délire'), whether Crane encountered the text in English or French is unimportant. However, Crane did read French, translating his own versions of Laforgue: 'Locutions des Pierrots', *The Double Dealer*, 1.3 (1921), p. 82. I have followed the Blackmores' translation, but substituted 'shimmers' for the cognate for 'scintille', 'scintillate'.

[107] Crane, 'Modern Craft', *The Pagan*, 2.9 (1918), p. 37; Crane, 'Legende', *The Modernist*, 1.1 (1919), p. 28.

[108] Moréas, 'The Symbolist Manifesto', p. 51.

a song . . . is *like* a bird'.[109] In *The Pagan* poems there is little of the sustained, confident and often surreal metonymy of later texts, developed through his attention to contemporary French experiments. While there are glimpses of the associative mode of the 'logic' in the 'dawn's broken arc' in 'Postscript' (*The Pagan*, April–May 1918), which suggests the gradual, curved line of the watery rise of the winter sun,[110] there is not yet the densely packed, self-consciously disorientating metaphors of his later poems.

Crane's *Pagan* poems were written at the height of the popularity of the Imagist aesthetic. The journals that Crane was reading carefully, including *Others*, *The Modern School*, *The Little Review* and *Poetry*, were at this time centres of Imagism. For its February 1914 number, *The Glebe* published *Des Imagistes*, edited by Ezra Pound and published by Alfred and Charles Boni from their famous bookshop on Washington Square. This publishing move assuredly tied the Imagist movement to Greenwich Village and foreshadowed the aesthetic sensibilities of Boni and Liveright's list in the 1920s.[111] This was reflected in Bruno's journals, which showed a sustained interest in, as the editor put it, 'Imagism and Ezra Poundism'.[112] *The Pagan*'s contents, by contrast, highlight the ways in which Imagist ideas were debated through what might be termed creative criticism. While publishing a variety of experiments in Imagism, *The Pagan* also often featured poetry that interrogated the tenets of the Imagists, as outlined variously in prose by Pound, Flint and Aldington. These poems critiqued ideas associated with Imagism through facetious comment and parody, and through poems that assimilated Imagist and 'post-Decadent' tendencies.

Testament to his unpartisan editing policy, Kling published Imagist poems alongside criticism of Imagist tenets and advocates. This critical engagement with Imagism shaped Crane's own complicated negotiation of Imagist techniques; his experimentation with Imagist ideas was far from a straightforward emulation; rather he combined sparse Imagistic forms with *fin-de-siècle* subjects. Imagism was often satirised in *The Pagan*: one contribution, 'To the Author of Lustra', admonishes 'Ezra / You idle roamer in classical banalities',[113] while Winthrop Parkhurst's 'Vers Libre' mocks Pound's imperative that poets detail 'instance[s] of time' in free verse with the sideswipe 'each kiss a bad poem / Without rhyme

---

[109] Crane, 'Forgetfulness', *The Pagan*, 3.4–5 (1918), p. 15.
[110] Crane, 'Postscript', *The Pagan*, 2.12–3.1 (1918), p. 20.
[111] *The Glebe: Des Imagistes-An Anthology*, ed. Ezra Pound (New York: Albert and Charles Boni, 1914).
[112] Guido Bruno, 'In Our Village: Spring and Poets', *Bruno's Weekly*, 2.14 (1 April 1916), pp. 593–4. Aldington, for instance, was mentioned or appeared twenty times in *Bruno's Weekly*. Data gathered using the Blue Mountain Project.
[113] Max Light Sonin, 'To the Author of Lustra', *The Pagan*, 3.6 (1918), p. 22.

or reason'.[114] Appearing alongside 'Vers Libre' was a prose piece that made a similar comment on the 'cardinal points' of Imagism, and referenced Pound's 'credo' in his 'A Few Don'ts by an Imagiste': 'The credo exhausted my breath already.'[115] 'Flimagism' by John R. McCarthy in the summer 1920 number parodies the pared-down Imagist aesthetic:

> Beans
> Beans
> And a little pork
> Done to a good hard brown.
>
> Beans
> *Hell –*
> How is a good free-poet
> To sing without beans?[116]

McCarthy's bathetic reduction of Imagism to stylistic redundancy (one stranded word per bare line) and domestic mundanities provides a mordant retort to Aldington's claim in *Greenwich Village* in July 1915 that Imagist techniques offered the 'ideal of style . . . for our time', and the Imagist indictment of traditional models as 'often totally unsuited to the matter treated'.[117]

Pound's split from Imagism, explained in a letter to Harriet Monroe in January 1915, reveals the extent to which its aesthetic principles had become the orthodoxy of the avant-garde. Pound wrote that 'Imagism' had degenerated into 'Amygism' (a joke aimed at Amy Lowell's supposed over-exposure in literary journals), and the popularity of the form had, as Pound wrote, resulted in 'a democratic beer garden'.[118] Elitist as his comments seem, they illustrate how widespread this poetic style had become in certain quarters. *The Pagan* printed a large proportion of work in this Imagist vein, such as Kling's own 'Une Vie', from September 1916 – the number Crane compliments in his letter printed in the journal:

> Childhood—April—Russia
> How can skies
> Be so blue,

---

[114] Winthrop Parkhurst, 'Vers Libre', *The Pagan*, 4.6 (1919), p. 11.
[115] C. Kay Scott, 'Imagists', in 'Amazon Forests', *The Pagan*, 4.6 (1919), pp. 12–17 (p. 15).
[116] John R. McCarthy, 'Flimagism III', *The Pagan*, 5.3/4/5 (1920), p. 20.
[117] Aldington, 'The Imagists', p. 54.
[118] Pound to Monroe, c. January 1915, in *The Selected Letters of Ezra Pound 1907–1941*, ed. D. D. Paige (New York: New Directions, 1971), p. 48.

> And sunlight
> So golden?
> Cloud-drifts
> So white—
> And state-roads so muddy?[119]

Crane, as the *Pagan* poems attest, was not immune to these influences, and the sparser impulse of the Imagist form tempered the 'superfluous' tendencies of his early verse. As well as Taggard's rich phrase 'an imagist in amber', Antonio Marichalar commented in *Revista de Occidente* that Crane 'was, before now, an Imagist poet', collaging images into a kind of 'patio'.[120]

Crane's opening lines in 'October–November' recall Kling's 'Une Vie', complete with hyphens, but he cannot resist swapping the trochees for a lively dactylic metre. Crane begins with the subject of his poem, the 'sun', in the fashion common to Imagism, whereby the article is removed. This was unusual for Crane, and asserts his attempt to write in an Imagist mode. In contrast, his other *Pagan* poems open with 'Up', 'The anxious', 'Though' (twice), 'Sinuously' and 'Vault'.[121] This same impulse to emulate characteristics of Imagist poetry directs his subject, observing light patterns over 'instances of time', and his use of purely descriptive lines such as 'Then the moon', and the swift move in time-frame at the beginning of the second stanza with 'Now'.[122] Yet Crane's affinities with the previous generation of poets dominate the poem, and the two conflicting strands of influence clash. Crane's 'external analogies' are hardly going 'in fear of abstractions', to borrow from Pound's 'Don'ts' and F. S. Flint's 'Imagisme', and are at odds with central Imagist premises of the 'direct treatment of the thing'.[123] Crane's poem contains 'superfluous' images that are not 'contributing to the presentation': 'delirium', 'scintillate' and 'dance' all indicating the same movement.[124] It is hardly surprising, then, that in 1917 Pound, who was then the foreign editor at Margaret Anderson's *Little Review*, wrote to Crane following Anderson's acceptance of 'In Shadow', registering his distaste

---

[119] Kling, 'Childhood–April–Russia', from 'Une Vie', p. 7.
[120] Antonio Marichalar, 'La estética de retroceso y la poesía de Hart Crane', review of Crane, *White Buildings* (1926), *Revista de Occidente*, 5.47 (1927), pp. 260–3 (trans. Camilla Sutherland).
[121] Crane, 'The Hive', *The Pagan*, 1.11 (1917), p. 36; Crane, 'Annunciations', *The Pagan*, 1.12–2.1 (1917), p. 11; Crane, 'Modern Craft', p. 37; Crane, 'Postscript', p. 20; Crane, 'Carmen de Boheme', p. 2; Crane, 'To Potapovitch [*sic*] (de la Ballet Russe)', p. 80.
[122] Crane, 'October–November', p. 33.
[123] Pound, 'A Few Don'ts', p. 201; F. S. Flint, 'Imagisme', *Poetry*, 1.6 (1913), pp. 198–200 (p. 200).
[124] Pound, 'A Few Don'ts', p. 200.

for Crane's poetry: 'Lover of Beauty is all very egg; there is perhaps better egg, but you haven't yet the ghost of a sitting hen or an incubator about you.'[125]

The assimilation of Imagist and *fin-de-siècle* forms in Crane's early verse, apparently so distasteful to Pound, must be considered alongside Kling's editorial practices. Kling's poem 'The Theatre' begins with a description of 'A naked bosomed female / On a stage', and the 'flush of feeling' of her audience, but slips into:

> Men and women
> (Upright citizens)
> Laugh . . . . . .[126]

where the lines are stripped of detail and 'ornament'.[127] Monnie Laib's 'Twilight' from December 1917 contains Symbolist-informed tropes similar to 'October–November', even down to the palette, but also displays a comparable affinity with Imagist forms:

> The last tinted rays
> In the west
> Are fading, dying . . .
> Threads of purple
>
> Threads of gold
> Quiver through the air . . .[128]

Clearly, Crane was working within a particular model of fashionable 'post-Decadent' verse that assimilated these two modes. In 'Echoes', published in *The Pagan* in October 1917, Crane again employs Wildean tropes. The poem opens with rain upon the glass, describing changing colours under the 'sunlight', and its eventual evaporation:

> Slivers of rain upon the pane,
> Jade-green with sunlight, melt and flow.
> Upward again: —they leave no stain
> Of storm or strain an hour ago.[129]

---

[125] Pound to Crane, n.d., c. 1918; Unterecker, *Voyager*, p. 89.
[126] Joseph Kling, 'The Theatre', *The Pagan*, 1.1 (1916), p. 3.
[127] Pound, 'A Few Don'ts', p. 202.
[128] Monnie Laib, 'Twilight', *The Pagan*, 2.6 (1917), p. 11.
[129] Crane, 'Echoes', *The Pagan*, 2.6–7 (1917), p. 39.

The poem echoes a contribution to *The Pagan* by Ovro'om Raisin in the July 1916 number:

> Like tristful tears
> The raindrops trickle down
> The window-pane,
> Tracing symbols fraught
> With melancholy meaning . . .?
>
> 'The streets are wet
> And your boots are torn'[130]

While Raisin's poem seems to have been Crane's starting point (and, like Raisin, he mixes the abstract 'tristful' with description, 'The streets are wet'), 'Echoes' still seems rooted in Decadent imagery, with 'fragile', 'cool roses' and eyes as 'opal pools' (recalling a number of descriptions from Wilde, for example, eyes as 'opals that burn always'), and the poem cleaves conservatively to rhyming couplets.[131] Despite Crane's attempts to pare back his language, these images are still cast in abstractions, for instance the 'arms' as 'circles of roses', or the dried rivulets becoming the 'stain' of the 'storm'.[132]

'The Hive', published in *The Pagan* in March 1917, shows Crane starting to move beyond imitation. Rather, he self-consciously dramatises his frustration with his inability to discipline the associations of his chosen subject at this point in his career. The poem reads:

> Up the chasm-walls of my bleeding heart
> Humanity pecks, claws, sobs and climbs;
> Up the inside, and over every part
> Of the hive of the world that is my heart.
>
> And of all the sowing, and all the tear-tendering,
> And reaping, have mercy and love issued forth.
> Mercy, white milk, and honey, gold love—
> And I watch, and say, 'These the anguish are worth.'[133]

Crane is not naïve about the hackneyed nature of that fourth line where the poet is fashioned as the 'vates', the interpreter or prophet scrying the 'world'.

---

[130] Ovro'om Raisin, 'Tamud-Student's Monody', *The Pagan*, 1.3 (1916), p. 41.
[131] Ibid.; Wilde, *Salomé*, p. 74.
[132] Crane, 'Echoes', p. 39.
[133] Crane, 'The Hive', p. 36.

In later poems he uses these clichéd motifs knowingly (fashioning himself as the 'famished kitten' on a step in New York in 'Chaplinesque'), without the need for the kind of declarative defensiveness of the last phrase: '"These the anguish are worth."'[134] Here, Crane is concerned with the dangers of cliché in adopting a prophetic voice, which becomes a dominant pose in the opening poem of *The Bridge*, 'To Brooklyn Bridge', an effort to 'lend a myth to God'.[135]

In 'The Hive' the geometry of the honeycomb metaphor also reflects Crane's increasingly self-conscious interest in his associative, complex form marrying aspects of the *fin de siècle* to Imagism. He plays on the dual meaning of 'humanity' as humankind/society and benevolence/empathy, concepts that, again, are bifurcated throughout the poem, ending on the uncertain but empathetic note of the poet's 'anguish' at placing himself as an interlocutor for 'the hive of the world'. At the start of the poem, the cells of the honeycomb are filled with these individual qualities of 'humanity' struggling for air, or the polyvocal struggle of thought. This idea of the poet as vessel is consistently undermined by an implication of self-interest ('tear-tendering', 'reaping') as the poet elicits ('issue[s] forth'), with deliberate irony, an anxious discussion of formal properties from this traditional conception of the poet as 'vates'. Kling's editorial decisions heighten these implications: 'The Hive' was followed by Routledge Curry's 'Veni, Vidi, Vici', in which a woman saves a child from traffic: 'I saw / Another woman / Snatch a curly headed bit / Of humanity.'[136] The young child in the poem is somehow synecdochic: a part of this whole, 'humanity'. It is an idiomatic trope, and a saccharine image. Crane, by contrast, puts pressure on the hackneyed associations of the word, meticulously dividing it into the component parts ('mercy', 'heart', 'love', 'anguish'), which form the geometry of the hive. He emphasises the noun's dual meaning as a way of articulating his own unease. Despite the complexity of the internal metaphors, the metaphor of the 'heart', punning, as Crane frequently did, on his own name (Hart/heart), remains tired. It is, somewhat perversely, precisely the inability to control these layered associations – his frustrations in struggling towards poetic maturity emphasised in his pun – that seems to have pushed Crane to his accomplished later experiments with an associative form.

These formal concerns are literalised in the quoted final phrase of 'The Hive'. In 'Modern Craft', published in the January 1918 number of *The Pagan*, Crane is working in a similar reflexive mode. He is declarative, but, crucially, as well as the somewhat tired borrowings of nineteenth-century tropes, he 'make[s] sexuality rather than its sublimation central to his text'

---

[134] Crane, 'Chaplinesque', *Gargoyle*, 1.6 (1921), p. 24.
[135] Crane, 'To Brooklyn Bridge', *Complete Poems*, pp. 43–4 (p. 44).
[136] Routledge Curry, 'Veni, Vidi, Vici', *The Pagan*, 1.11 (1917), p. 37.

(as Yingling writes), growing increasingly confident in his developing associative form:[137]

> Though I have touched her flesh of moons,
> Still she sits gestureless and mute,
> Drowning cool pearls in alcohol.
> O blameless shyness; —innocence dissolute!
>
> She hazards jet; wears tiger-lillies; —
> And bolts herself within a jewelled belt.
> Too many palms have grazed her shoulders:
> Surely she must have felt.
>
> Ophelia had such eyes; but she
> Even, sank in love and choked with flowers.
> This burns and is not burnt . . . My modern love were
> Charred at a stake in younger times than ours.[138]

As with 'Echoes', there is a glimmer of Crane's new style here in the striking metaphors, with 'She hazards jet' ('jet' meaning both the gems on her belt and her fashion, style, mode: she dresses quickly, as if observed) and 'bolts herself' firmly and chastely 'within her jewelled belt', guarding against those 'Too many palms' that have 'grazed her shoulders'. The rhythms are roughened, resisting a clear metre. Line openings shift between stressed and unstressed first feet; the first line is iambic, while the second is broken into three uneven feet, with 'Still' as an isolated stressed syllable creating a pause at the start of the line.

'Modern Craft' is a poem about inaction in various forms as Crane comments on his own work, vainly 'search[ing] for a modern muse', as Yingling has suggested.[139] Light is shed on 'Modern Craft' through its resonances with another of Crane's *Pagan* poems, 'The Bathers', published in the December 1917 number. In 'The Bathers', 'Still she sits gestureless and mute' refers to Venus and her unnamed companion, with its similarly static, Pygmalion-esque 'ivory women by a milky sea', and the awkward, aphoristic description of Venus in the last lines: 'She came in such still water, and so nursed / In silence, beauty blessed and beauty cursed.'[140] The nudity of the first line of 'Modern Craft' feels

---

[137] Yingling, *Hart Crane and the Homosexual Text*, p. 244.
[138] Crane, 'Modern Craft', p. 37.
[139] Yingling, *Hart Crane and the Homosexual Text*, p. 243, n. 4.
[140] Crane, 'The Bathers', *The Pagan*, 2.8 (1917), p. 19.

forced; 'flesh of moons' is obvious, even vulgar, draining the description of any erotic charge as Crane seems to reach for Laforgue, of whom, significantly in terms of Crane's use of 'emergent and vestigial styles', he wrote in 1922 that his 'affection' was 'none the less genuine for being led to him through Pound and T. S. Eliot than it would have been through Baudelaire'.[141] In 'Modern Craft' Crane seems to have in mind Laforgue's line 'Dans ce halo de chair en harmonies lactées!. . .' ('In that halo of flesh where milk harmonies well!. . .').[142] In another poem in *The Pagan*, 'Postscript', Crane's concerns about his 'gestureless and mute' poetry are once again figured as 'marble':

> Though now but marble are the marble urns,
> Though fountains droop in waning light, and pain
> Glitters on the edges of wet ferns,
> I should not dare to let you in again.[143]

He alludes in frustration to Keats's 'Ode on a Grecian Urn', lamenting his inability to bring his own 'marble men and maidens' (Keats's phrase) to life: they remain, he repeats, 'but marble . . . the marble urns'.[144]

In both 'Postscript' and 'Modern Craft', Crane's concerns with his poetic ability become intertwined with sexual anxiety. This is apparent in 'I should not dare to let you in again', and in the final line of 'Modern Craft' which Yingling reads as 'a line whose power of surprise derives from its frankness and from its break with the earlier subjects of the poem', a 'feeble protest about the burning of homosexuals in a former historical period'.[145] I would suggest that, given the poem's links to 'Postscript', Crane is also suggesting the 'burn' of unfulfilled desire, which finds a corollary, even a metaphor, in his poetic goals, here 'crafting' the modern love poem – a link Crane would make throughout his career. It wasn't until the mid-1920s that he began sustained experimentation with the associative mode of his 'logic of metaphor' as a coded way of representing his homosexual relationships in a censorious society. In 'For the Marriage of Faustus and Helen', first published as a whole in 1924 after Crane had given serious thought to ideas that would form his associative poetic, he offers an attempt at a solution:

---

[141] Crane to Allen Tate, 16 May 1922, *O My Land*, p. 85.
[142] Jules Laforgue, 'Ève, sans Trêve' ('Eve No Reprieve'), in *The Complete Poems*, trans. Peter Dale (London: Anvil Press Poetry, 2004), pp. 366–7.
[143] Crane, 'Postscript', p. 20.
[144] John Keats, 'Ode on a Grecian Urn', in *The Complete Poems*, ed. John Barnard (Oxford: Oxford World Classics, 1988), pp. 344–6 (p. 345).
[145] Crane, 'Modern Craft', p. 37; Yingling, *Hart Crane and the Homosexual Text*, p. 113.

> *There is a world dimensional for*
> *Those untwisted by a love of things irreconcilable.*[146]

Though melancholic, here there is less of the 'anguish' of 'The Hive' and 'Modern Craft'. The 'logic', in his later poetry, provided Crane with this means of 'reconciling' his poetry with his male subjects using this associative, 'dimensional' model. Whereas in the *Brunos* Crane was working within a recognisable coded queer aesthetic, poems in *The Pagan* begin to combine the process of writing about sexuality in a homophobic society with the process of writing itself, an early attempt to 'untwist' the 'love of things irreconcilable'.

A 'Training School' for Transnational Modernism

In *The Awakening Twenties*, Munson remembers *The Pagan* as a 'training school' for the young editors of the 'exile' journals of the 1920s.[147] The significance of *The Pagan* was, for Munson, negligible in terms of the ultimate trajectory of Crane's career, but apparently formative for the development of his poetry. Munson adds that it was Kling's 'insensitivity to the new writers of *The Little Review*' that led to Crane's eventual disenchantment with the journal. While this oversimplifies Crane's complex affiliations during these years, Munson's overall point rings true: Crane's increasing interest in avant-garde experiments led to his disenchantment with *The Pagan* as the 'post-Decadent' aesthetic of the Village began to lose its appeal. Crane started looking for new publishing outlets. Initially he sent work to New York's *The Modernist* and the New Jersey-based *Modern School*, before looking to journals with broader readerships outside New York City and its environs. In the early 1920s Crane appeared in New Orleans's *Double Dealer*, Vanderbilt's *The Fugitive*, *The Dial* and, after 1922, the 'exile' magazines and other journals in their networks: *Gargoyle*, *Secession*, *Broom*, *1924*, *S4N* and, later in the decade, *transition*.

As contributions to *The Pagan* attest, Kling was paying close attention to literary developments in Europe. However, although Imagist, post-Symbolist and, later, Dadaist poetic forms were highlighted by *The Pagan*, they were treated with caution. Kling's editing practices show a suspicion of arbitrary formal experimentation, and he made this stance clear through parodies of calligrammes in editorial segments. As early as 1915 in Stieglitz's *291*, New York journals had been publishing calligrammatic poems influenced by the European literary avant-garde, with, for instance, J. B. Kerfoot's 'Bunch of Keys', in which the text is arranged to visually represent the subject.[148] Perhaps

---

[146] Monroe, 'A Discussion', pp. 34–41; Crane, 'For the Marriage of Faustus and Helen' [Faustus II], *Secession*, 7 (winter 1923–24), pp. 1–4 (p. 1) [italics in original].

[147] Munson, *Awakening Twenties*, p. 76.

[148] J. B. Kerfoot, 'A Bunch of Keys', *291*, 1.3 (1915), back cover.

responding as much to the offerings in *291* as those in European publications, in July 1918, in a number that featured Crane both as editor and contributor, Kling's 'As It Seems' appeared: an ode to waffles and syrup with the text shaped into a phallus.[149] As early as September 1916, a calligrammatic experiment appeared in *The Pagan* by 'Ben S.' (Kling's pseudonym), in which banal adjectives for Kling at ages 'Twenty' and 'Thirty-Two' are pointlessly grouped into two columns.[150] As these parodies show, Kling believed that form must elucidate content, and the simple visual reflection of the subject was in his view a gimmick. He was more sympathetic to the aims of 'machine-age' poetry – what Dickran Tashjian terms 'skyscraper primitivism' (in fact a pejorative term in the period), the aesthetic of 'those American painters and poets who were affected by Dada's fascination with the machine and who in turn celebrated modern American technology'.[151] Cityscape poems, more in the vein of Carl Sandburg than the overtly Dadaist experiments of *Broom* and *Secession*, were a frequent presence in *The Pagan*, but Crane did not fully experiment with these ideas until he became involved with the 'exile' journals, though he does mention 'ragtime and dances' and 'city, your axles need not the oil of song' in 'Porphyro in Akron' (*The Double Dealer*, August–September 1921) and 'the fury of the street' in 'Chaplinesque' (*Gargoyle*, December 1921).[152] Despite the irreverence of the calligrammes published in *The Pagan*, its attention to these forms enables Crane's interest in post-Symbolist literature to be pinpointed earlier than his reading of Apollinaire (which Unterecker dates from 1919).[153] Crane and Munson (the latter went on to found and edit *Secession*) met at Kling's office and shared his views on form.

As well as introducing Crane and Munson to Dadaism (and possibly fashioning their cautious approach), Kling's presentation of American poetry as a transnational venture seems to have been a key feature of *The Pagan* as a 'training ground'. Crucial to Kling's transnational understanding of the poetic 'renascent period' was his own Russian background and his Greenwich Village location. The social make-up of the Greenwich Village area – not just the literary tourists drawn to the self-mythologised Village – was crucial to Kling's editing of the magazine, informing his conception of modern literature. In contrast to primarily monoglot mainstream journals, Kling reflected the sizeable

---

[149] Joseph Kling, 'As It Seems', *The Pagan*, 3.3 (1918), p. 35.
[150] Joseph Kling as 'Ben S', 'Twenty', *The Pagan*, 1.5 (1916), p. 37.
[151] Munson uses the phrase in 'Skyscraper Primitives', *The Guardian*, 1.5 (1925), pp. 164–78; Dickran Tashjian, *Skyscraper Primitives: Dada and the American Avant-Garde, 1910–1925* (Middletown, CT: Wesleyan University Press, 1975), p. ix.
[152] Crane, 'Porphyro in Akron', *The Double Dealer*, 2.8–9 (1921), p. 53; Crane, 'Chaplinesque', p. 24.
[153] Unterecker, *Voyager*, p. 146.

German-, Polish-, Italian- and Russian-speaking population of his New York.[154] Kling invariably used these translated texts to open their respective numbers, framing the pieces that followed. Translations appeared from French, Hungarian, Polish, Russian, Norwegian, Chinese, German, Turkish, Yiddish, Danish, Swedish, Spanish, Italian, Japanese and 'Indian Poems From the Sioux'.[155] The latter reflected a broader interest among contemporary magazines, which Crane would dubiously appropriate for 'Powhatan's Daughter'.[156] Polyglottism was a social and political issue that Kling foregrounded in his magazine, calling to mind Randolph Bourne's famous essay in *The Atlantic Monthly*, 'Trans-national America', in which Bourne celebrates polyvocality and calls for a 'spiritual welding' of the 'young intelligentsia'.[157]

As in the *Salomé* review, Kling left words and fragments deliberately untranslated. In a number that showcases Jewish literature, he published his own 'In Re Judea et Al' (as 'Nichel') and plays with the word 'Americanism':

> Americanism!   Americanism!
> Americanism!   Americanism!
> Americani . . . .[158]

This chanting results in 'Americanism!' being truncated in its final iteration to 'Americani' in a 'polyglot discordance', to borrow Cristianne Miller's useful phrase.[159] 'Americanism', 'a word, phrase, or other use of language characteristic

---

[154] Rosenwaike, *Population History of New York City*, pp. 93, 95.

[155] For instance, Fyodor Sologub, 'The White Dog', *The Pagan*, 1.2 (1916), pp. 3–9; Octave Mirbeau, 'The Pocketbook', *The Pagan*, 1.4 (1916), pp. 10–31; Gabriele D'Annunzio, 'Francesca da Rimini', *The Pagan*, 1.7–8 (1916), pp. 3–30; D'Annunzio, 'The Hero', *The Pagan*, 3.2 (1919), pp. 12–15; Anton Chekhov, 'Dushitka', *The Pagan*, 2.5 (1917), pp. 3–11; Knut Hamsun, 'The Conqueror', *The Pagan*, 1.3 (1916), pp. 3–10; W. Perzynski, 'The Murder', *The Pagan*, 1.6 (1916), pp. 3–6; Ovro'om Raisin, 'Silent Footsteps', *The Pagan*, 1.6 (1916), pp. 25–7; Unsigned, 'Indian Poems from the Sioux', trans. Mary Katherine Reely, *The Pagan*, 2.11 (1918), pp. 21–2.

[156] See Alice Corbin Henderson, 'Poetry of the North American Indian', review of *The Path on the Rainbow: An Anthology of Songs and Chants from the Indians of North America*, ed. George W. Cronyn (1918), *Poetry*, 12.1 (1919), pp. 41–7. See Robert Dale Parker on appropriation and 'alternative survivances' (Gerald Vizenor's term) in 'Modernist Literary Studies and the Aesthetics of American Indian Literatures', *Modernism/modernity*, 5.4, available at <https://doi.org/10.26597/mod.0189> (accessed 18 March 2021); Gerald Vizenor, *Manifest Manners: Postindian Warriors of Survivance* (Hanover, NH: Wesleyan University Press, 1994).

[157] Bourne, 'Trans-national America', pp. 86–97.

[158] Joseph Kling, 'In Re Judea et al', *The Pagan*, 1.3 (1916), pp. 43–4 (p. 43).

[159] Cristianne Miller, 'Tongues "loosened in the melting pot"', *Modernism/modernity*, 14.1 (2007), pp. 455–76 (p. 462).

of, peculiar to, or originating from the United States', is transformed from a singular collective into the Italian masculine plural noun: 'Americans' becomes 'Americani'. Kling's subtle point here is that the modern American idiom is, ideally, plural and polyglot. Similarly, Kling's own 'Pedagoguesesque' (a poem from 'Une Vie') perhaps pre-empts Crane's 'Chaplinesque', creating a pun that sits between English and French (suggesting 'Pedagogues que').[160]

Kling's playful use of cognates and words that sit between translations may have also influenced the young Eugene Jolas, later the founding editor of *transition*, whose theory 'Revolution of the Word' operates similarly. Jolas's poetry advocates a kind of literary Esperanto, as he writes in 'Rodeur': 'I mute in rain wind crow darkling / Nowhere stop you walkst in fir / Haende tasten apportez-moi du vin'.[161] Building on nineteenth-century experiments in dialect, vernacular and orthography, traced by Gavin Jones in *Strange Talk*, Kling's focus on works in translation, and deliberate non-translation of phrases in his editorials, are testament to his conviction that an American modernism or 'a renascent period in American poetry' (the famous phrase from the first editorial of James Oppenheim, Waldo Frank and Van Wyck Brooks's *Seven Arts*) must be transnational, multilingual.[162] As Cristianne Miller has explored, similar impulses informed the editorial practices of the magazine *Others*, whereby contributors can be seen to 'celebrate a linguistic and cultural mixing echoing the popular idiom of America as a melting pot and affiliated with the figure of the immigrant'.[163]

Kling's richly polyglot magazine exposed Crane to the European avant-garde and provided a 'training ground' for future editors of magazines in which Crane published, such as Munson, Josephson and Jolas, that was crucial in providing Crane with an exemplary transnational model of poetic practice, in which assimilation and juxtaposition, 'collage, polyglossia, syncretic allusiveness' were key. Crane's engagement with these modes permeated his work, but can perhaps be most keenly glimpsed in a light-hearted 1923 fragment, written on a postcard to Charlotte Rychtarik, 'Well/Well/Not-At-All':

leonarda-della-itchy-vinci
es braust ein Ruf wie
      DONNERHALL
pffffff ![164]

---

[160] Kling, 'Pedagoguesque', in 'Une Vie', pp. 17–18.
[161] Eugene Jolas as 'Theo Rutra', 'Rodeur', in 'Poems', *transition*, 7 (October 1927), pp. 144–5 (p. 144).
[162] Gavin Jones, *Strange Talk: The Politics of Dialect Literature in Gilded Age America* (Berkeley, CA: University of California Press, 1999); James Oppenheim, Waldo Frank and Van Wyck Brooks, 'Editorial', *The Seven Arts*, 1.1 (1916), pp. 52–7.
[163] Miller, 'Tongues "loosened in the melting pot"', p. 456.
[164] Crane, 'Well/Well/Not-At-All', *Complete Poems*, p. 208.

Disenchantment: Leaving the Village

In February 1919 Crane wrote to Zigrosser, editor of *The Modern School*, 'A Monthly Magazine Devoted to Libertarian Ideas in Education', chasing up the publication of his poem 'To Portapovitch'. As far as Crane was concerned, the publication of the poem in *The Modern School* was merely opportunistic, marking his attempts to distance himself from Kling's 'mysterious aesthetic touchstones' in *The Pagan*, which had been his mainstay until 1919, and to find a publisher for a poem that Kling had rejected, as also had *The Little Review* and *The Liberator*.[165]

Zigrosser accepted the poem, but Crane clouded the issue by impulsively suggesting that Rockwell Kent might illustrate the text, as he had Wallace Stevens's 'Earthy Anecdote' for the July 1918 number.[166] Crane felt that his poem was 'particularly suitable for accompanying illustration.'[167] It was this 'crowning illustration' of Kent's, Crane said in a letter of 30 December 1918, that had 'tempted [him] to submit [a] lyric for like treatment', hinting at his future interest in ekphrastic poetry, as well as a more general sense of his personal interest in the non-textual, material aspects of publication. In a subsequent letter from 12 February, keen to secure publication, Crane clarified that he simply wanted the poem in *The Modern School*, with its 'fine typography and woodcuts' and impressive roll call of contributors.[168] The journal was the mouthpiece for the Modern School, based in New Jersey's Stelton anarchist colony, and Zigrosser, who expanded its purview into the arts, had been room mates with Randolph Bourne at Columbia.[169] The Modern School programme, of which Emma Goldman was a key advocate, aimed to unseat the traditional American schooling system, which it saw as a 'powerful instrument for the perpetuation of the present social order with all its injustice and inequality'.[170]

The Modern School shared aesthetic similarities with the Village magazines; perhaps unsurprisingly, the school had originally been based in the Village at St Mark's Place. Munson deemed it a journal of 'real distinction', partly due to its beautiful printing. It devoted most of its pages to innovative teaching methods, particularly learning through play and physical movement, including eurhythmics, and the importance of sex education. As Zigrosser put it, his aim was to 'make a beautiful thing' that would reflect the holistic educational methods of

---

[165] Crane to Zigrosser, c. late January 1919, box 9, folder 346, Zigrosser papers.
[166] Wallace Stevens, 'Earthy Anecdote', ill. Rockwell Kent, *The Modern School*, 5.7 (1918), p. 1.
[167] Crane to Zigrosser, 30 December 1918, box 9, folder 346, Zigrosser papers.
[168] Crane to Zigrosser, 12 February 1919, box 9, folder 346, Zigrosser papers.
[169] Paul Avrich, *The Modern School Movement: Anarchism and Education in the United States* (Oakland, CA: AK Press), p. 125.
[170] Ibid., pp. 172–5.

the Modern School movement, while also providing 'a medium of expression for creative thinkers and artists. It deals with radical ideas in education, and by education I mean every activity that broadens and enhances life.'[171] The journal also published regular articles on Irish independence, the activities of the US anarchist movement, literary criticism, some poetry, prose and reviews. Its contributors included Stevens, Maxwell Bodenheim, Padraic and Mary Colum, Kent, Kreymborg, Munson, Rabindranath Tagore, Man Ray (who had been a student at the Village's Modern School),[172] Padraic Pearse, Lola Ridge and Crane himself.

Enquiring whether Zigrosser wanted to see more of his poetry, Crane emphasised the unpartisan stance he had developed at *The Pagan* on avant-garde movements within contemporary poetry: 'I have no very strict prejudices regarding either vers libre or the established conventional.' Crane fired off this letter in a fit of pique after Kling had rejected 'To Portapovitch'.[173] Writing on *Pagan* letterheaded paper, Crane declared his frustrations with Kling and advertised his position as 'Associate Editor', stamped in the margin alongside 'E. O'Neill', presumably Eugene, who also published in *The Pagan*, and was originally tasked with writing the introduction for *White Buildings* (the introduction did not appear, and O'Neill was replaced by Allen Tate). Further emphasising what Crane hoped would be interpreted as an outsider status fitting for the magazine, he speculated, correctly, that his work was unwelcome at *The Little Review* due to 'Mr Pound's rabid dislike of my things'.[174] Zigrosser accepted the poem, and 'To Potapovitch [sic] (de la Ballet Russe)' appeared, with the title misspelled, in the March 1919 issue. The poem was written for Stanislav Portapovitch of Diaghilev's Ballets Russes, with whom Crane, Carl Schmitt and Portapovitch's wife, Anna, had spent the summer of 1917 at Long Beach, when Portapovitch taught Crane the gotzotsky – his party trick.[175] Crane's poem, with its 'vault[ing]' movements, was complemented by an article on 'Ferrer School Entertainments' on the opposing page which detailed 'those few and fugitive performances' of the children's 'acting, dancing, singing' that seem 'prompted by the joy of life'.[176]

Like *The Modern School*, James Waldo Fawcett's *The Modernist* declared its commitment to be 'radical in policy: international in scope', 'devoted to the common cause of toiling people', 'overthrowing old falsehoods' and to act as

---

[171] Zigrosser as quoted in ibid., p. 172.
[172] Ibid., pp. 172–5.
[173] Crane to Zigrosser, c. late January 1919, 12 February 1919, box 9, folder 346, Zigrosser papers.
[174] Crane to Zigrosser, 12 February 1919, box 9, folder 346, Zigrosser papers.
[175] Unterecker, *Voyager*, pp. 92–3.
[176] Crane, 'To Portapovitch [sic] (de la Ballet Russe)', p. 80; John Edelman, 'Ferrer School Entertainments', *The Modern School*, 6.5 (1919), pp. 81–2.

'a forum for active minds and vital art'.[177] The journal (which only managed a single issue) self-consciously declared 'modernism' to be art that 'interpret[s] the ideals and events which we ourselves have a part, the service of humanity'.[178] Crane's initial interest in Fawcett's journal was, as with *The Modern School*, opportunistic. These forays should not, then, be read as an attempt by Crane to ally his poetry with radical politics. In fact, after *The Modernist* was published in November 1919, with Crane's 'Interior', 'Legende' and 'North Labrador', he attempted to distance himself from the journal entirely, and he seemed surprised that Fawcett had credited him with helping to edit the magazine by printing his name on the masthead. It was, he told Munson, a 'jelly like mass', and he was 'quite astonished by the amount of literary rubbish [Fawcett] had managed to get into its confines'. Crane even considered writing 'a letter withdrawing [his] contributions' but was swayed by his 'dumb animal affection' for 'Waldo' and, for the want of other suitable outlets, the opportunity 'simply to have [his poetry] published'.[179]

Crane did, however, plan to send *The Modern School* more work, but suffered a period of writer's block, and Zigrosser stopped editing the journal early in April 1919.[180] While irritated by the sting of Kling's rejection, it had become necessary for Crane to expand his publishing networks beyond the Village. His submissions to *The Modern School* and *The Modernist* were partly a reflection of the wider changes in the literary climate. After these brief engagements, Crane turned his attentions to *The Dial* and *The Little Review*, journals that could offer him exposure and cultural capital in a non-programmatic environment. It was not, though, until the editors and contributors who had cut their teeth at *The Pagan* began to found journals in the early 1920s that Crane would find receptive and sympathetic outlets for his poetry with *Broom* and *Secession*; both had significant influences on his poetic evolution. While throughout the late 1910s Crane was wrestling with how *fin-de-siècle* elements could be incorporated into his verse, in the early 1920s he was attempting to tackle the new influences of the 'machine age' – as is clear in 'Porphyro in Akron' and 'For the Marriage of Faustus and Helen'. His early experiments, in 'Carmen de Boheme' and 'C33', were highly imitative, while

---

[177] Unsigned, 'Platform', *The Modernist*, 1.1 (1919), unpaginated.

[178] Fawcett, secretary to the feminist Margaret Sanger, was also a regular contributor to *Bruno's Weekly*; see, for example, 'Poems and Other Things', *Bruno's Weekly*, 3.6 (22 July 1916), p. 860. Biographical detail from Victoria Kingham, 'Audacious Modernity', in Brooker and Thacker (eds), *The Oxford Critical and Cultural History of Modernist Magazines, Volume II: North America 1894–1960*, pp. 398–419 (p. 419).

[179] Crane's letter also makes his editing role seem minimal. As he told Munson, 'your connection with it resulted in a waste of time'; Crane to Munson, *O My Land*, p. 26.

[180] Allan Antliff, 'Carl Zigrosser and *The Modern School*: Nietzsche, Art, and Anarchism', *Archives of American Art Journal*, 34.4 (1994), pp. 16–23 (p. 23).

his initial attempts to engage with 'machine-age' poetry were laced with irony. In 'For the Marriage of Faustus and Helen', skyscrapers are 'metallic paradise[s]', and the poem leaps from 'asphalt' to 'clouds'.[181]

Crane's aesthetic shifted decisively from the *fin-de-siècle*, post-Decadent poetry of his early work published in Greenwich Village, but remained influenced by transnational artistic currents. As he began to draw on the poetic experiments of the European avant-garde, introducing the Surrealist-informed 'logic of metaphor' and 'machine-age' ideas to his poetry in the 1920s, there remained a line of influence drawn from his earliest work. These new experiments were first tested in the 'exile' journals, published from Paris, Vienna, Rome and Berlin, by editors who had mingled with Crane in the Village. Given the necessary interest of 'the logic of metaphor' in intertextual allusion – as well as the individual associative qualities of words and phrases – analysing Crane's formative use of 'borrowing' and allusion in the late 1910s is crucial to unpicking the genealogy of the 'logic', a form based on collage principles, as it developed in the mid-1920s. Crane integrated this collage-like principle into the microstructures of his later poetry, utilising this technique of juxtaposition so that isolated metaphors are made up of minute, juxtaposed images that use surreal combinations to create the overall impression of the object in question. There was, in essence, a clear link between his post-Decadent early work and his strikingly distinct mature modernist verse.

Nevertheless, Crane never quite managed to struggle free from critical opprobrium rooted in his juvenilia in Village magazine circles, as in Yvor Winters' famous assessment in *Primitivism and Decadence: A Study of American Experimental Poetry*, which includes the unpalatable equation of Crane's homosexuality with a general 'decadence' of character and lack of discipline that reveals itself in his poetry.[182] Marianne Moore, who edited *The Dial* from 1925 to 1929, famously reduced 'The Wine Menagerie' from 49 to 18 lines for the May 1926 number, turning the poem into a meditation on the 'thresholds' of poetic practice rather than desire, as in Crane's original text. When questioned about the edit by Donald Hall, Moore echoed Winters. Revealing perhaps more about her own poetic process than Crane's, she complained to Hall that Crane was unable to self-edit, 'to be hard on himself', something she found rooted in a lack of discipline that she linked to his homosexuality and alcoholism. Alluding to his 'wild parties', she added that he was 'in both instances under a disability with

---

[181] Crane, 'Porphyro in Akron', p. 53; Crane, 'For the Marriage of Faustus and Helen' [Faustus II], pp. 3, 1.

[182] Yvor Winters, *In Defense of Reason: Primitivism and Decadence, a Study of American Experimental Poetry* (Denver, CO: Alan Swallow, 1947), p. 590.

which I was unfamiliar'.[183] Unpicking Crane's periodical networks, the history of his publications and interactions with journals, works to shed considerable light on his complex poetry, and challenges some of the more crude shibboleths of his reception history, which have their roots in his association with the radical, bohemian and sexually liberal post-Decadent journals of Greenwich Village in the 1910s.

---

[183] Ibid., p. 590; Moore, 'The Art of Poetry No. 4', p. 60.

2

'ARE YOU FUTURISTIC OR ARE YOU NOT?': ADVERSARIAL EDITING AND EUROPEAN AVANT-GARDES

> Opposition is true friendship
>
> William Blake[1]

On a damp November afternoon in 1923, the editors of two rival literary magazines squared off against each other in a sodden field in Woodstock, New York. The 'parley' instigated by the co-editor of *Broom*, Matthew Josephson, was ostensibly to resolve long-standing tensions with Gorham Munson, founding editor of *Secession*. The quarrel had emerged during their time in Paris editing 'exile journals', *Broom* co-editor Malcolm Cowley's term for Anglophone magazines founded and edited by Americans in Europe.[2] In the autumn of 1921 Munson had moved to Paris, where, furnished with a letter of introduction from Hart Crane, he was introduced to Josephson and Cowley. The three whiled away the hours at La Rotonde, eating, drinking and playing dominoes with a fellow 'exile', the photographer Man Ray, and the Parisian Dadaists Tristan Tzara, Louis Aragon and André Breton. In those Parisian years they sat at Gertrude Stein's feet in her salon on the rue de Fleurus, met James Joyce – emaciated in his mouldy hotel room in the septième – and discussed publishing with little magazine 'schoolmaster' Ezra Pound – occasionally flanked by Ernest Hemingway, then working for the International News Service, but

---

[1] William Blake, 'The Marriage of Heaven and Hell', *Selected Poems*, ed. G. E. Bentley (London: Penguin Classics, 2006) p. 56.
[2] Cowley, *Exile's Return*, pp. 96–7.

already deemed to be 'something new in American literature' by his mentor.[3] The aesthetic theories of both Munson and Josephson were formed in the crucible of the theatrically fractious circles of Paris Dada, an arena of conflict that had a deep bearing on the emergence of Hart Crane's distinctive poetic voice.

Like Hemingway, Cowley had returned to Paris after serving as an ambulance driver in the First World War. In its aftermath, publishing in Greenwich Village had grown increasingly difficult as a result of wartime censorship laws; 'salvation' was to be found only 'by exile' via the French Line Pier.[4] Such was the ubiquity of Village exiles in Paris that they frequently sent themselves up in their own magazines: 'bored, drinking too much, they analyse their use of adjectives in casual conversation, blithely moving from city to city and purchasing *objets d'arts* and other curios'.[5] *Secession*, founded in Paris, and *Broom* in Rome, were forged in the complex literary dynamics of post-war Europe, shifting business headquarters from Paris, to Rome, Berlin, Vienna and the Tyrol as editors followed the exchange rate, keeping printing costs low.[6]

Munson and Josephson's quarrel maps on to the split in Dada between André Breton and Tristan Tzara early in 1922: Munson sided with Breton, Josephson with Tzara. According to Munson, Josephson 'had swallowed Dada calipash and calipee', contributing enthusiastically to Tzara's single-issue magazine *Le Coeur à Barbe* in which Breton's pontifical edicts were lambasted. After Josephson was appointed literary editor of *Broom*, founded in November 1921 by Harold Loeb (the original for Hemingway's antisemitic portrayal of Robert Cohn in *The Sun Also Rises*) with assistance from Alfred Kreymborg and Lola Ridge (who resigned over Loeb's publication of Stein), the magazine shifted taste to an American Futurist aesthetic and layered 'machine-age' details.[7] Munson, by contrast, was increasingly enamoured with how Breton shepherded Dada's 'haw haws' into a set of aesthetic principles.[8] In *Secession*, Munson was 'working in a scholastic direction, trying to formulate more clearly a literary aesthetics'.[9] *Secession* published poems experimenting with metaphorical formations alongside long critical essays examining their construction and effects.

Shortly before the 'duel', at Cowley's request the 'Broomides' and 'Secessionists' met for a 'unity meeting' in a speakeasy on Prince Street in New York.

---

[3] Ibid, pp. 119–20.
[4] Ibid., p. 74.
[5] Norman H. Matson, 'Expatriate', *Gargoyle*, 2.1–2 (1922), pp. 18–22.
[6] Gorham Munson et al. [the editors], 'Peculiar Arithmetic', *Secession*, 2 (July 1922), p. 53.
[7] Ridge to Loeb, 2 January 1923, in Belinda Wheeler and Lola Ridge, 'Lola Ridge's Pivotal Editorial Role at *Broom*', *PMLA*, 127.2 (2012), pp. 283–91 (pp. 288–91).
[8] Crane to Munson, 23 January 1922, *O My Land*, p. 81.
[9] Munson, *Awakening Twenties*, p. 161.

Fuelled by home-brewed moonshine, Cowley and Josephson sought to amalgamate the two financially troubled and censor-hounded journals, smoothing out factional differences in order to mount an avant-garde 'attack on the New York literary scene – on the establishment'. For the Broomides, such an assault on the literary establishment meant Dadaist nihilistic 'gestures' and tongue-in-cheek poetic experiment. As Cowley wrote in his memoir, the transition from 'exile' journal to New York required 'courts-martial of the more prominent critics, burlesques of Sherwood Anderson, Floyd Dell, Paul Rosenfeld and others – all this interspersed with card tricks, solos on the Jew's harp, meaningless dialogue and whatever else would show our contempt for the audience and sanctity of American letters'.[10]

This held no attraction for Munson, who, like Crane, had an investment in sincerity and 'the passionate apprehension of life'.[11] The unity gathering took place without him, since he was convalescing in Woodstock after a debilitating bout of flu. Instead, he sent a letter, half of it in blank verse, in which he repeated his call for a literature that would 'bring back significance to life' and attacked Josephson as an 'intellectual faker'. For the Broomides, these were 'fighting words'.[12] Cowley read the letter aloud, his impression of Munson growing more ridiculous with each line, provoking the Secessionists. The purpose of the meeting foundered: Kenneth Burke regaled the group with chatter about his dog; Glenway Westcott complained of their inability to 'preserve ordinary parlor decorum'; and Crane paced around the restaurant, pouring glasses of wine and muttering 'Parlor, hell parlor'; Hannah Josephson called for order; Isidor Schneider was overwhelmed by the noise. The evening ended when a group of 'apprentice gangsters ... natives of Prince street' offered to either pack the group off in taxicabs or 'fight [them] at the drop of a hat'.[13]

Munson and Josephson's argument began during the latter's tenure as an assistant editor at *Secession*, clashing over their 'opposing critical [and] aesthetic doctrines' in *Broom* and, later, other publications that emerged within their broader networks: *S4N, 1924* and *Aesthete, 1925*. Josephson's idea for a 'duel' was premised as a way to settle the aesthetic disputes between the factions, but in reality it is best seen as a type of artistic performance, a stylised 'significant gesture' in the manner of the Dadaists: '*action*, action designed to subvert men's minds by laughter and ridicule, by generating a mood of disgust everywhere', wrote Munson, paraphrasing Aragon: 'If a man wrote a review of

---

[10] Cowley, *Exile's Return*, p. 180.
[11] Ibid., p. 179; Munson, *Awakening Twenties*, p. 184.
[12] Munson, *Awakening Twenties*, p. 184.
[13] Cowley, *Exile's Return*, pp. 182–3.

you which you resented, you didn't meet him with literary weapons; you went forth and wrecked his office as Aragon had once done.'[14]

These absurd macho performances might seem like amusing but insignificant anecdotes, inconsequential to Crane's poetic development.[15] In fact, Crane had a surprising stake in them. This chapter uncovers the aesthetic experiments that lay at the heart of the *Broom–Secession* wars, revealing a strand of US modernism and a community of writers closely engaged with European avant-gardes. In turn, it argues that the conflictual aesthetics of both factions incisively shaped Crane's poetry, drawing the young poet out of a creative rut and into the fertile transnational 'exile' networks of post-war Parisian, German, Viennese and Roman little magazines.

I use the term 'adversarial editing' to theorise the aesthetic identity of certain little magazines formed in direct opposition to their contemporaries within the literary field. Adapting Chantal Mouffe's useful analysis of political disagreement, the engagements between these literary factions are understood as belonging to an 'agonistic' model of conflict. Agonism, as opposed to antagonism, is not a struggle between enemies, but a 'struggle between adversaries', which presupposes a degree of mutual respect: 'the opponent is not considered an enemy to be destroyed but as an adversary whose existence is perceived as legitimate'.[16] Crane was at the centre of these vexatious yet fruitful adversarial encounters. His review 'Knitting Needles and Poppycock', which I found during my research, shows how he directly intervened in particular debates within and between magazines, but as this chapter explores, aesthetic negotiations of those arguments are the very substance of his poetry in the early 1920s. Put simply, he takes ideas of poetic experiment and form from *Secession* and applies them to the machine-age subjects inspired by his reading of *Broom*. Here Paul Giles's discussion of *The Bridge* as a Surrealist work presents a useful foothold for my argument that Crane charted a distinct path between *Broom*'s 'love of the machine' and Dadaist collage principles (henceforth, I use the contemporaneous umbrella term, American Futurism) and *Secession*'s fascination with proto-Surrealism and experiments in metaphor.[17]

More than most major modernist poets (with perhaps the exception of T. S. Eliot), Crane's poetry is seen as a self-conscious product of 'The Tradition': Harold Bloom's passionate advocacy of Crane and his insistence on the

---

[14] Munson, *Awakening Twenties*, p. 185.
[15] See David Hopkins, *Dada's Boys: Masculinity After Duchamp* (New Haven, CT: Yale University Press, 2007), on slippages between heterosexual masculinity, homosociability and homosexual identity.
[16] Mouffe, *For a Left Populism*, p. 31.
[17] Giles, 'La Revolution Surréaliste', in *The Contexts of 'The Bridge'*, pp. 134–62.

Shelleyan character of his poetry is an exemplar of this tendency.[18] In *Hart Crane's Poetry*, John T. Irwin's focus on mythic and canonical intertextuality leads to the argument that Crane's celebrated logic of metaphor owed debts to Symbolism. This is the usual reading of Crane's poetic inheritance, as suggested in other fine interpretations of his work by Yingling, Tapper and Reed.[19] Lauren Berlant wrote that intimacy 'names the enigma of [a] range of attachments', that it 'poses a question of scale that links the instability of individual lives to the trajectories of the collective'.[20] Periodicals bear the traces of intimacies between individuals, collectives, sub-groups and coteries. Often unstable, both in editorial terms, publication schedules and contributors and in the uneasy aesthetic alliances they represent, periodicals raise similar questions relating to the individual and the collective. How can we determine such groups? How might Crane's poetry have been shaped by these shifting communities? How might his poetry relate to larger coteries of writers?[21] Through my discussion of Crane's negotiation of various communities, I show that his poetry is directly responding to contemporary developments in the European avant-garde. This is an intimate, coterie poetics that holds in tension the individuality of Crane's own craft with the aesthetic 'trajectories' of the collective groups.

This navigation between aesthetic positions is expressed in the publication history of 'For the Marriage of Faustus and Helen' and 'Voyages', published variously in *Secession*, *Broom*, *1924* and *The Little Review*.[22] Crane used periodical publication to fuse material and aesthetic experimentation: the blueprint for the deconstruction and reconstruction of *The Bridge* between its magazine and volume forms. Both sequences first appeared in fragmentary forms published piecemeal among this cluster of transnational 'exile' magazines. Their scattered publication not only highlights Crane's maturing style, featuring the 'logic' and 'machine-age' details, but raises critical theoretical questions surrounding the fragment and the assembled text. This moment was a watershed in Crane's realisation that publishing might become part of a poem's form, or emphasise its status as collage and fragment.

---

[18] Bloom, *The Anatomy of Influence*, pp. 271–8.

[19] Irwin, *Hart Crane's Poetry*; Yingling, *Hart Crane and the Homosexual Text*; Tapper, *The Machine that Sings*; Reed, *Hart Crane: After his Lights*.

[20] Berlant, 'Intimacy', p. 283.

[21] I am indebted to Lytle Shaw's *Frank O'Hara: The Poetics of Coterie* (Iowa City, IA: University of Iowa Press, 2006), which first alerted me to ways of reading coterie poetics.

[22] Crane, 'The Springs of Guilty Song', *Broom*, 4.2 (1923), pp. 131–2; Crane, 'For the Marriage of Faustus and Helen' [Faustus I], *Secession*, 6 (September 1923), pp. 1–4; Crane, 'For the Marriage of Faustus and Helen' [Faustus II], *Secession*, 7 (winter 1923–24), pp. 1–4; Crane, 'Voyages' ['II', 'III', 'V', 'VI'], *The Little Review*, 12.1 (1926), pp. 13–15; Crane, 'Poster' ['Voyages I'], *Secession*, 4 (January 1923), p. 20; Crane, 'Voyages' ['IV'], *1924*, 4 (December 1924), p. 119.

INTERLUDE: *THE FUGITIVE*, *THE MEASURE* AND *THE DOUBLE DEALER*

At the start of the decade, Crane suffered a period of intense writer's block: he managed just two lines between November 1920 and February 1921, when he began 'Black Tambourine', feeling that he had few responsive outlets for his poetry.[23] He found the newly resurrected *Dial* 'safe . . . despite its protests to the contrary', marred by its 'deep and dirgeful attitude'. *The Little Review*, co-edited by Margaret Anderson and Jane Heap, fared little better in his (misogynistic) estimation, being 'overly temperamental in its tastes'.[24] With rejections piling up at both journals, and having severed ties with *The Pagan*, he made one-off appearances in *The Modern School* and *The Modernist*. His letters describe opportunistically 'selling' his poems to the 'uneven' *Doubler Dealer* and *The Measure*, and he did not build a particularly fruitful relationship with either journal.[25]

Based in New York, *The Measure* was widely distributed, stocked in bookshops across the US, and in London and Paris. Relatively traditional in its tastes, in their first issue *The Measure*'s editors provocatively singled out disfavoured poets. They 'would not accept the works of Amy Lowell and Louis Untermeyer. We prefer Conrad Aiken', suggesting a rejection of the Village aesthetic associated with the former.[26] The journal was edited by a nine-person board that included Maxwell Anderson, Padriac Colum, Louise Townsend Nicholl and Genevieve Taggard. Crane's involvement with *The Measure* was, nonetheless, very much the product of his Village connections, enabled by his friend, the Irish poet and playwright Colum. 'A Persuasion', then, appeared in the October 1921 issue.[27] Meanwhile, although it published 'Porphyro in Akron', the New-Orleans based *Double Dealer* was perhaps of greatest significance to Crane in that it was through the publication of his translation of Laforgue's 'Locutions des Pierrots' in May 1922 that he met Allen Tate, when the latter's 'Euthanasia' appeared on the following page, initiating their correspondence.[28]

Tate was at the time involved with the Southern Agrarian Fugitive group, helping to edit their magazine from Vanderbilt. Crane's dealings with *The Fugitive* and its brand of Southern reaction were minimal, but they did cement his friendship with Tate. *The Fugitive* enabled publication of a few poems that

---

[23] Unterecker, *Voyager*, pp. 187–8; Mariani, *Broken Tower*, p. 74.
[24] Crane to Wiegand, January 20, 1923, *O My Land*, pp. 120–2.
[25] Crane to Munson, 9 September 1921, *Letters*, p. 64; to Munson, 25 December 1921, *O My Land*, p. 76.
[26] Front matter, *The Measure*, 1.1 (1921).
[27] Crane, 'A Persuasion', *The Measure*, 1.7 (1921), p. 14.
[28] Crane, 'Locutions des Pierrots', *The Double Dealer*, 3.17 (1922), p. 261; Allen Tate, 'Euthanasia', *The Double Dealer*, 3.17 (1922), p. 262.

had been hard to place, and 'Stark Major' secured him a spot on the magazine's Nashville Prize shortlist. With the judges chaired by Munson, Crane had perhaps felt his win was assured; he even wrote to his friend to cajole him, emphasising his need for 'free dinners', adding that 'the extra hundred is worth having these days!'[29] Laura Riding ultimately beat him to the $100 prize. Like this prize entry, Crane's publications in *The Fugitive* were opportunistic. He did not read *The Fugitive* with enthusiasm. With its medieval ballads and Southern Agrarian nostalgia, *The New York Times* described the first issue of the journal as 'extremely mediocre'.[30] It was, at best, populated by 'gift book phrases about moonlight and roses', at odds with Crane's increasing interest in American Futurist approaches.[31]

'The "arty" book stores', he told Munson in January 1922, 'bulge and sob' with the weight of 'magazines', and the 'mediocre' or 'safe' journals operating in the US would 'take your work however good or bad it is'.[32] Crane needed the literary community and friendship, the 'visionary company' that he had found in his first years at *The Pagan*, characterised by fast-paced debate and experiment, in order to fully develop his unique approach to poetic language. He was once again on the threshold of just such a reinvigorating scene.

Broom and Secession: Tensions over American Futurism

That necessary reinvigoration came through the first wave of the 'exile journals', *Broom*, *Secession* and *Gargoyle*. The magazines that made up this constellation emerged in the early 1920s as the world of Greenwich Village publishing began to unravel. In 1921 *The Quill*'s Arthur Moss left the Village for Paris, where he founded *Gargoyle*. This first generation of 'exile journals' inspired the later avant-garde periodicals *transition* and *larus: the celestial visitor*, in which Crane also appeared.[33] For a short period in 1921, Munson joined Moss as an assistant editor, briefly providing Crane with another publishing outlet. *Gargoyle*'s contributors included Cowley, Robert Coates, H.D., Wyndham Lewis (whose Vorticism also appeared in *Broom*), Pablo Picasso, Laurence Vail, Man Ray, Georges Braque, Fernand Léger and Henri Matisse. After Moss rejected 'Garden Abstract' for the first issue, Crane submitted four poems to Munson in November 1921 for consideration. Munson accepted all but 'Black Tambourine', which eventually found a home at *The Double*

---

[29] Crane to Munson, 28 October 1923, *Letters*, p. 155.
[30] As quoted in John L. Stewart, *The Burden of Time: The Fugitives and Agrarians* (Princeton, NJ: Princeton University Press, 1965), p. 25.
[31] Ibid.
[32] Crane to Munson, 23 January 1922, box 19, Crane papers.
[33] *larus* also had an editor, J. S. Mangan, in Lynn, Massachusetts. Front matter, *larus: the celestial visitor*, 1.2 (1927); Crane, 'March', *larus: the celestial visitor*, 1.2 (1927), p. 14.

Dealer.[34] *Gargoyle* published 'Chaplinesque' in December 1921; the poem had been hard to place, and had already been returned by *The Double Dealer*, *The Little Review*, *The Dial* and *The New York Post*.

In the late summer of 1922, the journal published two of Crane's strange, quiet lyrics, 'The Great Western Plains' (for which Crane was paid $1) and 'The Fernery'.[35] Both poems are preoccupied with memory – ideas that Crane would return to in 'My Grandmother's Love Letters' and 'The Mango Tree'. The final stanza of 'The Great Western Plains' reads, 'Indeed, old memories come back to life; / noses pressed against the glass', a Yeatsian/Keatsian image that shows the kernel of the later, more consummate poem. While Munson's role at *Gargoyle* offered Crane a testing ground, he rapidly lost interest in Moss's journal. It had not lived up to the transatlantic energy it promised, becoming 'ineffectual . . . not worth 35¢', as he told Munson.[36] Crane would soon look to the magazines that emerged in its wake.

Broom and *Secession* were founded soon after *Gargoyle*, with their inaugural issues in November 1921 and April 1922, respectively. Both were edited from Paris and drew on a similar pool of contributors as their predecessors in the early 1920s. In January 1922 Crane wrote to Munson that he was 'either bewildered or else indifferent', faced with the 'deluge of production' with 'so little at stake'.[37] He needed the discursive atmosphere of a magazine with shared (though not identical) aesthetic interests to push his poetry, the kind of transnational creative community he had experienced at *The Pagan* in the late 1910s. Bored with the offerings available on New York news-stands, he increasingly looked to the European avant-garde for cues. He wrote to Munson, recently relocated to Paris, 'send me some poetry. It's sure to be better than anything the magazines offer here.'[38]

Munson's *Secession* was founded in the atmosphere of Parisian Dada, and he even credited Josephson with helping him sketch out the purview of the magazine.[39] The review was to be 'intransigent, aggressive, unmuzzled'.[40] Like *Broom*, then based in Rome and still edited by Loeb, *Secession* was to be published from Europe, moving printing locations in pursuit of favourable

---

[34] Crane to Munson, c. June 1920, 21 November 1921, *Letters*, pp. 40, 71; Crane, 'Black Tambourine', *The Double Dealer*, 1.6 (1921), p. 232.
[35] Crane to Munson, Thursday, late August 1922, *O My Land*, p. 101; Crane, 'Chaplinesque', p. 24; Crane, 'The Great Western Plains', *Gargoyle*, 1.3 (1922), p. 7; Crane, 'The Fernery', *Gargoyle*, 1.4 (1922), p. 19.
[36] Crane to Munson, 25 May, *O My Land*, p. 87.
[37] Crane to Munson, 2 February 1922, box 19, Crane papers.
[38] Crane to Munson, 26 November 1921, *Letters*, p. 70.
[39] Munson, *Awakening Twenties*, pp. 161–2.
[40] Ibid., p. 164.

post-war exchange rates: '*Secession* is printed in Central Europe which gives it the advantage of a peculiar arithmetic: $5.00 = $25.00 $30.00 = $150.00'.[41] Munson aggressively outlined the magazine's ethos in an 'Announcement' circulated prior to the first number.[42] *The Little Review*, he wrote, was overly 'personal', 'represent[ing] nothing but the wandering preferences of its editors', a dismissal with an undertow of misogyny similar to that of Crane. He chided *The American Mercury*, a magazine for 'adolescents', and singled out Louis Untermeyer and Paul Rosenfeld as 'custodians' of 'the general flabbiness of American criticism'. The 'unmuzzling' continued in the first issue of *Secession* with his 'Exposé No. 1', which took aim at *The Dial*, which was printing a 'catholic' and 'diffuse assortment of culture'.[43] *The Dial*'s eclectic approach was, for the 'exiles', its chief deficiency after its take-over by Scofield Thayer and James Sibley Watson. Its failure to support the 'new generation of American writers' was encapsulated in its awarding Sherwood Anderson, 'an established writer', the first *Dial* prize; Anderson had published six books, and had magazines 'eager for his work', Munson wrote.[44]

Secession's most immediate adversary, however, was *Broom*, which was 'not doing much sweeping'.[45] By 1921, Munson wrote, *Secession* had become 'necessary' after the 'final disappointment of *Broom*', which appeared to have 'joined the anthology classification' (*Broom* shifted its focus to 'machine-age' modernism shortly after Munson made this tart comment).[46] In contrast to this moribund catholicity, *Secession* would represent a new generation of writers and their blasts against the status quo:

> SECESSION Instigated in Paris, opens fire this spring at Vienna, will march on Berlin, and eventually establish itself in New York. *Secession* is an organ for the youngest generation of American writers who are moving away from the main body of intelligent writing in the United States since 1910. They are defining a new position from which to assault the last decade and to launch the next. 'Form, simplification, strangeness, respect for literature as an arts with traditions, abstractions . . . these are the catchwords that are repeated most often among

---

[41] Munson et al. [the editors], 'Peculiar Arithmetic', p. 53.
[42] Gorham Munson, '*Secession* Announcement', c. spring 1922, box 1, folder 1, Crane family papers.
[43] Gorham Munson, 'Exposé No. 1', *Secession*, 1 (spring 1922), pp. 22–4 (p. 22).
[44] Ibid., p. 23.
[45] Matthew Josephson, *Life Among the Surrealists* (New York: Holt, Rhinehart and Winston, 1962), p. 154.
[46] Loeb had ignored Munson's offer to help edit the magazine, drawing his ire. *Awakening Twenties*, p. 163.

the younger writers.' – Malcolm Cowley. *Secession* aims to be the first gun of the younger generation. It will publish stories, poems, criticisms, insults and vituperations by Slater Brown, Kenneth Burke, Donald B. Clark, Malcolm Cowley, Hart Crane, E.E. Cummings, Matthew Josephson, Marianne Moore, Wallace Stevens and by certain allied Frenchmen, Guillaume Apollinaire, Louis Aragon, André Breton, Paul Eluard, Philippe Soupault and Tristan Tzara. It will, in its early numbers, expose the private correspondence, hidden sin and secret history of its American contemporaries, *The Dial, Little Review, Broom, Poetry*, et cetera. It already notes in current literature very much that demands hilarious comment.[47]

Josephson's name in this roll call suggests the slipperiness of the two factions in their earliest phase, as Tashjian discusses in *Skyscraper Primitives: Dada and the American Avant-Garde*.[48] *Secession*'s affiliation with 'certain allied Frenchmen', outlining its plans for 'significant gestures', 'accusations' and 'hilarious comment', placed the magazine among the literary avant-garde, antagonising those with a broader appeal and higher circulation. With a $20.00 budget and circulation of between 300 and 500, these strategic shots across the bow offered Munson free marketing.[49] He immediately received the responses he desired, with Jane Heap's 'Exposé' in *The Little Review* in its spring–summer 1922 issue insinuating that *Secession*'s attacks were motivated by the 'numerous rejection slips' these magazines issued.[50] Controversy proved a successful tactic and became key to the method of aesthetic debate in the journal. Writing in *The Saturday Review* in 1937, Munson declared that the editor of an underfunded, small-circulation magazine might yet attract 'writers with "names"' if 'the controversy is sharp enough to draw them in'.[51]

Munson quickly appointed Josephson as a fellow 'director' of *Secession* – the terminology was borrowed from French journals – in order to 'represent more fully' Josephson's brand of 'machine-age' modernism.[52] Josephson's involvement spanned only three issues, from August 1922 to January 1923. His hand in the magazine fuelled the scepticism of Crane, who worried that, under his influence, the journal would be in thrall to the 'insane jumble' of Dada. Crane

---

[47] Munson, '*Secession* Announcement'.
[48] Tashjian, *Skyscraper Primitives*, p. 228.
[49] Munson, *Awakening Twenties*, p. 167; Josephson recalls 300 in *Life Among the Surrealists*, p. 231.
[50] Jane Heap, 'Exposé', *The Little Review*, 8.2 (1922), pp. 46–7 (p. 46).
[51] Gorham Munson, 'How to Run a Little Magazine', *The Saturday Review*, 15.22 (26 March 1937), pp. 3–4, 14 (p. 14).
[52] Matthew Josephson, 'Made in America', *Broom*, 2.3 (1922), pp. 226–70 (p. 269).

claimed to have swung 'by the straight and narrow path . . . to the south of the village DADA' and, 'abashed', would rather 'posture' with 'reverence before the statues of Ben Jonson, Michael Drayton, Chaucer, sundry others'.[53] Though he remained characteristically ambiguous about the place of his own work in the journal, Crane was soon so convinced of the magazine's value that he acted as an informal distributor for it, sympathetic to the magazine's combination of, as he put it to Charmion von Wiegand, 'tradition while at the same time being far more daring in its experiments than *The Dial*'.[54] He published two spirited defences of *Secession* in *The Little Review* and Woodstock's *1924*, a magazine funded by Otto Kahn.[55] The latter essay, a piece I have found and identified, defends *Secession* against one of its chief critics, Amy Lowell, using a pseudonym taken from a phrase in 'For the Marriage of Faustus and Helen', 'Religious Gunman'.[56]

Munson's journal declared literary allegiances by publishing Anglophone writers alongside Europeans. These 'Frenchmen' were to be 'allies', not 'leaders'. And Munson quite literally meant male writers based in Paris; Marianne Moore was the only woman to appear in the journal – revealingly, this was in a number edited by J. B. Wheelwright while Munson was in New York.[57] Prefiguring New York as the final location for *Secession* (a plan Josephson and Cowley copied after moving to *Broom*) was an attempt to state the importance of the city as a global literary centre. As Josephson wrote, using distinctly Futuristic terminology, in 'Apollinaire: Or Let Us Be Troubadours' in the first number of *Secession*:

> the conviction comes that Americans need play no subservient part in this movement. It is no occasion for aping European or Parisian tendencies. Quite the reverse, Europe is being Americanized. American institutions, inventions, the very local conditions of the United States are being duplicated, are being 'put over' daily in Europe. One has only to visit Berlin, for instance, in 1922 to witness this phenomenon. The complexion of the life of the United States has been transformed so rapidly and so daringly that its writers and artists are rendered a strategic advantage. They need only react faithfully and imaginatively to the brilliant minutiae of

---

[53] Crane to Munson, 23 January 1922, *O My Land*, p. 81.
[54] Munson, 'Exposé No. 1', p. 22; Crane to Wiegand, 20 January 1923, *O My Land*, p. 121; Crane to Munson, 29 September 1922, *Letters*, p. 101; Crane wrote to Tate urging him to contribute, 16 May 1922; on distribution, to Munson, 25 May 1922, *O My Land*, pp. 83, 87.
[55] Edwin Seaver, *So Far So Good: Recollections of a Life in Publishing* (Westport, CT: Lawrence Hill, 1986), pp. 99–100.
[56] Crane as 'Religious Gunman', 'Knitting Needles and Poppycock', pp. 136–9.
[57] Matthew Josephson, 'Apollinaire: Or Let Us Be Troubadours', *Secession*, 1 (spring 1922), pp. 9–13 (p. 13); Marianne Moore, 'Bowls', *Secession*, 5 (July 1923), pp. 12–13.

her daily existence in the big cities, and in the great industrial regions, athwart her marvellous and young mechanical forces.[58]

Munson and Josephson were in effect restating the cultural project that had guided an earlier generation of magazines: these early position pieces announce *Secession*'s aim to work against what Randolph Bourne identified in the *Atlantic Monthly* in 1914 as a 'cultural humility' in American writing that could 'only have the effect of making us feeble imitators'.[59] This concept was crucial to the founding of Bourne's own journal, *The Seven Arts*, as well as *The Pagan* and *Others*, and it informed the editing policy of *The Dial* and *Poetry*, although expressed differently in the 'exile' journals; Munson cited Bourne as a predominant intellectual influence for the 'exile' generation in *The Awakening Twenties*.[60]

Like *Secession*, *Broom* was launched and published from the 'revered places' of Europe, and distributed in the US, Italy, France, the Netherlands and the UK, announcing its selection from the 'continental literature of the present time the writers of exceptional quality [. . .] these will appear side by side with the contemporary effort in Great Britain and America'.[61] Cultural confidence was once again critical: as Loeb put it to Cowley in 1922, 'above all [*Broom* is] a positive note to contrast with the persisting weeping over the fact that America is not Europe'.[62] The first issue was printed in Rome in November 1921, complete with a frontispiece from the Italian Futurist painter Ernesto Prampolini printed on 'fine paper', with full-page inserts of reproductions of paintings including Joseph Stella's *Brooklyn Bridge*, and sold at an expensive 50¢ per copy.[63] Financed partly by Loeb's selling of his share in the Sunwise Bookshop, then, later, his inheritance (his mother was Rose Guggenheim), the journal was initially edited by Loeb and Kreymborg, whom Loeb appointed in the hope that his 'established literary reputation would help the magazine off the ground'.[64] As Munson recalled, perhaps selectively, it started as 'a sort of clearing house', with a 'catholic' and 'anthological editing policy'.[65] *Broom*'s early numbers featured contributions from Conrad Aiken, Amy Lowell, Lola Ridge, Louis Untermeyer, Sherwood Anderson, Wallace Stevens and Harold Monro. The journal's

---

[58] Josephson, 'Apollinaire', p. 13.
[59] Randolph Bourne, 'Our Cultural Humility', *The Atlantic Monthly*, 114.3 (1914), pp. 503–7 (p. 506).
[60] Munson, *Awakening Twenties*, pp. 23–32.
[61] See front matter, *Broom*, 1.1 (1921).
[62] Loeb to Cowley, 2 May 1922, box 1, folder 11, Loeb/*Broom* correspondence.
[63] Harold Loeb, *The Way It Was* (New York: Criterion Books, 1959), p. 75; Stella, *Brooklyn Bridge*, painting; photographic reproduction in *Broom*, 1.1 (1921), p. 2.
[64] Loeb, *The Way It Was*, pp. 2–6.
[65] Munson, *Awakening Twenties*, p. 168.

early iterations prized literary criticism, Aiken's 'The Function of Criticism', Untermeyer's 'Einstein and the Poets' and Emmy Veronica Sanders's 'America Invades Europe' all appearing in the inaugural number.[66] This focus on criticism, and the manner of contributors associated with the journal, shifted sharply after the third number – a move that led to Kreymborg's resignation after its publication in January 1922.

Loeb's change in editorial policy effectively formed a new journal; as Hoffman, Ulrich and Allen note, *Broom* was actually 'two magazines under one name'.[67] The new-look run of *Broom* featured Cowley and Josephson as assistant, then, later, full editors, with contributions from William Slater Brown, Gertrude Stein, Jean Cocteau, reprints from Guillaume Apollinaire and Philippe Soupault, as well as Yvor Winters, William Carlos Williams and Virginia Woolf. Loeb's new ideas for the journal were very much influenced by Josephson and were articulated in his essay 'The Mysticism of Money', which discusses a literature that might embrace 'advertising', 'curved belt lines of machinery' and the 'possibility of steel' architecture in 'geometrical forms' that 'rise in great tooth like rows, incisors and molars, cubes and pyramids'. Like Crane outlining the thinking behind 'For the Marriage of Faustus and Helen', Loeb comments on the possibilities of 'a combination of advertising and talking machines', of the 'barbaric totem beat with the exotic accompaniment of gongs, conches, syrens and voices', of 'jazz tunes', and of a 'narrative technique' in which 'the essential ingredient is speed'.[68] Arguments over 'machine-age' modernism, or American Futurism, would come to define the 'exile' journals, and would shape Crane's poetry through his engagement in their debates. While *Broom* committed itself to this new aesthetic, a split emerged at *Secession*. Josephson was increasingly interested in the literary uses of 'industrial' tropes and 'mechanical forces', while Munson viewed *Secession* as a 'technical journal' that would focus on 'form and strangeness'.[69] Crane's poetry, as it developed after Greenwich Village, was positioned somewhere between the concerns of these two editors, effectively transcending the limited creative vistas of each.

The contours of arguments about American Futurism appear in a flurry of activity in the magazines after Lowell's 'Two Generations in American Poetry', an article for *The New Republic* in 1923, which attacked Munson for an overly theoretical 'mathematic[al]' approach, prompting Crane's

---

[66] Conrad Aiken, 'The Function of Criticism', *Broom*, 1.1 (1921), pp. 33–8; Louis Untermeyer, 'Einstein and the Poets', *Broom*, 1.1 (1921), pp. 84–6; Emmy Veronica Sanders, 'America Invades Europe', *Broom*, 1.1 (1921), pp. 89–93.

[67] F. J. Hoffman, C. F. Ulrich and C. Allen, *The Little Magazine: A History and Bibliography* (Princeton, NJ: Princeton University Press, 1947), p. 261.

[68] Harold Loeb, 'The Mysticism of Money', *Broom*, 3.2 (1922), pp. 115–30 (pp. 115, 125). See Josephson, *Life Among the Surrealists*, pp. 167–71.

[69] Gorham Munson, 'The Mechanics for a Literary *Secession*', S4N, 3.21 (1922), pp. 1–9 (p. 7).

response in *1924*.⁷⁰ The editorial differences between Munson and Josephson were clear from the first issue, although Josephson was not officially a 'director' until the second number. Coming out in April 1922, *Secession* coincided with, and in some ways responded to, the arguments between Breton and Tzara in *Littérature* and *Le Coeur à Barbe*. These two journals charted a wrench that began the aesthetic shifts from Dada to Surrealism.⁷¹ Josephson, who socialised at 'Dada soirées', contributed to *Le Coeur à Barbe*, which Tzara intended to rally his supporters against Breton. It included a short manifesto signed by Tzara, Eluard and Georges Ribemont-Dessaignes: 'Le « *Coeur à Barbe* » ne contiendra ni littérature, ni poésie.'⁷²

Josephson's poetry adhered to the Dadaist line, his poem 'Do You Fear the Dark' in *Broom* incorporating advertising from a popular 'lamp with a clamp' and 'machine-age' details; Crane would do the same with 'Tintex', a clothing dye brand, in his poem 'The River', as John Baker has explored in detail.⁷³ Tzara's collage approach was also formative in Josephson's poetic thinking.⁷⁴ The essence of this was, as Tzara put it in his 1920 'How to Make a Dadaist Poem', 'Take a newspaper / Take some scissors'.⁷⁵ As Perloff writes, in 'Dada collage, pictorial composition gives way to a new emphasis on the materials, assembled themselves', producing 'subtle formal and material as well as semantic tensions'. Surrealist collage, Perloff writes, differs subtly, so that juxtapositions 'produce a fragmented narrative'.⁷⁶ Declaring his own allegiances, Josephson placed an advertisement for *Secession* in the pages of Tzara's *Le Coeur à Barbe*, a flourish that announced his intention to represent Dada in its pages.⁷⁷ He sought for Munson's magazine works that deployed new, mechanical, quotidian objects:

---

⁷⁰ Munson, *Awakening Twenties*, pp. 168–9; Amy Lowell, 'Two Generations in American Poetry', *The New Republic*, 37.470 (5 December 1923), pp. 1–3 (p. 3).
⁷¹ For a full account, see Alan Young, *Dada and After: Extremist Modernism and English Literature* (Manchester: Manchester University Press, 1983), pp. 110–26.
⁷² Crane to Munson, 23 January 1922, *O My Land*, p. 81; Tristan Tzara et al., 'Pour Faire Pousser le Coeur', *Le Coeur à Barbe*, 1.1 (1922), p. 1.
⁷³ Crane, 'The River', p. 113; John Baker, 'Commercial Sources for Hart Crane's "The River"', *Wisconsin Studies in Contemporary Literature*, 6.1 (1965), pp. 45–55. See Peter Riley on Crane's advertising career in *Against Vocation*.
⁷⁴ Matthew Josephson, 'Dada', box 13, folder 332, Josephson papers; Josephson, 'Do You Fear the Dark?', *Broom*, 5.2 (1923), pp. 95–6; Adjusto-Lite advertisement, 'The Lamp with a Clamp', *Popular Mechanics Advertising Section*, 5.38 (1922), p. 163.
⁷⁵ Tristan Tzara, 'How to Make a Dadaist Poem', in *The Dada Painters and Poets: An Anthology*, ed. Robert Motherwell (Boston, MA: G. K. Hall, 1981), p. 92.
⁷⁶ Marjorie Perloff, 'Collage and Poetry', in *Encyclopaedia of Aesthetics*, ed. Michael Kelly (New York: Oxford University Press, 1998), vol. I, pp. 384–7 (pp. 384–5).
⁷⁷ Unsigned, 'Dernière Heure', *Le Coeur à Barbe*, 1.1 (1922), back cover; Matthew Josephson, 'Beware of Editors', *Le Coeur à Barbe*, 1.1 (1922), p. 6.

for instance, Josephson's own 'The Oblate', which tracks a car's acceleration, juxtaposed (collage-like) against the passing details of the street. Tellingly, his main contribution to the second number was a translation (under the pseudonym 'Will Bray') of Tzara's 'Mr AA the Antiphilosopher' which, in the same issue, Munson pointedly eschewed: 'I do not, at present, vouch for the majority of Tzara's activities.'[78] As the fissures between the co-directors spread, Josephson's criticism and writing aligned him further with Loeb's new-look *Broom*. The factional identities could not be avoided. After Josephson and Cowley left *Secession*, Crane told Munson: 'We really have two groups to the former ONE of *Secession* and there is no use in trying to evade that fact,—as, obviously, you are not trying to do.'[79]

While Josephson privileged the use of 'industrial' tropes and 'mechanical forces', Munson, like Crane, was more interested in the problems of their formal application. *Secession*, he emphasised after Josephson's departure, was intended as a 'technical journal' concerned with poetic technique.[80] The uneasy truce between the former friends at an end, Munson wrote that he found works they had published such as Josephson's 'Peep Peep Parrish' to be 'tripe'; such 'machine-age' experiments were the equivalent of 'putting automobile goggles on Proteus', a 'verbose and inept transposition to an industrial city of Illinois'.[81] Munson penned a cutting review of Josephson's 1923 collection *Galimathias*, a volume that included calligrammes, dedications to Aragon and Jacques Baron, and a poem titled 'Toward Public Disgrace in a Streetcar' which, in prurient euphoria, apostrophises the possible dangers of the car: 'O my fellow passengers— / of the innumerable provocative impacts'.[82] Munson's review ran:

> It is easy to surmise that this lack of any fundamental attitude toward life, this indulgence in trivial fancy, make [Josephson] especially susceptible to influences which swallow him with little resistance. However, he has the cunning to pick influences new to American poetry, —*The Lay of Maldoro* [sic], Gertrude Stein, the Dadaists, —and so his work glitters with a novel reflected brilliance. At the same time one is depressed by an emptiness in back of his shrillest exclamations, the emptiness of one who

---

[78] Gorham Munson, 'A Bow to the Adventurous', *Secession*, 1 (spring 1922), pp. 15–19 (p. 17).
[79] Crane to Munson, 28 October 1923, *Letters*, p. 155.
[80] Munson, 'Mechanics', p. 8.
[81] Matthew Josephson, 'Peep Peep Parrish', *Secession*, 3 (August 1922), pp. 6–11; Gorham Munson, 'Interstice Between Scylla and Charybdis', *Secession*, 2 (July 1922), pp. 30–2 (p. 30).
[82] Matthew Josephson, 'The Oblate', *Secession*, 3 (August 1922), p. 14; Josephson, 'Toward Public Disgrace in a Street-Car', in *Galimathias* (New York: Broom, 1923), p. 29; Peter D. Norton, *Fighting Traffic: The Dawn of the Motor Age in the American City* (Cambridge, MA: MIT Press, 2008), p. 31.

cannot create his own artistic world and assimilate into it the stronger poets he reads.[83]

'Assimilation' is a key word in Crane's stake within these arguments: the difficulties of assimilating modern, mechanical details and subjects into the poet's own 'artistic world' was both a topic of debate and a source of experiment throughout *Secession*'s run, culminating with Waldo Frank's article 'For the Declaration of War', which criticised Dada as a response to the devastation of the First World War. Dada's nihilistic, splintering formal impulses, Frank wrote, were an attack on spiritual fellowship, 'an attempt to articulate the rejection of this first principle [. . .] Unity is truth. This is a universe, not a multiverse.'[84]

Crane's 'For the Marriage of Faustus and Helen' preceded Frank's essay in the same number and is illuminated when seen as a response to these debates. Like Munson, Crane was sceptical about 'machine-age' accoutrements until he began considering how they might be properly assimilated into his verse. After reading Josephson's first contribution to *Secession*, Crane wrote a mocking letter to Munson, stuffed with familiar and somewhat disingenuous disavowals of the current crop of magazines:

> But what has happened to Matty!?! And, —just why is Apollinaire so portentous a god? Will radios, flying machines, and cinemas have such a great effect on poetry in the end? [. . .] It is metallic and pointillistic— not derogatory terms to my mind at all, but somehow thin, —a little too slender and 'smart'—after all. O Matty must be amusing himself perfectly in Paris. And so he took you to be a real, honest-to-God disreputable and commercial editor! Serves you right, bad boy, following the primrose path of the magazines![85]

For Crane, the rage for contemporaneity was in itself 'a little too slender and "smart"': it clearly needed something else. Josephson's investigations were, by his own account, at times superficial: in 'Apollinaire', he emphasised the necessity of utilising the 'new poetic equipment of cinema, phonograph, Dictaphone, airplane, wireless', but, as regards 'form and technique', 'alliteration' and 'assonance with typographical arrangements' would be enough to 'give new visual and auditory sensations to the reader'.[86] Elsewhere, however, he

---

[83] Gorham Munson, 'Tinkering with Words', review of Matthew Josephson, *Galimathias* (1923), *Secession*, 7 (winter 1923–24), pp. 30–1 (p. 31).

[84] Waldo Frank, 'For the Declaration of War', *Secession*, 7 (winter 1923–24), pp. 5–14 (pp. 10, 12).

[85] Crane to Munson, 19 April 1922, *Letters*, p. 84.

[86] Josephson, 'Apollinaire', p. 13.

noted that Tzara's 'poems are as naturally expressive as Herrick's are of the 17th century', and 'the tramway gets into the very rhythm, form and texture of the poems', rather than just indicating '"I was in the tramway,"'[87] This aside seems to echo Crane (and even Munson) in exhibiting Josephson's anxieties regarding the need for proper 'assimilation' of machine-age apparatus.

For Crane, Josephson's Dadaist collage used quotidian details to give an impression of modernity, with formal details (alliteration and assonance) sprinkled among these 'surface phenomena'.[88] Crane paid attention to both sides of the debate, overcoming his total scepticism of 'Dada theories and other flamoodle' through his exposure to it in both *Broom* and *Secession*. He began creatively responding in his poetry to the crackling energy that this argument unleashed. His 1925 critical essay 'General Aims and Theories' picks up some of his intuitive critique of Josephson's 'thin' Futurism, and explores the nature of his own assimilative approach:

> it was my intention to embody in modern terms (words, symbols, metaphors) a contemporary approximation to an ancient culture or mythology that seems to have been obscured rather than illumed with the frequency of poetic allusions made to it during the last century. So I found 'Helen' sitting in a street car; the Dionysian revels of her court and her seduction were transferred to a Metropolitan roof garden with a jazz orchestra; and the katharsis of the fall of Troy I saw approximated in the recent world war.[89]

The cityscapes of 'For the Marriage of Faustus and Helen' create 'correspondences', a 'grafting process' as Crane termed it, between the myth and the modern landscape, with the aim – as also explored later in *The Bridge* – that cosmopolitan New York, in all its 'seething' detail, would be given the same depth and significance as Troy. Faustus's gaze lies on Helen unflinching, even as she flicks through banal 'newspaper advertisements . . . counting the nights'.[90]

The nature of Crane's development, and his experiments with assimilation, may be grasped through a comparison of 'For the Marriage of Faustus and Helen' with 'Porphyro in Akron', published in *The Double Dealer* in 1921. Taking Porphyro from Keats's 'The Eve of St Agnes' and transplanting him to the streets of Akron, Ohio, is deliberately comic here. Crane castigates the banality of everyday life in 1920s Akron, swapping Madeline's lute

---

[87] Crane to Munson, 19 April 1922, *Letters*, p. 84.
[88] Bourne, 'Trans-national America', pp. 86, 97.
[89] Crane, 'General Aims and Theories', p. 162; Crane to Munson, 19 April 1922, *Letters*, p. 84; Josephson, 'Do You Fear the Dark?', pp. 95–6.
[90] Crane, 'General Aims and Theories', p. 160.

and chambers for Fords, iceboxes and 'a shift of rubber workers'.[91] Notably, many of these quotidian objects and things of urban modernity such as those he derided in Josephson's work also appear in his later masterpiece, *The Bridge*. 'For the Marriage of Faustus and Helen', in contrast to the bathos of 'Porphyro in Akron', contains giddy allusions to 'flying machines', exalting 'metallic paradises' as Crane casts off his scepticism and tests out the possibilities of this mode. It was through his exposure to machine-age poetry such as Josephson's that he began to puzzle out how he might incorporate these ideas into his own work, as realised in the paeans to 'elevators', 'cinemas', 'subways', 'traffic lights', 'dim slogans' of advertisements, 'radio[s]', 'EXpress' [*sic*] and 'Overalls ads' in *The Bridge*.[92] The logic of metaphor is, then, best thought of as akin to Keats's 'negative capability' or Eliot's 'dissociation of sensibility' in that it is a piece of jargon that theorises and does things for the poet in question. As Hammer writes, the logic of metaphor is 'both an obstacle and an instrument' – and usefully so.[93] The logic of metaphor, which went through a new stage of development as Crane read *Secession*, gave him a set of principles of association. Through the paratactical movements of this micro form, Crane could approach subjects at a glancing angle, from the love poem to sketches of the machine age prompted by his reading of *Broom*.

Proto-Surrealism and 'the Logic of Metaphor'

The logic of metaphor has historically frustrated even the most devoted of Crane's critics. Examining the genealogy of the logic of metaphor helps to clarify its contested function. The concept developed throughout his career, beginning with his early interest in Imagism and Symbolism as demonstrated in the early Village poems and, in the 1920s, drawing on proto-Surrealist and Dadaist experiments in juxtaposed metaphor and collage, where ideas are placed in tension to create a given image.

From his time as Kling's assistant at *The Pagan*, Crane was attuned to the literary experiments of Paris Dada. He envied Sherwood Anderson's 1922 trip to Paris, which 'put him in direct touch with all the younger crowd in France'.[94] After he had taken up a poorly paid, entry-level position at the Cleveland advertising agency Corday and Gross that January, *Secession* and *Broom* invited the young poet into dialogue with the Parisian avant-garde.[95] That said, he was initially sceptical of attempts by US writers to adopt their ideas. As we have

---

[91] Crane, 'Faustus II', p. 1.
[92] Keats, 'The Eve of St Agnes', *Complete Poems*, pp. 312–24; Crane 'Porphyro in Akron', p. 53.
[93] Hammer, *Janus-Faced Modernism*, p. 178.
[94] Crane to Wiegand, 6 May 1922, *Letters*, p. 85.
[95] Unterecker, *Voyager*, p. 225.

seen, Crane viewed Josephson's 'machine-age' poems as period pieces.[96] It was, Crane told Munson, 'like coffee-twenty-four-hours afterward not much remains to work with'.[97]

Why, then, is Crane's epic *The Bridge* at first glance a paean to that same American Futurism – engineering, elevators, cinemas, subways, derricks? What enabled him to work effectively in this mode? As Crane read and published in the 'exile journals' of the early 1920s, he formulated his own sensitive response to arguments between the Dada-influenced 'machine-age' Broomides and proto-Surrealist Secessionists, developing his own assimilative mode that could incorporate these 'machine-age' details without turning the text into 'useless archaeology'.[98]

Key to this assimilation was Crane's critical doctrine, the logic of metaphor. His 'General Aims and Theories' and 'Letter to Harriet Monroe' have generally been analysed for their exegesis of the associational workings of the 'logic'. However, the poetic examples Crane works through have, curiously, been paid little attention. In both essays, he reaches for 'machine-age' metaphors to illustrate the possibilities of his associational method. Referring to 'For the Marriage of Faustus and Helen', he writes, 'So I found "Helen" sitting in a street car; the Dionysian revels of her court and her seduction were transferred to a Metropolitan roof garden.' But, he clarifies, 'what is interesting and significant will emerge only under the conditions of our submission to, and examination and assimilation of the organic effects on us of these and other fundamental factors of our experience'. The logic of metaphor was therefore essentially an act of reflective assimilation, mediating between tendencies in the transatlantic poetic avant-garde, and through a process that was equally Romantic organicism and modernist revisionism, achieving the significant poetic statement.

As method, the logic was a way of writing metonymically, able to slough off 'previous precepts or preconceptions' through unusual juxtapositions of ideas, creating ideas and images through 'thought extension' and association. Crane underlines this in his essay by deconstructing the aeroplane imagery in 'For the Marriage of Faustus and Helen':

> the speed and altitude of an aeroplane are much better suggested by the idea of 'nimble blue plateaus' – *implying* the aeroplane and its speed against a contrast of stationary elevated earth. Although the statement is pseudo in relation to formal logic – it *is* completely logical in relation to the truth of the imagination [. . .][99]

---

[96] Sanders, 'America Invades Europe', p. 89.
[97] Crane, 'General Aims and Theories', p. 161; Crane to Munson, 19 April 1922, *Letters*, p. 84.
[98] Crane, 'General Aims and Theories', p. 161.
[99] Ibid., p. 164.

The poetry and critical arguments published in *Secession* incisively shaped Crane's development of the logic of metaphor. Fine critics of Crane's poetry have traced Symbolist resonances in it. This line of thought sees the logic adhering to French forms, Crane's use of metaphor adapted from the Symbolist principle that 'the idea will never appear without the sumptuous clothing of analogy', reflecting his interest (counter to the precepts of Imagism) in producing the emotional 'effect' as well as describing the 'thing'.[100] True as this is to an extent, in his more mature poetry Crane moves away from the idea of metaphor as extraneous, ornamental 'clothing' to the very essence of poetry: its function as a sharpening, shifting – even refracting – of ideas: that 'single new *word*' he speaks of in the 'General Aims'.[101] This required the careful juxtaposition of uneasy ideas – a process informed by experiments in proto-Surrealism.[102] There is a clear shift from Crane's experiments in French Symbolism, the 'mad orange flare' or 'grape hung night' in 'Echoes' and other *Pagan* poems, and the more radical later experiments in which metaphors often resolve into balanced tensions between juxtaposed images ('metallic paradises' for high-rise buildings, 'choiring strings' for the harp-shaped cable structure of Brooklyn Bridge).[103]

Crane was exposed to new work by factions of Paris Dada through *Broom* and *Secession*, privy to – and part of – technical arguments over means and aims of constructing metaphors and poetic images in Munson's journal. Munson's editing selections, at least in the first two numbers solely under his control, were dominated by proto-Surrealist metaphorical experiments. He adopted Pierre Reverdy's principle (reiterated by Breton in his 1924 manifesto) that 'The image [. . .] cannot be born from comparison but from a juxtaposition of two more or less remote realities', a dictum that appears to have wielded significant influence over Munson's selections in the first four numbers of *Secession*.[104] This distinction between 'comparison' and the 'juxtaposition' of 'remote realities' is crucial to Crane's poetry, and shows its debt to the proto-Surrealist experiments he was encountering in the 'exile' journals. In its emphasis on juxtaposition, fusion and fruitful tensions, Munson interestingly pre-empts some of the impulses of the New Critics.

In the first number, edited solely by Munson, Aragon's 'Bottle Found at Sea' – which Crane described to Munson as 'quite a beautiful thing' – demonstrated Munson's initial interest in these metaphorical forms, as Aragon

---

[100] Moréas, 'The Symbolist Manifesto', p. 50.
[101] Crane, 'General Aims and Theories', p. 163.
[102] In doing so I am able to date this interest earlier than Giles in *The Contexts of 'The Bridge'*, his finely grained study of Crane, Surrealism (as it had developed by the late 1920s), Joyce and *transition*.
[103] Crane, 'Faustus and Helen', *Complete Poems*, p. 29; Crane, 'To Brooklyn Bridge', *Complete Poems*, p. 43.
[104] Pierre Reverdy, 'L'image', *Nord-Sud*, 2.13 (1918), pp. 3–8 (p. 3).

deploys disharmonious associations such as 'sponges of silence' to describe the removal – absorption – of sound.[105] In a subtle contrast, in 'Poem' in the third number of *Secession* (August 1922) Cowley uses a similarly metonymic construction with a description of 'fishcakes blossoming', which is both a literal description and is used as a metaphor to describe a floral pattern stitched on a cloth covering the hot plate. Here, the two juxtaposed ideas seem entirely unrelated (fish, flowers).[106] At a stretch the metaphor conveys the round shape and perhaps the texture of the flowers, but the juxtaposition is distracting rather than illuminating.[107] The absurdity of such disparate images strategically diverts attention from the idea that is being conveyed towards the construction of the metaphor.

Crane was interested in toeing a line between tense, surprising juxtapositions and a metaphor or image that, in its ridiculousness, becomes self-referential. These experiments are clear in 'For the Marriage of Faustus and Helen', where the defamiliarising technique is applied to the cityscape: skyscrapers become 'metallic paradises' 'scour[ing] the stars'. Crane employs this to great effect in *The Bridge*, beginning even with the 'cinema' in the 'Proem' where viewing the screen is described as 'foretold to other eyes on the same screen', so that the emphasis is placed on the communal experience ('other eyes') of the cinema, rather than its technological innovations.[108]

The difference between Crane's and Josephson's treatments of these ideas is clear in the publication of 'The Springs of Guilty Song' ('Faustus and Helen' Part II) in *Broom* alongside Josephson's American Futurist 'Pursuit':

> O whizzing dynamo set spinning the vast wheelbelts of this world
> the long rods in flight down the cool oiled cylinders.
> O heart O Vesuvius
> O destroying speed of descent and escape.
> O sun omnipotent motor drive with infinite velocity the solar orbs
> in accelerated dispersion. [original formatting][109]

Josephson's effort throws Crane's associative description of the cityscape in 'Springs' into relief, where he combines his experiments with Surrealist metaphor with his interest in how machine-age tropes might be assimilated into poetry. Crane sketches out the New York skyline with its 'metallic paradises' of

---

[105] Louis Aragon, 'Bottle Found at Sea', trans. Matthew Josephson, *Secession*, 1 (spring 1922), pp. 4–7 (p. 7).
[106] Malcolm Cowley, 'Poem', *Secession*, 3 (August 1922), p. 13.
[107] Ibid., p. 13.
[108] Crane, 'To Brooklyn Bridge', *The Dial*, 82.6 (1927), pp. 489–90.
[109] Matthew Josephson, 'Pursuit', *Broom*, 4.2 (1923), pp. 164–7 (p. 167).

skyscrapers that create this 'cultivated' sky, while the sounds of the city become 'catastrophes of drums' and 'hailed' 'groans' of 'Dionysian revels' that almost seem to shake the 'gyrating' steel 'awnings' of the skyscraper beneath Helen's 'Metropolitan roof garden'.[110] With the logic he could not only refresh the Helen myth, which he felt had been partitioned into quotes, half-baked and doled out in different poetic iterations ('an all-too-easily employed crutch for evocation'), but he could also apply it to American Futurist ideas, using quotidian, modern details without the disenchanting effect of referring to 'surface phenomena'.[111]

'For the Marriage of Faustus and Helen': Editing Accidents, Interventions and Form

The genealogy and publishing histories of the different variants of 'For the Marriage of Faustus and Helen' published in *Broom* and *Secession* reveal Crane's interest in larger-scale collage forms. The poem was printed in three versions as a result of a hitherto unexplored series of miscommunications with *Broom* and due to editing interventions by Wheelwright at *Secession*. After sending the first version of 'For the Marriage of Faustus and Helen' to *The Dial*, where it was rejected, and having consulted with Munson, Crane wrote to Josephson on 6 November 1922. He outlined his plans for the unfinished poem (Part III was still a sketch), but suggested that he might excise Part II. He suggested that Part II could be published on its own; 'I've called it "The Springs of Guilty Song" and let it go at that', he wrote.[112]

Judging from his next letter, Crane must have been persuaded by Josephson's reply to reverse his decision and reassemble the first two parts of the poem, with the third part completing the poem in its eventual volume form:

> My original conception of this poem makes it difficult to acceed [*sic*] to your suggestion about publishing it and the 'Brazen hypnotics' as parts I and II under the one heading. But go ahead. They fit well enough together, so far as that goes—my original conception is, of course, privy to myself. When it comes out in book form 'Faustus and Helen' will probably have the third part which I miss, alone, and which, so far, has only been sketched.[113]

Josephson did not receive Crane's response in time; *Broom* went to press with 'The Springs of Guilty Song' to 'make up the number', as Loeb put it in a curt

---

[110] Crane, 'Springs', p. 132; Crane, 'General Aims and Theories', p. 160.
[111] Crane, 'General Aims and Theories', p. 160.
[112] Crane to Josephson, 12 December 1922, and 6 November 1922, box 1, folder 13, Loeb/*Broom* correspondence.
[113] Crane to Josephson, 12 December 1922, box 1, folder 13, Loeb/*Broom* correspondence.

response. The printing error 'was in no way our fault', he added after Crane had responded angrily.[114] Furious with Loeb's denials, Crane told Josephson he would no longer submit to *Broom* because 'THE WORST WILLHAPPEN [*sic*] BY ALL MEANS ANYHOW'.[115]

Despite Crane's anger over the error, his impulsive letter to Josephson is nonetheless revealing of the poem's form and gestures towards his later publishing decisions for *The Bridge*, not only in terms of split publication, but the idea of saving the publication of the final, unifying section for the volume, as he did with the final fragment of *The Bridge*, 'Atlantis'. Crane's belief that the poem could be split, with the parts functioning independently, suggests that it was built to resemble more of a triptych than a conventional, cumulative sequence, foreshadowing *The Bridge*'s Cubist arrangement. The three parts of 'For the Marriage of Faustus and Helen' are not only able to function independently as discrete meditations (I on the lovers, II on Helen's court, III the 'religious gunman', war poem section), but use markedly different forms that map on to the *Broom* and *Secession* arguments. In Part I Crane lists 'baseball scores', 'stenographic smiles' and 'stock quotations', and Helen is found in her 'street car', essentially detailing the 'problem' as presented in *Broom* (that is, how to integrate the materiality of the machine age into poetry). In Part II Crane offers a first Secessionist solution: he so obfuscates the two characters and the cityscape they inhabit through the logic of metaphor that the section is at a remove from the 'For the Marriage of Faustus and Helen' context, standing 'perfectly on its own two feet'. 'The other [two] parts', which contain less abstract descriptions, were, Crane wrote, 'entirely unlike it'.[116] In Part III he offers something of an aesthetic compromise between the Broomide literalism of Part I and the Secessionist obfuscations of Part II. Helen is no longer 'her', but is renamed once again. She re-emerges amid the violence, where Troy finds a parallel in the recent world war. But here, unlike Parts I and II, this devastation is rendered through surprising but delicately revealing juxtapositions, such as a squadron of planes 'in corymbulous formations of mechanics,—' (resembling a flower in a corymb form, where each head blooms at the same height, such as a yarrow plant). For Crane these evasive, associative movements – the acts of interpretation – offer something of a balm (if not a stay) against violence and the glamorisation of the war machine (a hallmark of Josephson's writing). With the traumas of the war in mind

---

[114] Loeb to Crane, 20 March 1923, box 1, folder 13, Loeb/*Broom* correspondence.
[115] Frank to Crane, 21 February 1923, box 6, Crane papers; Crane's formatting, to Josephson, 2 March 1923, box 1, folder 13, Loeb/*Broom* correspondence.
[116] Crane, 'For the Marriage of Faustus and Helen' [Faustus II], p. 1; Crane to Munson, 4 June 1922, *O My Land*, p. 88.

('our flesh remembers') he offers a consolation in the final stanza: 'bleeding hands extend and thresh the height / The imagination spans beyond despair, / Outpacing bargain, vocable and prayer.'[117]

While the editing accident at *Broom* is revealing of the form of 'For the Marriage of Faustus and Helen', the interventions at *Secession* are part of a wider pattern in Crane's reception in the early 1920s, even before the publication of *White Buildings*. Entrusted to 'supervise' the printing of numbers five and six of *Secession* in Florence during Munson's absence, Wheelwright 'assumed editorial duties in the matters of revision, comment and acceptance'.[118] Wheelwright's 'garbled' (Crane's assessment) version of the poem removed Part II of 'For the Marriage of Faustus and Helen' (perhaps not understanding that Munson had secured permission from Loeb to reprint the poem),[119] introduced errors, and cut lines 32 ('the white wafer cheek of love, or offers words') and 53 ('That beat, continuous, to hourless days—') because he found them 'inessential', foreshadowing Moore's attempts to restrain 'The Wine Menagerie' in her edit of the poem for *The Dial*.[120] 'Still worse', for Crane, was Wheelwright's 'ill-advised' and unauthorised 'quotation from [Munson's] personal comment':

> Hart Crane's three poems for the Marriage of Faustus and Helen are to be read with reference to T.S. Elliot [*sic*]. In Munson's opinion they are an affirmation that reveals a sub-stratum of the *Waste Land* to be sentimentaly [*sic*], namely, that depression is a mark of aristocracy.[121]

Crane was concerned that the journal's readers and contributors would assume that this ridiculous note was authorised. Crane asked Munson to destroy all available copies of the journal to ensure that 'as many people in America are free from misconceptions about me as possible'.[122] Most irritating for Crane, who was fearful that 'Eliot's influence threatens to predominate the new English', was the reduction of his engagement with Eliot in 'For the Marriage of Faustus and Helen' to a comment on *The Waste Land* – a recurrent framework in criticism

---

[117] Crane, 'For the Marriage of Faustus and Helen' [Faustus II], p. 4,
[118] Gorham Munson, 'Explanatory', *Secession*, 7 (winter 1923–24), back pages.
[119] See Gorham Munson, 'Notes', *Secession*, 7 (winter 1923–24), front matter; Crane to Munson, 28 October 1923, *Letters*, p. 154.
[120] Wheelwright switches 'bluet' for 'blues', adds commas after 'unjubilant' and 'briefly', switches a comma to a full stop at 'tides', and misspells 'vine' as 'wine'.
[121] John Brooks Wheelwright, 'Note to "For the Marriage of Faustus and Helen"', *Secession*, 6 (September 1923), p. 4.
[122] Crane had yet to publish a volume. Though short, this was one of the first pieces of criticism of Crane to appear in print. Date of publication established by Crane's letters. The issue date is given as 'winter 1924'.

of Crane's long poems.[123] Rather, it was debates over European avant-gardes that allowed Crane to engage with but ultimately depart from Eliot. Through his attention to these lively journals, he could attempt a depiction of the modern city while working 'through' Eliot to a 'different goal', leaving behind the 'damned dead' world of *The Waste Land*.[124]

'FRIENDS MAKE A BIG DIFFERENCE': COTERIE POETICS AND 'VOYAGES' IN *SECESSION*, *1924* AND *THE LITTLE REVIEW*

Crane's 'Voyages' sequence emerged in the same energising and receptive environment as 'For the Marriage of Faustus and Helen'. The first publication was in January 1923, with 'Voyages I' as 'Poster' in *Secession*. This was followed by 'IV' in the December number of *1924*. The remaining four poems ('II', 'III', 'V', 'VI') appeared in *The Little Review*'s 'America vs Europe' issue, edited by Josephson. At the same time, Crane published poems to artist-friends in Seaver's journal, dedicated to works by the Ohio painter William Sommer ('Sunday Morning Apples *To William Sommer*') and the sculptor Gaston Lachaise ('Interludium *to "La Montagne" by Lachaise*').[125] Whether or not he was worried about his over-affiliation with the 'exile' group, he was, nonetheless, firmly connected to their circles. The coterie established by the two ekphrastic poems is useful to bear in mind when thinking about the development and dissemination of 'Voyages'.

Edwin Seaver's *1924* was founded and edited from the 'artistic and literary' community of the 'Woodstock colony' in upstate New York. The zeitgeist, Munson suggests, of this 'foothill' in the Catskills was characterised by *1924* and Frank Schoonmaker's *Hue & Cry*, which expressed an interest in 'the new in arts and letters' and 'a revival of the spirit of Walt Whitman'.[126] The 'new' was represented by Seaver's continuation of *Broom* and *Secession*'s arguments, with both magazines on the point of insolvency. After *1924*, *Aesthete, 1925* would take up the baton, edited and assembled by Burke, Crane, Cowley, Josephson, Tate, Wheelwright, William Slater Brown and, by mail, Williams, with the group writing under the pseudonym 'Walter S. Hankel'. Crane was strategically unnamed in the magazine's notes, but his involvement with the magazine, which resolutely attacked Munson, ultimately severed their friendship.[127] 600 copies of *Aesthete, 1925*, a single-issue magazine, were sent

---

[123] Crane to Munson, 13 October 1920, *Letters*, p. 44.
[124] Crane to Munson, 5 January 1923, *O My Land*, p. 117; to Munson, 20 November 1922, *O My Land*, p. 108.
[125] Crane, 'Sunday Morning Apples *To William Sommer*', *1924*, 1 (July 1924), p. 1; Crane, 'Interludium *to "La Montagne" by Lachaise*', *1924*, 1 (July 1924), p. 2.
[126] Munson, *Awakening Twenties*, p. 291; Hoffman, Allen and Ulrich, *Little Magazines*, pp. 269–70.
[127] Crane's participation is recorded in Brown (ed.), *Robber Rocks*, pp. 42–3.

out in February 1925.[128] It has been speculated that Crane wrote 'Chanson' for *Aesthete, 1925* under the guise of Hankel. Weber points out that a copy of *Aesthete, 1925* had 'Crane' scrawled across the top of the page, and Josephson, in *Life Among the Surrealists*, suggests that Crane authored the text.[129] Susan Jenkins Brown, however, claims that the poem was written by her husband, William Slater Brown. The truth may be somewhere in between, with the group of editors writing the poem.[130]

Running from July to December, *1924* published a similar pool of contributors to *Broom* and *Secession*, featuring American writers working with European avant-garde influences alongside pieces that emphasised Seaver's interest in regional, 'localist', literature.[131] He mixed, for instance, his own creative-critical response to a local artist in 'The Paintings of Judson Smith' (in which he declares 'American! / Is the flavour of the pear [. . .] of these apples') with stories based in and around Woodstock, advertisements that asserted a nearby readership for the town's soda fountain services, insurers, weavers and sandwich shops, alongside an argument between Frank and Cowley over 'Seriousness and Dada', Crane's 'Voyages', and a letter from Pound offering a summary of the current Parisian literary scene.[132] The magazine ultimately ceased publishing after tensions once again rose between the Secessionist and Broomide factions, with Crane withdrawing poems from the journal 'out of loyalty to his two friends' and trying to broker another peace between Cowley, Josephson and Munson through letters.[133]

---

[128] Jack Selzer, *Kenneth Burke in Greenwich Village: Conversing with the Moderns, 1915–1931* (Madison, WI: University of Wisconsin Press, 1996), p. 51. The magazine, like *1924*, was in large part a response to Ernest Boyd's attack on the 'exiles' in 'Aesthete: Model 1924', *The American Mercury*, 1.1 (1924), pp. 51–6.

[129] "Walter S. Hankel" [perhaps Crane or W. S. Brown], *Aesthete, 1925*, 1.1 (1925), p. 27; Weber, *Hart Crane*, p. 242; Brown (ed.), *Robber Rocks*, pp. 42–3; Josephson, *Life Among the Surrealists*, p. 264.

[130] I have thus not listed this as a publication in the appendix. Butterfield, not realising the poem was a joke, comments on Crane's 'damp squib' in *The Broken Arc*, p. 95. I would hazard that Crane was involved with the 'Impure Pure Criticism' feature, particularly judging by the tone of its last piece, 'Meditations': 'I am often accused of being amateurish or immature . . .', *Aesthete*, p. 8.

[131] On localist modernism, see White, *Transatlantic Avant-Gardes*, pp. 81–109.

[132] Edwin Seaver, 'For the Paintings of Judson Smith', *1924*, 4 (December 1924), p. 127; Stark Childe, 'Tale of a Wooden Leg', *1924*, 1 (July 1924), pp. 25–9; Waldo Frank, 'Seriousness and Dada', *1924*, 3 (September 1924), pp. 70–3; Malcolm Cowley and Waldo Frank, 'Communications on Seriousness and Dada', *1924*, 4 (December 1924), pp. 140–2; Ezra Pound, 'A Communication from Ezra Pound', *1924*, 3 (September 1924), pp. 97–8.

[133] Mariani, *Broken Tower*, p. 170; Selzer, *Kenneth Burke*, pp. 47–52; Crane to Munson, *Letters*, p. 154.

Despite its clear importance for his poetry, Crane was ambivalent about the idea of writing within a coterie. *Broom* and *Secession* had thoroughly energised his writing, but he began to worry that it entangled him too closely 'to one group, faction "opportunity," or another'.[134] He was initially reluctant to give poems to Seaver, who tried to assure Crane that 'the magazine favors no group, and no individual'.[135] Crane's poems to artists in the group seem to register these mixed feelings: keeping him within discussion, but at a slight remove from the intense debates of *Broom* and *Secession*. It is significant, too, that when he did wade into the second round of arguments between Munson and Josephson and Cowley in *1924*, he wrote under the 'Religious Gunman' pseudonym. It was easily identifiable to a group intimately acquainted with 'For the Marriage of Faustus and Helen', but offered him an air of plausible deniability and a semblance of detachment from the increasingly heated debates.

His ekphrastic poems in *1924* to William Sommer and Gaston Lachaise speak to the magazine's investment in dialogue between visual and written arts. As Munson put it: 'this mood of the American risorgimento was most fully experienced at Woodstock [. . .] One of two art colonies in the East—the other being Provincetown.' Both poems make comment on, as Munson wrote, the 'exchanges of writers and artists' that 'enlivened [. . .] Woodstock in the twenties', and situate Crane within a responsive coterie.[136] Sommer was popular among the group, providing a frontispiece for *Secession*, issue 4. *Secession* and *1924* contributor William Carlos Williams had bought one of Sommer's paintings (with Crane as an intermediary) after it 'got under his underdrawers'.[137]

Crane had spent considerable time sending '27 Sommer things off to Anderson' at *The Little Review* and *The Dial*, and Munson had attempted to secure gallery space for Sommer in New York, but Sommer appeared resistant to exhibiting outside Ohio.[138] After Sommer took a job at the Otis Lithography Company of Cleveland, he painted only on Sundays – hence his series 'Sunday Morning Paintings'.[139] This may have resonated with Crane, who had scribbled down snatches of the 'Voyages' while working for his father's

---

[134] Crane to Munson, 8 December 1924, *O My Land*, p. 202.
[135] Perhaps irritated by contributors' notes that labelled him a 'Secessionist'. See Unsigned, 'Notes on Contributors', *The Fugitive*, 2.8 (1923), p. 127; Unsigned, 'Contributor's Notes', *S4N*, 4.26–9 (1923), pp. 50–1; Seaver to Crane, n.d. [late autumn 1924?], box 7, Crane papers.
[136] Munson, *Awakening Twenties*, p. 290.
[137] Crane to Munson, 12 October 1922, *Letters*, p. 102; William Carlos Williams, *Selected Letters*, ed. John C. Thirwell (New York: New Directions, 1984), p. 186; Munson, *Awakening Twenties*, p. 292.
[138] Mariani, *Broken Tower*, p. 79; Brown (ed.), *Robber Rocks*, p. 33.
[139] Unterecker, *Voyager*, p. 196.

confectionery business and, later, for advertising firms.[140] Crane's poem (which, in turn, receives a tacit response in Frank O'Hara's 'Why I am Not a Painter'), spins around 'apples', simultaneously as a nod to the painter's favourite still life subject, the 'valley . . . (called Brandywine)', where Sommer lived (Brandywine Creek), and Sommer's home-brewed 'aerial wine' (Crane's term for the bootlegged concoctions of cider the two drank together).[141] Their intimacy is recreated in the final line where Crane shouts 'The apples, Bill, the apples!' There is a sense here that Crane is directing the painter: 'Put them again beside a pitcher with a knife, / And poise them full and ready for explosion', referring to Sommer's untitled still life of a blue pitcher and apples.[142]

Paris-born Lachaise, meanwhile, trained at the École des Beaux-Arts and moved to New York in the 1910s. He was a frequent resident in Woodstock with his wife, Isabel Dutaud Nagle, and his stepson, the writer and artist Edward Nagle, classmate of e. e. cummings (both were contributors to this cluster of magazines). Crane treasured a bronze by the artist, a cast of his sleeping seagull, and had enjoyed 'danc[ing] around' with Isabel Dutaud Nagle until exhausted at a raucous Thanksgiving celebration in November 1923.[143] While Nagle is recorded simply as Lachaise's 'passion' and 'muse' in most sources, Louise Bourgeois has suggested a more collaborative relationship.[144] Crane even seems to suggest this in his poem, written as a dramatic monologue in what appears to be Lachaise's awestruck voice; the artist carves 'the arms / to spread; the hands to yield their shells' (the bronze casts), but this is not a silent, passive muse: 'Madonna, natal to thy yielding / still subsist I, wondrous'.[145]

The 'Voyages' were similarly embedded in contemporary literary and artistic dialogues. As Marc Simon has shown, the most famous and controversial example of this emerges in Crane's use of poems by Samuel Greenberg, Munson's

---

[140] Crane to Munson, Monday evening, January 1923, box 19, Crane papers.
[141] Frank O'Hara, 'Why I am Not a Painter', in *Selected Poems*, ed. Mark Ford (New York: Knopf, 2008), p. 113; Unterecker, *Voyager*, p. 202.
[142] Crane, 'Sunday Morning Apples', p. 1; William Sommer, *Untitled* [Still life with blue pitcher and apples], no date (c. 1923), oil on canvas, American Drawings and Paintings Collection, Princeton University Library. See Julie L. Mellby's note on the poem and painting at Princeton's Graphic Arts Collection blog, available at <https://www.princeton.edu/~graphicarts/2012/06/sommer.html> (accessed 23 July 2021).
[143] William Innes Homer, *Avant-Garde Painting and Sculpture in America: Exhibition Catalogue* (Newark, DE: University of Delaware Press, 1975), p. 88. Crane to Elizabeth Hart, 5 December 1923, *Letters*, p. 159.
[144] *Stieglitz and his Artists: Matisse to O'Keeffe*, ed. Lisa Mintz Messinger (New York: Metropolitan Museum of Art, 2011), p. 146; Louise Bourgeois, 'Gaston Lachaise's Obsession', *Art Forum*, 30.8 (1922), pp. 85–7.
[145] Crane, 'Interludium', p. 2.

friend and Woodstock resident. Greenberg died in August 1917 and his manuscripts were circulated around the Woodstock group.[146] It has been suggested that Crane plagiarised Greenberg's poems. As Mark Ford explores in his essay on the pair, Crane 'cannibalised' words and phrases from Greenberg, inserting these fragments into drafts of 'Voyages' and 'Emblems of Conduct'.[147] Simon suggests that Crane's investment in Greenberg's use of metaphor resulted in 'recurring phrases and lines' as he attempted to cultivate some of the late poet's 'verbal richness' and 'gusto'.[148] The coterie context is crucial to understanding Crane's engagement with the manuscript. The poems he published in this period in *1924* and *The Little Review* received responses from Seaver and Cowley containing and elaborating on Crane's own turns of phrase.[149] Simon writes that Crane found a 'model' in Greenberg 'suited to Crane's own genius', while Slater Brown suggested that 'Hart's relationship to Greenberg was in its small way rather like that of Baudelaire to Poe—kindred souls who wrote lines the other poet felt he had written himself.'[150]

As with 'For the Marriage of Faustus and Helen', the majority of the 'Voyages' poems were circulated in manuscript prior to their submission to journals. The poems were sent out in correspondence to the *Secession*, *Broom* and *1924* group as he worked through drafts, with versions posted to Munson, Jean Toomer and Waldo Frank in late 1923 and 1924.[151] When Crane began 'Poster' in September 1921 he did not intend to develop the single lyric into a six-part poem.[152] Two years later, after beginning 'Belle Isle' ('VI'), Crane began transforming the two poems into a sequence. Characteristically, the rest of the sequence was not written consecutively; Crane did not formulate an order for

---

[146] Marc Simon, *Samuel Greenberg, Hart Crane and the Lost Manuscripts* (Herndon, VA: Humanities Press, 1978), pp. 39–49.

[147] Mark Ford, 'Who Seeketh Thy Woob? Samuel Greenberg and Hart Crane', in *This Dialogue of One: Essays on Poets from John Donne to Joan Murray* (London: Eyewear, 2014), pp. 141–60.

[148] Crane as quoted in Simon, ibid., p. 47.

[149] Seaver's poem makes it possible to date 'V' to, at the latest, August 1924. Edwin Seaver, 'A Poem', *1924*, 2 (August 1924), p. 39; Malcolm Cowley, 'Hart Crane', in 'Anthology', *The Little Review*, 12.1 (1926), pp. 33–6 (p. 35); Cowley, 'Day Coach', *Secession*, 1 (spring 1922), pp. 1–5.

[150] Simon, *Samuel Greenberg*, p. 56; Brown as quoted in Simon, ibid.

[151] Kenneth Lohf, *The Literary Manuscripts of Hart Crane* (Columbus, OH: Ohio State University Press, 1967), p. 15; Crane to Jean Toomer, 23 November 1923 [includes 'This way when November takes the leaf'], box 8, Crane papers; Crane to Grace Hart Crane, 12 October 1923, *O My Land*, pp. 150–1; Crane to Alyse Gregory, 12 March 1924, box 2, folder 49, *Dial*/Thayer papers; Crane to Frank, 21 April 1924, *O My Land*, p. 188; Gregory to Crane, box 2, folder 50, *Dial*/Thayer papers.

[152] Unterecker, *Voyager*, pp. 262, 216; Crane, 'The bottom of the sea is cruel' ('I'), included in Crane to Munson, 1 October 1921, box 22, Crane/Munson correspondence.

the poems until 1925. After 'I', Crane composed 'VI' while at work at Corday and Gross. He submitted the poem to *Secession* in January 1923 with the weary comment: 'Don't mind rejecting it. God knows I'm not serious about it. I continued it while I should have been writing an ad this afternoon.'[153] He continued, noting cagily in the margin beneath the poem, which is more sexually explicit than his later draft, '[p]erhaps this is an impossible "story" to tell—yet I think the last three stanzas achieve a kind of revelation'.[154] While Crane was anxious about the roughness of the draft (correctly, for Munson returned the poem), he is hinting here at the 'impossib[ility]' of documenting his relationships in his poetry. Significantly, this draft is more explicit than the eventual 'Belle Isle'.[155] This issue became crucial to the later developments of the sequence, where he used his associative mode to present coded descriptions of his homosexual love affairs.

Cowley's response to the 'Voyages' in 'Hart Crane' was published alongside the original poems in the spring–summer 1926 number of *The Little Review*. Anderson and Heap's journal was his second choice; the 'Voyages' had been slated to appear with an accompanying essay from Tate in Philadelphia's *Guardian*, which had taken an interest in Munson.[156] The magazine's designated issue appeared without the 'Voyages' and, for Crane, 'unforgivably' advertised that the 'four remarkable poems by Allen Tate will appear in the next issue!'[157] Crane was furious and quickly dispatched the sequence to *The New Masses*, which was on the verge of its 1926 launch. *The New Masses* returned the poems, and Crane blamed the rejection of 'Voyages' on his association with Tate, who had criticised writers associated with *The Masses* group: 'Allen gave Untermeyer and Kreymborg such digs that it's not surprising that [the editor, James] Rorty summarily returned the mss. I shall be surprised if he fancies my work.'[158]

Josephson took the poems for a special issue of *The Little Review*. The number's title, 'America vs Europe', came from Heap, who had been critical of *Secession*. Heap blamed *Secession*'s attacks on journals with broader appeal,

---

[153] Crane, 'Belle Isle', enclosed in a letter to Munson, n.d. [c. January 1923], box 22, Crane/Munson correspondence.
[154] Ibid.
[155] For example, penetration in 'Down by the river at its base / And remembering that stream of pain / I press my eyes against the prow, / Waiting ... And you, who with me also / Traced that flood, — where are you now?'; then orgasm two stanzas later: 'that sharp joy brighter than the deck / That instant white death of all pain'.
[156] Munson, 'Skyscraper Primitives', pp. 164–7; Crane to Frank, 19 August 1925, *O My Land*, pp. 204–6.
[157] Crane to Slater Brown, 21 October 1925, *O My Land*, p. 207.
[158] Crane to Munson, 5 April 1926, *O My Land*, p. 239.

among which she grouped *The Little Review*, on the 'numerous rejection slips' received by their contributors.[159] Heap, Josephson notes in his memoir, thought 'it would be fun to publish your group and the French group against each other'.[160] That *The Little Review* was formative to Crane's career seems to be something of a critical misconception.[161] He did spend time at the offices during his early years in New York, but *The Little Review* sent back five of Crane's poems – around half of his total submissions to the journal. Anderson noted that she was not a 'great fan' of Crane's poetry in the early years of his career, while Pound (foreign editor from April 1917 to winter 1922) positively disliked it, writing to Anderson 'do not publish him'.[162] Nonetheless, the 'Contributors' Notes' in the spring–summer 1926 number appear as a retrospective attempt to claim Crane as a *Little Review* discovery: 'well known' to *The Little Review*'s 2,000 readership, 'he is one of our finest poets'.[163] 'Voyages' mark a change in attitude towards Crane at *The Little Review* after Pound's departure: this was underlined by a 1929 letter from Anderson to Crane requesting a 'démodé [. . .] adolescent' photograph to illustrate *My Thirty Years War*; she added (perhaps a little disingenuously, given that she later claimed that 'Hart Crane never said anything I wanted to hear'): 'I've come to like your poetry very much.'[164]

Once *The Little Review* regrouped after its trial over the serialisation of *Ulysses*, the journal attempted to reposition itself as a transatlantic magazine, boasting (somewhat dubiously) that it was 'the first magazine to reassure Europe as to America, and the first to give America the tang of Europe', having produced a number dedicated to Francis Picabia.[165] However, Heap's arrangement of the number as Josephson's 'group' against the 'French group' showed

---

[159] Heap, 'Exposé', p. 46. This prompted Crane's response: 'To J. H.', *The Little Review*, 9.1 (1922), p. 39.

[160] Josephson, *Life Among the Surrealists*, p. 291.

[161] For example, Alan Golding, '*The Dial*, *The Little Review* and the Dialogics of Modernism', *Little Magazines and Modernism*, 15.1 (2005), pp. 42–55 (p. 50).

[162] Pound to Anderson, 26 January 1917, in *Pound/The Little Review: The Letters of Ezra Pound to Margaret Anderson*, ed. Thomas L. Scott and Melvin J. Friedman (New York: New Directions, 1989), p. 6.

[163] Unsigned, 'Contributors' Notes', *The Little Review*, 12.1 (1926), p. 2; circulation figures from Brooker and Thacker (eds), *The Oxford Critical and Cultural History of Modernist Magazines, Volume II: North America 1894–1960*, p. 17.

[164] Anderson to Crane, n.d., c. autumn 1917, box 1, Crane papers; Margaret Anderson, *My Thirty Years War* (New York: Greenwood, 1930); Anderson quoted in Micir, *Passion Projects*, p. 100.

[165] Jane Heap, 'Ulysses', *The Little Review*, 9.1 (1922), pp. 34–5; Unsigned, 'Advance in Price', *The Little Review*, 7.3 (1920), unpaginated; *Little Review*, 8.2 [Picabia Number] (1922).

a misunderstanding of the aesthetic debates conducted between *Broom* and *Secession*.[166] As the splits between the American factions show, these debates did not cut across national lines. Rather, they were fought over transnational aesthetic principles that resisted nationalistic classifications.

Cowley's contributions offer creative-critical appraisals of the 'exile' group. His 'Anthology' contained poems to Crane, Josephson, Munson and Burke. Cowley satirises Munson's fondness for technical language, categories and mysticism ('Theory is better than practice. Words are the man'), which he contrasts against a pastiche of Josephson's Dadaist collage, juxtaposing telephone[s]', 'vulcanized rubber', 'Bowling Green[s]', 'Mr [Otto] Kahn', 'steel and copper', 'railways' and 'public utilities'.[167] Cowley's 'Hart Crane' and Seaver's 'A Poem' make similar borrowings from Crane. Both rely on imagery of hands and sea as instantly conjuring Crane. While Seaver's poem offers 'a tremendous / hiatus of sea [. . .] arms blossoming / Thy hands', Cowley writes, apparently in Crane's voice:

> Jesus I saw crossing Times square
> with John the Baptist and they bade me stop
> their hands touched mine
>
> Visions from the belly of a bottle
>
> The sea white white
> the flower in the sea
> the white fire glowing in the flower
> and sea and fire and flower one
> the world is one, falsehood and truth
> one, morning and midnight, flesh and vision
> one
>
> I fled among the avenues of night
> interminably and One pursued
>
> My bruised arms in His arms nursed
> my chest against His bleeding chest
> my head limp against his shoulder[168]

---

[166] Unsigned, 'Contributors' Notes', p. 2.
[167] Cowley, 'Matthew Josephson', in 'Anthology', pp. 34–5; Cowley, 'Gorham Munson', in 'Anthology', p. 35.
[168] Cowley, 'Hart Crane', pp. 35. Retitled 'The Flower in the Sea' in Malcolm Cowley, *Blue Juniata: Poems 1919–1929* (New York: Jonathan Cape and Harrison Smith, 1929).

Crane's images of hands are 'fold[ed]' throughout the 'Voyages' sequence: 'fingers', 'fold', 'caresses', 'palms' 'gathering', 'caught', 'pieties of lovers' hands', 'rich palms', 'close round one instant', 'wind', 'stroke', 'reliquary hands', 'touch', 'strangle', 'Knowing I cannot touch your hand' (which nods to 'Faustus and Helen', 'There is some way, I think, to touch / Those hands of yours that count the nights'), 'lift', 'twine'.[169] The importance of this image is made clear in the final lines of 'III' where this image 'binds' with the title: 'Permit me voyage, love, into your hands...'.[170] As in this line – and, through the oblique Shakespearean allusion to 'holy palmers' kiss' through the pun – hands are tactile, but they are also pleading.

Cowley explicitly draws on central images of the 'Voyages' to establish the parody, but he also, tongue in cheek, amplifies Crane's coded images – which, in turn, borrow from Whitman. The 'flower in the sea' and 'flower one' are borrowed from 'Voyages II' ('Voyages I', in *The Little Review* arrangement) where Crane writes 'In these poinsettia meadows of her tides [. . .] crocus lustres' and 'Close round one instant in one floating flower'.[171] 'Pursued' recalls the narrative of seduction and consummation in the sequence – and Crane had even written a directive note in his jotter on these poems: '"O pursued lumine"—Whitman'.[172] Cowley's veiling of the sexual as religious is deliberately uncompelling. In the homoerotic embrace between Jesus and John the Baptist in Cowley's final lines, Cowley is thinking of Crane's 'mingling / Mutual blood' in 'IV' from *1924*, and Crane's broader Whitmanesque practice of using religious figures as erotic proxies.[173] In 'Voyages', the erotic becomes religious as 'mingling blood' recalls the Christian sacrament. Eroticism is, unlike earlier poems such as 'C33' or 'Modern Craft', redemptive in these poems, after Ephesians 1:7: 'in him we have redemption through his blood'.

In 'IV', drawing on this language, Crane barely disguises the moment of consummation at the centre of the series with a Swinburnian flourish:

---

[169] Crane, 'Poster', p. 20; 'Voyages' ['IV'], p. 119; 'Voyages II' ['I' in *TLR*], p. 13; 'Voyages III' ['II' in *TLR*], pp. 13–14; 'Voyages V' ['III' in *TLR*], p. 14.

[170] Crane, 'Voyages III' ['II' in *TLR*], p. 14; 'Voyages V' ['III' in *TLR*], pp. 15–16; 'Voyages VI' ['IV' in *TLR*], p. 15.

[171] Crane, 'Voyages II' ['I' in *TLR*], p. 13.

[172] Crane's various distillations of Whitman can be found in his Notebook, box 10, Crane papers. See Davies, *Whitman's Queer Children*, and Stephen Guy Bray, 'Crane on Whitman', in *Loving Verse: Poetic Influence as Erotic* (Toronto: University of Toronto Press, 2006), pp. 61–85.

[173] See M. Jimmie Killingsworth, *Whitman's Poetry of the Body: Sexuality, Politics, and the Text* (Chapel Hill, NC: University of North Carolina Press, 1989).

> In signature of the incarnate word
> the harbor shoulders to resign in mingling
> mutual blood, transpiring as foreknown
> and widening noon within your breast for gathering
> all bright insinuations that my years have caught
> for islands where must lead inviolably
> blue latitudes and levels of your eyes,—[174]

'In signature of the incarnate word' sits, characteristically, between meanings. As Cowley's parody highlights, Crane is paraphrasing the biblical phrase 'and the word was made flesh'.[175] But this was also how he described his lover, Emil Opffer, in a letter to Waldo Frank. The 'word made flesh' or 'incarnate' ('invested, embodied with flesh') is Crane's muse for this particular 'Voyages' poem, Opffer – Crane wrote 'EO' beneath 'IV' in his own typed manuscript copy of *White Buildings*.[176]

'All the drama of Hart's turbulent personality was there in the strange images of those verses', wrote Josephson of the connections between the 'Voyages' and Crane's relationships, adding that he felt that Crane had been 'unreconciled to the anxieties of his position'. Crane's sexuality was an open secret in his circle, unremarkable to some friends, but resulting in cruelty from others – something which is borne out in early criticism of his poetry.[177] For Crane, the act of writing became bound up with this 'anxiety' about depicting his homosexuality in his poetry (the 'love of things irreconcilable' as he put it in 'Faustus and Helen'), and the 'Voyages' work through a series of comparisons between textual and physical 'anatomies'. With 'signature', Crane is flagging the 'insinuations' he makes in these stanzas, and nudges for a more explicit reading – in particular with the final images of 'receive' and 'secret oar'.[178] Crane is wry about this process of codification (it is there if you want to see it): 'And could they hear me I would tell them'.[179] 'Signature' suggests 'sign', the action or thing expressed, essentially metaphorically, through language. As such, 'word made flesh' or 'incarnate word' and 'in signature' play against each other in these poems. In the former ('word made flesh', 'incarnate word') the abstract is made physical,

---

[174] Crane, 'Voyages' ['IV'], p. 119.
[175] John 1:14.
[176] Crane to Waldo Frank, 21 April 1924, *O My Land*, p. 186; Crane, 'Voyages IV', *White Buildings* [typed MSS copy], box 10, Crane papers.
[177] Josephson, *Life Among the Surrealists*, p. 294; Mariani, *Broken Tower*, pp. 60–1; Williams refers to Crane's sexuality negatively in a letter to Ezra Pound, box 55, folder 2518, Pound papers; Winters, *Primitivism and Decadence*, p. 590.
[178] Crane, 'Voyages' ['IV'], p. 119.
[179] Crane, 'Poster', p. 20.

that is, a physical expression of the emotion (love/physical attraction). But for the latter ('in signature') we get the 'sign', or the process of writing, as the physical is made abstract (for example, sexual acts described in poetry).

Crane had already introduced this play on the 'incarnate word' in 'Voyages I'. Munson accepted the poem for his newly founded *Secession* in the summer of 1922. But, having shown the poem to Burke (who was then helping edit *The Dial*), the two suggested 'changes'. Crane, writing back, found them mostly 'beyond him', but did agree to change the title: 'you might name it "Poster" if the idea hits you. There is something more profound in it than a "stop, look and listen" sign.' The then title 'Poster' is nonetheless revealing, given Crane's comment that this would be a 'sign', and sets up the framework for the forthcoming poems.[180] From 'Voyages I':

> but there is a line
> you must not cross nor ever trust beyond it
> spry cordage of your bodies to caresses
> too lichen-faithful from too wide a breast [. . .][181]

Immediately after the 'you' of the poem is introduced – delayed until the 13th line – we get this salient, compressed, physical image of tensed muscles (responding to touch) in the third line. But as in 'IV', and Crane's line from 'The Wine Menagerie', 'new thresholds, new anatomies', the phrase is doubled, commenting on the poem's language and addressing Crane's 'slants' between meanings. '[A]natomy' refers as much to the body as it does the act of writing poetry, his use of the 'logic' and the boundaries of the associationally constructed image. He ends the 'Voyages' with the same statement:

> The imaged word, it is, that holds
> Hushed willows anchored in its glow.
> It is the unbetrayable reply
> Whose accent no farewell can know.[182]

Here 'imaged word' is synonymous with his descriptions in letters of the 'word made flesh'. Crane comments on the necessity of this codification with 'hushed' and 'unbetrayable'. This was rooted in a very practical concern. The majority of the 'Voyages' were written after the summer of 1922, when a love affair resulted in Crane being blackmailed. He was forced to hand over $10 of his $25 weekly salary, under the threat of his father being informed of the

---

[180] Crane to Munson, Monday, 1921, *Letters*, p. 99; Crane/Munson correspondence.
[181] Crane, 'Poster', p. 20.
[182] Crane, 'Voyages VI' ['IV' in *TLR*], p. 15.

brief – and much-regretted – relationship.[183] This written threat haunts these poems, as Crane worries in the final line of 'I', written almost a year before 'VI': 'the bottom of the sea is cruel'.

Central to Cowley's creative-critical response in his poem is his suspicion of this associative 'logic' as it operates in the 'Voyages' – despite his own similar experiments in *Secession* – and his amusement at unpicking Crane's coded descriptions of his partners (Emil Opffer, whose 'bright hair' appears in 'Voyages V', was in Crane and Cowley's social circle).[184] Cowley first toys with Crane's use of metonymy: 'sea and fire and flower one', and then, 'world is one . . . flesh and vision one'.[185] Cowley's joke here is how we get from the first object, the 'sea', to the end point: 'flesh'. This is the most basic associative relationship in the 'Voyages', as Crane finds the rhythms of the body and the sea interchangeable, like Whitman's twenty-nine bathers. This joke at the expense of the fabric of Crane's verse taps into contemporary assessments of Crane's 'unintelligible' logic as 'confused' and 'confounding', to borrow from Eastman and Monroe.[186] In his review of *White Buildings* in *Poetry*, Winters made a similar point, noting that these lyrics create 'a series of perceptions so minute and so thoroughly insulated from each other that little unifying force or outline results'. Winters' charge that the poems are too fragmentary to be intelligible is familiar, foreshadowing his comments on *The Bridge*. In both cases, Winters' emphasis on a lack of cohesion seems to owe something to their gradual publication.[187]

As with *The Bridge* and 'For the Marriage of Faustus and Helen', the individual publications show Crane's experimentation using fragmentary forms to construct a long poem. These individual publications illustrate the ability of the sequence to operate in both discrete lyrical parts and different arrangements, with Crane content for the four poems in *The Little Review* to appear without 'I' and 'IV'. The sequence in *The Little Review* is markedly different to *White Buildings* as it opens *in medias res* with the first line of 'II': '—And yet this great wink of eternity'.[188] The sequence, then, begins with a compressed metaphor, in which Crane is not only describing the horizon (the curved, 'wink' shape of a vast seascape) but is also implying the atemporality of these love poems – something his biographers have linked to Opffer's sailing schedule, with stretches of time at sea then intense weeks with Crane.[189] In contrast, the *White Buildings*

---

[183] Mariani, *Broken Tower*, pp. 95–6.
[184] See ibid., pp. 90–3, 152–3; Crane, 'Voyages V' ['III' in *TLR*], p. 14.
[185] Cowley, 'Hart Crane', p. 35.
[186] Monroe, 'A Discussion', pp. 34–41; Eastman, 'The Cult of Unintelligibility', pp. 632–9.
[187] Winters' formatting in 'Hart Crane's Poems', review of Crane, *White Buildings* (1926), *Poetry*, 30.1 (1927), pp. 47–51 (pp. 47, 49).
[188] Crane, 'I' ['II' in *TLR*], p. 13.
[189] Mariani, *Broken Tower*, p. 157.

arrangement begins with a placing line: 'Above the fresh ruffles of the surf'.[190] '[A]bove' forces the reader to take in two different viewpoints (the natural eyeline and the gaze 'above' that, as directed by Crane) looking just above the surface of the water (and thus to the horizon), not directly on the 'fresh ruffles'. While still elusive, the line is rooted by the 'Bright striped urchins', the physical action of 'crumbl[ing] fragments of baked weed' and the sketched-out beach scene, before ending with the final line 'The bottom of the sea is cruel', which introduces the more abstracted poems that follow.

The Little Review sequence and the individual publications of 'I' and 'IV' both highlight the individual lyrical forms within the 'Voyages' sequence – after all, Crane did not originally imagine that 'Poster' would become the first of a set of six poems.[191] This invites a re-examination of the initial contexts of these poems as discrete lyrics – assembled into a coherent sequence – rather than, say, a cumulative narrative progression. This approach complicates the common reading of the full sequence as predominantly dedicated to Crane's relationship with Opffer, and takes note of the specific local genealogy of the lyrical sections of the text.[192] Crane had several muses: one, a ship's officer; another man whose affair with Crane ended, in his words, in 'appalling tragedy'; and, of course, Opffer. Crane's relationship with Opffer began in the spring of 1924. While 'IV' is certainly concentrated on Opffer, the casting of a single unity or cumulative narrative from these poems with specific local genealogies is, then, somewhat dubious. Publishing the 'Voyages' within the literary networks of *Secession, 1924* and *The Little Review* challenged Crane to consider individual responses to the poems as they appeared. Judging by the relative level of activity on the sequence in 1924, it seems that 'Voyages' dominated Crane's writing – and thus, his correspondence – during this year.

Recontextualising Crane's poetry among the 'exile' journals, and publications within their shared networks, sheds light on some of its most complex aspects. The 'logic' was developed, first of all, through his reading of *fin-de-siècle* poetry, and was shaped by the 'post-Decadent' contributions to Greenwich Village journals, particularly *The Pagan*. However, the previously unacknowledged influence of proto-Surrealist experiments with metaphor on Crane's associative mode cannot be ignored. This influence is not only clear in Crane's poetry, but can be found in his close engagement with this group of journals and the 'technical' debates conducted between *Secession, Broom, S4N* and *1924*. Crane's use of 'the image' develops from weaker comparisons such as 'trees that *seem* dancing', '*like* ancient lace' [my emphases],[193] and

---

[190] Crane, 'Voyages I', *Complete Poems*, p. 34.
[191] Unterecker, *Voyager*, p. 262.
[192] Ibid.
[193] Crane, 'October–November', p. 4; Crane, 'Carmen de Boheme', p. 2.

through his engagement with the 'exile' journals it matures so that, to quote from Breton's 1924 *Manifeste*, it resists 'comparison'.[194]

The 'logic', with its built-in resistance to easy paraphrase, allowed Crane to use 'machine-age' details without their inclusion resulting in 'surface phenomena', turning the work into a 'picture of the "period"'; the idea was to employ 'the machine that sings' fully integrated into the body of the text.[195] These developments introduced difficulties when Crane sought to publish in *The Dial* and *Poetry*, as a result of both his use of experimental forms and his association with specialist, avant-garde journals. But, as the 'Voyages' demonstrate, the logic of metaphor became an exciting tool for Crane to explore an erotic poetic language, setting up an analogy between the 'anatomy' of the text and the physical body that would continue to preoccupy his writing.[196] This associational mode, built as it was in lively, responsive writing communities, both registers the practical impossibilities of a literal erotic language and the intimacy that comes from attempting to unravel its elusive movements.

---

[194] Breton, André, *Manifeste du surréalisme; Poisson soluble*, p. 17.
[195] Crane, 'Cutty Sark', *Poetry*, p. 28.
[196] On Crane's enmeshed ideas of the body and text, see Tapper, *The Machine that Sings*.

3

'CHAMPION MIXED METAPHORS': GRADUATING TO *THE DIAL* AND *POETRY*

'Words are constructive / when they are true; the opaque allusion—the simulated flight / upward—accomplishes nothing.' So writes Marianne Moore in 'Picking and Choosing'.[1] Published in *The Dial* in 1920, the poem provides a remarkable statement on her poetic technique and a premonition of her distinctive, creative work as the editor of that same magazine. Editing is a creative-critical practice. For Moore, writing and editing were synonymous with revision, as is demonstrated in both her poetry and throughout her tenure at *The Dial*, as Bonnie Costello and Victoria Bazin have argued.[2] In her poetry and at *The Dial*, Moore's editing demonstrates complex, interacting aesthetic principles. For Moore, Crane's poetry was bristling with 'wrong meanings' and artificial gestures.[3] Editing Crane's poetry, then, required the careful imposition of discipline, at odds with his associational forms. Moore's edit of Crane's 'The Wine Menagerie' (retitled 'Again' by Moore) might be seen as a material example of Emily Dickinson's lines of influence colliding. Here principles of indeterminacy and fluidity, 'dwell[ing] in possibility' (Crane) collided with precision and restraint: the prudence of the microscope (Moore).[4]

---

[1] Marianne Moore, 'Picking and Choosing', *The Dial*, 68.4 (1920), pp. 421–2 (p. 421).
[2] Bonnie Costello, *Marianne Moore: Imaginary Possessions* (Cambridge, MA: Harvard University Press, 1981), p. 237; Bazin, *Modernism Edited*, pp. 107–39.
[3] Moore, 'Picking and Choosing', p. 421.
[4] Emily Dickinson, 'I dwell in Possibility—', in *Complete Poems*, ed. Thomas H. Johnson (London: Faber and Faber, 1970), p. 327; Dickinson, 'Faith is a Fine Invention', ibid., p. 87.

In 1926 Crane had two notorious disagreements with editors. Despite their own aesthetic quarrels, Marianne Moore's and Harriet Monroe's views converged when it came to Crane's poetry.[5] Crane had fraught interactions with Moore at *The Dial* and with Monroe at *Poetry* over editing interventions made to, respectively, 'The Wine Menagerie' and 'At Melville's Tomb'. Monroe agreed to publish 'At Melville's Tomb' on the condition that Crane provide a gloss of his 'confused', 'champion mixed metaphors' for publication alongside the poem in the October number of the magazine.[6] Moore's famous edit of 'The Wine Menagerie', meanwhile, brought the poem down from 49 to 18 lines for the May 1926 number of *The Dial*.[7] Both Crane's response to Monroe's and Moore's edits have received significant and useful critical commentary.[8] But the ways that both interventions set critical precedents for criticism of his work, formulating an influential language for dealing with his poetry, have yet to be explored. This chapter offers a new framework for the development of his reception history and the resulting shibboleths that remain in criticism of his work.

Monroe's explicit request that Crane paraphrase his 'confused mixed metaphors' and Moore's changes to 'The Wine Menagerie' form a similar critique, with the latter brought to bear on the poem through excisions and rearrangements. The two interventions run in parallel, showing a shared scepticism of Crane's associatively built 'logic of metaphor'. The edits to 'The Wine Menagerie' shadow Moore's own sense of 'the connection between criticism and creation'. The mid-1920s editorial cultures of *The Dial* and *Poetry* helped shape descriptions of Crane's Surrealist-influenced poetry as 'confused' and lacking 'discipline' in subsequent criticism, with a number of contemporary reviews alluding to Monroe's comments in *Poetry*. Irrespective of Moore's own sexuality, her criticisms of Crane in her 1974 *Paris Review* interview map on to a culture of homophobia: the unpalatable equation of Crane's homosexuality with a general 'Decadence' of character and lack of discipline that reveals itself in his poetry.[9] Building on the earlier discussion of Crane's poetry among post-Decadent and exile magazines, and his continuing association with the Village's queer poetry networks, here I foreground how his associations with these journals affected his uneasy reception at *The Dial* and *Poetry* in the mid-1920s.

---

[5] See Robin G. Schulze's 'Textual Darwinism: Marianne Moore, the Text of Evolution, and the Evolving Text', *Text*, 11 (1998), pp. 270–305 (p. 293).
[6] Monroe, 'A Discussion', p. 35.
[7] Crane and Moore, 'Again', *The Dial*, p. 370.
[8] See Introduction, n. 40.
[9] Using Sedgwick's definition of queerness, Elien Arckens discusses Moore's 'less rigid model' of sexuality in '"In This Told-Backward Biography": Marianne Moore Against Survival in Her Queer Archival Poetry', *Women's Studies Quarterly*, 44.1/2 (2016), pp. 111–27.

Crane's restrained first submissions to *The Dial* and the wide acclaim of 'My Grandmother's Love Letters' as his first supposedly mature poem show a brief entente with the journal;[10] Crane's later, more recognisable style of juxtaposed metaphor was met with consistent rejections.

Crane's publications in *The Dial* and *Poetry* paved the way for appearances in, to borrow Jane Heap's term, the 'smart journals' (*The Saturday Review*, *The Nation* and *The New Republic*) but Moore's and Monroe's responses set the tone for refrains in criticism of Crane's work as 'difficult' or opaque – a common reading, even from his most ardent admirers.[11] In this chapter I offer a corrective to such critical stereotypes – so deeply entrenched that they emerge in crib-sheet study guides – showing the origins of these tropes in early negative reactions to his poetry, and beginning to trace their reproduction in twentieth- and twenty-first-century literary criticism. Crane's own defence in his *Poetry* letter can, I argue, be reclaimed as a vital deflation of Moore's and Monroe's critiques, one which he was forced to articulate in the real-time argumentative literary culture of periodicals.

'My first "litry" money': 'My Grandmother's Love Letters', 'Pastorale' and 'Praise for an Urn' in *The Dial*

Louise Bogan suggested that *The Dial* exposed 'the obvious distinction between the American avant-garde and American conventional writing'.[12] Bogan was referring to the catholic editing principles that underscored *The Dial*'s aesthetic, even through the tenures of Scofield Thayer and James Sibley Watson's managing editors, Gilbert Seldes, Alyse Gregory and, finally, Marianne Moore. Appointed in 1925, Moore was declared full editor on the masthead in January 1927, but, as Jayne E. Marek has demonstrated, she had considerable control over the editing of the journal from the outset.[13] Thayer and Watson purchased the magazine late in 1919, and, the following January, ushered in the new decade with its first issue. They announced that *The Dial* would offer space to 'inevitable' and 'impossible pieces' that 'would not be acceptable elsewhere' while ensuring that established writers should share space with their younger counterparts.[14] In practice, as Thayer and Watson wrote in a private 'Statement of Intent', this meant printing 'highly significant, imaginative work by such a

---

[10] On 'My Grandmother's Love Letters' as a marker of his poetic 'maturity' see, for example, Mariani, *Broken Tower*, p. 36.

[11] 'Smart journals' being Jane Heap's term in 'Exposé', pp. 46–7. On appraisals of 'difficulty', see Introduction.

[12] Bogan quoted in Moore, 'The Art of Poetry No. 4', p. 58.

[13] Marek, *Women Editing Modernism*, pp. 138–66.

[14] Scofield Thayer, 'Comment', *The Dial*, 68.3 (1920), p. 408.

poet as Ezra Pound side by side' with 'a poet like Edwin Arlington Robinson'.[15] In Bourdieu's terms, cultural capital was to be transferred from the established to the emerging writer, via the magazine.

To consider *The Dial* mainstream, however, is not only to divorce the journal from the reality of the early twentieth-century literary marketplace, but to view 'conventional writing' as anything that is not explicitly 'avant-garde' in the theoretical, rather than historically determined, sense, resting on retrospective claims based on the fact that now-canonical poets were published in it. Indeed, Crane had already accrued twenty-seven publications by the time he first appeared in the magazine in 1920 with 'My Grandmother's Love Letters', while H.D.'s first appearance in the November 1920 issue was her 51st periodical publication. Eliot had well over 100 publications before appearing in *The Dial* with 'The Possibility of Poetic Drama'.[16] *The Dial* was not, in general, offering space to truly unknown writers, as its competitor *The New Republic* enjoyed pointing out.[17] This arrangement may well have made its more experimental contributions more palatable to its readers, but it is not sufficient to show that *The Dial* had an overly weighted hand in the canonisation of these specific works, or, indeed, that '*The Dial* helped to canonise what *The Little Review* helped to discover', as Christina Britztolakis writes.[18] 'Imagine anybody's calling it conservative three years ago', wrote Cowley. 'The public which could call the *Dial* conservative was formed by reading the *Dial*.'[19] This, coupled with retrospective assessments of the later reputations of 'outlier' contributions, such as *The Waste Land*, *The Cantos* and even *The Bridge*, has led to assessments of *The Dial* as so 'mainstream' that it could be 'acutely conscious of its competition with *Vanity Fair*'.[20] While Thayer might have worried about *Vanity Fair* poaching his contributors, in practical terms the two magazines occupied very different spaces within the literary field: *The Dial* had

---

[15] Thayer and Watson, 'Statement of Intent'.
[16] Figures include prose, reviews, poetry and articles. T. S. Eliot, 'The Possibility of a Poetic Drama', *The Dial*, 69.5 (1920), pp. 441–7; see Donald Gallup, *T.S. Eliot: A Bibliography* (London: Faber and Faber, 1969), pp. 195–207; Michael Boughn, *H. D.: A Bibliography, 1905–1990* (Charlottesville, VA: University of Virginia Press, 1993), pp. 95–109.
[17] Nicholas Joost, *Scofield Thayer and "The Dial"* (Carbondale, IL: Southern Illinois University Press, 1964), pp. 250–1.
[18] Christina Britztolakis, 'Making Modernism Safe for Democracy: *The Dial*', in Brooker and Thacker (eds), *The Oxford Critical and Cultural History of Modernist Magazines, Volume II: North America 1894–1960*, pp. 85–103 (p. 86); Michael True quoted in Golding, 'Dialogics of Modernism', p. 46.
[19] Cowley to Thayer, 10 May 1923, box 2, folder 42, *Dial*/Thayer papers.
[20] Rainey, *Revisiting "The Waste Land"*, pp. 96, 98.

a fluctuating circulation, but it stood at around 9,500 in 1922, while *Vanity Fair* had 90,000 readers.[21]

Crane found *The Dial* 'safe' for a specific reason: it was not printing the experiments of his transnational network of writers. *The Dial* accepted poems from Crane in which he actively engages with the previous generation of Symbolists. *The Dial* did not meaningfully engage with the experiments of the European Dada movement and their American counterparts, even while Thayer was based in Vienna between July 1921 and October 1923.[22] This goes some way to explaining the magazine's lack of interest in Crane's Surrealist-influenced poetry. Tellingly, one of *The Dial*'s few direct references to Dada was in Paul Morand's 'epitaph' for the movement in his September 1924 'Paris Letter', marking the publication of *Le Manifeste du Surréalisme: Poisson Soluble*.[23] Thayer and Watson were also cautious when it came to the gaze of the New York Society for the Suppression of Vice; the less circumspect *Broom*, for instance, was suppressed by the US Postal Service.[24] *The Little Review*'s trial over the publication of sections of *Ulysses* (at which Thayer was present) highlighted the constraints of publishing, and the degree to which the Society was watching literary magazines. Thayer, for instance, requested changes to a story by Waldo Frank in which he deemed 'the sex is too thick'.[25] Nonetheless, as James Dempsey notes, Thayer and Watson allowed themselves occasional jokes at the expense of the censor, punctuating an essay by the head of the Society, John S. Sumner, with an erotic drawing of a 'voluptuous' nude by Crane's friend, Gaston Lachaise.[26]

Crane's first publication in the magazine was thanks to Thayer, who accepted 'My Grandmother's Love Letters' for the April 1920 issue. Seldes and Gregory, meanwhile, were hostile to his work, returning a batch of poems with the comment that they were 'unnecessarily obscure' – all but one were subsequently

---

[21] Rainey suggests 9,500 for *The Dial*, perhaps using an average for news-stand sales that modifies for the December peak following *The Waste Land* sales. See *Revisiting "The Waste Land"*, p. 91. Brooker and Thacker suggest a range of 4,000–30,000 for *The Dial* and estimate 90,000 for *Vanity Fair*; see Peter Brooker and Andrew Thacker, 'Introduction', in Brooker and Thacker (eds), *The Oxford Critical and Cultural History of Modernist Magazines, Volume II: North America 1894–1960*, p. 33. See also *The Dial* 'News Stand Sales', box 9, folder 327, *Dial*/Thayer papers.

[22] There were a few scattered exceptions, for example Jean Cocteau, 'Cock and Harlequin', *The Dial*, 71.1 (1921), pp. 52–62; Louis Aragon, 'Madame a sa Tour Monte . . .' *The Dial*, 72.1 (1922), pp. 20–8.

[23] Paul Morand, 'Paris Letter', *The Dial*, 78.3 (1924), pp. 239–43.

[24] Cowley, *Exile's Return*, p. 195.

[25] Dempsey, *Scofield Thayer*, p. 71.

[26] John S. Sumner, 'Adult or Infantile Censorship?', *The Dial*, 68.4 (1920), p. 381; Dempsey, *Scofield Thayer*, p. 71.

published in more experimental, smaller circulation magazines.[27] Rejections from Seldes were so predictable that in November 1923 Crane goaded him with a penis-shaped calligramme, adding that he eagerly 'awaited his comment'.[28] Seldes did commission Crane to write two 'Briefer Mentions', after the poet jokily urged him to 'provide me with sundry other pastime subjects which winter is icummin [sic] in and we ring the axe? I need these occasional bucks badly, the woods aren't half full of them.'[29]

The Dial poems, 'My Grandmother's Love Letters', 'Pastorale' and 'Praise for an Urn', are characterised by a restrained use of metaphor. 'Praise for an Urn: In Memoriam Ernest Nelson', with its traditional elegist's apology ('scatter these well meant idioms'),[30] was so well received by the editors that it was used in the clipsheet for the number (Weber, though, finds the poem 'mawkish').[31] 'My Grandmother's Love Letters', inspired, Crane told Munson, by Charles Vildrac, was published in the April 1920 issue; it opens:

> There are no stars to-night
> But those of memory.
> Yet how much room for memory there is
> In the loose girdle of soft rain.[32]

The night is cloudy with rain; stars are obscured or imagined. Despite the initial simplicity, there is a glimpse of Crane's associative mode in 'the loose girdle of soft rain'. And so the rain seems to encroach on all fronts, bringing with it an ability to provoke memories. From here, Crane shifts and tackles the problem suggested by that opening statement, where the fancies of recollection seem to project unseen stars on to the clouded, rain-smudged sky above. Crane drops into (for him) an unusually straightforward description:

> There is even room enough
> For the letters of my mother's mother,
> Elizabeth,
> That have been pressed so long
> Into a corner of the roof

---

[27] Gregory to Crane, 18 March 1924, box 2, folder 50, *Dial*/Thayer papers; Crane to Gregory, 12 March 1924, box 2, folder 49, *Dial*/Thayer papers. Returned poems: 'Recitative', 'Belle Isle', 'Possessions', 'In a Court', 'Lachrimae Christi' and 'Sunday Morning Apples'.
[28] Crane to Gilbert Seldes, box 2, folder 49, *Dial*/Thayer papers.
[29] Crane to Gregory, 12 March 1924, box 2, folder 49, *Dial*/Thayer papers.
[30] Crane, 'Praise for an Urn: To E.N.', *The Dial*, 72.6 (1922), p. 606.
[31] Joost and Sullivan, *"The Dial", Two Author Indexes*, p. 15; Weber, *Hart Crane*, p. 110.
[32] Crane, 'My Grandmother's Love Letters', *The Dial*, 68.4 (1920), p. 457.

> That they are brown and soft,
> And liable to melt as snow.³³

Here there is 'room' only for a physical description; the performance of the lines comes from the play on 'that', which drags the sentence through seven lines and the stuttering, repetitive music of the poem.

With its relative restraint and delicacy, 'My Grandmother's Love Letters' exhibits a different set of influences to the poems published in the 'exile' magazines, such as 'For the Marriage of Faustus and Helen' or 'Voyages' – poems written after his exposure to post-Dada poetic experiments. Shifts in Crane's poetry, particularly in the contrast between 'My Grandmother's Love Letters' and 'The Wine Menagerie' (the latter being unacceptable to Moore prior to her edits), highlight *The Dial*'s own ideas regarding modernist poetry's relationship to the literary past and acceptable demonstrations of influence. Although he was unspecific as to the exact nature of Vildrac's influence on 'My Grandmother's Love Letters', Crane seems to have had the French poet's concept of the 'rhythmic constant' in mind.³⁴ Vildrac's influence is, then, predominantly located in the formal properties of the poem, by contrast to Crane's sweeping, bombastic use of Baudelaire's *Les Fleurs du mal* in 'The Wine Menagerie', where imitation transforms into pastiche (Crane compared his poetry to Baudelaire's as early as 1921).³⁵ Vildrac, at least in Anglophone circles, had grown associated with the Imagists and practitioners of *vers libre*. Crane most probably encountered Vildrac through F. S. Flint or then *Dial* foreign editor (1920–23) Pound, who refers to Vildrac's 'Technique Poétique' in his advice on 'Rhythm and Rhyme' in 'A Few Don'ts From an Imagiste'.³⁶

The carefully assembled prosody of 'My Grandmother's Love Letters' may have appealed to Thayer, particularly given his interest in the French Symbolists (notably, 'Praise for an Urn' contains frequent nods to Laforgue's pierrots and 'dandies of the moon'). Tellingly, Crane's poem appeared in the same number as Witter Bynner's translations of Vildrac's 'An Inn' and 'A Castle in Spain' (in 1921 Crane would translate Vildrac, with the aim of placing the poems in *The Double Dealer*, which took his versions of Laforgue's 'Locutions').³⁷ The delicate homage in 'My Grandmother's Love Letters' turns on Crane's use of Vildrac's technique of a repeated pattern of rhythmic syllables, which

---

[33] Ibid.
[34] Crane to Munson, 14 April 1920, *Letters*, p. 37.
[35] Crane to Munson, 21 May 1920, *Letters*, pp. 57–8.
[36] Crane to Munson, 22 July 1921, *Letters*, p. 38; Pound, 'A Few Don'ts', p. 205.
[37] Witter Bynner, 'Poems and Translations', translation of Charles Vildrac, 'An Inn' and 'A Castle in Spain', *The Dial*, 68.4 (1920), pp. 473–8. See Charles Vildrac, *A Book of Love*, trans. Witter Brynner (New York: E. P. Dutton, 1923).

are based on the pattern made by the first name of his grandmother, Elizabeth
(˘ ˘ ˘ ˘) Belden Hart. Crane repeats these stresses inside the lines, often further
contained within phrases with, first, 'no stars to-night', 'for memory'; later, as
the pattern coheres, 'Elizabeth' is isolated on a single line. The poem is laced
with self-conscious interruptions ('and I ask myself', 'And so I stumble') as he
moves from the clarity of the letters to interpretation, 'like birch limbs webbing the air'.[38] In the final line the pattern of the rhythmic constant disintegrates, as he appears to admonish himself in his grandmother's voice, coupled
with 'pitying laughter'. While Irwin reads the poem as a retort to Grace Hart
Crane, 'reflecting Crane's hostility toward his mother at this period',[39] 'My
Grandmother's Love Letters' seems rather to see the poet shifting between personas as hostility is directed inwards. Crane, whose letters are littered with
self-castigation as to his 'foolishness', imagines the 'pitying' sounds that would
accompany any attempt to share his romantic life with his grandmother, to
'lead my grandmother by the hand / Through much of what she would not
understand'.[40] Indeed, shortly before Elizabeth Belden Hart's death in 1928,
Crane came out to his mother, which precipitated the final rupture in their
relationship. They did not lay eyes on each other again, nor was Crane able to
respond to his mother's letters.[41]

While using a more complex metaphorical language, 'Pastorale' (October
1921) turns on a similar sense of self-consciousness favoured at *The Dial*. Like
'My Grandmother's Love Letters', 'Pastorale' is preoccupied with memory
and its fruitful contradictions. 'What woods remember now / her calls, her
enthusiasms', writes Crane, as 'time' disintegrates and recollections are broken
down into imagistic 'smoky panels'.[42] Crane's comments on his own attempts
at restraint are central to the poem: 'If, dusty, I bear / An image beyond this',
he offers, aware of an 'Already fallen harvest' of unpicked ideas. Then comes
his inevitable 'pitying' admonishment: 'Fool'.[43] Well received at *The Dial*, these
poems illustrate Crane's movement away from the imitative poetry of the late
1910s in *The Pagan*, *Bruno's Weekly* and *Bruno's Bohemia*, but still have (as
Taggard noted in her review of *White Buildings*) some of the imagistic qualities of these early experiments. These *Dial* poems are, by contrast to the bold

---

[38] Crane, 'My Grandmother's Love Letters', p. 457.
[39] Irwin, *Hart Crane's Poetry*, p. 79.
[40] Crane to Munson, 6 February 1923, *O My Land*, p. 122; Crane, 'My Grandmother's Love Letters', p. 457.
[41] Unterecker, *Voyager*, pp. 534–41.
[42] Crane, 'Pastorale', *The Dial*, 71.4 (1921), p. 422.
[43] Crane, 'Pastorale'; Crane has himself as a similar 'fool' playing with language as 'whispers' surround him and he 'pivots' pointlessly in the final line. Crane 'The Wine Menagerie', *Complete Poems*, pp. 23–4.

metonymy of the 'exile' poems, laced with equivocations: he barely trusts his own metaphorical movements in 'Pastorale'. The complex structural patterns and ideas that were introduced through his experiments with the 'logic of metaphor' are not quite established here. Indeed, 'Sunday Morning Apples', published in *1924*, reconsiders the neuroticism of 'Pastorale' and its 'fallen harvest'. In lines that are at once about Bill Sommer's paintings and his own poetry, Crane offers a consolation to his younger self: 'The leaves will fall again sometime and fill / The fleece of nature with those purposes / That are your rich and faithful strength of line.'[44] The poet reminds himself in a 'ripe' period of writing activity, 'full and ready for explosion', that inspiration and confidence will return. And, as 'Sunday Morning Apples' suggests in its dedication to Sommer and Crane's disarming final shout, 'The apples, Bill, the apples!', this was often made possible through collaboration, finding inspiration and new ways of working through his engagement with his artistic communities.

This transition from tentative, self-conscious questioning to the bold, associative logic of metaphor is underlined in both of Crane's 'Briefer Mentions', short reviews written for *The Dial* in 1923. Crane's review of Romer Wilson's *The Grand Tour* speaks to his burgeoning work on *The Bridge* as he praises Wilson's 'piling up constantly to the end' with 'etchings, moods and anecdotes' and Romantic flights: 'this Elysian wind that sets my nerves quivering like an Aeolian harp', 'I soar up into the blue sky'.[45] Meanwhile, Crane expresses a revealing antipathy to Thomas Moult's selections in *Best Poems of 1922* (an anthology series). The anthology, he wrote, contained 'broadly accessible poetry', with contributions from the Georgians complemented by appearances from Richard Aldington, Carl Sandburg, H.D., Amy Lowell, Louis Untermeyer and Alfred Kreymborg. Cheekily, given that Moult notes the magazine source of each poem, with the majority of the American work coming from *Poetry* and *The Dial*,[46] Crane wrote that the anthology would 'confuse or destroy what incipient taste for contemporary poetry its more occasional readers may be nursing'. This chimed with Crane's increasing interest in transnational and regional literature (and their effective cohabitation in the 'exile' magazine networks). He was irritated by Moult's failure to distinguish between the American and British poets included, giving 'no guide to their nationality except what is revealed by the work itself'.[47] Crane's annoyance is useful in teasing out different strains of literary nationalism during the 1920s. *The Dial* and *Poetry* took a similar approach to dealing with an idea of American 'cultural humility'

---

[44] Crane, 'Sunday Morning Apples', p. 1.
[45] Crane, 'Briefer Mention: Romer Wilson', p. 198; Romer Wilson, *The Grand Tour* (London: Methuen, 1923), p. 21.
[46] *The Best Poems of 1922*, ed. Thomas Moult (Nendeln: Kraus Reprint, 1969), pp. vii–xiii.
[47] Crane, 'Briefer Mention: Thomas Moult', p. 200.

(drawing on Randolph Bourne), viewing the dual modes of the 'exile' contributors as incompatible.[48]

As Crane's poetry became increasingly influenced by European avant-garde experiments, one of the – in Moore's words – 'New York sophisticates', 'so near to Europe and so far from America!', *The Dial* grew increasingly impatient with his style.[49] As Burke wrote, in returning 'Recitative', 'You have set yourself a record of greater volume [. . .] with which the pedantic Wrigley daily-dozens do not fit.'[50] Moore's edit of 'Again', in this light, is useful not only in revealing the personal tastes that motivated her, but the wider attitude of *The Dial* towards the new, transnational inflections of Crane's poetry.

'OMISSIONS ARE NOT ACCIDENTS': MARIANNE MOORE EDITING CRANE

During her *Paris Review* conversation with Donald Hall, Moore discussed her notorious edit of 'The Wine Menagerie' and her broader view of Crane's poetry.[51] Pinning down Moore's own critical and creative principles, so bound together in her own work, explains the misreadings that led to the 'Again' edit, and her habit of suggesting 'improvements' to other *Dial* contributors such as Gertrude Stein, Archibald MacLeish and Conrad Aiken.[52] Moore's edit is itself a creative-critical reading of Crane's poetry. Her particular dislike of his associative use of metaphor (which she cut from 'Again') highlights the distinct poetic qualities Crane developed in the early 1920s. Revealing perhaps more about her own poetic process than that of Crane's poem, Moore complained to Hall that Crane was unable to self-edit, 'to be hard on himself'. To suggest that his poetic limitations lay in a decadence of character was to make a barely coded reference to his sexuality. Moore connects both Crane's homosexuality and his alcoholism to a lack of discipline that presented itself in his work. Discussing his work and 'wild parties', she added that he was 'in both instances under a disability with which I was unfamiliar'.[53]

'The Wine Menagerie' was written in 1925 during raucous fourth of July celebrations with Malcolm and Peggy Cowley. Drenched in the language of Crane's beloved *Les Paradis artificiels*, the poem recounts the weekend's heavy drinking (transferred from the Cowleys' house in Patterson to a dive bar in New York) and makes coded references to his romantic and sexual relationships.[54]

---

[48] Bourne, 'Our Cultural Humility', p. 506.
[49] Harriet Monroe, 'Why Not Laugh?', *Poetry*, 33.4 (1929), pp. 206–9 (p. 209).
[50] Burke to Crane, 14 July 1927, box 2, folder 49, *Dial*/Thayer papers.
[51] Moore, 'The Art of Poetry', pp. 59–60.
[52] Bonnie Costello, 'Editing *The Dial*', in *Selected Letters of Marianne Moore*, ed. Bonnie Costello (London: Penguin, 1997), p. 213.
[53] Moore, 'The Art of Poetry', p. 60.
[54] Crane refers directly to *Les Paradis artificiels* by its subtitle, 'Petits Poëmes en prose', in a letter to Frank, 19 August 1926, *O My Land*, p. 271; Mariani, *Broken Tower*, p. 180.

The poem went against Moore's 'strong opinions about order, decorum, and duty', views that 'provide a moral thread traceable through the pattern of her work', as Jayne Marek puts it, referring to how Moore's Presbyterian faith influenced her poetry.[55] But Moore's edit was not simply an attempt to censor the aspects of the poem that she might have found unpalatable. While she does remove the speakeasy setting, her main quarrel with the poem was with Crane's use of an associative, dense metaphorical form. For Moore, Crane's inability to exercise restraint and self-edit resulted in his use of 'multiform content' (the associative logic) with a corresponding 'lack of simplicity and cumulative force'.[56]

Moore's sense of the symbiosis of critical and creative work is neatly conveyed in her review of T. S. Eliot's *The Sacred Wood* for *The Dial*:

> in what it reveals as a definition of criticism it is especially rich. The connection between criticism and creation is close; criticism naturally deals with creation but it is equally true that criticism inspires creation. A genuine achievement in criticism is an achievement in creation; as Mr Eliot says, 'It is to be expected that the critic and the creative artist should frequently be the same person.'[57]

This preoccupation is clear even in Moore's first publications in Bryn Mawr's student magazine *Tipyn o'Bob*, of which she was also on the editorial board. Although ostensibly fiction, a number of Moore's short stories in the magazine ('The Discouraged Poet', 1907, and 'Pym', 1908) reflect on her own developing writing practices and critical principles and emphasise her sense of craft, work and apprenticeship. Moore's charge of a '*lack* of simplicity' in her letter to Crane is revealing in this sense, suggesting that simplicity is somehow missing, a quality that must be worked at, acquired.[58] In her story 'Pym', a student begins to revile her 'feminine writing', recognising her need for precision, noting in her diary the need to 'say things to the point', that good writing should be '*toil*' [Moore's italics]. She begins to develop a suspicion of artifice: 'Nothing done for effect, is worth the cost', she writes, likely with the previous generation of poets in mind. Crucially, though, 'Pym' argues that precision and

---

[55] Marek, *Women Editing Modernism*, p. 139.
[56] Moore to Crane, 13 August 1925, box 2, folder 49, *Dial*/Thayer papers.
[57] Marianne Moore, 'The Sacred Wood', review of T. S. Eliot, *The Sacred Wood* (1920), *The Dial*, 70.3 (1921), pp. 336–9 (p. 336).
[58] See Marianne Moore, 'The Discouraged Poet', in *The Complete Prose of Marianne Moore*, ed. Patricia C. Willis (London: Faber and Faber, 1987), pp. 8–9; Moore, 'Pym', *Complete Prose*, pp. 12–16.

restraint is learned, is teachable: 'Again' was for Moore, perhaps, a didactic moment.[59]

Moore's poetry makes this '*toil*' clear through collage forms, and the close knitting of her creative and critical writings. Her instructively titled 'Picking and Choosing' appeared in the same number as 'My Grandmother's Love Letters' (April 1920), and asserts her creative methods, as scholars of Moore have noted.[60] Working as creative criticism, in the poem Moore takes quotations from her own critical prose and weaves them into the fabric of the poem:

> Literature is a phase of life: if
>   one is afraid of it, the situation is irredeemable; if
> one approaches it familiarly,
>   what one says of it is worthless. Words are constructive
> when they are true; the opaque allusion—the simulated flight
>
> upward—accomplishes nothing. Why cloud the fact
>   that Shaw is self-conscious in the field of sentiment but is
>   otherwise re-
> warding? that James is all that has been
>   said of him, if *feeling* is profound? It is not Hardy
> the distinguished novelist and Hardy the poet, but one man [. . .]
>
> 'interpreting life through the medium of the
>   emotions.'[61]

The poem takes from her own *New York Times* review of Robert Lynd's *Old and New Masters in Literature* (October 1919), where she writes: 'To apply Hudson's definition of a poet, Hardy is an "interpreter of life through the medium of emotions"; the verse is, if you like, a variation on the prose; superfluous if one does not care for the prose, indispensable if one does.'[62] This quotation works as another reflective statement on allusion and the allusive fragment: 'allusion' serves a clear purpose here. And, in reaching back to the prose, Moore invites a comparison between Hardy's 'verse' as a 'variation on the prose' and her own.

---

[59] Moore, 'Pym', *Complete Prose*, pp. 13, 14, 16.
[60] For example, Evan Kindley, 'Picking and Choosing', in *Poet-Critics and the Administration of Culture* (Cambridge, MA: Harvard University Press, 2017), pp. 17–35; Bazin, *Modernism Edited*, p. 7.
[61] Moore, 'Picking and Choosing', p. 421.
[62] Marianne Moore, 'Old and New Masters in Literature', *Complete Prose*, pp. 41–3.

Moore's reviews show her sympathy towards work that reflected similar interests. In a review penned for *Broom*, she commented on the 'exacting' tenor of H.D.'s *Hymen* and (echoing Pound's sculptural metaphors in 'A Retrospect') praised her 'chiselled ivory of speech'.[63] Writing in *Contact*, she praised William Carlos Williams's *Kora in Hell* as 'crisp', 'precise', 'secure', 'rooted', admiring the poet's 'compression, color, speed accuracy and that restraint of instinctive craftsmanship'. As in 'Pym', the gendered language is worth noting here: the masculine 'vigor' of Williams's poetry precludes 'anything dowdy or labored' – poetry as a shabbily dressed labouring (in either sense) woman, without brightness.[64] For Crane, Moore's criticisms of other poets exhibited a kind of literary transference. In a letter to Waldo Frank after Moore had returned 'Passage', he copied out Moore's original comment (it was *Dial* policy to use the editorial 'we' in letters, a feature Crane parodied in a letter to Seldes):[65] 'We could not but be moved, as you must know, by the rich imagination and sensibility in your poem, "Passage". Its multiform content accounts, I suppose, for what seems to us a lack of simplicity and cumulative force.'[66] Moore, Crane wrote, 'might be rather speaking of her own poems with such terms'.[67] This symbiotic understanding of criticism and editing (often represented through collage forms) was part of Moore's literary practice. For Moore, H.D., Williams and Eliot were 'craftsmen'; Crane was unable to self-edit, to 'chisel' at his work and, as she told Hall, 'be hard on himself'. In *The Sacred Wood* review, Moore paraphrases Eliot's own essay on Jonson as she makes more general, admiring comments on the volume. She notes how Eliot illustrates the 'case between brilliance of surface and mere superficiality'.[68] This 'case' forms the basis of the criticism that she makes against Crane, finding his associative mode to be a form of decadence 'done for effect' or, as Williams claimed Moore described it, 'fake knowledge'.[69]

The language of these reviews forms part of Moore's critical code for 'modern poetry', with similar descriptions of 'exactness', 'praiseworthy opacity', 'directness', 'keen[ness]' 'compact[ness]' in later critical pieces, including in

---

[63] Marianne Moore, '*Hymen*', review of H.D., *Hymen* (1921), *Broom*, 4.2 (1923), pp. 133–5.
[64] Moore, 'Pym', *Complete Prose*, p. 13; Moore, '*Kora in Hell*', review of William Carlos Williams, *Kora in Hell: Improvisations* (1920), *Contact*, 1.4 (1921), pp. 5–8 (p. 5).
[65] Crane to Seldes, 21 November 1923, box 2, folder 50, *Dial*/Thayer papers.
[66] Moore to Crane, 13 August 1925, box 2, folder 50, *Dial*/Thayer papers.
[67] Crane to Frank, 19 August 1925, *O My Land*, p. 205.
[68] Moore, '*The Sacred Wood*', p. 336.
[69] Williams to Pound, commenting on Moore's views of Crane, 12 July 1928, box 55, folder 2518, Pound papers.

The Dial, both before and during her tenure as editor.[70] In contrast to the 'secure', 'rooted', 'concise' poetry she admired, Crane was 'vapid' and not 'well reefed'; he was fluid, unanchored and 'yield[ing]' – coded feminine, and, with the same sleight of hand as in her comments in *The Paris Review*, revealing of her suspicions of Crane's queer modernism.[71]

Moore's concept of self-editing and her commitment to provisionality, famously revising 'Poetry' from thirty-two to just three lines for her 1967 *Complete Poems*, might help to explain her willingness to suggest edits for *Dial* contributors.[72] As her borrowing of 'verbal delicacies' (to adopt Fiona Green's wonderfully suggestive phrase) from other sources for her poems suggests, Moore had a rather flexible notion of authorship.[73] A case in point, Tara Stubbs notes, is her 1954 play, *The Absentee*. Moore claimed that her play was a 'new dramatic version' of Maria Edgeworth's 1812 novel, despite the fact that she could only have seen Edgeworth's 'sketch' of the novel, given that the manuscript did not survive.[74] As with Edgeworth's text, Moore may have felt that she was extending rather than curtailing projects through her changes. Correspondingly, Moore insisted that she welcomed editing suggestions for her own poems: 'if you have the genius of an editor you are blessed', she told Donald Hall with a hint of self-congratulation. '*The Times*, *The Herald Tribune*, *The New Yorker*, have a number of times had to patch and piece me out.'[75]

While 'Again' is an infamous example of Moore's alterations to *Dial* contributions, perhaps because it constitutes a biting appraisal of Crane's poetic mode, she also asked – with varying levels of compliance – for edits from Robert Hillyer, Archibald Macleish, Pound, Aiken and Stein, as Costello, Marek and Bazin have discussed.[76] Moore requested changes to further submissions from Crane. He refused her acceptance of 'At Melville's Tomb' if he 'omit the fourth stanza' (the poem, of course, went to *Poetry*). On his submission of 'The Mermen' in 1928,

---

[70] See Marianne Moore, '*Natives of Rock*', review of Glenway Westcott, *Natives of Rock: Poems 1921–1922* (1925), *The Dial*, 81.1 (1926), pp. 69–72; Moore, 'Poet of the Quattrocento', *The Dial*, 82.3 (1927), pp. 213–15.

[71] Moore, '*Kora in Hell*', p. 5; Moore to Watson, 9 March 1927, *Selected Letters*, p. 213.

[72] Marianne Moore, *The Complete Poems* (London: Faber and Faber, 1967), p. 36.

[73] Fiona Green, 'The Magnitude of their Root Systems: "An Octopus" and National Character', in *Critics and Poets on Marianne Moore*, ed. Linda Leavell, Cristianne Miller and Robin G. Shulze (Lewisburg, PA: Bucknell University Press, 2005), pp. 137–49 (p. 137).

[74] Tara Stubbs, 'One Title, Three Works?', in *Romantic Ireland from Tone to Gonne: Fresh Perspectives on Nineteenth Century Ireland*, ed. Paddy Lyons, Willy Maley and John Miller (Cambridge: Cambridge Scholars, 2013), pp. 246–53 (p. 247); Marianne Moore, *The Absentee* (New York: House of Books, 1962).

[75] Moore, 'The Art of Poetry', p. 60.

[76] Costello, 'Editing *The Dial*', pp. 211–14; Marek, *Women Editing Modernism*, pp. 160, 197; Bazin, *Modernism Edited*, pp. 140–64.

Moore asked if he might alter 'the construction of the first stanza' to remove the word 'solve', tellingly questioning his use of words 'so far removed from each other as not to be conspicuously related'. Crane did not agree with the changes; the original version of the poem was published.[77] By contrast, he left a minor change in 'To Brooklyn Bridge' entirely at Moore's discretion.[78]

When Moore wrote to Crane with provisos for *The Dial*'s acceptance of 'The Wine Menagerie', she asked if he would 'permit us to make certain changes in it which we are venturing to present to you'. The letter continues:

> It is so much our wish not to distort or to interfere with an author's concept, that we thought to take no liberty and to relinquish the poem; we feel, however, that you may concur with us in the changes we suggest. In that case, might we use 'Again' as a title?[79]

The 'changes' Moore suggested that she claimed would not 'interfere' with Crane's concept reduced the poem from 49 to 18 lines and removed all references to its subject (a dive bar), thus forcing the title change. In contrast to Moore's revisions, Thayer and Watson's position on editing submitted manuscripts was clear; they suggested that editors limit changes to 'grammatical editors'; 'if a passage in a manuscript is obscure', their procedure entailed asking the author 'if he so desires, to express it more clearly'.[80] Moore's edits demonstrate her autonomy as editor of *The Dial*, though she may have felt that they were made, as Marek puts it, as an attempt to 'maintain the magazine's range of interests'.[81] Moore's response to 'The Wine Menagerie' is, though, unique among these requests for edits in its function as a comprehensive piece of creative criticism on Crane's use of linguistic forms.

Perhaps impulsively, Crane agreed, replying on the same day. He wrote to Moore, agreeing to the new title and to the idea that 'Again' contained 'the essential elements of the original poem'. And, he wrote, 'inasmuch as I admire the sensibility and skill of your rearrangement of the poem I shall be glad to have it so printed in *The Dial*'.[82] Crane's comment that he admired the 'skill' of Moore's 'rearrangement' of the text suggests that he was a careful reader of

---

[77] Moore to Crane, 26 June 1928, box 2, folder 50, *Dial*/Thayer papers; Crane to Moore, 28 June 1928, Moore to Crane, 2 July 1928, box 2, folder 50, *Dial*/Thayer papers.
[78] Crane to Moore, 12 August 1926, box 2, folder 50, *Dial*/Thayer papers.
[79] Moore to Crane, 10 November 1925, box 2, folder 50, *Dial*/Thayer papers.
[80] Moore reiterates this in 'The Art of Poetry', p. 59. Scofield Thayer and James Sibley Watson, 'General Instructions for Editorial Department', box 9, folder 318, *Dial*/Thayer papers.
[81] Marek, *Women Editing Modernism*, p. 161.
[82] Crane to Moore, 10 November 1925, box 2, folder 50, *Dial*/Thayer papers.

Moore's poetry and prose. In 'Again', he may have spotted the same process of collage and reassembly as in her own work, calling the text a 'happy mixture' in a letter from May 1926. Along with his more positive appraisals, he nonetheless complained profusely about the edit to his friends, including Richard and Charlotte Rychtarik, Winters, Josephson and Frank; perhaps he realised the magnitude of Moore's criticisms of his poetic style embedded in the edit after his hasty acceptance of the changes.[83]

With the omission of six whole stanzas and half of the ninth stanza, 'Again' reads as follows:

> What in this heap in which the serpent pries,
> Reflects the sapphire transepts round the eyes—
> The angled octagon upon a skin,
> Facsimile of time unskeined,
> From which some whispered carillon assures
> Speed to the arrow into feathered skies?
>
> New thresholds, new anatomies,
> New freedoms now distil
> This competence, to travel in a tear,
> Sparkling alone within another's will.
>
> My blood dreams a receptive smile
> Wherein new purities are snared. There chimes
> Before some flame a restless shell
> Tolled once perhaps by every tongue in hell.
> Anguished the wit cries out of me, "The world
> Has followed you. Though in the end you know
> And count some dim inheritance of sand,
> How much yet meets the treason of the snow."[84]

By cutting the first three stanzas, Moore removes Crane's initial contextualisation of the poem in a bar and the dense metaphors of the 'mustard scansions of the eyes', the 'leopard ranging', 'glozening decanters', and the bartender's smile drawn out with 'forceps' – which seems to borrow from Baudelaire's

---

[83] Crane to Charlotte and Richard Rychtarik, 1 December 1925, *O My Land*, p. 210.
[84] Crane and Moore, 'Again', *The Dial*, p. 370. Hereafter, my quotations from 'The Wine Menagerie' (unless stated otherwise) come from a fair manuscript version of the poem from 1925, presumably the version Crane sent Moore. Crane, 'The Wine Menagerie', box 1, folder 1, Crane Collection, Austin. Referred to henceforth as 'The Wine Menagerie MS'. Dated by Lohf as 1925, *Literary Manuscripts*, p. 11.

'un charmant sourire', the 'charming', slightly patronising 'smile' of 'les divinités mythologiques' (the mythological gods) in *Les Paradis artificiels*.[85] These changes, as Burke put it, resulted in an edit that 'took all the wine out of the menagerie'.[86]

Moore, who had praised Stevens's 'winter-starved metaphors' in the January 1924 number of *The Dial*, exhibits a thorough scepticism of Crane's associative mode in 'Again',[87] thoroughly restructuring the poem, grouping the text into three contained parts that work through three ideas, and imposing (with some slight deviations) a ten-syllable, syllabic form on the poem, as well as a couplet rhyme scheme.[88] In its original form, 'The Wine Menagerie' ranges (like the poem's leopard 'always in the brow') and drifts between different, loosely connected images, reflecting the speaker's obvious intoxication (the 'me' of Crane's poem comes in stanza two; the first sense of voice in Moore's edit ['My blood'] occurs in the final stanza). Crane has Baudelaire's 'Enivrez-vous' in mind, in which the drunken voice initially attempts to orientate himself through his attention to 'le vent, la vague, l'étoile, l'oiseau, l'horloge' ('the wind, the wave, the star, the bird, the clock') before giving up: 'enivrez-vous sans cesse!' ('be drunk continually!').[89] As a form of linguistic collage emphasised by allusion, Crane's juxtaposition of images endeavours to remove 'previous precepts or preconceptions' from the subject conveyed in the poem, creating the 'single *new word*' [italics in the original], as he explains in 'General Aims and Theories' when discussing his placing of Helen of Troy in modern-day New York City.[90]

Moore's first stanza, meanwhile, deals with the image of the 'serpent' that 'pries' within a 'heap' of jewels. Her second verse picks up on Crane's reflections on his own poetic process, selecting Crane's erotically ambiguous line, 'New thresholds, new anatomies', and makes it the centre of the poem. Devoid of context, the line becomes a reflection on poetic craft, its promise and limitations. As Yingling writes, 'The Wine Menagerie' hinges on this line, a poem in which 'sex is tested as poetic inspiration'. It works through ideas present in

---

[85] Moore and Crane, 'Again', *The Dial*, p. 370; Crane, 'The Wine Menagerie MS'; Charles Baudelaire, *Les Paradis artificiels: Petits Poëmes en prose* (Paris: Editions Baudinière, 1900), p. 35.

[86] Edward Brunner, *Splendid Failure: Hart Crane and the Making of "The Bridge"* (Chicago: University of Illinois Press, 1985), p. 264.

[87] Marianne Moore, '*Harmonium*', review of Wallace Stevens, *Harmonium* (1923), *The Dial*, 76.1 (1924), pp. 84–91 (p. 89).

[88] Moore began experimenting with syllabics in the early 1920s. See Margaret Holley, 'The Model Stanza: The Organic Origin of Moore's Syllabic Verse', *Twentieth Century Literature*, 30.2–3 (1984), pp. 181–91 (p. 181).

[89] Charles Baudelaire, 'Enivrez-Vous' ('Be Drunken'), trans. Arthur Symons, in *Baudelaire: His Prose and Poetry*, ed. T. R. Smith (New York: Boni and Liveright, 1919), pp. 57–8 (p. 57).

[90] Crane, 'General Aims and Theories', p. 161.

'Voyages' and 'For the Marriage of Faustus and Helen' where Crane elides distinctions between textual and erotic bodies: 'the word made flesh' ('Voyages'), 'the love of things irreconcilable' ('Faustus and Helen'). Significantly, Yingling makes the 'thresholds' line the jewel in the title of his seminal monograph, *Hart Crane and the Homosexual Text: New Thresholds, New Anatomies*, reclaiming this crucial line – and indeed Crane's queer poetics – from Moore's edit.

Minor changes to the first stanza of 'Again' unseat an interesting use of the 'logic' present in the original. Crane writes in 'The Wine Menagerie':

> What is it in this heap the serpent pries—
> Whose skin, facsimile of time, unskeins
> Octagon, sapphire transepts round the eyes;
> From whom some whispered carillon assures
> Speed to the arrow into feathered skies?[91]

By 'time unskeins' Crane means that time unwinds; or, at least, his narrator is incapable of experiencing time pass with any semblance of accuracy. At this moment, Crane shifts to Baudelaire's *Les Paradis artificiels: du vin et du haschisch*. Crane was most probably reading Baudelaire in the French, given his translations of Jules Laforgue's 'Locutions des Pierrots' for *The Double Dealer*, but Boni and Liveright had issued an edition of *Baudelaire: His Prose and Poetry* in 1919. While Baudelaire offers a similar description of 'l'horrible fardeau du Temps' ('the horrible burden of Time') in 'Enivrez-Vous', Crane draws more from the 'splendid visions' and temporal disintegration of *Les Paradis artificiels* where 'Le temps avait complètement disparu' and 'Vous avez jeté votre personnalité aux quatre vents du ciel, et maintenant vous avez de la peine à la rassembler et à la concentrer' ('Time has completely disappeared [. . .] You have scattered your individuality to the four winds: how hard it is, now, to put it back together!)[92]

Crane wrote that the dismissal of the 'last generation' of Decadents was 'nostalgia for something always "new"'.[93] By 'nostalgia' Crane was referring to the cycle of a movement's definition in opposition to its predecessors, as in the Imagists' influential moves against 'superfluous word[s]' and 'ornament', all associated with Decadent poetry – an unpopular stance at both *The Dial* and *Poetry*.[94] Moore's seemingly inconsequential shifts in the opening of 'Again'

---

[91] Crane, 'The Wine Menagerie MS'.
[92] Baudelaire, *Les Paradis artificiels*, pp. 174–5; Baudelaire, *Artificial Paradises*, trans. Patricia Roseberry (Harrogate: Broadwater, 1999), pp. 61, 63.
[93] Crane to Munson, 5 January 1923, *O My Land*, p. 117.
[94] Pound, 'A Retrospect', p. 107. Echoed by Moore in 'Pym', *Complete Prose*, pp. 14, 16.

mute Crane's allusions to Baudelaire and the poem's sense of intoxicated atemporality. While Moore's edit prioritises the 'i' sounds of 'in', 'this', 'in which', 'pries' to link to 'skin', Crane had structured this stanza around a sibilant pattern that helps to reveal its sense. Moore's edit focuses on a pun between 'skin' and 'unskeined' but, in moving 'unskeined' into the past tense, she removes a crucial detail. Crane's sibilance creates a link between the associative construction of the poem and the metaphor of the snake's skin 'unskeining' as time disintegrates. The sibilance builds the 'anatomy' of the text in a manner analogous to the tiny scales that form the snake's skin, which is – as he pushes this further – analogous to the experience of time in the poem as tiny details stitched together to build up a larger form (an image that also recalls De Quincey's famous description of 'infinite declensions' of time in his *Confessions of an English Opium Eater*).[95] 'Unskeins' needs to be in the present tense for this metaphor of time 'unskein[ing]' and unravelling to work. A sense of temporality, even just of an event having happened in the past, is contrary to the point of this poem's efforts to resist temporal markers – something also interrupted in the edit when Moore changes the vague opening phrase of 'Invariably when' to 'What in'.

In 'The Wine Menagerie', time is non-linear (until he finally leaves the bar, stepping over Holofernes in the final stanza) and is constituted of parts signalled by passing images; in Crane's poem the various images show the attempt to reassemble the 'personality' thrown 'to the four winds' with drink. We can safely assume, I think, that the drinker is a cipher for Crane, who long suffered with his relationship with alcohol. The poem is structured according to the voice's stream of consciousness, which often dwells on images or evocations of his own sexual desire as he moves from the 'leopard' (his own desire: Crane cruising the New York docks)[96] to the 'snake' (the bartender) to the 'urchin' to 'Petrushka' – which alludes to Stravinksy's ballet of the same name. Time, for Crane's narrator, can 'unskein' or be viewed as the individual, hallucinatory components present in 'The Wine Menagerie', just as the snake skin can be viewed as individual scales (and, to take it further, abruptly shed, signifying death). Likewise, Crane's associative mode is both conducted on these small scales (as in that central complex metaphor, 'time unskeins') while also connecting the poem as a whole through linked associations and the phonics of the sibilant patterns. As in 'At Melville's Tomb' with its 'certain messages undelivered', Crane seems anxious about the potential opacity of the 'logic' and its ability to 'unskein' if these associations are missed by the reader (the death of

---

[95] Thomas De Quincey, *Confessions of an English Opium Eater and Other Writings* (Oxford: Oxford University Press, 2013), p. 150.
[96] Mariani, *Broken Tower*, pp. 137, 139, 266, 380, 424.

meaning). While Moore notices the reflective moment in 'New thresholds, new anatomies', this particular analogy to Crane's method goes, apparently, unnoticed, or was deemed too 'multiform' and complex.

Moore also removes another queer turn in the poem, the self-address in the penultimate stanza, describing how he 'pivots' as he leaves the bar. The dancerly 'pivot' comes from Crane's self-comparison to 'Petrushka's Valentine', a character from Stravinsky's ballet. Crane saw his beloved Stravinsky conduct in New York in February 1925, and, as Irwin has usefully noted, this stanza re-enacts the composer's *Petrushka*, named after the folkloric 'Punch' figure.[97] In Stravinsky's ballet, originally danced by the Ballets Russes, three puppets compete for affection as the 'Ballerina' is courted by 'The Moor' and 'Petrushka'.[98] In Crane's rendering, he places himself as 'Petrushka's Valentine': the Ballerina. This image performs the 'New thresholds, new anatomies' line as Crane switches genders, casting himself in the female role and subverting the 'erotic triangle' of the original ballet.[99] Like Whitman in 'The Sleepers' declaring 'I am the actor, the actress', 'I am she who adorn'd herself', this is employed as a way of simultaneously declaring, albeit in a coded manner, the poem's subtle play with gender and attraction.[100]

Moore's edits remove this discursive allusive process of codification and interpretation, forcing the 'New thresholds, new anatomies' metaphor to function only as a comment on the poem's construction and the 'anatomy' of the text. Tapper reads the lines as penetrative, whereby the 'eroticised bodies are cleansed of their stigma' in an 'epiphanic moment'.[101] In Moore's edit, this reading is lost. There is no sense, as in the original and as is characteristic of Crane's writing, of the continuity between textual and physical body. While Moore might take this 'surgical' approach to minimal limits, Crane revels in multifarious comparisons and allusions to Baudelaire, Isaac Watts, the Book of Judith and Stravinsky. Underpinning the use of collaged metaphors and allusions is an interest in different types of fragment forms. For both Crane and Moore, this impulse may have been derived from their poetic development at the height of Imagist fashions in which, as Andrew Clearfield puts it, the poem can become a 'collage of images' without the expected 'formal, visual or semantic ordering'.[102]

---

[97] Irwin, *Hart Crane's Poetry*, pp. 318–20.
[98] Richard Taruskin, 'Stravinsky's *Petrushka*', in *Petrushka: Sources and Contexts*, ed. Andrew Wachtel (Evanston, IL: Northwestern University Press, 1998), pp. 67–115.
[99] Eve Kosofsky Sedgwick, *Between Men* (New York: Columbia University Press, 1985), p. 21.
[100] Walt Whitman, 'The Sleepers', in *Leaves of Grass*, ed. Jerome Loving (Oxford: Oxford University Press, 2009), pp. 325–32 (p. 326).
[101] Tapper, *The Machine that Sings*, pp. 65, 47.
[102] Andrew Mark Clearfield, *These Fragments I Have Shored: Collage and Montage in Early Modernist Poetry* (Ann Arbor, MI: UMI Research Press, 1984), p. 127.

Moore's comments suggest a misreading of Crane's associative 'logic of metaphor', implying that he lacked an editing process, the paring down of a final draft. In 'Again' she attempts to supply that missing stage of work on 'The Wine Menagerie'. Her underestimation of the thought behind the 'logic' may have stemmed from emphases in reviews and contributors' notes on Crane's lack of formal education. Crane's schooling was erratic from a young age; his mother withdrew him from school to accompany her on trips on several occasions. He spent the winter of 1914–15 at the Hart family estate on the Isle of Pines (meaning that he had to cram for exams in the New Year), and spent much of 1916 travelling from Chautauqua to San Francisco, across the Pacific Northwest and into Canada. Just after Christmas in 1916, and following his parents' divorce, he finally dropped out of East High School and headed to New York.[103] Contributors' comments often picked up on this. At the end of the decade, in *Twentieth Century Poetry*, the editors Drinkwater, Canby and Benét noted that Crane's 'academic education was early broken, which is linked to his "well-nigh baffling" poems'. Perhaps with Moore's notorious edit in mind, the anthology's editors even snobbishly contrast the two poets in these terms, with the Bryn Mawr-educated Moore's chemist-like fastidiousness (Moore majored in history, economics and political science) lined up against a long description of Crane's work as a manual labourer: 'he has been successively employed as: mechanic, bench-hand, shipyard bolter-up, newspaper reporter, hod carrier, book clerk, shipping clerk, and advertising copy-writer'.[104]

Building on Hammer's discussion of Crane's 'Janus-faced' modernism, and the 'opposing forces' of his poetry, in *Transmemberment of Song* Lee Edelman considers Crane's poetry as 'the site of a heated ideological battle to define the nature of literary modernism and its relationship to the literary past in general and to romanticism in particular'.[105] The idea of Crane's poetry representing contested aesthetic ground applies to its immediate reception. This 'battle' over the influences of 'literary modernism' can be seen played out in the 1920s via Moore's edit of 'Again'. Crane and Moore's clash over the edit was, at least in part, rooted in their different ideas about a viable literary past, and what Moore deemed to be legitimate or illegitimate influences. Here, though, the question is not so much about Crane's relationship with 'romanticism', but his interest in Decadent poetry which grew out of his engagement with the Greenwich Village journals. Pound was a dominant presence in both *The Dial* and *Poetry* during the 1910s and 1920s and, as Vincent Sherry puts it, drew 'forceful' distinctions

---

[103] Unterecker, *Voyager*, pp. 35–52.
[104] The editors, 'Hart Crane', in *Twentieth Century Poetry*, ed. John Drinkwater and William Rose Benét (New York: Houghton Mifflin, 1929), p. 572.
[105] Edelman, *Transmemberment of Song*, p. 259.

between modernist experiments and 'the artifice of written literature among Nineties poets'. Making claim to his supposed wrench in literary tradition, Pound wrote: 'And in the face of this are we in the heat of our declining youth expected to stretch the one word *merde* over eighteen elaborate paragraphs?'[106] These distinctions, writes Sherry, have become the 'truism of literary history' of '[Pound's] own decade'.[107]

Crane's poetry, like that of Charlotte Mew or Iris Tree, resists such easy categorisations. 'The Wine Menagerie' revels in its allusions to Baudelaire's *Les Fleurs du mal* and *Les Paradis artificiels*. Moore was averse to Crane's obvious interest in Baudelaire, while her precursors in *The Dial*'s editorial chair appreciated his nods to Symbolism via Vildrac. The more subtle implications of Moore's dislike of Crane's 'artifice' play into this 'truism' – and a perception of the relationship between literary history and modernism that was more widely broadcast by *The Dial*. As Moore's edit implies, Crane's obvious engagement with Decadence in 'The Wine Menagerie' through his use of Baudelaire would not have sat well with the literary tastes of the journal. Although *The Dial* printed translations from Rimbaud and Valery, and poetry that was subtler in its borrowings from the French Symbolists (with Eliot, 'apprenticed' to Laforgue being an obvious example here),[108] its contributions exhibited a scepticism towards the 'artifice' of Decadence and its frequently homophobic association with moral 'decay', 'attributed to those aspects of character and activity that are manifestly counter-conventional, sometimes scandalous'. Indeed, these associations of Decadence are perhaps Crane's main focus in 'The Wine Menagerie'.[109] *The Dial* did not publish, like *The Pagan* or Bruno's journals, the nostalgic 'post-Decadent' modernism of Greenwich Village that was central to Crane's poetic development. *The Dial* preferred, as its contributors' lists show, experiments in a more straightforwardly Imagistic vein, local and national subjects, and writers who were, at least ostensibly, sceptical about the 'artifice' of the Decadents. This worked, perhaps according to the Imagists' conception of modern poetry, as a way of distinguishing, as Pound put it in the first number of *The Egoist*, the 'younger' writers from 'that disastrous decade'.[110] A review of Oscar Wilde's 'The Portrait of Mr. W. H.' in the September 1921 number of *The Dial* contained a final comment, revealing established homophobic patterns of contemporary criticism, that 'discipline

---

[106] Pound quoted in Vincent Sherry, *Modernism and the Reinvention of Decadence* (Cambridge: Cambridge University Press, 2014), p. 2.
[107] Ibid., p. 1.
[108] David E. Chinitz, *T. S. Eliot and the Cultural Divide* (Chicago: University of Chicago Press, 2005), p. 34.
[109] Sherry, *Modernism and the Reinvention of Decadence*, p. 37.
[110] Ezra Pound, 'Ferrex on Petulance', *The Egoist*, 1.1 (1 January 1914), pp. 9–10 (p. 9).

was a mere name to him'.[111] Aiken's scathing review of *White Buildings* seems symptomatic of *The Dial*'s tastes, and further highlights Crane's uneasy position at the journal, with its comments on 'unreflecting indulgence[s]' and his 'affectation'.[112]

Crane retained the sense of pressure that Moore put on the poem. A comparison of his 1925 version of 'The Wine Menagerie' with the *White Buildings* text also reveals some post-*Dial* edits in which Crane seems to clarify ideas further. Perhaps with Moore's criticisms in mind, the majority of these changes come in the first three stanzas, which Moore cut entirely. Crane changes, for instance, 'deep cynosures' to 'liquid' to make it more obvious that he is still describing the 'decanters' in the preceding lines.[113] Close attention to Moore's dealings with Crane reveal her preferences for material for *The Dial*, for instance the kind of forms and influences and affiliations that she wished her contributors to display, as a way of situating the aesthetic interests of the magazine, while her shifting of Crane's allusions also worked to introduce these visual correlations, creating a network of correspondences between contributions to the journal. As Moore commented on her approach to editing: 'Didn't Aristotle say that it is the mark of the poet to see resemblances between apparently incongruous things?'[114]

CRITICAL NARRATIVES: HARRIET MONROE'S 'DISCUSSION WITH HART CRANE'

'Take me for the hard-boiled unimaginative unpoetic reader', wrote Harriet Monroe to Crane in a letter published alongside his first poem in *Poetry*, 'At Melville's Tomb'. '[And] tell me', she added, 'how *dice* can *bequeath an embassy* (or anything else).' 'Your ideas and rhythms interest me', Monroe continued, before asking Crane to 'justify the poem's succession of champion mixed metaphors' in this public forum.[115] Crane submitted the poem to *Poetry* in the spring of 1926, and it was published in October.[116] While Winters' letters to Monroe show his 'efforts to convince H. M. that she ought to publish Hart Crane' as early as 1923, there is no evidence that Crane sent work to *Poetry* prior to this submission; Monroe did not solicit poetry from Crane at any point

---

[111] Charles Hooley [as Charles Vale], 'A Brilliant Failure', review of Oscar Wilde, *The Portrait of Mr W. H.* (1921), *The Dial*, 71.3 (1921), pp. 359–64. Pseudonym found in Nancy Milford, *Savage Beauty: The Life of Edna St. Vincent Millay* (New York: Random House, 2001), p. 104.

[112] Aiken, 'Briefer Mention: *White Buildings*', p. 432.

[113] Crane, 'The Wine Menagerie MS'; Crane, 'The Wine Menagerie', *Complete Poems*, pp. 23–4 (p. 23).

[114] Moore, 'The Art of Poetry', p. 58.

[115] Monroe's emphasis, 'A Discussion', p. 35.

[116] Most likely in late April, judging by his submission to *The Calendar* and Monroe's discussion with Winters in May. See Crane to Frank, 19 June 1926, *Letters*, p. 258.

during his association with the journal.[117] However, Morton Dauwen Zabel, her associate editor from 1928, was more sympathetic to Crane's poetry – Zabel assumed the full editorship in 1936, after Monroe's sudden death in Arequipa, Peru, while travelling to Machu Picchu.[118] Zabel sought out Crane's writing, admitting that he was accepting his submissions with 'somewhat keener interest' than his superior.[119] Although Monroe accepted 'At Melville's Tomb', she did so only after Winters had persuaded her of Crane's talent. And even then, it was with the caveat that Crane write a gloss. The result, 'A Discussion with Hart Crane', was printed alongside the poem in the October 1926 issue.[120] Monroe, like Moore, expressed frustration with Crane's associative mode, conveyed to readers through editing interventions; the 'Discussion' makes explicit the implicit criticisms of the 'Again' edit. The 'Discussion' framed Crane as a writer of 'confused' poetry in need of 'explaining in prose'. Winters initially saw Monroe's dismissal of Crane as evidence of *Poetry*'s increasing irrelevance among avant-garde literary circles: 'you are about three movements behind the times', he told Monroe in June 1927.[121]

The 'Discussion' usefully forced Crane to publicly articulate his poetic theories. Significantly, he uses the phrase 'the logic of metaphor' publicly here for the first time. The exchange also shows how a major editor shaped his immediate reception (Taggard refers directly to the 'prose controversy' in her review of *White Buildings*).[122] Despite Crane's dismissal of Monroe's worries, the exchange, alongside Moore's edit, inaugurated a critical language for dealing with Crane. This interaction set a precedent for his treatment in reviews and articles published in *Poetry* during Crane's lifetime. *Poetry* is unique among Crane's publishers in that it also published highly influential critical articles on his work, laying out still-dominant frameworks for the analysis of his poetry. Yvor Winters' 'The Progress of Hart Crane' (June 1930) echoes Monroe's statements. The review, which 'astonished' Crane, argued that *The Bridge* was 'confused', lacking 'narrative framework' and 'formal unity'.[123] Crane's shock was due partly to the fact that Winters had historically defended him in letters to Monroe, and urged her to accept any sections of *The Bridge* sent to the

---

[117] Winters to George Dillon, 31 May 1938, in *Dear Editor: A History of Poetry in Letters*, ed. Joseph Parisi and Stephen Young (New York: W. W. Norton, 2002), pp. 329–30 (p. 329).

[118] Daniel Cahill, *Harriet Monroe* (New York: Twayne, 1973), p. 129.

[119] Zabel to Crane, 3 November 1931, box 7, Crane papers. Zabel was referring to Crane's forthcoming review of James Whaler's *Green River*, and other reviews commissioned by Zabel.

[120] Winters to Monroe, 27 November 1926, in Parisi and Young (eds), *Dear Editor*, p. 277.

[121] Winters to Moore, 28 June 1927, in Parisi and Young (eds), *Dear Editor*, p. 278.

[122] Taggard, 'An Imagist in Amber', p. 4.

[123] Winters, 'Progress', pp. 133, 158; Crane to Isidor Schneider, 8 June 1930, *O My Land*, p. 431.

magazine.[124] Then, three months after Crane's death in April 1932, Allen Tate's 'Hart Crane and the American Mind' popularised the description of *The Bridge* as a 'grand failure'. Developing lines of criticism evident in Winters' article, Tate presented a view of Crane's poetry that further reinforced Monroe's criticisms, but added a series of troubling retrospective readings. One of Tate's most disturbingly influential assertions was that Crane's death could, in part, be blamed on the idea that 'he could no longer believe in even his lyrical powers', with Tate linking the 'fragmentary' vision of the poem to what he called Crane's 'blind desire for self-destruction'.[125] 'His sensational death was morally appropriate', Tate concluded, leaning into the narrative he had constructed, 'and I think it has some significance as a symbol of the "American" mind.'[126]

In January 1932, shortly before he left Mexico City for New York, Crane wrote to Zabel expressing his hope that *Poetry* might manage to struggle through a period of financial difficulty. While he admitted that he had 'been at times one of its most rabid critics', he added that:

> the fact remains that it has been absolutely unique in modern literary history. It has blazed more than one trail and exposed countless stupidities; and its critical standards, especially of late, have been a challenge to those of any magazine printed in English. I'm not a Christian Scientist, but I can't help thinking that, granted H. M.'s continued interest and admirable enthusiasm, a way will be found to keep it alive beyond the 20-year limit.[127]

While his view of the magazine had no doubt warmed Zabel's appreciation of his poetry, Crane's appreciation stemmed from the journal's 'unique' longevity ('20-year limit' refers to *The Little Review*'s demise in 1929; *The Dial* also ceased publishing in the year of the financial crash).[128] Established in 1912 to 'give poetry her own place, her own voice', when 'most magazine editors say

---

[124] Winters to Monroe, 11 May 1926, in Parisi and Young (eds), *Dear Editor*, pp. 275, 280; Winters to Monroe, 27 November 1926, ibid., p. 277; Winters to Monroe, 31 July 1928, ibid., pp. 279–80.

[125] Tate, 'American Mind', pp. 211, 214.

[126] Winters, 'Progress', pp. 153–65; Tate, 'American Mind', pp. 210–16. The phrase 'grand failure' originates from Cowley's review of *The Bridge*, 'A Preface to Hart Crane', review of *The Bridge*, New Republic, 62.803 (23 April 1930), pp. 276–7 (p. 266).

[127] Crane to Zabel, 7 January 1932, box 1, folder 18, Zabel papers.

[128] Prior to this, *The Little Review* had appeared irregularly as a quarterly throughout the 1920s after the *Ulysses* trial in 1921. The last number was 12.2 (May 1929: Confessions and Letters Number). Thayer had decided he no longer wanted to foot the bill for *The Dial*'s huge deficit. Joost, *Thayer and "The Dial"*, pp. 255–6

that there is no public for poetry in America',[129] unlike many of its contemporaries, *Poetry* was still active in 1932. It is still, at the time of writing late in 2020, a major international force in Anglophone poetry; in 2003 Ruth Lilley's $200,000,000 endowment enabled the magazine to establish the Poetry Foundation, 'an independent literary organization committed to a vigorous presence for poetry in our culture'.[130] More unstable journals with a smaller readership, such as *Others*, *Secession*, *1924* and *S4N*, had, on average, lifespans of around two years. Monroe carefully financed the magazine through donations,[131] and generally refused to give its pages over to particular groups, at least after Pound's involvement (*Poetry* was briefly dominated by Pound's Imagist cluster of poets during his appointment as foreign editor). Combined with careful financial planning, this inattention to coteries, while irritating for Crane in the early 1920s (and perhaps lending the magazine a conservative sheen), ultimately seems to have ensured its longevity. Crane was, too, in a very different position to his early interactions with *Poetry*; by 1932 he had published two volumes, with *Key West* in its last stages.

Implicit in Crane's letter is the necessity for catholic journals, like *Poetry*, to offer a broader range of writers, before these more factional, specialised journals could stake out their own positions in the field. *Poetry* quickly amassed an eclectic range of contributors. Pound appeared in the first issue and later, as foreign editor between 1912 and 1917, secured a number of impressive contributions for the journal, including T. S. Eliot's 'The Love Song of J. Alfred Prufrock'. Other *Poetry* contributors included Padraic and Mary Colum, Countee Cullen, John Gould Fletcher, Robert Frost, Ford Madox Ford, Langston Hughes, James Joyce, Amy Lowell, Edna St. Vincent Millay, Marianne Moore, Carl Sandburg, Wallace Stevens, Arthur Symons, Rabindranath Tagore, William Carlos Williams and W. B. Yeats. *Poetry* is also notable for its dedicated 'Women's Numbers' (to Pound's chagrin), while standard issues were relatively well populated by female poets, including in the review pages.[132]

Poetry had a number of distinguished contributors with, as Crane notes in his letter, an increasing number of critics – some of whom became influential commentators on his own work, such as R. P. Blackmur, Winters and Tate. By the 1920s a great deal of the poetry in the magazine seemed, in Crane's

---

[129] Harriet Monroe, 'The Motive of the Magazine', *Poetry* 1.1 (1912), pp. 26–8 (p. 27).
[130] Unsigned, 'About Us', *Poetry Foundation*, available at <https://www.poetryfoundation.org/foundation/about> (accessed 10 December 2021).
[131] Monroe had founded the journal in 1912, financing it through a system of $50 annual endowments from 100 donors. Cahill, *Harriet Monroe*, p. 129.
[132] On Pound and 'Ladies' Numbers', see Cahill, *Harriet Monroe*, p. 73. A third of the space in the October 1926 number (29.1) was given over to women, for instance.

eyes, conservative.[133] Monroe's continued attention to experiments in Imagism, which had been fashionable in the early 1910s, popularised through, among others, *The Little Review* and *Others*, dated the publication. The rise of Imagism had created, as Pound put it to Monroe as early as 1915, a 'democratic beer garden'.[134] As Alice Corbin Henderson pointed out to Monroe's biographer, she had fairly fixed editing principles throughout her tenure, which resonated with Pound's writings on Imagism. Monroe's editing principles, Henderson recalled, emphasised 'structure'; she disliked 'the padding of lines', 'any poeticises', 'propaganda poetry', 'overstatement', 'typographical idiosyncrasies', 'personal verse or verse in dubious taste' and 'conversation[al] language'.[135] Monroe's preferred 'tangent of the modern movement' followed these principles, which had 'stripp[ed] the art bare' of 'rhetoric, eloquence, grandiloquence, poetic diction' and the 'frills and furbelows which had over-draped, over-ornamented its beauty'.[136] For Winters, this made *Poetry*'s selections 'about three movements behind the times'.[137]

In an article titled 'Why Not Laugh?', published in January, Monroe belatedly commented on the 'New York sophisticates' – of whom Crane the '*Secessionist*' was, presumably, one – who were 'so near to Europe and so far from America!': 'And the movements and groups and isms, born to save the world or the day or the art—futurism, cubism, impressionism, symbolism, imagism, realism, *sur-réalisme*—is there not always one of these revolutions to laugh at.'[138] *Poetry* seemed concerned that the American poets experimenting with these forms were in some way 'servile' (as Crane put it) and too 'near' to European letters – a fundamental misunderstanding of the transnational founding principles of *Secession*, *Broom*, *Gargoyle* and *transition*, which highlighted the mutual influences between American writers and their 'allied Frenchmen'.[139]

In 'Looking Backward' in the October 1928 number, Monroe discussed *Poetry*'s then sixteen-year career, and subtly linked the poetic move away from 'the simplification process' of the magazine's early years towards 'unintelligibility' to the 'oscillations' of French poetry. Monroe picked out journals that frequently published work in translation from Europeans for negative

---

[133] Crane to Burke, 28 September 1926, *O My Land*, p. 276.
[134] Pound to Monroe, January 1915, *Selected Letters of Ezra Pound*, p. 48.
[135] Cahill, *Harriet Monroe*, p. 85.
[136] Harriet Monroe, 'Looking Backward', *Poetry*, 33.1 (1928), pp. 32–8 (pp. 35–6).
[137] Winters to Monroe, 27 November 1926, in Parisi and Young (eds), *Dear Editor*, p. 277; Winters to Monroe, 28 June 1927, ibid., p. 278.
[138] Monroe, 'Why Not Laugh?', p. 209. Monroe's comment appeared eight years after Munson and Josephson discussed the founding of *Secession*, and fourteen years after Stieglitz founded his Dadaist *291* in New York.
[139] Crane to Munson, *Letters*, p. 35.

comment – *The Little Review*, *The Fugitive* and *transition* – and noted that the 'groups' they were publishing '[we] might reasonably call the Intellectualists if we had a Frenchman's talent for labels'; they were working against the dominant impulse in the early years of her journal, which attempted to bring poetry 'closer to life, to modern subjects, people and interests'.[140] Monroe went on to single out poets whom she found particularly guilty of perpetuating the fashion for 'unintelligibility', naming the 'later Ezra Pound of the *Cantos*', William Carlos Williams, Hart Crane, Allen Tate, Laura Riding and Yvor Winters, all of whom she deemed 'scornful of the *profanum vulgus*'.[141] Monroe picks up on the association of these poets with the European, avant-garde, small readership journals, adding that:

> Once more we have 'the doctrine of folding-in, the closure, the eso-teric—the aristocrat conception of the Poet, the ancient spirit of caste.' The poet deliberately aims at being unintelligible to all but specialists, deliberately discards all the common aids which the ordinary reader is accustomed to, such as punctuation, capitalization, grammar, syntax, sentence-structure, etc., telescoping the English language into hints, exclamations, tip-toeing the high spits of his mood.[142]

For Crane, Munson and Josephson, however, this was a point of pride, with Crane referring to the founding of *Secession* as emblematic of a developing 'aristocracy of taste' within the US poetry scene.[143] Crane was, then, with his reputation as a 'Secessionist' and his more general association with the 'exile' journals, exactly this kind of 'scornful', 'specialist' poet.[144]

Monroe's criticisms in 'Looking Backward' on the return to this kind of aestheticism resonate with her specific complaints about Crane in the 'Discussion'. The complex, associative metaphors of 'At Melville's Tomb' were anathema to Monroe's preference for 'stripped', 'bare' poetry. She singled out the following lines as particularly objectionable:

> And wrecks passed without sound of bells,
> The calyx of death's bounty giving back
> A scattered chapter, livid hieroglyph,
> The portent wound in corridors of shells.[145]

---

[140] Monroe, 'Looking Backward', pp. 35–6.
[141] Ibid.
[142] Ibid.
[143] Crane to Munson, 16 May 1922, *Letters*, p. 87.
[144] Monroe, 'Looking Backward', pp. 35–6.
[145] Crane, 'At Melville's Tomb', p. 25.

Monroe wrote:

> [T]ell me how *dice* can *bequeath an embassy* (or anything else) and how a calyx (*of death's bounty* or anything else) can give back a *scattered chapter, livid hieroglyph* and how, if it does, such a *portent* can be *wound in corridors* (of shells or anything else).[146]

Monroe's arch, faux-naïve tone does not mask her misreading of this stanza, and, indeed, the poem as a whole. In this self-conscious moment, Crane is articulating the formal properties of the 'logic of metaphor'. Again, here he links the 'logic' (as a form of collage through juxtaposed metaphors) to his interest in fragment forms with the phrase 'scattered chapter'. 'Hieroglyph' operates as his fairly simple analogy for the process of poetic association.

In his response, Crane dutifully explains this process to Monroe, noting that his gloss is necessarily a 'poor substitute for any organized conception that one has fancied he has put into the more essentialized form of the poem itself'.[147] That is to say, the intricate workings of a poem should not be capable of paraphrase. A 'hieroglyph' as a figure replacing a word is a precise, convincing analogy for Crane's logic, which, through its associative construction, he aimed to use to craft a 'single new word', a fresh and surprising way of articulating ideas. Crane explains further, parsing the 'dice' image:

> Dice bequeath an embassy, in the first place, by being ground (in this connection only, of course) in little cubes from the bones of drowned men by the action of the sea, and are finally thrown up on the sand, having 'numbers' but no identification. These being the bones of dead men who have never completed their voyage, it seems legitimate to refer to them as the only surviving evidence of certain messages undelivered.[148]

The 'surviving evidence of certain messages undelivered' of the 'wreck' is analogous to Crane's concern for exactly the kind of reading dramatised by Monroe. Here readings of the poem have the potential to be lost ('undelivered') through the self-conscious risks that Crane takes with his compressed metaphors through their own 'scattered' links and associations.

Crane begins his response to Monroe with a literal explanation of 'the double ironic sense' of the meaning of 'calyx' as 'both a cornucopia and the vortex made by the sinking vessel', but then goes on to explicitly outline the metaphorical construction of the poem, noting that Monroe's attachment to 'rigid

---

[146] Monroe's emphasis, 'A Discussion', p. 35.
[147] Ibid., p. 35.
[148] Ibid., p. 38.

significations' was 'quite outside the issues of my own aspirations'.[149] Crane is careful to mention the importance of discussions in other literary journals in shaping his 'dynamics of metaphor', and, significantly, he uses the phrase 'the logic of metaphor' publicly here for the first time. Most probably he had debates aired in *Secession*, *Broom* and *1924* in mind when he added that, 'This argument over the dynamics of metaphor promises as active a future as has been evinced in the past.'[150]

Just as Moore had suggested that Crane omit the fourth stanza (a quarter of the poem) on his submission of 'At Melville's Tomb' to *The Dial*, this stanza bore the brunt of Monroe's complaints.[151] After his subtle suggestion that Monroe might not be apprised of the discussions he had in mind as they were active in avant-garde journals, Crane moves on to Monroe's 'arbitrary concerns' over particular images, including 'how a *portent* could possibly be wound in a *shell*', by comparing metaphors from Blake and Eliot:

> I ask you how Blake could possibly say that 'a *sigh* is a *sword* of an Angel King'. You ask me how *compass, quadrant and sextant 'contrive'* tides. I ask you how Eliot can possibly believe that 'Every street *lamp* that I pass *beats* like a fatalistic *drum!*' Both of my metaphors may fall down completely. I'm not defending their actual value in themselves; but your criticism of them in each case was levelled at an illogicality of relationship between symbols, which similar fault you must have either overlooked in case you have ever admired the Blake and Eliot lines, or have condoned them on account of some more ultimate convictions pressed on you by the impact of the poems in their entirety. [emphases in original][152]

Crane is questioning the grounds of Monroe's objections to his 'obscurity' and 'illogic' – terms that have become clichés of criticism of his poetry. The question of whether or not a poetic image is or is not logical is irrelevant for Crane. He is more interested in the 'interplay [of] metaphor'. 'Bones' cannot literally 'bequeath' an 'embassy' of ideas that can reconstruct the 'scattered chapter' of the history of the wreck, but his meaning is nonetheless clear. Crane's approach to Monroe's accusations of illogic is to dismiss the claim on the grounds on which it is based, questioning the appropriateness of these types of requirements for poetry.[153] This was, significantly, picked up on in articles by Max Eastman on

---

[149] Ibid., pp. 35–6.
[150] Ibid., p. 36.
[151] Moore to Crane, 10 December 1923, box 2, folder 50, *Dial*/Thayer papers.
[152] Monroe, 'A Discussion', p. 37.
[153] Eastman, 'The Cult of Unintelligibility', pp. 632–9.

Crane's 'unintelligibility', which also cited Joyce and Stein. In the first of Eastman's attacks, he quoted 'At Melville's Tomb' in full to make his point, before launching into a page-and-a-half-long critique of the poem, which included a paragraph on Crane's exchange of letters with Monroe.[154]

Criticism of Crane has become entangled in what is or is not 'obscure' or 'logical' or a 'failure'. These charges imply that there is an ideal that Crane's poetry is being measured against, and against which it is found lacking, that is, an ideal poetic logic or success, or a particular allowable kind of difficulty for some, but not all, poets. Crane himself made this clear through examples taken from a poet whom he assumed Monroe admired, Blake (who received regular critical attention in *Poetry*),[155] and from Eliot, a relatively established poet already venerated by Crane's avant-garde contemporaries.[156] While accounts of Monroe's and Moore's interventions have, perhaps rightly, expressed affront regarding the edit and the 'Discussion', it remains the case that equally censorious questions abound even in recent criticism of Crane (rooted in these same dubious desires for poetic rationality and 'restraint').

Monroe's interrogation of Crane's use of metaphor annoyed Winters. As well as being a contributor, Winters acted as an occasional, although unofficial, editorial advisor.[157] In July 1928 Monroe wrote a letter to Crane on his recent submission, 'Moment Fugue', that echoed the points made in the 'Discussion', and which Crane forwarded to Winters. Posing as 'Cerberus', Monroe asked to be 'throw[n] a sop', something to placate her desire to worry at the poem, requesting that Crane point out its 'verbs and subjects'. She included her own 'attempts' to paraphrase the text, and finished with the suggestion that Crane 'send the poem back, just a little changed', asking him to consider the virtues of 'intelligibility'.[158] This obtuse response so irritated Winters that he replied on Crane's behalf, enclosing a sarcastic gloss that mimicked Monroe's tone in the 'Discussion'. Winters 'parse[d] the thing', as requested, and facetiously took note of each part of speech used in the poem: 'the syphilitic (adj. used as noun)', 'selling—pres. part. mod. subj.'.[159] Crucially, he referred to Crane's assimilative mode – often incorporating *fin-de-siècle* details – as he commented that Monroe, like Moore with her edits of 'The Wine Menagerie', had:

---

[154] Eastman, 'Poets Talking to Themselves', p. 563.
[155] For example, then foreign editor, Pound, on Blake: 'divinely sent to deliver us' from 'imaginative reason', '*Odes et Prières*', review of Jules Romains, *Odes et Prières* (1913), *Poetry*, 2.5 (1913), pp. 187–9 (p. 187).
[156] See Martin Dodsworth, 'Contemporary Reviews', in *T. S. Eliot in Context*, ed. Jason Harding (Cambridge: Cambridge University Press, 2011), pp. 349–58.
[157] Winters to Monroe, 27 November 1926, in Parisi and Young (eds), *Dear Editor*, p. 277.
[158] Monroe to Crane, 18 July 1928, box 7, Crane papers.
[159] Winters to Monroe, 31 July 1928, in Parisi and Young (eds), *Dear Editor*, pp. 279–80.

decided early in your editorial career that all the poetry of the past was ipso facto affected and ridiculous and hence not to be read [. . .] See any English classics for precedent. Or simply see any of the English classics for a few elementary notions of style in general.[160]

For Winters, Monroe's 'sidestepping' of Crane was indicative of her wider 'alienat[ion] of the best poets of [the] generation' and was, as he put it rather emphatically, indicative of the magazine 'sliding' to the 'dogs' as a result of its inability to react to changes in literary movements and magazine culture.[161]

Despite Crane's rebuttal, Monroe's questions were reiterated by a number of reviews of *White Buildings* and, four years later, *The Bridge*. As Taggard made clear in her review of *White Buildings*, the 'Discussion' was crucial to her understanding of Crane's poetry. Taggard makes much of Crane's 'mistake of explaining in prose what his verse was trying to do'. 'However sincere his explanation,' she writes, 'it was a mistake to make it.'[162] The idea that 'no poem should require such a defense' demonstrates the effectiveness of the 'Defence' in framing readings of Crane's poetry in relation to modernist criticism of Decadent excess, with Taggard's review paraphrasing Monroe's open letter: 'He proceeds from one mixed metaphor to another, image on image, and we almost allow him his way with us because he makes together with a confusion of images, a perfect gaunt and stately music.'[163] The majority of the reviews of *White Buildings* echoed this sentiment. *The Yale Review* snarkily commented that 'what we could understand of "White Buildings" seemed often redolent of poetry, but there was much that we could not understand, even after three readings'.[164] *The New York Times* found the volume 'esoteric' and 'incomprehensible so far as the actual thought-content goes'.[165]

The Dial perhaps best expressed the formula. While admitting the beauty of the 'Voyages' sequence, Conrad Aiken's anonymous review noted Crane's 'affectations of idiom', 'indulgence' and – again mingling comments on personality with criticism – complained of his 'straining and self-conscious and disingenuous precocity', concluding that Crane was nothing but a 'high-class

---

[160] Ibid.
[161] Winters to Monroe, 1 October 1930, 28 January 1931, in Parisi and Young (eds), *Dear Editor*, pp. 291, 245.
[162] Taggard, 'An Imagist in Amber', p. 4.
[163] Ibid.
[164] Frederick E. Pierce, 'Four Poets', *The Yale Review*, 1.17 (2 October 1927), pp. 166–9 (p. 167).
[165] Herbert Gorman, 'Tradition and Experiment in Modern Poetry', review of Crane, *White Buildings* (1926), *New York Times*, 27 March 1927, p. 2.

intellectual fake'.[166] Aiken echoes the sentiments of Moore's edit and her sense of Crane's poetic theories as 'false knowledge', and pre-empts Winters' reading in *Primitivism and Decadence*.[167] In 'The Significance of *The Bridge*', Winters' comments are complicated by his ideas about 'the morality of poetry', and, as such, contain similarly troubling undercurrents as Moore's, where Crane's homosexuality is equated with a general sense of 'decadence' of character and lack of discipline that then reveals itself in his poetry.[168] His comments on Crane's 'obscurity' and 'figurative' use of 'term[s] [. . .] that he has probably never endeavoured to define', and his 'gift of style without the gift of thought', reflect these early reactions to Crane's borrowings from the unfashionable 'disastrous decade', despite Crane's emphasis on the influence of Whitman and Emerson on *The Bridge*.[169]

Not all of Crane's reviewers followed this pattern. More positive appraisals were found in the *Times Literary Supplement* in an unsigned article most likely written by Edgell Rickword, who regularly reviewed American poetry for the *TLS*, as well as a three-page 'nota' from Antonio Marichalar in Madrid's *Revista de Occidente* which drew attention to the 'synthetic construction' of Crane's 'visionary' poetry, comparing him to Whitman and Blake.[170] In his 1927 review of *White Buildings* in *The New Republic*, Waldo Frank mounted a defence against the negative appraisals of the volume. Frank asserted that 'the obscurity of Hart Crane is his creative temper. If you go in a geometrical mood to Michelangelo, you will find them, too, obscure.'[171] In other words, Frank allows Crane the sense of mastery over his subject familiar to other 'difficult' poets (what Seamus Heaney, writing on 'Yeats as an Example', calls 'the faith that artistic process has some kind of absolute validity').[172]

---

[166] Thomas Francis Parkinson, *Hart Crane and Yvor Winters: Their Literary Correspondence* (Berkeley, CA: University of California Press, 1978), p. 52; Aiken's authorship is verified in the *Dial* archives by an autographed galley proof dated 14 February 1927, box 9, folder 305, *Dial*/Thayer papers.

[167] Winters, *Primitivism and Decadence*; Williams to Pound, commenting on Moore's views of Crane, 12 July 1928, box 55, folder 2518, Pound papers.

[168] See Winters' disbelief at Crane's claim to him in a letter that he had 'never in his life done anything of which he had been ashamed', Winters, *Primitivism and Decadence*, p. 590.

[169] Ibid., pp. 597, 600.

[170] Unsigned, '*White Buildings*', review of Crane, *White Buildings* (1926), *Times Literary Supplement*, 24 February 1927, p. 130. The *Times Literary Supplement Index* does not list an author. *TLS Index*, I (A–K) (Reading: Newspaper Archive Developments, 1978), p. 363. Marichalar, 'La estética de retroceso', pp. 260–3; Winters, 'Hart Crane's Poems', pp. 47–51.

[171] Waldo Frank, 'The Poetry of Hart Crane', *The New Republic*, 50.641 (16 March 1927), pp. 116–17.

[172] Seamus Heaney, 'Yeats as an Example', in *Preoccupations: Selected Prose 1968–1978* (London: Faber and Faber, 1985), pp. 98–114 (p. 99).

The Dial and *Poetry* both had significant roles in shaping Crane's poetic reputation, enabling his transition to larger circulation journals such as *The Saturday Review*, *The New Republic* and *The Nation*. Moore and Monroe helped carve out a critical language for dealing with his poetry, colouring how he was received in articles and reviews of *White Buildings*, *The Bridge* and even the 1933 *Complete Poems*. This no doubt affected the wider arc of his career, as he began to appear in less specialised journals with broader readerships. *The Dial* and *Poetry* were crucial to the publication of *The Bridge* during the late 1920s, and would have been sympathetic to its American subject matter. Crane's affiliation with the 'exile' journals and the corresponding Surrealist-inflected developments in his poetry formed the basis of his uneasy relationships with *The Dial* and *Poetry* in the late 1920s.

An assessment of these relationships reveals the shifts in Crane's poetry, the reputations of *The Dial* and *Poetry*, and how their editors negotiated interactions with more specialised journals. Despite Crane's frustrations with the 'Again' edit, its publication did preface a series of appearances in *The Dial* after three years of rejections. This, alongside his newly established relationship with *Poetry*, gave Crane the necessary exposure to be able to publish in the 'smart journals', and, crucially, opened up new publishing opportunities for *The Bridge* beyond specialist, less widely read publications. In retrospect, thinking about Crane's canny knowledge of the literary field and his amusement in dispatching targeted parodies to editors, his submission of 'The Wine Menagerie' to Moore appears almost a provocation, similar to the satirical poem that he sent Seldes. The poem revels in Crane's new-found queer modernist poetics. His poetry, here, 'pivots', as it moves from the more subtle investigations of the early 'Voyages' poems and 'For the Marriage of Faustus and Helen', amassing and revelling in Decadent allusions and their associations as he teases out the contours – the thresholds and anatomies – of his queer poetry.

4

'A SCATTERED CHAPTER': PUBLISHING *THE BRIDGE*

> Each cited element breaks the continuity or the linearity of the discourse and leads necessarily to a double reading: that of the fragment perceived in relation to its text of origin; that of the same fragment as incorporated into a new whole, a different totality. The trick of collage consists also of never entirely suppressing the alterity of these elements reunited in a temporary composition.
>
> Group Mu, 'Collages'

> Like spears ensanguined of one tolling star
> That bleeds infinity—the orphic strings,
> Sidereal phalanxes, leap and converge:
> —One Song, one Bridge of Fire!
>
> Hart Crane, from 'Atlantis'[1]

In his 1930 review in *Hound & Horn*, Allen Tate offered the first of many pronouncements on *The Bridge*. Drawing together his frustration with the poem's form and Crane's reviewers, he wrote that the 'fifteen poems, taken as one poem, suffer from the lack of a coherent plot', adding that 'it is difficult to

---

[1] Group Mu, 'Collages', *Revue d'aesthetique*, 1.3–4 (Paris, 1978), as quoted in Perloff, 'Collage and Poetry', pp. 384–5. Crane, 'Atlantis', from *The Bridge, Complete Poems*, pp. 105–8 (p. 107–8).

agree with those critics who find the work a single poem and as such an artistic success'.[2] The poem appeared in two different forms: first, fragmented in periodicals, and then reassembled in the 1930 editions from Caresse Crosby's Parisian publishing house Black Sun and New York's Liveright.[3] Tate's remarks reflect how *The Bridge* was first presented publicly: thirteen fragments published in seven periodicals between 1927 and 1930, scattered between London, Paris, Chicago and New York.

Crane began work on *The Bridge* in 1923. In an interview to mark the poem's publication, he told *The Wilson Bulletin* that 'by the autumn of 1925, this plan [for the poem] had attained a definite pattern'; in March 1926 he outlined provisional sections in a letter to Otto Kahn.[4] Although Crane had a plan for the poem early on, the fragments were not published as they were completed, nor in the order that Crane designed for the volume edition. 'Atlantis' was the first section to be completed, but was not submitted for journal publication. Instead, the poem was saved for the volume, bringing together the reconstituted sequence in a poem in which the fragments of *The Bridge* 'leap and converge'.[5]

As Tate's review implies, Crane's publishing arrangement had an effect on the reception of the poem as a 'grand failure' – a phrase coined by Malcolm Cowley that became a truism in criticism of the poem, propagated by influential magazines such as *Poetry* and *Hound & Horn*. Rather than creating a sense of this publishing practice linking (or bridging even) distant magazines and artistic communities, for Tate, Cowley and other contemporary reviewers, receiving the poem piecemeal between 1927 and 1930 left its ruins on either side of the Atlantic. In this chapter, I will analyse the ways in which Crane fuses material and aesthetic experimentation in the poem, considering the relationship between the poem's experimental publication and its reception history. While Langdon Hammer has offered a remarkable deconstruction of Tate's view of Crane, the 'simple permanence' of his judgements and their broader implications for 'scholarship [of Crane] during the tenure of the New Criticism', here I situate *The Bridge* within its broader reception history among a range of critics.[6] Delving into the poem's periodical contexts reveals

---

[2] Allen Tate, 'A Distinguished Poet: *The Bridge*', *Hound & Horn*, 1.3 (1930), pp. 580–5 (pp. 580, 583).
[3] Crane, *The Bridge* (New York: Horace Liveright, 1930); *The Bridge* (Paris: Black Sun, 1930).
[4] As told to *The Wilson Bulletin for Librarians*; Unsigned, 'Hart Crane: Author of *The Bridge*', *Wilson Bulletin for Librarians*, 5 (October 1930), p. 104; Crane to Kahn, 18 March 1926, box 4, Crane papers.
[5] Crane to Frank, 26 July 1926, *O My Land*, p. 265.
[6] Hammer, *Janus-Faced Modernism*, pp. 35–6.

how fragmentary publication conditioned its immediate reception and played a part in establishing prevailing themes in Crane criticism. As Hammer notes, 'Crane's admirers usually have had to work to prove that (as Lee Edelman conveniently puts it) "the poetry was *not* incoherent, was *not* confused, was *not* seriously obscure"'.[7]

This chapter draws on a rich history of criticism on *The Bridge*, including Daniel Gabriel's reading of it as 'lyric-epic dialogism', and Yingling's suggestion that the scope of Crane's experiments was inhibited by the 'discourses of heterosexuality' inherent in the epic.[8] I share, however, Niall Munro's scepticism as to the usefulness of classifying *The Bridge* as an epic and, therefore, wrestling with whether or not the poem fits certain formal parameters.[9] As Paul Giles notes in *The Contexts of 'The Bridge'*, 'Crane learnt more from Dada and Surrealism than meets the eye'.[10] Giles, who considers *The Bridge* alongside Joyce's *Finnegans Wake*, offers a useful point of departure, situating Crane in a broader, transatlantic writing community. Crane expanded his experiments from linguistic to material forms, mixing his broad interest in European avant-gardes as he played with collaged, multi-perspectival poetic forms. Rather than adopting a defensive pose – that Crane was '*not* incoherent', that *The Bridge* is not a 'grand failure' and so on – I maintain my position that such arguments rest on a category mistake embedded in narratives of Crane's poetry.

Playing with fragments and fragmented forms, Crane's publishing practices constitute an aesthetic programme for *The Bridge*: the poem finds its form through dissemination and reconstitution via little magazines, a deliberately 'scattered chapter' (to quote a reflectively self-aware phrase from 'At Melville's Tomb').[11] Crane viewed the poem as an 'epic', 'a symphony', 'a fugue' – in other words, as complex, often multi-perspectival structures. Crane found an 'analogy' for the poem's form in 'the Sistine chapel' in a 1927 letter to Kahn. The chapel's vaulted ceiling and painted walls offer a grand narrative through compartmentalised, sectioned-off scenes: 'each is a separate canvas, as it were, yet none yields its entire significance when seen apart from the others'. For Crane, *The Bridge* sections work as fragments (the separate canvas), designed for reassembly. Crane worried about the 'unique problem of form' this presented, 'not alone in relation to the materials embodied within its separate confines, but also in relation to the other parts, in series, of the major design of the entire poem'.[12] For the fragment or fragmented poem, the idea of the relationship to

---

[7] Ibid., p. 35.
[8] Gabriel, *Modernist Epic*; Yingling, *Hart Crane and the Homosexual Text*, p. 199.
[9] Munro, *Hart Crane's Queer Modernist Aesthetic*, p. 95.
[10] Giles, *The Contexts of 'The Bridge'*, p. 134.
[11] Crane, 'At Melville's Tomb', *Poetry*, p. 25.
[12] Crane to Kahn, 12 September 1927, *O My Land*, p. 349.

the whole is central. We might think here of Samuel Taylor Coleridge's 'Kubla Khan, or, a Vision in a Dream, A Fragment' where the poem's central conceit is its unfinishedness. In this form of Romantic fragment, the 'very boundaries' of the text are 'seen to be contested and indeterminate' as the incompleteness of the poem is 'announced', as Michael Bradshaw writes.[13] This form makes 'an issue of incompletion, not only of apologising for, but actively displaying their failures to resolve texts—and publishing them'.[14]

Allusions, similarly, forge connections between art objects. Contained within the allusive moment is the question of whether the allusion is intended simply to conjure the isolated object referred to, the quoted phrase or lines, the text as a whole, or the writer's or artist's broader body of work. Crane plays with the gesture of allusion in *The Bridge*: the contact allusion brings about between texts. The fragments of *The Bridge*, broken up and distributed in their discrete periodical publications, reach for the other fragments of the poem through allusion and shared phrases and ideas, as well as the reconstituted text. Their reassembly, with the original aura of the periodical contexts still alive in them, creates a collage form in the final volume version. Publishing, then, becomes a theoretical reflection and extension of the fragmented patterns of images, rhythms and motifs in the poem.

In the material structure of *The Bridge*, Crane fully realised experiments prompted by the split publications of 'Voyages' and 'For the Marriage of Faustus and Helen'. I see the form of *The Bridge* as both demonstrating fruitful exchanges between Crane's various periodical cultures and as an experiment with the literary fragment and processes of reassembly. This unique claim has implications for other materially experimental long poems written in the twentieth century, such as Ezra Pound's *Cantos*, Louis Zukofsky's *A* or Diane di Prima's *Revolutionary Letters*.[15] The rejection of linear, narrative progressive structure (what Tate would call 'plot') in *The Bridge* in favour of a collaged, Cubist repetition of fragmentary images and rhythms is contextualised by the poem's dissemination in multiple periodicals. Close attention to the poem's original fragmentary publication history and its 'processes of transmission' challenges the idea of the poem as a failure of incoherence. Countering this interpretation, I provide a radical rereading of the poem through attention to its material and aesthetic experiments, seeing it as a collaged, Cubist work. Eschewing linearity or narrative, the

---

[13] Michael Bradshaw, 'Hedgehog Theory: How to Read a Romantic Fragment Poem', *Literature Compass*, 5 (2008), pp. 73–89 (p. 74).

[14] Ibid., p. 75.

[15] For example, the non-linear emergence of *A* in *Poetry*: Louis Zukofsky, 'A: Second Movement', *Poetry*, 40.1 (1932), pp. 26–9; 'A: 29', *Poetry*, 46.2 (1933), p. 312; 'A: 9', *Poetry*, 58.3 (1941), pp. 128–30; Ezra Pound, *The Cantos* (New York: New Directions, 1999); Diane di Prima, *Revolutionary Letters* (San Francisco: City Lights, 2021).

beauty of *The Bridge* emerges through juxtapositions, interlinked images and repeated rhythmic effects.

Periodical Publishing as Form

Crane's poetic experiments in *The Bridge* are extended and transformed through the material form of the poem, published in fragments in literary magazines. Reading the poem in its periodical contexts not only helps to accentuate its fine detail but illuminates its overarching form. The final poem emerges as a form of Cubist collage, which Marjorie Perloff distinguishes from similar Futurist, Dada and Surrealist forms. Here 'the objects, though disparate, are drawn from the same radius of discourse' so that 'the larger scheme into which these fragments are drawn is still that of a unified picture'.[16] Edits between versions in periodicals and the 1930 volume show Crane pinning down and refining ideas, as well as playing with periodical versions as variants, drawing out different resonances in the fragments through the surrounding magazine context, title changes and *The Bridge* sub-section groupings.[17] I understand the variations between periodical and volume versions as forming a set of complex formal poetic movements. Material and aesthetic forms work in tandem, creating links between the disparately published fragments. To borrow from the Group Mu on collage, this process invites a 'double reading', 'that of the fragment perceived in relation to its text of origin; that of the same fragment as incorporated into a new whole, a different totality'.[18] Or, in this case, there are two totalities presented by Crane: the webbed *Bridge*, published in fragments and connected through allusive gestures and patterns of ideas, and the 1930 version of the poem, reconstituted in volume form but retaining the relational, intimate aura of periodical publishing and the artistic communities represented by each journal.

The Bridge was composed between 1923 and 1929, with Crane making final adjustments to the poem right up until his submission of the manuscript to Caresse Crosby. The poem was published in seven journals as thirteen non-consecutive 'fragments', as Crane referred to the sections in letters (see Table 4.1).[19] *Poetry* issued two further reprints, publishing 'Cutty Sark' and 'To Brooklyn Bridge' after appearances in *transition* and *The Dial*, respectively. Crane frequently dispatched drafts of varying completion to friends as the poems developed, updating Frank most regularly.[20] Apart from a manuscript that Kenneth Lohf

---

[16] Perloff, 'Collage and Poetry', pp. 384–5.
[17] Ben Mazer's extremely useful edition presents the periodical variants, but in the order of the volume. Crane, *The Bridge: Uncollected*, ed. Ben Mazer (Asheville: Madhat, 2015).
[18] Group Mu, 'Collages', pp. 384–5.
[19] For example, Crane to Charlotte Rychtarik, 21 July 1923, *O My Land*, p. 159.
[20] Crane notes his use of Frank as a 'repository, 26 July 1926, *O My Land*, pp. 266, 265.

suggests was sent to Kahn in the winter of 1928–29, *The Bridge* was, it seems, not circulated in full prior to the publication of the 1930 volume.[21] Mirroring the magazine publication arrangements of the fragments, the assembled volume appeared in simultaneous editions on either side of the Atlantic. In February 1930 Crosby published 283 copies of the finely printed Black Sun volume, stunningly illustrated with Walker Evans's iconic photographs of Brooklyn Bridge and with titles set in poppy red type. Six weeks later, Liveright released 1,000 copies of the New York edition ahead of schedule, much to Crosby's irritation; she feared Liveright's early release would limit her own edition's reviews and sales.[22]

Crane no doubt appreciated the payments; with a $2000 loan from Kahn he was freer to choose aesthetically suitable, rather than simply well-paying, journals (though, as he wrote: 'It seems I have to pay $60 off the rest of my mortal term on life insurance to the Kahn estate, which, of course I was dumb

Table 4.1 *The Bridge*, Section Outline

Part	Section title	Subsection
Proem	To Brooklyn Bridge	
I	Ave Maria	
II	Powhatan's Daughter	1. The Harbor Dawn
		2. Van Winkle
		3. The River
		4. The Dance
		5. Indiana
III	Cutty Sark	
IV	Cape Hatteras	
V	Three Songs	1. Southern Cross
		2. National Winter Garden
		3. Virginia
VI	Quaker Hill	
VII	The Tunnel	
VIII	Atlantis	

[21] Lohf, *Literary Manuscripts*, pp. 27–54. The final MS: *The Bridge* [galley proofs], box 1, folder 2, both in Crane Collection, Austin.

[22] Caresse Crosby to Crane, 3 April 1930, box 6, Crane papers; Crane to Isidor Schneider, 1 May 1929, *O My Land*, pp. 405–6.

Table 4.2 *The Bridge*, Overview of Periodical Publication

Section	Date	Journal	Location
Southern Cross	April–July 1927	*The Calendar of Modern Letters*	London
National Winter Garden	April–July 1927	*The Calendar of Modern Letters*	London
Virginia	April–July 1927	*The Calendar of Modern Letters*	London
Cutty Sark	June 1927	*transition*	Paris
The Harbor Dawn: Brooklyn Heights	June 1927	*transition*	Paris
To Brooklyn Bridge	June 1927	*The Dial*	New York
Ave Maria	September 1927	*The American Caravan*	New York
Powhatan's Daughter [The Dance]	October 1927	*The Dial*	New York
Van Winkle	October 1927	*transition*	Paris
Cutty Sark	October 1927	*Poetry*	Chicago
The Tunnel	November 1927	*The Criterion*	London
The River	September 1928	*The Second American Caravan*	New York
Cape Hatteras	15 March 1930	*The Saturday Review*	New York
Eldorado [Indiana]	April 1930	*Poetry*	Chicago
To Brooklyn Bridge	November 1930	*Poetry*	Chicago

bell enough not to understand when he proposed it').[23] *The Calendar* paid 'a competitive rate of £3.3s for 1,000 words' and *The Dial* paid $40 for 'To Brooklyn Bridge' and $80 for the longer poem, 'Powhatan's Daughter'.[24] To contextualise: Crane was paid $100 in advance for *White Buildings*, around a fiftieth of the average household income in 1926 ($5,306.43).[25] *The Bridge* volume earned just $1 in 1934.[26] Despite Crane's money troubles, he chose for the majority of *The Bridge* fragments a magazine, *transition*, that could not pay

---

[23] Crane to Kahn, 12 September 1927, *O My Land*, pp. 344–50; Crane to Frank, 28 January 1928, *Letters*, p. 286.
[24] Harding, *The Criterion*, p. 47; Moore to Crane, 17 March 1927, box 2, folder 50, *Dial/Thayer papers*.
[25] Boni and Liveright contract, 9 July 1926, box 25, Crane papers; income statistics, Office of the Commissioner of Internal Revenue, *Statistics of Income from Returns of Net Income for 1926 Including Statistics of from Estate Tax Returns* (Washington DC: United States Government Printing Office, 1928), p. 3.
[26] Liveright Publishing Corporation royalty statement, box 25, Crane papers.

its contributors (Susan Jenkins Brown also recalls that Crane refused payment to churn out villanelles for the commercial magazine she was editing, *Telling Tales*).²⁷ Crane's priority was to place the sections in sympathetic journals, rather than seeking out magazine publishers with generous contribution rates.

The periodical form of *The Bridge* began with the 'Three Songs' in London's *Calendar of Modern Letters* in April 1927 and ended with the 'To Brooklyn Bridge' reprint in the November 1930 number of *Poetry*, on Crane's receipt of the journal's annual award. All but 'Quaker Hill' and 'Atlantis' were published in journals. A further three sections, 'The Dance', 'The Tunnel' and 'Van Winkle', were reprinted in four anthologies before the volume edition was published.²⁸ 'Cape Hatteras' and 'Eldorado' ('Indiana') followed the Black Sun and Liveright editions, appearing that spring in *The Saturday Review* and *Poetry*, respectively.²⁹ The fragmented format went against contemporary norms for publishing long poems. Standard procedure, among the 'variety of possibilities of modernist publishing', was via a sympathetic editor of a journal, with the text printed in one instalment (*The Waste Land* in *The Criterion* and *The Dial*) or, less commonly, serialised (Mina Loy's *Love Songs* in *Others*), in chapbook form (Ford Madox Ford's *Antwerp*, published by Monro's Poetry Bookshop Press), or as a single volume (Rilke's *Die Sonette an Orpheus*).³⁰

The publishing history of 'To Brooklyn Bridge' shows the interaction between the fragment and fragmented text. Crane had hoped that the proem might be the first of the fragments to be published, appearing (like *The Waste Land*) in *The Dial* and *The Criterion*. Despite sending back 'The Wine Menagerie' and 'Passage', Eliot had told Crane to 'let him see other things' that he was working on. Crane then sent 'Passage' to *The Calendar*, where it appeared in July 1926, and in August he sent Eliot 'To Brooklyn Bridge'.³¹ Writing to Frank days after sending the proem to *The Criterion* and *The Dial*, Crane noted that he 'probably [would not] let anything out of the bag on this side of the water, though, for sometime yet, it keeps too many question marks in my head, albeit a little

---

²⁷ Brown (ed.), *Robber Rocks*, p. 21.
²⁸ Crane, 'Powhatan's Daughter' ['The Dance'], in *Anthology of Magazine Verse for 1928 and Yearbook of American Poetry*, ed. William Stanley Braithwaite (New York: Harold Vinal, 1928), pp. 84–7; Crane, 'The Tunnel', in *Modern American Poetry and Modern British Poetry*, ed. Louis Untermeyer (New York: Harcourt, 1930), p. 529; Crane 'Van Winkle', ibid., p. 521.
²⁹ Crane, 'Cape Hatteras', *The Saturday Review*, 6.34 (15 March 1930), pp. 821–2; Crane, 'Eldorado', *Poetry*, 36.1 (1930), pp. 13–15.
³⁰ Ford Madox Hueffer [Ford], *Antwerp* (London: The Poetry Bookshop, 1915); Rainer Maria Rilke, *Die Sonette an Orpheus* (Munich: Insel-Verlag, 1923).
³¹ Crane to Frank, 12 August 1926, *O My Land*, p. 268.

change for the purse'.³² Eliot returned the poem six months after its submission, and *The Dial* published the piece over a year later.³³

Crane decided to split *The Bridge* publications even at this early stage, and wanted, ideally, 'To Brooklyn Bridge' to introduce the fragments that were to be published later. While Crane's term for the poem, 'invocation', is closely associated with the classical epic, he was drawing on a more recent history of 'invocation' poems, particularly in Romantic poetry, that experimented with the genre. In 'To Brooklyn Bridge', while Crane was, no doubt, gesturing to the epic convention, he seems to be specifically remembering Wordsworth's 'Introduction' to *The Prelude*, another long poem that evades strict generic classification.³⁴ Wordsworth's 'cherished fetters to unbind', 'But not on high, where madness is resented' become the 'unfractioned idiom', 'chained bay waters Liberty' and the 'bedlamite speed[ing] to thy parapets'.³⁵ The idea is more to introduce the central image of Brooklyn Bridge, and the allusions to the structure that resonate and connect the following sections, than to announce that the poem will be working strictly within the formal traditions of the conventional epic.

After the poem's delayed publication in *The Dial*, and silence from Eliot, Crane pragmatically decided to have the fragments printed in a non-linear fashion, avoiding the issues that might result from different acceptance and printing schedules at his chosen journals.³⁶ Given his precarious finances, the benefits of journal publication are clear: immediate and relatively generous pay (effectively selling *The Bridge* twice, once to journals and once to Liveright), as well as the prestige of publishing in journals such as *The Dial*. Crane sent 'To Brooklyn Bridge' to *The Criterion* and *The Dial*, to function in the manner

---

[32] Ibid.
[33] 'I must apologise for having kept the enclosed manuscript for so long.' Eliot to Crane, 24 January 1927, in *The Letters of T. S. Eliot, Volume 3: 1926–1927*, ed. Valerie Eliot, John Haffenden and Hugh Haughton (New Haven, CT: Yale University Press, 2012), p. 391. The editors of Eliot's letters note that this rejection was for 'The Wine Menagerie', 'Passage' and 'Praise for an Urn'. Looking at Crane's letters, in fact it seems that Crane submitted a different poem, 'To Brooklyn Bridge', to Eliot in August 1926. See Crane to Frank, 12 August 1926, *O My Land*, p. 269.
[34] See Masaki Mori on Wordsworth's 'Introduction' in *Epic Grandeur: Toward a Comparative Poetics of the Epic* (Albany, NY: SUNY Press, 1997), p. 103.
[35] William Wordsworth, 'Invocation to Earth', in *The Poetical Works of William Wordsworth* (London: Edward Moxton, 1837), vol. I, pp. 320–1; Crane, 'To Brooklyn Bridge', *The Dial*, p. 489.
[36] *The Dial* took around ten days to decide on a poem: the proem was submitted on 22 July 1926 and accepted on 5 August, box 2, folder 49, *Dial*/Thayer papers. Eliot took six months to return the same poem. Eliot to Crane, 24 January 1927, *Letters of T. S. Eliot, Volume 3*, p. 391.

of the Romantic fragment poem, but referring to an actual fragmented text – albeit an, at the time, incomplete one. However, *The Bridge* (as it appeared in journals) opened in London with the 'Three Songs', which, like the proem, gestures to the following sections through its unique note 'from *The Bridge*'. Crane's emphasis, however, was on the fragment's ability to be read as an isolated poem; he had told the editors of *The Virginia Quarterly* (who sent back the 'Three Songs') that they were welcome to 'drop the reference to *The Bridge*', if they preferred.[37]

But there was an aesthetic benefit in what had begun as a pragmatic choice of split, non-linear publication, just as Crane had discovered the usefulness of the fragmented versions of 'For the Marriage of Faustus and Helen' and 'Voyages'. *The Bridge* fragments share allusive gestures, forging links between the scattered poems. The densely allusive qualities of 'Cape Hatteras' guided Crane's decision to publish the poem even after the volume had appeared and offers an instructive example of the material and poetic form of the poem in its periodical form. In 'Cape Hatteras' Crane takes up Whitman's ideas of 'crossing', 'spanning' and 'bridging' from 'Passage to India'.[38] But he shifts from Whitman's characteristic panoptic and surveying gaze ('Have you reckoned a thousand acres much? Have you reckoned the earth much?') and narrows his focus to the unusual, chevron-shaped seventy miles of the North Carolina coast – that 'convulsive shift of sand'.[39] Crane borrows lines from 'Passage to India' as his epigraph to the section: 'The seas all crossed, / weathered the capes, the voyage done . . .' (with a schooner printed above the title and epigraph in *The Saturday Review*).[40] The poem is encircled by Whitman's presence through the epigraph and direct address to the poet in Crane's final lines ('My hand / in yours, / Walt Whitman— / so— ').[41] Crane is emphatic that *The Bridge* is written in hand with Whitman. The 'Song of the Exposition' is the other key intertext here, where Whitman writes:

> These triumphs of our time, the Atlantic's delicate cable,
> The Pacific railroad, the Suez Canal, the Mont Cenis and Gothard and
>   Hoosac tunnels,
>   the Brooklyn Bridge
> This earth all spann'd with iron rails, with lines of steamships threading
>   every sea,
> Our own rondure, the current globe I bring.[42]

---

[37] Crane to the Editors, 25 July 1927, box 11, folder 24, *Virginia Quarterly* papers.
[38] Whitman, 'Passage to India', in *Leaves of Grass*, pp. 315–23 (pp. 316–17).
[39] Whitman, 'Song of Myself', in *Leaves of Grass*, pp. 29–79 (p. 30); Crane, 'Cape Hatteras', p. 821.
[40] Whitman, 'Passage to India', p. 318; Crane, 'Cape Hatteras', p. 821.
[41] Crane, 'Cape Hatteras', p. 822.
[42] Whitman, 'Song of Exposition', in *Leaves of Grass*, pp. 157–65 (p. 163).

The impulse to 'span' and connect literary networks, expressed practically through the disseminated publication, intersects with Crane's ideas for the mythical potential of America. Crane had Whitman in mind here, but in disassembling this long poem, spreading its publications and then having them 'converge' via 'Atlantis' in the volume form of *The Bridge*, Crane gives this mystical idea its practical application. Crane's invocation of Whitman in 'Cape Hatteras' aims to ensure that his presence is felt in the poem as a whole, and so Whitman becomes one of the links between ideas and sections, allusions to the poet providing some of the 'spanning' architecture of *The Bridge*.

In 'Eldorado/Indiana', meanwhile, Crane holds the periodical and volume form in tension, an example of how the two versions of *The Bridge* can invite complementary but distinct readings. As 'Eldorado', the poem's emphasis is placed on Crane's allusion to the colonial El Dorado legend through his exploration of the 1849 Gold Rush. The title borrows from Poe's own 'Eldorado' poem, creating more obvious links between the fragment and the various allusions to Poe in *The Bridge* (like the repeated allusions to Whitman and Melville in the poem, creating a structure through links between fragments). Crane entwines Sir Walter Raleigh's descriptions of 'that great and golden city of Manoa, which the Spaniards call El Dorado' in *Discoverie of Guiana* with Poe's critique of the myth in 'Eldorado' (Poe's poem was printed in the first number of *transition* in April 1927, alongside Crane's *Bridge* offcut, 'O Carib Isle').[43] In reference to Poe's poem, Jerome McGann describes 'the critical position the poem is taking toward a pair of his favorite subjects: self-delusion and crass American materialism', which Crane hints at as he describes the 'dream' of the town 'shambling in the nuggets' wake'.[44] Crane's dating of the poem in 1860 has implications for this reading, five years after the publication of the first edition of *Leaves of Grass* (and the year the third edition was printed). The suggestion, then, is that it is the American poetic tradition that is being 'loosed from the clay', implicitly dismissing the Native American cultural history that Crane leans on both in the poem and elsewhere in this sub-section of *The Bridge* ('Powhatan's Daughter').

As 'Indiana', the poem is rooted in Larry's point of departure rather than where he hopes to arrive, muting the poem's debt to Poe and the El Dorado myth. Fixing the poem at the homestead with its 'lintel' and 'wiry vine', the newer title focuses on the mother's lament for her son. Crane had initially planned the poem as a narrative spoken by a father, as he told Kahn:

---

[43] Sir Walter Raleigh, *Discoverie of Guiana*, ed. Joyce Lorimer (London: Ashgate, 2006), p. lxxxii; Edgar Allan Poe, 'Eldorado', in F. Boillet, 'The Methodological Study of Literature', *transition*, 1 (April 1927), pp. 57–8 (p. 57); Crane, 'O Carib Isle', *transition*, 1 (April 1927), pp. 101–2. See Brunner, *Splendid Failure*, for a detailed discussion of the poem's composition and variants.

[44] Jerome McGann, *Edgar Allan Poe: Alien Angel* (Cambridge, MA: Harvard University Press, 2014), p. 128.

It will be a monologue of an Indiana farmer; time, about 1860. He has failed in the gold-rush and is returned to the soil. His monologue is a farewell to his son, who is leaving for a life on the sea . . . It is a lyrical summary of the period of conquest, and his wife, the mother, who died on the way back from the gold-rush, is alluded to in a way which implies her succession to the nature-symbolism of Pocahontas.[45]

In the late 1920s Crane's relationships with his parents inverted. His once disconnected and often fraught relationship with his father improved, much to the younger Crane's delight and surprise. At the same time, his connection with his mother utterly disintegrated after their final fight in California (the two were estranged at the time of his death). It seems significant, then, that Crane abandoned the monologue, delivered by an unnamed mother, though traces of the original plan for the poem remain. The final cry of 'Indiana', 'oh I shall always wait', then, almost seems to be spoken by Grace. Tennessee Williams seems to have felt the same; he tearfully – albeit rather drunkenly – read 'Indiana' on the Bill Boggs show, comparing the dynamic of his parents to that of Crane's. After introducing the poem with a discussion of his wish to have his remains sunk 'close to the submerged bones of Hart Crane', Williams lingers over 'Indiana'. The playwright acts the poem; he shapes the mother's voice so that her call in the last lines is marked by a manipulative sharpness ('Come back to Indiana – not too late!' appears as a threat, in Williams's voice). The poem becomes a mutually defensive conversation between parent and child about the poet's career (recalling Crane's letters to and from his father, and therefore the original plan for the monologue). The line 'golden syllables loosed from the clay' transforms here: writing is work, physically dug from the 'clay', but artistic achievement transforms into something mythic, impossible and resting on 'gilded promise' with no hint of material success.

Crane had particular reasons for retaining 'Quaker Hill' and 'Atlantis' for the volume. 'Quaker Hill', which he considered an 'accent mark' rather than a 'major section' of the poem, was simply completed too late. He finished edits on 26 December 1929 and immediately wrote to Crosby: 'I am hastily enclosing the final version of "Quaker Hill," which ends my writing on *The Bridge*.'[46] Downgrading the poem to an 'accent mark', Crane suggests that it did not operate successfully as a discrete fragment. This was perhaps because the final lines of 'Quaker Hill' work to introduce 'The Tunnel' and, with it, Crane's vexed engagement with Eliot. The poem's initial perspective of 'August Antarctic skies', 'mapled vistas' and a 'glance' that 'could cross the borders of three states' slowly lowers to the poem's final lines: 'Leaf after autumnal leaf / break

---

[45] Crane to Kahn, 12 September 1927, *O My Land*, pp. 345–6.
[46] Crane to Caresse Crosby, 26 December 1929, *O My Land*, p. 421.

off, / descend—'. While introducing the perspectival shift necessary for the following poem, here Crane also suggests lines from Eliot's 'The Fire Sermon': 'the last fingers of the leaf / Clutch and sink into the wet bank'.[47] Crane has these allusions dominate the poem here as he recreates Eliot's subterranean locations, as 'descend— / descend—' recalls 'and down we went', 'stairs unlit'.[48] But this also works as reflective comment on the 'descent' into the different, more pessimistic poetic mode of 'The Tunnel', which engages with, in Crane's words, the 'damned dead' tone of *The Waste Land*.[49]

The first of the fragments to be completed was the last poem in the sequence, 'the mystic consummation toward which all the other sections of the poem converge', 'Atlantis'.[50] As Crane wrote to Frank when he sent him a draft of the poem in 1916, 'a bridge is begun from the two ends at once!'[51] At the time, Crane had been reading Lewis Spence's eccentric *Atlantis in America* which outlines (in pseudo-scientific terms) Spence's investment in the sunken 'great island continent' that enabled one 'type of culture' to 'reach the shores of America as well as those of Europe.'[52] Crane described Spence's writing as 'full of exciting suggestions', finding in Atlantis a symbol of 'convergence', fitting for *The Bridge*'s transnational influences and for the particular, assimilative function of the final poem in the volume sequence.[53] The idea that 'Atlantis' would provide a point of unification for *The Bridge* guided Crane's decision not to publish the poem separately. In 'Atlantis', Crane begins weaving together the *Bridge* fragments in the self-conscious opening line: 'Through the bound cable strands, the arching path'.[54] 'Atlantis' provides the 'arching path' of the poem, created through strands 'bound' together, images and tropes collected and reconstituted in the last pages of the poem; the last collage piece that unifies the various ideas alive in the composition.

Harold Bloom wrote that '[a]ll of Crane's poetry, like Whitman's, is labyrinthine, a single poem, leaves of grass transmembered into one song, one bridge of fire'.[55] The lines from 'Atlantis' that Bloom draws on here provide an analogy for the particular structure of *The Bridge*. In language familiar from his descriptions of the poem in letters, Crane writes:

---

[47] Crane, 'Quaker Hill', from *The Bridge*, *Complete Poems*, p. 94; T. S. Eliot, *The Waste Land*, in *Complete Poems and Plays* (London: Faber and Faber, 1969), pp. 59–80 (p. 67).
[48] Eliot, *The Waste Land*, pp. 61, 69.
[49] Crane to Munson, 20 November 1922, *O My Land*, p. 108.
[50] Crane to Kahn, 18 March 1926, *O My Land*, p. 232.
[51] Crane to Frank, 3 August 1926, *O My Land*, p. 266.
[52] Lewis Spence, *Atlantis in America* (London: E. Benn, 1925), p. 13.
[53] Crane to Susan Jenkins Brown, 22 May 1926, *O My Land*, p. 254; Crane to Frank, 18 January 1926, ibid., p. 226.
[54] Crane, 'Atlantis', from *The Bridge*, *Complete Poems*, pp. 105–8 (p. 105).
[55] Bloom, *The Anatomy of Influence*, p. 273.

> Like spears ensanguined of one tolling star
> That bleeds infinity—the orphic strings,
> Sidereal phalanxes, leap and converge:
> —One Song, one Bridge of Fire! [. . .][56]

The fragments, published independently, are these 'spears', bloody from their extraction from the 'star', that then 'converge' as the 'One Song, one Bridge' in the reassembled text ('One arc synoptic of all tides below', as Crane writes elsewhere in the poem). The poem, seen in this light, becomes a Cubist 'convergence' of its fragments, eschewing linear form and the 'formal unity' expected by the poem's reviewers.[57] For Crane, thinking of Schlegel's concepts of the fragment and the whole, there is an interest in 'the mass of poetry' as 'a sea of struggling forces in which the particles of dissolved beauty, the pieces of shattered art, clash in a confused and gloomy mixture', where the 'whole' is made up of 'chaotic', contradictory stances.[58] It would, though, be erroneous to say that Crane was, strictly, a Cubist or, in terms of his use of metaphor, a Surrealist. Never a poet who desired to be part of 'any group', Crane assimilated forms that he found interesting into his writing indiscriminately – as demonstrated by the complex aesthetics of *The Bridge*.

The seeds of Crane's interest in the possibilities of these inter-art forms were perhaps planted through his friendship with the painter and writer Carl Schmitt, who he met in 1916. By early 1923 he had met Alfred Stieglitz and begun to associate with his circle, and his archive bears traces of a friendship with Georgia O'Keeffe. As George Knox notes, Crane was well acquainted with New York's plastic and graphic arts scene through Stieglitz, Lachaise and Isabel Dutaud Nagle, and parties at *The Little Review* offices, where Crane remembered first meeting Joseph Stella in the early 1920s (the autumn 1922 number was dedicated to the painter).[59] Crane habitually discusses visual art in his letters, even commenting on inter-art approaches and 'Gerty Stein' and 'her announced desire to break up poetry into an idiom corresponding to cubism, etc.'[60] Crane found ways to articulate the form of *The Bridge* through his knowledge of Analytical Cubism (Cubism's first phase), which sought to break down the object into multiple, contrasting and overlapping perspectives.

---

[56] Crane, 'Atlantis', pp. 105–8 (pp. 107–8).
[57] Winters, 'Progress', p. 153.
[58] Schlegel as quoted and discussed in Philippe Lacoue-Labarthe and Jean-Luc Nancy, *The Literary Absolute: The Theory of Literature in German Romanticism* (Albany, NY: SUNY Press, 1978), p. 51.
[59] George Knox, 'Crane and Stella: Conjunction of Painterly and Poetic Worlds', *Texas Studies in Literature and Language*, 12.4 (1971), pp. 689–707 (p. 691).
[60] Crane to Munson, 9 February 1923, *O My Land*, pp. 126–7.

More specifically, Crane was drawn to Stella's paintings, which integrated the Futurist presentation of dynamic modern construction and machinery and early Cubist play with perspective. Like Crane, he worked in series, producing multiple images of Brooklyn Bridge over his career. The 1919–20 version that Crane saw shows a dizzying, layered view of John Roebling's bridge from above, its sides impossibly visible through the railings and the New York skyline fragmented through and below the wires. Crane hoped to have the image as the frontispiece to *The Bridge*, having first seen the painting and essay in Charmion von Wiegand's copy of Stella's 1919 'privately issued monograph', *New York: Five Oils*.[61] Later, the painting appeared in monochrome in *The Little Review*'s 'Stella Number'. In 1929, and at Crane's request, Stella's *Brooklyn Bridge* was reproduced in *transition* with Stella's note on the work, '*Brooklyn Bridge* (A Page from My Life)', together with experimentally composed photographs of 'Manhattan: 1929' by Gretchen and Peter Powel.[62]

Crane allied the 'smashed', 'splintered' aesthetic of Stella's painting, 'modelled on the bridge's cables', to the structure or 'pattern' of his own project: 'It is a remarkable coincidence that I should, years later, have discovered that another person, by whom I mean you, should have had the same sentiments regarding Brooklyn Bridge which inspired the main theme and pattern of my poem.'[63] There is a correlation between the visual effects of Stella's painting and the structure of *The Bridge* as a 'fragmented whole', emphasised by its publication. Stella, like Crane, chose to refract the depiction of the city across different studies (just as Crane segmented his long poem into distinct lyrics), in a set of paintings that made up his *Five Oils* series. Crane's idea for the structure of *The Bridge* was, as he wrote in letters and reiterated in 'Atlantis', to have the fragments 'converge' in a manner analogous to a Cubist painting where multiple, conflicting perspectives on the same object are presented at once.

Cubism as a literary concept was active in journals from as early as 1907. A short story included in *Camera Work*, the journal of Crane's friend and correspondent Alfred Stieglitz, described four pairs of eyes creating a single 'converging gaze', looking at the same hand from different corners of a room.[64] In *Blast*'s July 1915 'War Number', Jessie Dismorr described Fleet Street as 'curiously exciting' with 'so many perspective lines, withdrawing, converging, they indicate evidently something of importance beyond the limits of sight'.[65]

---

[61] Joseph Stella, *New York: Five Oils* (New York: Joseph Stella, 1919).
[62] Joseph Stella, '*Brooklyn Bridge* (A Page from My Life)', *transition*, 16–17 (June 1929), pp. 86–8; Gretchen Powel and Peter Powel, 'Manhattan: 1929', photograph, reproduction, ibid., pp. 72–3.
[63] Crane to Stella, 24 January 1929, *O My Land*, p. 395.
[64] J. B. Kerfoot, 'The Cloak Room Mystery', *Camera Work*, 19 (July 1907), pp. 28–31 (p. 30).
[65] J. Dismorr, 'London Notes', *Blast*, 2 [War Number] (July 1915), p. 66.

Crane's interest in the poetic expression of Cubism may have stemmed from his reading of *The Pagan*, Bruno's journals and *Others* in the 1910s.[66] Stevens's 'Thirteen Ways of Looking at a Blackbird' (*Others*) is divided into thirteen numbered sections that create a collage-like, Cubist view of a blackbird - much like the painter Marguerite Zorach's front cover for the magazine two months later, which shows what appears to be a streetlamp and streams of light from multiple planes of vision, or Agnes Ernst Meyer's 'Mental Reactions' in *291*, in which she combines rotating, line-drawn images with text that drops and moves along and around the shapes.[67] Stevens's subtly facetious title indicates the prevalence of this kind of Cubist experiment; the title anticipates prior knowledge of similarly structured texts.[68]

This affiliation with Cubism was not lost on Crane's early reviewers, while poetic Cubism is now familiar ground, thanks to work on William Carlos Williams and the '"founding mother" of American cubist poetry', Gertrude Stein, among others.[69] Writing just weeks after the Liveright volume was released, Percy Hutchinson wrote a review in *The New York Times* titled 'Hart Crane's Cubistic Poetry in *The Bridge*'. Hutchinson commented on a 'theory' of 'cubism in poetry' that he found embedded in the form of Crane's poetry:

> it would call for just such work as Hart Crane has given us—the piling up of startling and widely disparate word-structures so that for the mind the cumulative result is very like the cumulative result of skyscrapers for the eye when looked on through a mist. If this conclusion is in any degree correct, then 'The Bridge' is to be regarded as a successful piece of work. The totality of tonal variations and tonal massings, plus the occasional pictorial achievements, give to the entire piece indisputable weight.[70]

The Bridge is structured with different, even disparate scenes that are connected through repeated images, and rhythmic and linguistic structures that build into the 'panoramic' but disconnected and fragmented 'sleights' that sketch out this 'body of America'.

---

[66] Examples include William Carlos Williams, 'To A Solitary Disciple', *Others*, 2.2 (1916), pp. 145–7; Kreymborg, *Mushrooms*.

[67] Marguerite Zorach, front cover, *Others*, 5.3 (1919); Agnes Ernst Meyer, 'Mental Reactions', *291*, 2 (April 1915), p. 3.

[68] Wallace Stevens, 'Thirteen Ways of Looking at a Blackbird', *Others*, 4.2 (1917), pp. 25–7.

[69] Bram Dijkstra, *Cubism, Stieglitz and the Early Poetry of William Carlos Williams* (Princeton, NJ: Princeton University Press, 1978); Jacqueline Vaught Brogan, *Part of the Climate: American Cubist Poetry* (Berkeley, CA: University of California Press, 1991), p. 8.

[70] Hutchinson, 'Hart Crane's Cubistic Poetry in *The Bridge*', p. 2.

Crane takes Cubist poetry beyond play with perspective and visualisation and transfers these processes to the material form of the text, scattered across periodicals. The fragments, through their disparate publications, tend towards one point ('Atlantis') through referential processes, from 'I started walking home across the bridge' ('Cutty Sark', *transition* and *Poetry*) to 'The Harbor Dawn' (*transition*) which first appeared with the subtitle 'Brooklyn Heights', invoking the bridge, and a cipher for Crane close to that same spot in 'The Tunnel' (*The Criterion*), 'Here by the river that is East', to the repeated and overly jaunty rhythms of 'Van Winkle' (*transition*) which re-emerge in 'The Tunnel', 'Cutty Sark' and 'Virginia'.[71] Viewing the poem as fragments, experimenting with material poetic forms, sheds light on its reconstituted structure. This sense of a poem that might forge connections, spanning and linking ideas, was paramount for Crane. As he told Tate, in a weary response to his *Hound & Horn* review, 'I shall be humbly grateful if *The Bridge* can fulfil simply the metaphorical inferences of its title . . .'[72]

THE TRANSATLANTIC *BRIDGE*: LONDON, PARIS, CHICAGO, NEW YORK

The allusive flights between *Bridge* fragments spanned magazines on both sides of the Atlantic, appearing in *The Calendar of Modern Letters* and *The Criterion* (London), *transition* (Paris), *Poetry* (Chicago), and *The Dial*, *The Saturday Review* and the short-lived annual, *American Caravan* (all in New York). Recontextualising parts of *The Bridge* within their transatlantic first publications shows Crane's dialogue between the 'mystical synthesis of America' and European avant-gardes, part of the ongoing negotiation between European and American literary traditions and experiments.

Among the journals active on the London literary scene in the late 1920s, *The Calendar* and *The Criterion* stand out for their engagement with modernist literature – though the two magazines printed different constellations of American writers. As Jason Harding writes, 'Eliot declined submissions from William Carlos Williams, Gertrude Stein, John Crowe Ransom, Allen Tate, Laura Riding, R. P. Blackmur and F. Scott Fitzgerald' – many of whom appeared in *The Calendar*.[73] While *The Calendar* was available in New York, Boston and San Francisco, *The Criterion* was less widely available. Although Faber had tried to sell the journal in the United States, it had not been popular.[74] Rickword,

---

[71] Crane, 'Cutty Sark', *transition*, p. 118.
[72] Crane to Tate, 13 July 1930, *O My Land*, p. 432.
[73] Harding, *The Criterion*, pp. 55, 163. A version of this section appeared in my *PN Review* article, 'Hart Crane "from this side": Edgell Rickword and *The Calendar of Modern Letters*', *PN Review*, 46.4 (2020), pp. 52–4.
[74] Harding, *The Criterion*, p. 55.

as noted earlier, was probably the anonymous reviewer of Crane's first collection, *White Buildings*.[75] Other publications, such as *The London Mercury*, were hostile to the kind of writing Rickword and his associate editors wanted to publish: 'They wrote things like "You can't get blood out of a Stein"', as Rickword later told Michael Schmidt and Alan Young in an interview in *Poetry Nation*.[76] In a 1973 interview, Rickword described *The Calendar* as 'sort of a discontented club, discontented with all the established novelists and literary cliques' – including that gathered around *The Criterion*. The 'anti-modernist' and 'anti-American' stance of other British journals, he added, was crucial to *The Calendar*'s conception of the 'sluggishness' of the British literary scene (Eliot, similarly, found the contemporary literary atmosphere 'shrivelled').[77] *The Calendar* tackled this 'sluggishness' in its 'Scrutinies' column, in which the editors established their own 'standards of criticism'. The aspiration was in part, as Rickword's biographer Charles Hobday put it, to pierce the 'inflated reputations' of 'their elders . . . a guilty generation that had sent them to war'.[78]

In comparison with *The Criterion*, Rickword's magazine was sympathetic to Crane's poetry, and to American poetry more generally. Crane was, though, keen to receive Eliot's seal of approval. He read Eliot's rejection letters with an amusing if unwarranted optimism. After 'To Brooklyn Bridge' was politely returned, he told Harry and Caresse Crosby that Eliot 'urges me to contribute' to a future issue.[79] Although Eliot wrote to Crane's mother Grace after his death in 1932, telling her that 'much of his work I admired very much. There are very few living poets in America of equal interest to me', he returned all but one of Crane's five submissions.[80] 'The Tunnel', the section of *The Bridge* in which Crane is most engaged with Eliot, was the only poem accepted for publication in *The Criterion*. But the admiration in Eliot's letter to Grace Hart Crane does, nonetheless, seem to have been sincere. Eliot is likely to have had Crane in mind as he was writing lines from 'Burnt Norton' in 1935: 'descend lower, descend only', recalling the final moments of Crane's 'Quaker Hill': 'descend—/ descend', which preface his conversation with Eliot in 'The Tunnel'.[81]

Herbert Read's 'Foreign Reviews' feature in the back pages of *The Criterion* was attentive to continental European and American avant-garde literature,

---

[75] Unsigned, '*White Buildings*', *TLS*, p. 130.
[76] Rickword, interviewed by Michael Schmidt and Alan Young, 'A Conversation with Edgell Rickword', *Poetry Nation*, 1 (1973), pp. 73–89 (p. 78).
[77] Ibid., p. 78; Eliot as quoted in Harding, *The Criterion*, p. 7.
[78] Charles Hobday, *Edgell Rickword: A Poet at War* (Manchester: Carcanet, 1989), p. 86.
[79] Crane to Harry and Caresse Crosby, 30 August 1929, *O My Land*, p. 415.
[80] See Appendix 3.
[81] Crane, 'Quaker Hill', *Complete Poems*, p. 94; T. S. Eliot, 'Burnt Norton', *Complete Poems and Plays*, pp. 171–6 (p. 174).

with a particular interest in the American Futurist magazines. Read followed *Broom*, *Secession* and *1924* through reviews, and in February 1924 commented revealingly (though incorrectly) on *Secession*'s issue from the previous September: '"For the Marriage of Faustus and Helen" by Hart Crane has been excised by the censor, leaving rather a dull number.'[82] In July 1926 *The Calendar* published three of Crane's poems, 'At Melville's Tomb', 'Praise for an Urn' and 'Passage', and, as Crane told Frank, 'At Melville's Tomb' and 'Passage' had been hard to place in the US.[83] Indeed, Rickword was so interested in Crane's poetry after this first submission that he requested a copy of *White Buildings* and then, albeit unsuccessfully, attempted to secure its publication with *The Calendar*'s publisher, Wishart.[84] It is likely that Laura Riding introduced Crane to *The Calendar*. Like other American poets, Crane found *The Calendar* a 'very decent quarterly' and more hospitable than *The Criterion*, which he nonetheless deemed 'representative of the most exacting literary standards of [the] times'.[85]

There are curious affinities between the different poetic sensibilities of Crane and Rickword. Both sought to keep their metaphysics warm, to paraphrase Eliot, by turning to the Elizabethans, Rickword perhaps for the satiric energy of the age, while Crane was attracted to their burnished, luminous forms. Both poets were conscious of publishing under regimes of censorship (*The Calendar* had published one of the first critical studies of the Marquis de Sade). Crane's poetry demonstrates his dances with Comstock in such coded poems as his elegy for Oscar Wilde 'C33', and in 'Voyages', which dwells on his relationship with Emil Opffer, and even his depiction of cruising in 'The Tunnel' ('searching, thumbing the midnight on the piers'). Rickword, meanwhile, satirised puritanical attitudes to literature in poems such as 'The Handmaid of Religion':

> Neither barbarians nor malaria
> destroyed Rome's grip on her vast area,
> but naughty novels sold in shops
> unhindered by censorious cops.[86]

Crane's 'Three Songs' are erotic, with 'Southern Cross' mixing spiritual strains with more earthly stirrings, while 'National Winter Garden' and 'Virginia' are,

---

[82] Herbert Read, 'Foreign Reviews', *The Criterion*, 2.6 (1926), p. 226. The 'censor' was probably, in fact, Munson, who excised the error-riddled 'Faustus' from as many copies of *Secession* as he could. Crane to Munson, 28 October 1923, *Letters*, p. 154.

[83] Crane to Frank, 19 June 1926, *O My Land*, p. 257.

[84] Rickword to Crane, 24 December 1926, box 7, Crane papers.

[85] Crane to Frank, 19 June 1926, *O My Land*, p. 257; Crane to Otto Kahn, 12 September 1927, ibid., p. 348.

[86] Edgell Rickword, 'The Handmaid of Religion', in *Behind the Eyes: Collected Poems and Translations* (Manchester: Carcanet, 1976), pp. 104–6 (p. 105).

like Rickword's 'pornology' in 'The Handmaid of Religion', burlesques on sexual mores. As he writes in the second song, 'National Winter Garden':

> Outspoken buttocks in pink beads
> Invite the necessary cloudy clinch
> Of bandy eyes . . . No extra mufflings here:
> The world's one flagrant, sweating cinch.[87]

One of the often-overlooked elements of Crane's poetry is its bawdy humour. As John T. Irwin notes, at the end of the poem Crane makes 'an ironic, obscene reference to Whitman's free passage in terms of a bowel movement'.[88]

The opening of the periodical version of *The Bridge* was, then, strikingly different to that of the volume's proem, 'To Brooklyn Bridge', where a seagull on the wing dips and pivots, 'building high / Over the chained bay waters'.[89] By contrast, the opening lines of 'Southern Cross', the first of the 'Three Songs from *The Bridge*' are:

> I WANTED you, nameless Woman of the South,
> No wraith, but utterly—as still more alone
> The Southern Cross takes night
> And lifts her girdles from her, one by one
> Close, cool,
>   high from the smoking lice
> Of slower heavens,
>   vaporous scars!
> Eve! Magdalene!
>   or Mary, you?[90]

Again, the periodical form usefully reroutes a reading of *The Bridge*. Rather than significantly altering the emphases of the poem, opening with the 'Three Songs' simply highlights its erotic, coded undercurrents. From this position, the seagull's flight in 'To Brooklyn Bridge' can be read against the erotic language of 'Voyages', where, similarly, a bird flies across the horizon, 'parting' the sea and sky with 'gulf on gulf of wings' – a symbol of waiting, of erotic expectancy. The bridge is, indeed, a romantic symbol in Crane's letters. In his correspondence with Frank he intertwines recent memories of Opffer ('the Word made Flesh') and Brooklyn Bridge, describing their walks home 'hand in hand across the most

---

[87] Crane, 'National Winter Garden', *The Calendar of Modern Letters*, 4.1 (1927), p. 109.
[88] Irwin, *Hart Crane's Poetry*, p. 122.
[89] Crane, 'To Brooklyn Bridge', *The Dial*, p. 389.
[90] Crane, 'Southern Cross', *The Calendar of Modern Letters*, 4.1 (1927), pp. 107–8 (p. 107).

beautiful bridge in the world, the cables enclosing us and pulling us upwards'.[91] The subtle eroticism of the proem complicates the address of 'Thee, across the harbor' in 'To Brooklyn Bridge' and, therefore, other moments of address in the fragments, as in 'The Tunnel'. Similarly to 'For the Marriage of Faustus and Helen', this moment of erotic connection is figured as a gaze ('And why do I often meet your visage here, / Your eyes like agate lanterns—on and on'), while elsewhere Crane plays on the ambiguities of gender in 'our' ('Kiss of our agony').[92] These moments allow for, as Yingling has written, the 'unconscious of the text' to emerge, hinting at the possibilities Crane saw in the queer epic.[93]

'The Tunnel', the section of *The Bridge* most engaged with *The Waste Land*, was published in *The Criterion* in November 1927. The vexed nature of Crane's attempts to grapple with Eliot are thrown into relief when the poem is read apart from *The Bridge*; we see Crane 'descend' in 'Quaker Hill' to (as he saw it) the subterranean, 'damned dead' frame of reference of *The Waste Land* in 'The Tunnel', and then emerge, 'Through the bound cable strands', aloft, and writing in his own striking and euphoric idiom, in 'Atlantis'. The commuters of 'The Tunnel' recall those of *The Waste Land* 'flow[ing] over London Bridge', but Crane inverts the image to the subterranean subway system: the New York City subway, twenty-three years old at the time of publication of 'The Tunnel'.[94] Crane follows the subway's geography closely. Where the commuter walks 'underneath the L for a brisk / Ten blocks or so', Crane is pinpointing the location exactly at Broadway, where the L train would have briefly emerged, elevated above the street.[95] But Crane follows a single commuter instead of Eliot's anonymous crowd on London Bridge. Although Crane relies on the mytheme of descent, he is careful (in the first half of the poem) to avoid closely aligning 'the commuter' to paradigmatic moments of descent to the underworld, such as Odysseus or Aeneas, or to the bathos of Eliot's Tiresias, transplanted from Thebes, 'below the wall', to a London bedsit, watching the uncomfortable encounter between the 'house-agent's clerk', 'young carbuncular' and 'the Typist'.[96]

The nature of this moment of descent is ambiguous, but this is less obvious in its *Criterion* context; the equivocal tone here depends on links (often rhythmic patterns) to other sections of *The Bridge*. As Crane's commuter ventures into the subway he is greeted by the rhythms of jazz music (immediately familiar from 'Van Winkle' and 'Cutty Sark') rather than shades or scenes of pathos. He 'press[es] the coin' into 'the turnstile' and the form shifts back to the patterns of the weary second stanza ('Then let you reach your hat / and go. As

---

[91] Crane, 'Voyages IV', *Complete Poems*, p. 37; Crane to Frank, 21 April 1924, *Letters*, p. 187.
[92] Crane, 'The Tunnel', *The Criterion*, 6.5 (1927), pp. 398–404.
[93] Yingling, *Hart Crane and the Homosexual Text*, p. 199.
[94] Eliot, *The Waste Land*, p. 62.
[95] Crane, 'The Tunnel', p. 398.
[96] Eliot, *The Waste Land*, p. 68.

usual') where Crane writes in trochees, their strictness sounding tired in their emphasis of the routine: 'as usual'. The fifth stanza reads:

> And so
> of cities you bespeak
> subways, rivered under streets
> and rivers . . . In the car
> the overtone of motion
> underground, the monotone
> of motion is the sound
> of other faces, also underground—[97]

Crane switches between iambic and trochaic metres that, though unsettled with the switch at 'subways', gradually shift into a stricter iambic pattern that, yet, becomes more lively and syncopated through the repeated 'o' and 'ou' sounds – where echoing forces those tones to prominence. The repeated but shifting sounds in 'overtone', 'motion', 'underground', 'monotone' work as a kind of poetic form of modulation, which, in its jazz form, sees the repetition of key musical phrases, but transposed or rhythmically altered. Crane's reported speech (recalling Eliot's use of the demotic in 'A Game of Chess' and 'Sweeney Agonistes')[98] relies on this device of modulation to give the sense that he is capturing the contemporary vernacular, with jazz rhythms used to emulate the patterns of modern speech.

> And repetition freezes. 'What

> 'what did you want? getting weak on the links?
> Fandaddle daddy don't ask for change—IS THIS
> FOURTEENTH? it's half past six she said—if
> you don't like my gate why did you
> swing on it, why *didja*
> swing on it
> anyhow—'

> And somehow anyhow swing—

> The phonographs of hades in the brain
> Are tunnels that re-wind themselves, and love
> A burnt match skating in a urinal—[99]

---

[97] Crane, 'The Tunnel', p. 399.
[98] Eliot, *The Waste Land*, pp. 64–6; Eliot, *Poems, 1920, Complete Poems*, pp. 37–58.
[99] Crane, 'The Tunnel', p. 400.

The commuter appears to understand the percussive aural landscape of the subway through the musical language of jazz. '[P]honographs of hades' ironically connects the descent to the subway to the mytheme of the descent to hell. Crane's line is delivered with a smirk. Like Eliot, Crane 'plays upon the relationship between popular culture and "high browed" culture' with 'O O O O that Shakespeherian Rag', paraphrasing contemporary views on jazz.[100] In March 1921 *The New York Tribune* claimed that in the US, 'no one [would] put even a passing word in defence of jazz. Only the devil's advocate could do that.'[101] These comments echoed a wider racist discourse, as documented by the progressive newspaper *The Dallas Express* in May 1921. *The Dallas Express* noted that Dr John Dill Robertson (Chicago's health commissioner) had 'decreed jazz is all wrong. Jazz must be sent to the devil to keep the white people from going to him.'[102] 'The phonographs of hades' shows a similar 'studied irreverence' to Eliot's 'Shakespeherian ragging',[103] as Crane puns on the popular ragtime record 'Swing on the Gait', with the suggestive line 'if you don't like my gate why did you / swing on it'.[104]

The syncopation in these lines verges on ragtime, even the rhythms of scat singing (the first known scat recording was Al Jolson's in 1911),[105] formed through the use of consonance and repeated unstressed syllables to the end of the line 'Fandaddle daddy don't ask for change—'. 'Fandaddle', it seems, is Crane's neologism, combining fandangle, panhandle/handler and daddy – the latter meant in its slang sense as a male lover. 'And somehow anyhow swing—' works as an interjection, possibly the commuter's voice as he recognises the swung formulations in the overheard conversation and slips into the form himself, after the initial antiquated and awkward 'Bespeak'. The 'swing' is embedded in the line as Crane employs a duplication of swinging rhythms and forms. The shift from 'anyhow' back to 'somehow' and 'anyhow' again is another

---

[100] Hugh Haughton, 'Allusion: The Case of Shakespeare', in *T. S. Eliot in Context*, ed. Jason Harding (Cambridge: Cambridge University Press, 2011), pp. 157–68 (p. 163).

[101] R. A. Parker, 'Paris, Madly Jazzing, Sees Jazz as the Music of the Future', *New York Tribune*, 20 March 1921, p. 7.

[102] A.N.P., 'They Say Now That Jazz Beat the Kaiser', *The Dallas Express*, 21 May 1921, p. 1.

[103] Jason Harding, 'T. S. Eliot's Shakespeare', *Essays in Criticism*, 62.2 (2012), pp. 160–77 (p. 162).

[104] 'Swing on the Gait' was a record put out by Caroll Gibbons and his quintet around the same time as Crane was writing the poem. Brian A. L. Rust and Sandy Forbes, *British Dance Bands on Record: 1911–1945* (London: General Gramophone Publications, 1987), p. 1349. Susan Jenkins Brown discusses his use of 'pop lyrics and rhythms', noting Irving Caesar's 'What Do you Do Sunday, Mary' in 'Virginia', Brown (ed.), *Robber Rocks*, pp. 110–11.

[105] 'Scat Singing', in *Encyclopaedia of African American Popular Culture*, ed. Jessie Carney Smith (Denver, CO: Greenwood, 2011), p. 1251.

type of modulation, as the metrics shift from dactyl to iamb to dactyl. This jazz form, carefully explicated in 'The Tunnel', was, for Crane, '[s]omething clean, sparkling, elusive!', and is part of his anxious dialogue with the 'damned dead' world of *The Waste Land*; it works through a process of adopting some techniques familiar from Eliot, but, in the first half of the poem, shifting the tone to the euphoric, even cacophonic strains of 1920s New York; the 'descent' into the subway, rather than being banal, alleviates the boredom of the workplace routine described in the opening lines.

'The Tunnel' functions differently in its fragment form in *The Criterion* than in its appearance in the reassembled *Bridge*. This is, to a large extent, due to this complex patterning between the 'interwoven strands' of the sections. The most obvious point here is that the placement of 'The Tunnel' in *The Criterion* highlights its complicated engagement with *The Waste Land*. The final lines of the poem, in particular, are revealing of the different readings prompted by 'The Tunnel' in its fragment and assembled forms:

> And this thy harbour, O my City, I have driven under,
> Tossed from the coil of ticking towers . . . To-morrow,
> And to be . . . Here by the River that is East—
> Here at the waters' edge the hands drop memory;
> Shadowless in that abyss they unaccounting lie.
> How far away the star has pooled the sea—
> Or shall the hands be drawn away, to die?
>
> Kiss of our agony Thou gatherest,
>   O Hand of Fire
>   gatherest—[106]

In its *Criterion* context we are left in *The Bridge*'s version of the *Purgatorio*, at the river's edge, riffing on Eliot, with the 'tugboat, wheezing wreathes of steam' that resembles Eliot's 'boat [. . .] beating obedient / To controlling hands' and the 'sweat[ing]' river with 'barges' that 'drift / With the turning tide'.[107] In the final lines ('O hand of Fire / gatherest—') Crane was remembering Eliot's 'O Lord Thou pluckest me out . . . burning' (which also alludes, as Eliot points out in his notes, to 'Saint Augustine's *Confessions*, again').[108]

---

[106] Crane, 'The Tunnel', p. 402.
[107] Dante Alighieri, *The Divine Comedy: Purgatory*, ed. and trans. Mark Musa (London: Penguin, 1985); Eliot, *The Waste Land*, pp. 74, 69, 70, 266, 273, 268–9.
[108] Eliot, *The Waste Land*, p. 70; Eliot, 'Notes on *The Waste Land*', *Complete Poems*, pp. 76–80 (p. 79).

In the assembled poem it is clear that this engagement with Eliot in 'The Tunnel' is part of a wider intertextual dialogue; 'Cape Hatteras', for instance, is in close dialogue with Whitman, and 'Cutty Sark' with Melville and, through its calligramme form, Apollinaire – as Crane wrote to Rickword, the poem was intended to resemble 'ships [that] meet and pass in line and type'.[109] Illustrating the different ways that these allusions function in their fragment and assembled forms, in *The Bridge* these last lines from 'The Tunnel' equally recall Crane's from 'Ave Maria':

> And kingdoms
> > naked in the trembling heart—
> Te Deum laudamus
> > O Hand of Fire[110]

Spoken here by Christopher Columbus, this multilayered allusion signals the literary politics at stake here by associating Eliot's phrase with the beginning of the European colonisation of the Americas. 'The Tunnel', too, sees a 'Wop washerwoman' fashioned as a latter-day Columbus ('O Genoese' – Columbus was born in Genoa, and this was Whitman's moniker for the colonist), and this allusion, in the assembled form, is anticipated by lines in 'Ave Maria', published in *The American Caravan* two months before 'The Tunnel' appeared in *The Criterion:*

> I thought of Genoa: and this truth, now proved,
> That made me exile in her streets [. . .][111]

Without the accompanying lines from 'Ave Maria', this link to Columbus is lost – and so is Crane's wry comment on the dominance of European forms and touchstones in American letters. *The American Caravan*, 'a yearbook conducted by literary men in the interests of growing American literature', also took 'The River' for its 1928 edition.[112] 'The River', with its 'slogans of the year' for 'Tintex—Jalapac—Certain-teed Overalls ads', 'playbill[s]' and 'RADIO ROARS IN EVERY HOME WE HAVE', was, like 'Ave Maria', complemented by its appearance in 'Yearbook of American Literature'.[113] The annual aimed

---

[109] Crane to Rickword, 7 January 1927, box 19, Crane papers.
[110] Crane, 'Ave Maria', *The American Caravan*, 1 (September 1927), pp. 804–6 (p. 806).
[111] Irwin has also noted this allusion in *Hart Crane's Poetry*, p. 100.
[112] *The American Caravan*, 1 (September 1927), front pages.
[113] Crane, 'The River', pp. 804–6.

to showcase new, experimental American writing that illustrated contemporary 'American life', alongside established poets such as Robert Frost.[114]

The tradition of the European epic, as Crane saw it, was exemplified rather than challenged by the expatriate Eliot's 'damned dead' *Waste Land* earlier in the decade. Crane, though, aimed to transplant some of the structural framework of the epic to a distinctly US setting, utilising both key historical figures and events, and the quotidian details of turnstiles, tickets, 'shoes, umbrellas'. Crane is scathing about the advertisements in the train, perhaps because of his own background working in advertising, contrasting the near spiritual meeting of 'eyes like agate lanterns' across the train carriage with 'the toothpaste and the dandruff ads'.[115] However, the moment of the 'eyes meeting' is not deflated by the 'dandruff ads', but manages to surpass the surrounding banality of the carriage, with this moment ending ecstatically:

> And did their eyes like unwashed platters ride?
> And Death, aloft—gigantically down
> Probing through you toward me, O Evermore![116]

Here, the 'eyes', 'probing through you toward me', recall lines from the opening section of 'Faustus and Helen':

> Then I might find your eyes across an aisle,
> Still flickering with those prefigurations—
> Prodigal, yet uncontested now,
> Half-riant before the jerky window frame.
>
> There is some way, I think, to touch
> Those hands of yours that count the nights
> Stippled with pink and green advertisements.[117]

As in work in *Secession* and *Broom*, these everyday details are utilised for contrast rather than bathos. In its fragment form here, there are optimistic hints in the text, but the underground landscape of the subway does not give way to the 'bound cable strands' and 'the arching path' of the 'Atlantis' section. As a fragment, this section does not – as Crane hoped *The Bridge* would – go 'through' Eliot to the 'ecstatic goal' of 'Atlantis'. In this form, isolated from its wider context, 'The Tunnel' seems absorbed with, in Crane's words, Eliot's

---

[114] The editors, *The American Caravan*, 1 (September 1927), ix.
[115] Crane, 'The Tunnel', p. 400.
[116] Ibid.
[117] Crane, 'Faustus II', p. 1.

'steady pessimism'.[118] Essentially, the whole process of the poem's engagement with *The Waste Land* is not revealed here. Working 'through' Eliot was key to Crane's understanding of what the capabilities of the American long poem or the 'modern equivalent' of the epic might be.

Michael Roberts, in his note on Crane in the 1936 *Faber Book of Modern Verse*, misquotes Allen Tate's 'Retroduction to American History' with the line 'the Parthenon / in Tennessee stucco / Art for the sake of death'. Roberts omits 'Tennessee' from the line, a detail we need so as to be able to make a revealing distinction between Crane's 'ecstasy' and Tate's cynicism.[119] Crane's long poem is populated by Rip Van Winkle from Washington Irving's 1819 story (in the same poem, Crane cannot resist mentioning 'Sleepy Hollow'), Columbus, Walter Raleigh, Thomas Jefferson and his daughter, Mary, and Pocahontas. Although Crane invokes the bloody colonial history of the Americas, he is, as Reed points out, generally 'disquietingly uncritical in his embrace of the founding myths of the U. S.'[120] Crane's use of these figures asserts his belief that modern poetry can utilise both the 'American mythos' and quotidian details, in contrast to the bathos of Tate's 'Retroduction', where 'Hermes decorates / a cornice on the Third National Bank'. The 'cinema' and the subway are, then, as capable a subject as the magisterial Brooklyn Bridge or the Southern Cross. For Crane, *The Bridge*, with its American subject, is not Tate's 'stucco' nor a cheap imitation of classical marble, but is carving out its own space through its experimentation with the long-form poem.

Although 'The Tunnel's' appearance as a fragment in *The Criterion* might have downplayed the complexity of Crane's engagement with Eliot (by comparison with the assembled volume), and the 'Three Songs' seem somewhat arbitrarily linked in *The Calendar*, the aesthetic affiliations of *The Bridge* are drawn out by the appearance of fragments in *transition*. Founded and edited by Eugene Jolas with assistance from Elliot Paul, Robert Sage and, briefly, Matthew Josephson and Harry Crosby, *transition*, like *Gargoyle*, *Secession* and *Broom*, intended to 'join' an 'international' body of literature by printing work from 'different continents' 'side by side' 'in a language Americans can read and understand'.[121] Like Pound's *Exile*, *transition* was founded after Ernest Walsh's *This Quarter* (an Anglophone journal based in Monte Carlo) went into hiatus in 1926.[122] In practice, though, the overwhelming majority

---

[118] Crane to Wiegand, 20 January 1923, *O My Land*, p. 121.

[119] *The Faber Book of Modern Verse*, ed. Michael Roberts (London: Faber and Faber, 1936), p. 10; Allen Tate, 'Retroduction to American History', in *Collected Poems 1919–1976* (New York: Farrar, Straus and Giroux, 2007), pp. 11–12 (p. 11).

[120] Reed, *Hart Crane: After his Lights*, p. 139.

[121] Eugene Jolas and Elliot Paul, 'Introduction', *transition*, 1 (April 1927), p. 137.

[122] *The Ezra Pound Encyclopaedia*, ed. Demetres P. Tryphonopoulos and Stephen J. Adams (Westport, CT: Greenwood Press, 2005), p. 288; Eugene Jolas, *The Man from Babel*, ed. Andreas Kramer and Rainer Rumold (New Haven, CT: Yale University Press, 1998), p. 90.

of *transition*'s 'international' contributions came from the West – primarily America and France. Jolas's interest in founding a transatlantic journal came, as his biographers have pointed out, from his childhood spent between the US and the multilingual 'European frontier-land' of Alsace-Lorraine, speaking what he referred to as a 'frontier patois'.[123]

Jolas's journal, with contributors ranging from Ernest Hemingway and Robert Graves to Philippe Soupault, Hans Arp and André Breton, was (relatively speaking) more of a broad church than *Littérature* or *La Révolution Surréaliste* (which almost exclusively printed works from Surrealist circles), but was still closely affiliated with the French Surrealists – to the extent that the journal was known, contemporaneously, as 'the American surrealist review'.[124] Based in Europe, these magazines did not simply offer 'reports from abroad' that were motivated by dissatisfaction with the US literary scene. Rather, they resisted views such as that of Van Wyck Brooks, who wrote in 1922 that 'what immediately strikes one, as one surveys the history of our literature during the last half century, is the singular impotence of its creative spirit'.[125] The journal's wide range of contributors ensured that *transition* (mirroring Jolas's own writing) maintained 'intellectual independence from the main Surrealist camp'. This was, in part, due to the journal's emphasis on the 'American mythos' (Jolas's phrase), which made 'Van Winkle' an especially good fit.[126] With its engagement in debates surrounding directions of influence between US and European writers, *transition* was naturally hospitable to *The Bridge*, Crane's long poem which promised 'a spiritual and natural' representation of 'the body of America'.[127] These fragments from *The Bridge* demonstrated in the pages of *transition* how this literary exchange, so often discussed in the journal, could be manifested in poetry.

Recontextualising parts of *The Bridge* back to their first publication in *transition* highlights how the 'mystical synthesis of America' can be seen in close dialogue with European avant-gardes. Crane appeared in half of the issues published in the journal's first run between April 1927 and June 1930, and it was through *transition* that he met Harry and Caresse Crosby in 1929.[128] Crane

---

[123] Jolas, *The Man from Babel*, pp. xxi, 2. See Dougald McMillan, *Transition 1927–1938: The History of a Literary Era* (London: Calder and Boyars, 1975), p. 9.

[124] Cowley, *Exile's Return*, p. 97.

[125] Cowley responds directly to these comments from Van Wyck Brooks's essay 'The Literary Life' in *Exile's Return*, pp. 75–6.

[126] Kramer and Rumold, paraphrasing Jolas, *The Man from Babel*, p. xix; Jolas, 'Super Occident', *transition*, 15 (February 1929), pp. 11–18.

[127] Crane to Kahn, 18 March 1926, *O My Land*, p. 232.

[128] Crosby helped to edit the journal from June 1929. The final number was dedicated to the poet after his death and included Crane's 'To the Cloud Juggler', *transition*, 19–20 (June 1930), p. 223.

agreed to put out a limited edition of *The Bridge* with the Crosbys – aiming for an aura of similarity to the volume form of *The Waste Land*, which, in 1922, came out with Boni and Liveright, and a year later as a limited edition with the Hogarth Press. 'The limited edition', notes Rainey, 'occupied a middle position within the larger tripartite structure of avant-garde and modernist publication (between journal and commercial edition).'[129]

transition offered Crane an opportunity to reconnect with the European avant-garde, building on his close relationship with *Broom* and *Secession* in the early 1920s. His trip to Europe has become notorious for his misbehaviour, beginning a pattern of erratic conduct and imprisonment that would continue during his time in Mexico City. On 8 December 1928 Crane boarded the RMS *Tuscania* for England. In London he met Laura Riding and Robert Graves and Rickword, visited the theatre, played darts and drank with charwomen and veterans of the Somme – he drank too much and quickly abandoned London and sailed from Dover to Paris in the New Year.[130] In Paris, Crane met *transition* editor Eugene Jolas and many of the magazine's contributors – Stein, André Gide, Kay Boyle, Philippe Soupault and Harry and Caresse Crosby. Crane was, for a moment, mixing with the much-romanticised 'lost generation', revelling in the city's delights, visiting Stein and Toklas at 27 rue de Fleurus. As he wrote to Sam Loveman: 'Painters, translations, lobsters, absinthe, music, promenades, oysters, sherry, asprin, pictures, Sapphic heiresses, editors, books, sailors. And How!'[131] As it often did, the bacchanalia quickly got out of hand, developing into scandal. Crane was unable to pay a bill at the Café Sélect and was accosted by a waiter, whom Crane then punched, starting a brawl in the restaurant. He was arrested, having also struck a gendarme. Crane was imprisoned for six days in La Santé, Paris – the jail that had housed Apollinaire (the French poet had, supposedly, had a hand in the theft of the *Mona Lisa*). The US press got hold of the story via the *Herald Tribune* and so, almost immediately after his release, Crane returned on the USS *Homeric*, rather than heading on to Marseilles as planned.[132]

While in Paris, Crane found confirmation that there were like-minded writers among the *transition* group. His meeting with the Crosbys was particular useful, securing publication of the first edition of *The Bridge* with their Black Sun Press. *transition* was closely allied to the Surrealists, as Jolas's declaration 'Revolution of the Word' makes clear. The principle of the 'Revolution of the Word' was developed while editing *transition* and is as revealing of Jolas's editing principles as his prose. Pushed to its logical conclusion, the 'Revolution of

---

[129] Rainey, *Institutions*, p. 104.
[130] Mariani, *Broken Tower*, pp. 317–18.
[131] Ibid., pp. 319–23. Crane as quoted in Mariani, ibid., p. 320.
[132] Ibid., pp. 327–8.

the Word' advocates a kind of literary Esperanto, as demonstrated in Jolas's 'Rodeur': 'I mute in rain wind crow darkling / Nowhere stop you walkst in fir / Haende tasten apportez-moi du vin'.[133] The June 1929 *transition* 'Proclamation' outlines the 'Revolution' in detail. Crane added his signature to the published document, later pleading intoxication after he was 'received amid a shower of ironic comment' in New York for his participation.[134] The 'Revolution of the Word' and Surrealism proper both work through juxtapositions and collage effects, but Surrealist aesthetic principles are designed to create disorientation or a radically different perspective on the chosen object, while, for Jolas, the 'Revolution of the Word' emphasised the writer's 'right to use words of his own fashioning'. Through the amalgamation of different languages and cognates, meaning is 'expressed' almost entirely through the juxtaposition of sounds rather than contrasting, or even unsuited, images that resist easy interpretation. Eastman, writing in *Harper's*, commented on the 'unintelligibility' of the *transition* set of writers (singling out Crane and Joyce in particular), an accusation that Harry Crosby repudiated in the June 1929 number of *transition*.[135] As Crosby made clear in his response to Eastman in 'Observation Post', the last proposition from the 'Proclamation' was key: 'The plain reader be damned.'[136] As he wrote of the 'fresh vision' of Crane's poetry: 'he is dynamic energy, concentration, fresh vision, a migratory crane flying above the worn-out forest of the poetic phrase, above the false and stagnant pools of artificiality'.[137]

As he explained in his autobiography, Jolas's interest in Crane was rooted in similarities he found between the 'Revolution of the Word' and Crane's own logic of metaphor, with the 'Revolution' taking ideas present in the 'logic' to their extremes. Jolas noted happily that Crane kept 'notebooks [that] were filled with unusual esoteric words which he would eventually incorporate in the stanzas of his poem'.[138] Discussions of Jolas's concept in *transition*'s first run, which included pieces by Breton, Aragon and Soupault as well as Marinetti's 'futuristic theory of "words in liberty"', made *transition* sympathetic to Crane's own experiments with language (as Paul Giles has explored in detail), the details of which were outlined in his 'Discussion' with Monroe in October 1926.[139]

---

[133] Jolas as 'Theo Rutra', 'Poems', p. 144.
[134] Eugene Jolas, 'Proclamation', *transition*, 16–17 (June 1929), unpaginated; Jolas, *The Man from Babel*, p. 111.
[135] Eastman, 'The Cult of Unintelligibility', pp. 632–9; Harry Crosby, 'Observation Post', *transition*, 16–17 (June 1929), pp. 197–205 (p. 201).
[136] Jolas, 'Proclamation', unpaginated.
[137] Crosby, 'Observation Post', p. 201.
[138] Jolas, *The Man from Babel*, p. 120.
[139] Eugene Jolas, 'The Revolution of Language and James Joyce', *transition*, 11 (February 1928), pp. 109–12 (p. 112); see Giles, *The Contexts of 'The Bridge'*, for further discussion of Crane, Joyce and *transition*.

Indeed, Jolas and his associate editor Elliot Paul (editor from April 1927 to summer 1928) cited Crane, along with Stein, Joyce, Breton, Leon-Paul Fargue and August Stramm, as one of the writers 'showing us the way' to write a poetry of 'freer association', of 'new words, new abstractions, new hieroglyphics, new symbols, new myths'.[140] The associative metaphors Crane employed, adapted from – as Jolas put it – 'the revolution of the surrealists', made *transition* particularly sensitive to, and a keen publisher of, his poetry, with Jolas soliciting his contributions.

Crane partnered his interest in Cubist forms with his use of calligrammes. The calligramme, which abandons linear poetic structures, was popularised by Apollinaire's 1918 volume in which this form of visual poetry, he hoped, would allow for the 'simultaneous' appreciation of text and image.[141] Designed as a calligramme, 'Cutty Sark' works similarly to Cubist forms in *The Bridge*; the multi-perspectival form builds up Crane's 'phantom regatta seen from Brooklyn Bridge' while illustrating the narrator's 'frontiers' of the 'mind' with his fractured, escaping thoughts that seem like 'running sands sometimes'.[142] Variants between 'Cutty Sark' in *transition* and the volume text show Crane building the fractured sense of the sailor's narrative as he adds caesura to his speech. Crane introduces hyphens to the line 'It's S.S. Ala—Antwerp—' to make it clear that '*Ala*' is the sailor struggling to remember the ship's name. 'Cutty Sark', which Crane also referred to as a 'fugue' (interestingly while he was writing 'Moment Fugue', also published in *transition*), is polyphonic and counterpointed; 'two voices' ('the derelict sailor and the description of the action') are used to amass a disjointed, multi-perspectival view of the 'lovely ghosts' of the ships and naval histories, as the narrative jumps (or tacks even) from the Cutty Sark's employment as a tea clipper ('Sweet opium and tea, Yo-ho!') to other journeys: 'clipper dreams', 'wink[ing] round the Horn / to Frisco, Melbourne'.[143] The italicised sections weave in and out of the narrative as accompanying mystical 'hallucinations incident to rum-drinking in a South Street dive'.[144] These lines work as interjections, emphasised by their heavily patterned rhythms, in stark contrast to the surrounding lines:

> [. . .] then Yucatan selling kitchen-ware beads
> have you seen Popocatepetl birdless mouth
> ashes sifting down

---

[140] Eugene Jolas and Elliot Paul, 'Suggestions for a New Magic', *transition*, 3 (June 1927), pp. 178–9 (p. 179).

[141] S. I. Lockerbie, 'Introduction', in Guillaume Apollinaire, *Calligrammes*, trans. Anne Hyde Greet (Berkeley, CA: University of California Press, 1980), p. 3.

[142] Crane to Rickword, 7 January 1927, box 19, Crane papers.

[143] Crane, 'Moment Fugue', *transition*, 15 (February 1929), p. 102; Crane, 'Cutty Sark', *transition*, 3 (June 1927), pp. 116–19 (p. 118).

[144] Crane to Kahn, 12 September 1927, *Letters*, p. 347.

> And then the coast again"
> *Rose of Stamboul O coral queen*
> *teased remnants of the skeletons of cities*
> *and galleries, galleries of watergutted lava*
> *snarling stone—green—drums—drown—*
> Sing! [original formatting][145]

The evenly patterned stresses work in contrast to the body of the text and, as a result, link to a wider pattern of similar interjections in 'Van Winkle', 'The Tunnel' and 'The Harbor Dawn'.

In the volume form Crane added a gloss that, in some ways, emphasises the fractured nature of the poem, rather than attempting to secure its parts into a streamlined whole. Shortly before sending *The Bridge* proofs to Caresse Crosby at Black Sun, Crane added italicised marginalia (which he called a 'gloss' in the printer's notes) that narrated the text and made the links between the sub-sections clear.[146] For instance, in 'Powhatan's Daughter', the marginalia to 'Van Winkle' ends: 'Like Memory, she is time's truant, shall take you by the hand . . .' This is continued in the following sub-section, 'The River', with 'and past the din and slogans of the year—'. In contrast, between 'Ave Maria' and 'Powhatan's Daughter' Crane added:

> *Columbus,*
> *alone, gazing*
> *toward Spain,*
> *invokes the*
> *presence of*
> *two faithful*
> *partisans of*
> *his quest . . .* [original formatting] [147]

and then:

> '*—Pocahuntus* [sic], *a well-featured*
> *but wanton young girle . . . of the age*
> *of eleven or twelve years* [. . .][148]

The links here are deliberately fractured, with '—' as an obvious interjection, as the marginalia unexpectedly work against making the parts cohere.

---

[145] Crane, 'Cutty Sark', *transition*, p. 117.
[146] Crane, *The Bridge* [MS], box 9, Crane papers.
[147] Crane, 'Ave Maria', *Complete Poems*, pp. 47–50 (p. 47).
[148] Crane, 'Powhatan's Daughter', *Complete Poems*, pp. 51–4 (p. 51).

They offer only the occasional clarification of details in the particular section rather than attempting to link them together (as between the sub-sections, 'Van Winkle', 'The River' and 'The Dance' previously), and seem motivated by a similar ironic impulse to disorientate as in Eliot's footnotes to *The Waste Land* – in Crane's case, this could also be a somewhat facetious reaction to accusations of 'obscurity' and 'unintelligibility' in reviews.

Adopting the Cubist, fragmented form was, effectively, Crane's avowal that a full representation of America – or indeed, of any nation or vast subject – in all of its infinite possibilities was impossible, but the Cubist aesthetic, at least, acknowledges this problem. For Crane this bears comparison to the poetic fragment, which also implicitly acknowledges the impossibility of capturing grand or abstract subjects, as encapsulated by the titles of Shelley's 'Fragment: To the Moon', or 'Misery—A Fragment'.[149] Incompleteness was another issue taken up by contemporary critics of *The Bridge*, and distilled into the well-worn notion of Crane's poetic failure. This form complements Crane's more general interest in problems of expression. Just as the Cubist aesthetic gestures towards unfilled spaces and undocumented perspectives (through, in painting – as an analogy – unused space), so does Crane's logic of metaphor acknowledge the gap between signified and signifier. A concept that Crane articulated on the back of a letter to Otto Kahn in April 1926 highlights this further. Crane's 'image circuit', expressed through geometric shapes, is defined as 'Recognition [. . .] aroused by relationships between objects'. Crane describes one of the products of the associative logic of metaphor: the apprehension of 'two images' at once. He illustrates the point with the example 'sky is a dome' – a Shelleyan image, as in 'the sunless sky [. . .] the dome of gold', 'the steep sky's commotion [. . .] the dome of a vast sepulchre'.[150] On a small scale (for example, 'empty trapeze of your flesh') Crane employs a collage method with more in common with Surrealism. In this metaphor, 'trapeze' is not 'drawn from the same radius of discourse', just as the 'harp' (swapped metonymically for 'bridge' in the proem) is not semantically related to 'bridge'; 'trapeze' is not semantically linked to 'flesh', but the word does convey something of the swinging movements of the dancer in 'National Winter Garden' as her body bends and shifts almost as if controlled by an external force.[151] By adopting an associative method Crane highlights what he saw as the arbitrary (but interesting) connections between words and things.

---

[149] Percy Bysshe Shelley, 'Fragment: To the Moon', 'Misery—A Fragment', in *The Complete Poetical Works*, ed. Thomas Hutchinson (Oxford: Clarendon Press, 1904), pp. 615, 555–6.

[150] Crane to Kahn, 10 April 1926, box 4, Crane papers; Shelley, 'Lines Written Among the Euganean Hills', *Complete Poetical Works*, pp. 550–4 (p. 550); Shelley, 'Ode to the West Wind', ibid., pp. 573–5 (p. 573).

[151] Crane, 'National Winter Garden', p. 109.

'The cult of failure': Reviews and Reception

The Bridge has become synonymous with failure.[152] Forming its own critical tradition, the word abounds unselfconsciously in relation to Crane: 'Grand Failure', 'Splendid Failure', 'Poetics of Failure', 'Reclaiming Hart Crane's "Splendid Failure"', 'The Cult of Failure'.[153] Writing in *The New Republic*, Cowley unknowingly laid the foundations for this reading:

> 'The Bridge' is a unified group of fifteen poems dealing primarily with Brooklyn Bridge. But the bridge itself is treated as a symbol: it is the bridge between past and future, between Europe and the Indies; it is the visible token of the American continent [. . .] We might well conclude that such an attempt was foredoomed to failure [. . .] In its presumptuous effort the poem has succeeded—not wholly, of course, for its faults are obvious; but still it has succeeded to an impressive degree.[154]

Crane's friends may have been writing with the poet's own letters in mind, in which, as the poem developed, he constantly fretted that 'the poem will be a huge failure!'[155] Irrespective, other reviewers became equally preoccupied with this idea, though the parameters according to how the poem had 'failed' were, as to be expected, debated according to the preferences of the reviewer in question. Writing in *The Outlook* one month before Tate's article in *Hound & Horn*, Louise Townsend Nicholl (who, like Crane, had contributed to *The Double Dealer* and helped edit *The Measure*) wrote:

> I do not question the publisher's statement, 'No poem written since Walt Whitman's *Leaves of Grass* expresses a more inclusive scope or loftier intention.' Crane's work is full of vision and ideas. But he does not, for the most part, make them into poetry, into the unforgettable and inevitable.[156]

---

[152] Tate, 'American Mind', p. 215; Cowley, 'Preface', p. 276.
[153] Brunner, *Splendid Failure*; Susan M. Schultz, 'The Success of Failure: Hart Crane's Revisions of Whitman and Eliot in *The Bridge*', *South Atlantic Review*, 54.1 (1989), pp. 55–70; Joseph Riddel, 'Hart Crane's Poetics of Failure', *ELH*, 33.4 (1966), pp. 473–96; Mike Field, 'Reclaiming Hart Crane's "Splendid Failure"', *Arts and Sciences* (fall 2011), available at <http://krieger.jhu.edu/magazine/2011/10/reclaiming-hart-cranes-splendid-failure/> (accessed 5 December 2015); Laura Riding and Madeleine Vara, 'The Cult of Failure', *Epilogue*, 1.1 (1935), pp. 60–6. Howard Moss commented that 'Hart Crane's "magnificent failure" in attempting to create *The Bridge* has become both a legend and a platitude'; 'Disorder as Myth: Hart Crane's *The Bridge*', *Poetry*, 62.1 (1945), pp. 32–45 (p. 32).
[154] Cowley, 'Preface', p. 276.
[155] Crane to Charlotte and Richard Rychtarik, 2 March 1926, *O My Land*, pp. 228–9.
[156] Louise Townsend Nicholl, 'Spring Poetry', *The Outlook and Independent*, 155.4 (1930), pp. 146–7 (p. 146).

Demonstrating how quickly this appraisal of the poem became consolidated, in July Benét echoed Winters and Nicholl in *The Saturday Review*, commenting that although Crane had 'failed in creating what might have been a truly great poem [. . .] it is a most interesting failure'.[157] Then, in *The Bookman* (New York) in September, Odell Shepard commented on Crane's 'failure' to 'reveal something about America', describing his poetry as a 'tirade' of 'bombastic nonsense' and 'a constant succession of loud noises, pulling itself along like a gasoline engine by a series of explosions'.[158]

Although some negative reviews can be attributed to a sense that *The Bridge* had failed to address its subject, for Allen Tate and Yvor Winters the problems were formal and, particularly for Winters, moral.[159] Bearing in mind how Tate and Winters received the poem, first through frequently circulated manuscripts and then in these sporadic magazine appearances, Crane's emphasis on the capability of these portions to function alone exaggerates the structurally fragmentary nature of his poem. In a cutting review that appeared in *Poetry* in June 1930, Winters describes the poem as, intriguingly, a series of 'magnificent fragments', after opening his review with the complaint that the poem: 'has no narrative framework and lacks the formal unity of an epic . . . the poem is not a single lyric, it is rather a collection of lyrics on themes more or less related and loosely following out of each other'.[160] Crane found the review symptomatic of Winters' 'pedantry' and 'pretentious classification' of the poem's genre – an assessment that may have been informed by the poem's fractured emergence through literary journals. Writing to Tate in July 1930, Crane commented that Winters' review in *Poetry* had bred a number of similar complaints. Crane felt that Taggard's review of *White Buildings* in *The New York Herald Tribune* simply copied Winters' review of the same volume in *Poetry*, and he dismissed her claims as simply 'conducting her education in public'.[161] Mariani goes further, noting that Taggard also seems to ape Aiken's short review in *The Dial*, which maintained that Crane was a 'high class intellectual fake'.[162] The similarities between the vague charges made against *The Bridge* in reviews are striking, and likely the result of the close network of Crane's reviewers who were, in some cases, editing the same journals, such as Tate, Blackmur and Winters

---

[157] William Rose Benét, 'Round About Parnassus', *Saturday Review of Literature*, 6.50 (5 July 1930), p. 1176.
[158] Odell Shepard, 'Hart Crane', *The Bookman*, 72.1 (1930), pp. 86–7.
[159] Winters, *In Defence of Reason*, pp. 54–5. See Yingling on Winters' homophobia and *The Bridge*, *Hart Crane and the Homosexual Text*, pp. 60–4.
[160] Winters, 'Progress', p. 164.
[161] Crane to Tate, 13 July 1930, *O My Land*, p. 432.
[162] Mariani, *Broken Tower*, p. 268.

all at *Hound & Horn*.¹⁶³ A number of critics seem to obliquely suggest this, with Cowley's unexplained side note that the poem's 'faults are obvious' in an otherwise positive review, or Benét's almost identical, and equally unsupported, comment on *The Bridge*'s 'obvious faults' or, slightly differently, in *The Bookman*, his 'defects'.¹⁶⁴

In 'Hart Crane and the American Mind', written shortly after Crane's death in 1932, Tate engaged with the debates conducted by Crane's contemporary reviewers. In his first review in *Hound & Horn*, Tate praised Crane's technique and 'vision of a heroic American past'. Like Cowley, who described 'a unified group of fifteen poems dealing primarily with Brooklyn Bridge', Tate summarised *The Bridge* as 'a collection of fifteen poems grouped in eight sections and tied together by a single theme'.¹⁶⁵ In this later review in *Poetry*, Tate revises his opinion and seems to have shifted towards Winters' school of thought. Discarding his impression of the poem's 'technical proficiency', Tate writes that though *The Bridge* was 'presumably' intended as an 'epic', the 'incoherent . . . framework' of the poem made it a 'magnificent failure' of the genre.¹⁶⁶

A common worry for critics of Crane has been how to address these contemporaneous charges of the poem's 'failure', 'defects' or 'incompleteness' which were laid out almost immediately after its publication. Although Crane's critics have occasionally reflected on the prevalence of these appraisals, criticism, as Hammer flagged in 1993, has remained preoccupied with defences against them – for example, *The Bridge* does not fail as an 'epic' if it is considered a Wagnerian epic, or if the 'logic' is seen as a grand scheme that can make the poem cohere if the reader fills in the gaps.¹⁶⁷ Both complaints of 'failure' and 'incompleteness', as well as being vague, contain the strange suggestion that *The Bridge* was being measured against an ideal, imaginary version of the poem that did not materialise – but that Crane might have imagined in letters – rather than approaching the published text in its own right. As Tate laments in 'Hart Crane and the American Mind', 'he wrote to me that he feared his most ambitious work, *The Bridge*, was not quite perfectly realised [. . .] This vagueness of purpose [. . .] he never succeeding in correcting.'¹⁶⁸

---

[163] There is a striking theme of musical analogies in the reviews. Vincent McHugh notes Crane's 'symphonically attuned', 'rhapsodic' form; Vincent McHugh, 'Crane's *Bridge*: Mighty Symbol of the Nation', *New York Evening Post*, 19 April 1930, p. 11.
[164] Cowley, 'Preface', p. 275; Benét, 'Round About Parnassus', p. 1176; Shepard, 'Hart Crane', p. 86.
[165] Cowley, 'Preface', p. 266; Tate, 'A Distinguished Poet', p. 580.
[166] Tate, 'A Distinguished Poet', pp. 580–5; Tate, 'American Mind', p. 215.
[167] Reed, *Hart Crane: After his Lights*, pp. 126–66; Beckett, 'The (Ill)ogic of Metaphor', pp. 57–80.
[168] Tate, 'American Mind', pp. 210, 213.

Much like Monroe's imprecise complaints about Crane's 'confused metaphors', critical accounts of his poetry have struggled to define what, exactly, a poetic failure is, or how it can be determined that a poem is 'incomplete'. Determining artistic failure and incompleteness are most likely broader epistemic impossibilities. It does seem, though, that this sense of 'incompleteness' or Crane's 'failure' to make the parts cohere stems from the poem's fragmented appearances in journals, coupled with occasionally bombastic, and often multifarious, claims that frequently emphasised commonalities between *The Bridge* and classical epic forms, claims which Crane made for the poem *to* his critics, Cowley, Frank, Tate and Winters, in his private correspondence but, crucially, never publicly.

In 'At Melville's Tomb' a sailor stares 'beneath the wave[s]', and imagines the stories of the sailors 'drowned' at sea (now 'bones' ground into 'dice' by the tides), and the shared stories of how their ships were 'wreck[ed]' into 'scattered chapter[s]' – with the odd, 'obscured' details dropped into the poem: 'coil' (coiled ropes), 'lashings' and 'compass, quadrant and sextant'. But this fracturing, or 'scattering' – which so irritated Harriet Monroe – does not empty these stories of meaning; rather, these 'obscured' tales become 'livid hieroglyphs' and 'portents'.[169] The recalibration of these 'bones' into 'dice' and 'hieroglyphs' means that these remains are seen to be oddly capable of associative meanings, even imbued with prophetic qualities that are more than the sum of their parts. This, in miniature, articulates Crane's thoughts on fragmentary forms.

Rather than an expression of disruption or chaos (or a kind of reaction to the 'crisis of modernity', as has been noted of *The Waste Land*),[170] this process of fragmentation, on its smallest scales with the 'logic' and in the larger structure of *The Bridge*, highlights the allusive gestures operating between sections; the fragment forms, by nature, gesture to each other. *The Bridge* contains the principles of the logic of metaphor at scale. I can, then, usefully disagree with Yingling's assertion that the 'contradictions' implicit in Crane's working within a heteronormative epic tradition are at the root of the poem's 'failure to cohere'.[171] In fact, the wellspring of *The Bridge* is Crane's queer poetics – that necessarily fugitive but exhilarating and vibrant process of association. I return again to Amin, Musser and Pérez's statement: 'queerness is best understood as a series of relations to form'.[172] I would say, however, that the reception of the

---

[169] Crane, 'At Melville's Tomb', *Poetry*, p. 25.
[170] Aleida Assman, 'T.S. Eliot's Reinvention of Tradition', in *T.S. Eliot and the Concept of Tradition*, ed. Giovanni Cianci and Jason Harding (Cambridge: Cambridge University Press, 2007), pp. 13–24 (p. 23).
[171] Yingling, *Hart Crane and the Homosexual Text*, p. 199.
[172] Amin, Musser and Pérez, 'Queer Form', p. 228.

poem was thoroughly rooted in a conservative understanding of poetic form and the long poem that was averse to the radical movements of *The Bridge* and, as explored elsewhere in this book, was hostile to expressions of queerness in Crane's poetry. At scale in *The Bridge* in its periodical forms, associational links are encouraged through the scattered publications by highlighting numerous connections between sections across different journals –with Crane perhaps counting on shared readerships. This creates a Cubist, collaged form – also expressed in the minutiae of the verse – in contrast to the consecutive form of the volume. Utilising literary institutions, the fragments of *The Bridge* were not 'shored' but scattered and reassembled, converging in the volume form of the poem with 'Atlantis'.

5

'THEY HAVE BEEN LOST': A YEAR IN MEXICO CITY

'Mexico killed Hart', declared fellow Guggenheimer Lesley Simpson, in one of the crudest summaries of Crane's final year.[1] Crane's time in Mexico has generally been considered to have been deeply unproductive and self-destructive.[2] He arrived in Vera Cruz from New York, via Havana, on 12 April 1931, making his way to Mexico City by train. His trip was funded by a Guggenheim Fellowship – the only major award of his career.[3] Dispatched to the committee on 29 August 1930, Crane's application outlined a vague plan to explore European literary traditions 'classical and Romantic' (his 'plans for work' section simply requested 'European study and creative leisure for the composition of poetry').

---

[1] Unterecker, *Voyager*, p. 760.
[2] Mariani, *Broken Tower*, p. 391.
[3] Unterecker, *Voyager*, pp. 655–6; Mariani, *Broken Tower*, p. 367. He did win *Poetry*'s 1930 award.

His resulting work, he wrote, would contrast European strands of influence with 'emergent features of a distinctly American poetic conversation', continuing themes from *The Bridge* and his negotiation with Eliot.[4] Crane's application was supported by references from Waldo Frank, Otto Kahn and Eda Lou Walton, a professor of English at NYU. Crane was informed of his success in a letter dated 13 March 1931.[5] At the last minute, however, after discussions with recent returnees Malcolm Cowley and Waldo Frank (Frank having published *America Hispana* that January), Crane spontaneously decided to travel to Mexico.[6] He hoped to research and write a long poem that he had first imagined during work on *The Bridge*, centring on Cortés's violent colonisation of Mexico. Crane met with the Guggenheim Foundation Fund's principal administrator, Henry Allen Moe, and was assigned to a group of Latin American Fellows.[7]

The Guggenheim was one of a handful of markers that Crane's reputation was rising. In the last years of his life he published in nationally distributed, mass-circulation magazines and was featured in *Vanity Fair* in 1929. This chapter discusses this shift in his reputation through an examination of his engagement with the 'smart journals', his attempts to raise his profile as a reviewer with new commissions at *Poetry*, and his drawing together of *Key West: An Island Sheaf*.[8]

Crane's letters, read alongside 'Nopal' which I have identified in the archive of his friend, former IRA Assistant Chief of Staff Ernie O'Malley, offer their own resistance to the prevailing narrative of his time in Mexico City, and the ease with which this year has been read back retrospectively from his death in April 1932.[9] 'Nopal' is a key finding of my research: a lost fragment from Crane's planned (but unrealised) Mexican epic that reflects the practices of the Mexican muralists as Crane shifts subtly from Cubist to Churriguresque experiments in perspective. I have verified the authorship of the poem with the generous help of Ernie O'Malley's son. Cormac O'Malley has confirmed that, as well as stylistic features typical of Crane, the unusual typeface and paper of 'Nopal' is, among Ernie O'Malley's files, unique to a clutch of poems typed out by Crane for O'Malley's safe keeping, the details of which O'Malley recorded in a letter

---

[4] Crane, 'To the John Simon Guggenheim Memorial Foundation', 29 August 1930, *O My Land*, pp. 434–5.
[5] Hammer and Weber, editorial note, *O My Land*, p. 447.
[6] Unterecker, *Voyager*, p. 650; Waldo Frank, *America Hispana, a Portrait and a Prospect* (New York: Charles Scribner and Sons, 1931).
[7] Unterecker, *Voyager*, p. 650.
[8] By *Key West* I refer to both *Key West* and what Simon refers to as the 'Folder Subsection'. See Simon, 'Notes', in Crane, *Complete Poems*, p. 238.
[9] Crane, 'Nopal'.

to Harriet Monroe.[10] Crane and O'Malley shared an enthusiasm for contemporary plastic arts. O'Malley's own writings on Mexican art and culture provide an unprecedented insight into Crane's Mexico year and the literary and artistic networks between Latin America and the US in which he operated.

The conventional narrative of Crane's Mexico period holds that his last year was sterile, creatively speaking. Until now, the only known poems written during this year are the much-celebrated 'The Broken Tower' and a handful of intriguing fragments: 'Purgatorio', 'Havana Rose' and 'The Circumstance'. It has been assumed that he did little to no work on his projected new poem. As well as 'Nopal', O'Malley's letters to Monroe mention a cache of lost poems, further challenging this assumption. Stripping the year of its accumulated mythology, what emerges from Crane's letters is his vigorous enjoyment of his surroundings with, for the first time in his life, a reasonable income and a stable place to live.[11] While characteristically changeable in mood, his correspondence with friends in the US nonetheless conveys a sense of excitement and a deep interest in Mexican culture. Crane's diary-like letters are peppered with allusions to Anita Brenner, the Mexican American writer and anthropologist. Crane attempts to describe his experiences through Brenner's anthropological framework, particularly her reading of Mexican religious, social and artistic culture as a 'crossing of threads'.[12] Remarkable for their detail and exuberance, alongside his reviews, his lucid, compelling letters home must have been what gave Frank great hope for Crane's development as a prose writer. As Crane wrote to his dear friend Sam Loveman, '[h]appiness continues, with also all of the gay incidentals of a Mexican Easter – exploding Judases, rockets, flowers, pappas [*sic* – a pun on the Spanish for potatoes] . . . mammas, delicious and infinitesimal children wearing masks and fireman's helmets, flowers galore and a sky that carried you ever upward'.[13] By introducing a new poem, 'Nopal' and exploring Crane's artistic community in Mexico, this chapter offers a new narrative of his last years, unpicking the myth-making narratives laid out in the days and months following his death.

NATIONAL RECOGNITION: *THE NATION*, *THE NEW REPUBLIC* AND *THE SATURDAY REVIEW*

Towards the end of the 1920s Crane was feeling 'optimistic' as his poetry began to receive attention beyond the avant-garde journals that had launched

---

[10] Cormac O'Malley, pers. comm., 28 April 2019; O'Malley to Monroe, c. January 1935, box 23, folder 25, O'Malley papers.
[11] Mariani, *Broken Tower*, p. 373.
[12] Crane to Frank, 13 June 1931, *Letters*, p. 372; Anita Brenner, *Idols Behind Altars* (New York: Harcourt, Brace, 1929), p. 40.
[13] Crane to Loveman, 27 March 1932, *O My Land*, p. 517.

his career.¹⁴ In 1929 *Vanity Fair* declared Crane one of five 'Singers of the New Age', 'as aspiring and as clear-cut as the skyscrapers of which he writes'. Shortly before his journey to Mexico City, *Poetry* had awarded Crane its $200 Helen Haire Levinson Prize for *The Bridge*, while *The Nation* included him on its 1930 cultural 'Honor Roll' for the same work: 'a poem unusual in technique, original in imagery, and affirmative in tone'.¹⁵ Along with the Guggenheim Fellowship, these notices were signs of Crane's changing status. He was now, at least according to *Vanity Fair*, 'an acknowledged leader among the younger Americans'.¹⁶

With the knowledge that it had taken almost seven years to get from planning *The Bridge* to publication, Crane imagined that a collection of short poems rather than his projected new epic would be his next book.¹⁷ The collection, *Key West*, contains offcuts from *The Bridge* and a set of poems which he began on the Isla de la Juventud (then the Isle of Pines) in 1926.¹⁸ With the exception of 'Imperator Victus', the poems in the *Key West* file had all been published in periodicals, beginning in April 1927 with 'O Carib Isle' in *transition*. The volume was in an unstable form at the time of Crane's death. His manuscripts of the *Key West* poems appear in fair draft, with Crane's characteristic worrying at occasional details and turns of phrase through edits on the typescript: between *transition* and his *Key West* file, the 'dozen turtles' of 'O Carib Isle' became 'tortoises' and then a single 'huge terrapin'.¹⁹

Characteristically, Crane had also been playing with the arrangement of the poems since their inception, with a handful of the *Key West* poems contained in a sequence 'East of Yucatan', published in the December 1927 issue of *transition*.²⁰ Most trickily, Crane's copies of the nineteen poems are housed in a manila folder with the title '*KEY WEST*', but only thirteen poems appear on the contents page.²¹ As such, Simon arranges the volume in two parts, *Key West: An Island Sheaf*, and '*KEY WEST*: Folder Subsection'.²² Brom Weber's

---

[14] Crane to Harry and Caresse Crosby, 30 August 1929, *O My Land*, p. 415.
[15] Unsigned, '1930 Honor Roll', *The Nation*, 132.3419 (17 January 1931), p. 8.
[16] Unsigned, 'Singers of the New Age', p. 89.
[17] As he told family friend Glenn Whistler, after news of his Guggenheim. Recorded in Grace Hart Crane's letters and quoted in Crane, *Complete Poems*, ed. Simon, p. 239.
[18] The island was renamed by Fidel Castro in 1978. See Michael E. Neagle, *America's Forgotten Colony: Cuba's Isle of Pines* (New York: Cambridge University Press, 2016).
[19] Crane, 'O Carib Isle', *transition*, pp. 101–2; Crane 'O Carib Isle', in *Key West: An Island Sheaf* [Lohf C1], box 9, Crane papers.
[20] Crane, 'East of Yucatan': 'I Island Quarry', 'II Royal Palm', 'III Overheard', 'IV El Idiota', 'V The Hour' [an early version of 'The Hurricane'], *transition*, 9 (December 1927), p. 136.
[21] Hammer's explanation of this issue is clear: 'Note on the Texts', in *Complete Poems and Selected Letters*, pp. 772–3.
[22] The subsection contains 'Key West', '—And bees of paradise', 'To Emily Dickinson', 'Moment Fugue', 'By Nilus Once', 'To Shakespeare', *Complete Poems*, pp. 126–31.

revised edition of the 1933 Liveright edition (1968) and Langdon Hammer's Library of America edition (2006) follow Waldo Frank's editing decisions on this detail, without separating the final six poems in a 'Subsection'.[23] While preserving the instability of the text in the editing arrangement is useful in Simon's edition, it seems likely that Crane intended the nineteen poems (at least) to be part of the same collection, with sections working through themes and preoccupations, perhaps in distinct sequences, as in 'Voyages' or 'For the Marriage of Faustus and Helen'.[24]

While Crane was unsure of the final form of the volume, the original publishing contexts of individual poems shed light on the aesthetic concerns of the book and his sense of his career trajectory. *Key West* shows his balancing act, with poems in avant-garde and small-circulation journals (*transition*, *Contempo*) and established, higher readership magazines (*The New Republic*, *The Nation*, *Poetry*). It is significant that *transition* is the most frequent presence in the collection. As discussed in relation to *The Bridge*, Crane appeared regularly in the magazine in the late 1920s. In 1929 he visited Paris, where he met *transition* editor Eugene Jolas and many of the magazine's contributors.[25]

The *Key West* poems are marked by self-conscious experimentation with Surrealist forms of language, pushing the logic of metaphor in new directions. The sections removed from *The Bridge*, 'O Carib Isle' and 'The Mango Tree', are remarkable for their engagement with Surrealist forms. Both poems show Crane working differently than in *The Bridge*, where he builds large-scale formal and thematic structures. 'O Carib Isle' offers a neat, self-conscious argument about theories of metaphor (echoing 'At Melville's Tomb') while 'The Mango Tree', in some ways a Surrealist reworking of 'My Grandmother's Love Letters', is arranged as a bold calligramme – a tree with a root that seems to trail ('come on') on to the following page.[26]

Crane's experiments with distinctly Surrealist, collaged forms emerge in *Key West* through studies in landscape and lyric. First published in *transition*'s first number (April) and then *Poetry* (October) in 1927, 'O Carib Isle' shows Crane positioning Surrealist experiments centre stage. As he recalls in *The Man From Babel*, Jolas solicited contributions from 'Surrealist friends' for the first issue – a list that included Crane and James Joyce (extracts from *Finnegans Wake* were

---

[23] See, for example, Frank to Grace Hart Crane, n.d., c. January 1933, box 25, Crane papers; Grace Hart Crane's copy of *Key West* [Banner Note Book: 'Hart Crane's Poems, Original MS, GHC'], box 9, Crane papers; Waldo Frank and Grace Hart Crane's 1932–33 correspondence, box 25, Crane papers.
[24] Unterecker wondered if 'Key West' would become a 'portion' of the lyrics, in one sequence within a larger collection. Simon, 'Notes', in Crane, *Complete Poems*, p. 239.
[25] Crane to Isidor Schneider, 1 May 1929, *O My Land*, p. 406.
[26] Crane, 'The Mango Tree', *transition*, 18 (Dreams Number) (November 1929), p. 95.

published as 'Work in Progress').[27] Crane's and Jolas's mutual interest came from their similar understanding of poetic language, rooted in their involvement in the Dadaist and proto-Surrealist circles of the early 1920s. Jolas's idea that poetry must find its energy through the search for a 'freer association' of words mirrors Crane's privileging of 'associational meanings' and the 'connotations of words'. In 'O Carib Isle' Crane, once again, walks a line between defamiliarisation and clarification. He juxtaposes images: the rhythmic tremors of plants caught by the ocean wind become 'lyric palsy of eucalypti', for instance, while the gaze of the poem moves from one strange impression to another:

> The tarantula rattling at the lily's foot,
> across the feet of the dead, laid in white sand
> near the coral beach, —the small and ruddy crabs
> flickering out of sight, that reverse your name; —
>
> and above, the lyric palsy of eucalypti, seeping
> a silver swash of something unvisited . . . Suppose
> I count these clean, enamel frames of death,
> brutal necklaces of shells around each grave
> laid out so carefully. This pity can be told . . .[28]

While 'At Melville's Tomb' appeared in Crane's first collection and 'O Carib Isle' was to be collected into a projected third volume, it was first published just one year before. There is a clear trajectory through the *White Buildings* and *Key West* poems. The poems of the late 1920s show a continuation of the same self-conscious, Surrealist poetic project established through Crane's interest in the 'exile' journals. 'O Carib Isle' offers a similar argument about poetry as 'At Melville's Tomb'. The 'dice of drowned men's bones' ('At Melville's Tomb') become 'the clean enamel frames of death' ('O Carib Isle'). The 'livid hieroglyph' carved into 'corridors of shells' of the earlier poem is rendered as a 'name' drawn in the 'white sand' that is 'reverse[d]' by the 'flickering' movements of the 'small and ruddy crabs' scuttling on the beach. The name 'reverse[d]' in the sand (in his second draft, the crabs 'anagrammatise' the letters)[29] is, like the 'hieroglyph' of the earlier poem, a self-conscious symbol: deciphering, mimicking the processes of association required to unpick Crane's complex metaphors.[30] This mimics the disorientating, often unrelated juxtapositions of Surrealist experiments in metaphor, which work to draw attention to

---

[27] James Joyce, 'Work in Progress', *transition*, 1 (April 1927), pp. 9–30.
[28] Crane, 'O Carib Isle', *transition*, p. 101.
[29] As used in 'O Carib Isle', *Complete Poems*, pp. 111–12.
[30] Crane, 'O Carib Isle', *transition*, p. 101.

the constructedness of the thing. Crane – characteristically – offers something of a compromise in his poetry, but in the *Key West* poems he pushes this to its limits through descriptions of eerie, dreamlike landscapes. The comparisons might be strange, but ultimately they work to clarify the image, rather than to create distance between the object and the description.

This is a movement that can be tracked through the poems gathered in *Key West*, as crabs seem to write, and spiders spin 'good underdrawers for owls', and an 'elephantine' tree rears its 'frondings' and sighs.[31] In 'A Name for All', first published in *The Dial* in April 1929, Crane offers a similar set of questions to 'O Carib Isle':

> Mammoth and grasshopper that flee our page
> And still wing on, untarnished of the name
> We pinion to your bodies to assuage
> Our envy of your freedom – we must maim[32]

Both Shakespeare and Stein are present here as Crane worries at the naming of things, exploring the possibilities of the logic of metaphor as a tool to escape the 'pinion' of naming, describing. He adds later 'Names we have, even, to clap on the wind; / But we must die, as you, to understand.' And in the final stanza Crane drifts into sleep: 'I dreamed that all men dropped their names, and sang / As only they can praise.' This idea of artistic action (singing) surpassing intellectual argument is scattered through the collection; in this case, the worry over what might be lost through representation or description – to 'pinion', for Crane, means to lose meaning. His poetry finds its energy in indeterminacy, approaching the object at a slant. His associative form 'sings' when approached in good faith. There is, then, both a preoccupation with Monroe's 1926 'Discussion' and also a sense that Crane wished to move beyond such questions.

'Old Song' and 'The Hurricane' were both published in *The New Republic*.[33] During these years, Crane was helped by the appointment of his friends to key editing roles at higher-circulation journals, with Cowley as *The New Republic*'s literary editor from 1929, Josephson a regular contributor to *The Saturday Review* and Morton Dauwen Zabel, his new ally as the associate editor of *Poetry*, a regular reviewer at *The Nation*, alongside Tate.[34] Crane's

---

[31] Crane, 'O Carib Isle', *Complete Poems*, p. 111; 'The Mango Tree', ibid., p. 115; 'Royal Palm', ibid., p. 122.

[32] Crane, 'A Name for All', *Complete Poems*, p. 119.

[33] Crane, 'Old Song', *The New Republic*, 51.662 (10 August 1927), p. 309, 'The Hurricane', *The New Republic*, 67.869 (29 July 1931), p. 277.

[34] Malcolm Cowley, *Conversations with Malcolm Cowley*, ed. Thomas Daniel Young (Jackson, MS: University of Mississippi Press, 1986), p. 131.

publications in *The Dial* and *Poetry* facilitated his appearances in the 'smart journals', *The Saturday Review, The Nation* and *The New Republic*. On 29 June 1927 'To Emily Dickinson' appeared in *The Nation*, followed by 'Old Song' in *The New Republic*. In March 1930 *The Saturday Review* published 'Cape Hatteras'. In July 1931 *The New Republic* published 'The Hurricane', followed by 'The Broken Tower' in June 1932. Crane had sent the poem to Cowley shortly before his death.[35] Crane's poem appeared with ex-Secessionist John Wheelwright's elegy 'To Hart Crane'.[36]

These larger-circulation journals opened up Crane's poetry to an almost incomparably larger audience and tended to publish work by established poets; Moore first appeared in *The Nation* in 1936, and in *The New Republic* in 1943. *The Saturday Review of Literature*, a supplement to the *New York Evening Post*, had a circulation of around 20,000. In 1925 *The New Republic* had around 14,500 subscriptions, but, during the 1920s, could sell 45,000 copies of a single issue, while *The Nation* had a circulation of around 25,000.[37] For Crane, the appointment of friends and acquaintances to powerful roles within these magazines, alongside his growing reputation, enabled access to their pages.

The transition from smaller-readership journals to exposure in more mainstream publications had its difficulties. Crane was surprised when *The Saturday Review* accepted 'Cape Hatteras', referring to the journal as 'the old enemy camp'.[38] Benét had written of his interest in 'The Tunnel', but deemed the poem 'by no means great', adding that 'a good many poems have been written about travelling underground, and a few about travelling under the river, in this Manhattan, but we give Crane best'.[39] *The Saturday Review* was, though, sympathetic to the 'machinery' and 'taut motors' of 'Cape Hatteras'.[40] *The Saturday Review*'s hostility to *White Buildings* tapped into an underlying theme in Monroe's and Moore's reactions to Crane's poetry that crept into contemporaneous assessments

---

[35] Crane, 'The Broken Tower', *The New Republic*, 71.914 (8 June 1932), p. 91; Crane to Cowley, 27 March 1932, *O My Land*, pp. 516–17.

[36] John Wheelwright, 'To Hart Crane', *The New Republic*, 71.914 (8 June 1932), p. 91.

[37] Data from Eric Pace, 'Norman Cousins', obituary, *The New York Times*, 1 December 1990, available at <http://www.nytimes.com/1990/12/01/obituaries/norman-cousins-75-dies-edited-the-saturday-review.html> (accessed 27 August 2018); David W. Levey, *Herbert Croly and "The New Republic"* (Princeton, NJ: Princeton University Press, 2014), p. 288; D. D. Guttenplan, *"The Nation": A Biography* (New York: Nation Publishing, 2015), unpaginated ebook.

[38] Crane to Caresse and Harry Crosby, 30 August 1929, *O My Land*, p. 415.

[39] William Rose Benét, [as 'The Phoenician'], 'The Phoenix Nest', *The Saturday Review*, 4.23 (31 December 1927), p. 496.

[40] For example, Matthew Josephson, 'A Modern Joan of Arc', review of Joseph Delteil, *Joan of Arc* (1925), *The Saturday Review*, 47.2 (19 June 1926), p. 869.

of his work: the sense that he was, as Monroe put it, writing for a specific and sympathetic audience of small readership, avant-garde journals and was otherwise 'unintelligible to all but specialists'.[41] Reviews in *The Saturday Review* and *New York Herald Tribune* echoed the sentiment, asserting that coterie poetics were the ruin rather than foundation of his poetry. Benét, writing in the former, complained that Crane was 'clapped for' only in 'the most select circles', while Taggard's *Herald Tribune* article made the odd, infantilising claim that 'Mr Crane needs rescuing from his admirers.'[42]

Max Eastman's twin essays in *Harper's*, 'The Cult of Unintelligibility' (1929) and 'Poets Talking to Themselves' (1931), crystallised this idea. The latter, published while Crane was in Mexico, provoked a biting, perceptive response from Anita Brenner.[43] In the later essay, Eastman singled out writers affiliated to European avant-gardes of various stripes: Crane, cummings, Joyce, Stein and Edith Sitwell, all of whom he deemed 'uncommunicative', withholding meaning from his hypothetical reader. Eastman makes an explicit and somewhat chauvinistic connection between affiliation with the avant-garde 'exile' journals and perceptions of 'unintelligibility' or specialism. Here Eastman curiously reasserts the avant-garde credentials of his 'Unintelligibles', while, at the same time, resting his essay on the fact that the group had acquired the name recognition necessary for a non-specialist essay in *Harper's*.

In the 1931 essay, Crane's poetry offers an almost erotic frustration for Eastman. 'Does it not tantalize you with a certain resistance?', writes the critic. Eastman's analysis departs from an anecdote, recalling a conversation with Crane; the two had sat with an unnamed 'red-lipped girl who had brought us together'. Beginning with the tint on the lips, this mouth becomes a central metaphor in the essay, transferring from 'girl' to poem. This is the source of the erotic charge of Eastman's critique but, along with it, attributes to Crane a particular, feminised inarticulacy. Crane's poetry, he writes, 'gazes out of the page significantly and in my direction but will not open its lips, will not make friends – will not, as we say, "come out with it"'.[44]

Brenner's unpublished response, 'Give to Caesar', is important not just for her dismantling of Eastman's argument but for her clear irritation at his choice of metaphor.[45] As much as it was, in Crane's words, a 'dissertation' on the poet,

[41] Monroe, 'Looking Backward', pp. 35–6.
[42] William Rose Benét, 'The Phoenix Nest', *The Saturday Review of Literature*, 3.36 (2 April 1927), p. 708; Taggard, 'An Imagist in Amber', p. 4.
[43] Brenner, 'Give to Caesar', p. 3, box 13, Crane papers.
[44] Eastman, 'Poets Talking to Themselves', p. 563.
[45] I am indebted to Camilla Sutherland's models for understanding gendered reviewing cultures in the Latin American context. See Camilla Sutherland, '"El pájaro de cuatro notas": The Reception of Argentine Women Writers and Artists' Work in Avant-garde Magazines (1920–1930)', *Journal of Iberian and Latin American Studies*, 23.3 (2017), pp. 399–416.

it was also a missive.⁴⁶ 'Give to Caesar', as well as its biblical connotations, can be read as an imperative, a command to 'give', to pass on, the manuscript to the self-appointed arbiter of 'intelligible' poetry. Brenner sent the piece to *Harper's* but it was refused.⁴⁷ Typed next to the title, she prefaces the essay with an 'Old Spanish proverb': 'No hables de lo que no entiendes' ('Don't talk about what you don't understand'). While tongue in cheek, this gesture is, nonetheless significant as she stakes her ground as a female and Mexican critic, noting the comparative ease with which Eastman published (his 'privilege' in dispatching his 'distinguished wisecracks' for *Harper's*), and the Anglophone nature of his cultural worldview as she wearily urges him towards other 'literatures', 'Eskimo, Pueblo Indian, Aztec, Polynesian, African'.⁴⁸

Brenner is attuned to the ways Eastman's mouth metaphor devolves into a heterosexist reading of Crane's poetry (echoing the broader interpretative trend outlined in previous chapters). Brenner appropriates and transforms the offending image. She declares, first, Eastman's twin essays to be a collective 'yawn', and offers him in return her own 'shrill female scream' – that is, a feminine, responsive criticism. Moving on, Brenner makes the subtext of Eastman's critical writings on Crane explicit, paraphrasing his essay: 'it makes no sense; and it makes no sense because the heads of those writers are addled, they are hysterical, infantile, psychopathological'.⁴⁹ Elsewhere she mocks the 'daringly sceptical' tone of Eastman's essay, which, she writes, amounts to 'a brave parade of bland detached analyses in a scientific manner'. She picks out the kernel of Eastman's argument, that 'the only valid function of words, is to convey information' – that the idea presented should be immediately obvious, without thinking through processes of association or decoding images. 'Mr Eastman cannot conceive of a man alone in a desert carving a statue without some thought in his head of showing it to somebody', she writes.⁵⁰

Brenner resists Eastman's conception of critical articulacy – 'speaking'. Her aesthetic views are strikingly similar to Crane's. In both the initial tone (that 'scream') of her essay and in its content she questions Eastman's poetic logic and his conception of 'scientific' analyses. Crane clearly enjoyed Brenner's 'pertinent' analysis of his poetry and her attack on, in his words, a critic as 'damned unscrupulous and canaille as Eastman'. On 8 January 1932 he sent the essay to Monroe's associate editor, Morton Dauwen Zabel, hoping that *Poetry* might print it (unlikely, he added, given its ten-page length).⁵¹ Brenner's unpublished essay is

---
⁴⁶ Crane to Zabel, 8 January 1932, *O My Land*, pp. 499–500.
⁴⁷ Ibid.
⁴⁸ Brenner, 'Give to Caesar', p. 3.
⁴⁹ Ibid., p. 4.
⁵⁰ Ibid., p. 7.
⁵¹ Crane to Zabel, 8 January 1932, *O My Land*, pp. 499–500.

an interesting artefact, showing Crane's position within the literary field towards the end of his life: both sufficiently established to be the subject of an attack in a mainstream journal, and unable to publish a detailed retort in a magazine of a similar stature. The essay, too, did not fit the conventional narrative of Crane's poetry, resisting as it did the very premise of a poetic logic. Resting in Crane's archive, this energetic essay offers a counter-narrative to the interpretative conventions that grew around the poet's writing in his own lifetime, while staking out Brenner's own ground for a feminist criticism that seeks to revel in Crane's unfixed poetry. Her form of feminist critique (the 'scream') works to reclaim the free, associative movements of Crane's 'song', '[a]bove all reason, lifting'.[52]

Ernie O'Malley and the Unfinished Mexican Epic

In 'Nopal', Crane settled on a unifying symbol for his new epic poem. As he told *El Universal* in an interview syndicated in publications across South America, his new project was to be a 'portfolio' of 'song patterns', 'dramatic cantos' in 'symphonic voices' on the 'physiognomy of the Mexican landscape'. In its brief exploration of key themes, 'Nopal' recontextualises the 'Purgatorio', 'Havana Rose' and 'The Circumstance' fragments by showing the possible directions of his new project.[53] Travelling with the buying power of the US dollar, Crane stayed at the Hotel Panuco, then with the writer and fellow 1931 Guggenheim awardee Katherine Anne Porter. The two fell out almost instantly as a result of Crane's erratic behaviour. Crane quickly moved to a spacious house in Mixcoac, 'an old-fashioned Mexican residence of 8 rooms, 3 servants, a luxurious garden with a goat, fighting cock, cat, Spitz dog and occasional scorpion—all for $50 a month'.[54] He immersed himself in researching the theme of his new poem, attempting to learn Spanish. Crane's letters record his notes on Stuart Chase's *Mexico: A Study of Two Americas* and other books by two Mexico City acquaintances, Carleton Beals (*Mexican Maze*) and Brenner (*Idols Behind Altars*) – the former two featuring fine illustrations by Diego Rivera, while Brenner's is accompanied by photographs by Edward Weston and Tina Modotti. In Taxco, Crane befriended William Spratling, the silversmith and artist whose own *Little Mexico* was published in 1932,[55] through whom he met

---

[52] Crane, 'The Idiot', *Complete Poems*, p. 118.
[53] Unsigned, 'Sr. Hart Crane, distinguido literato norteamericano, que se encuentra en México en viaje de estudio', interview, *El Universal*, 18 April 1931. Translated by Camilla Sutherland.
[54] Crane to Caresse Crosby, 31 March 1932, *Letters*, p. 406; Unterecker, *Voyager*, pp. 659–62.
[55] Crane to William Wright, 21 September 1931, *O My Land*, p. 480; Crane to Frank, 13 June 1931, ibid., pp. 468–70; Stuart Chase, *Mexico: A Study of Two Americas* (New York: Macmillan, 1931); Carleton Beals, *Mexican Maze* (Philadelphia, PA: J.B. Lippincott, 1931); Brenner, *Idols Behind Altars*; William Spratling, *Little Mexico* (New York: Cape and Smith, 1932).

David Siqueiros in the autumn of 1931.[56] Crane's papers show his interest in revolutionary ballads (known as *corridos*), printed on brightly coloured broadsides, and the local literary and artistic culture of Mexico City.[57] Siqueiros, who Crane housed along with his then-wife, the writer Blanca Luz Brum, at the Mixcoac house during the painter's inner exile, was an entry way to knowledge of complex local and national politics (an obituary noted that Crane 'felt society needed to be changed' and was 'vastly excited by hearing that writers were becoming revolutionary').[58] A copy of *Grito*, the organ of the UEPOC (the Pro-Worker and Peasant Student Union), in Crane's Mexico documents contains a handwritten note from the painter, chasing money from the poet.[59]

Crane travelled regularly, visiting Taxco, Tepoztlán and Cuernavaca. He enjoyed hiking alone, but was frequently guided by new friends: Siqueiros; Moisés Sáenz, a member of the Guggenheim selection committee and former sub-secretary in the Department of Public Education in Plutarco Elías Calles's post-Revolutionary government; Spratling, for whom Crane house-sat later in 1931; as well as Milton Rourke, a young archaeologist from Wisconsin.[60] His letters suggest intense vitality and periods of immersive research, hiking, visiting numerous festivals and churches; 'what gold and decorations I saw defies description', he wrote.[61] He collected 'serapes, leather work, pottery, embroideries, lacquers, etc.' and dressed the house with 'fresh bunches of lilies, tube roses, violets, nasturtiums, etc., every day from the garden'.[62] He attended digs with Rourke and the two visited the fiesta of Tepoztécatl, the Aztec god of pulque, where Crane was invited to beat the ceremonial drum at dawn.[63] As well as numerous affairs with men (he wrote that both his 'travels' and 'sex life' would fill 'a book'), in the last months of his life he embarked on an open relationship with Peggy Cowley – his first and only known relationship with a woman – which was both a source of joy and, increasingly, difficulty.[64] His letters take pains to note the personal, rather than intellectual, nature of his experiences, avoiding laying claim to expert knowledge of Mexican and Native American history or culture. As Susanne Hall points out, the letters 'often insist

---

[56] Unterecker, *Voyager*, p. 694.
[57] Unsigned broadsides (c. 1931), 'La Persecusion de Villa', 'Los Combates de Celaya', 'Corrido de Los Temblores..!', all box 10, Crane papers.
[58] Unterecker, *Voyager*, pp. 701–2; Unsigned, 'Death of a Poet', *The New Republic*, 70.910 (11 May 1932), pp. 340–2 (p. 341).
[59] Siqueiros to Crane [written on *Grito*], c. 1931, box 8, Crane papers.
[60] Crane to O'Malley, 19 July 1931, box 3, folder 42, O'Malley papers; Mariani, *Broken Tower*, pp. 370, 383.
[61] Crane to Loveman, 10 March 1932, *O My Land*, p. 513.
[62] Crane to Grunburg, 20 March 1932, *O My Land*, p. 514.
[63] Mariani, *Broken Tower*, pp. 383–5 (p. 513).
[64] Crane to Grunberg, 20 October 1931, *O My Land*, p. 485.

that his addressee consult the work of a historian or anthropologist instead'.[65] As he wrote in April 1932, the month in which he died, 'it takes a great while to know anything very definite about Mexico. I do know, however, how emphatically I love it – population, customs, climate, landscape and all.'[66]

Crane's friendship in Mexico with the Irish republican Ernie O'Malley goes some way to explaining the subtle shifts in the direction of his poetry in the last year of his life. After his release from prison for his part in the anti-Treaty campaign in the Irish Civil War, O'Malley began a long exodus. His post-Civil War travels from Ireland to Catalonia (where he helped the Independence movement), Italy, Germany, Holland, Belgium and North Africa were marked by a continued interest in folklore and institutions, literary and plastic arts. Having travelled to the US to fundraise for Éamon de Valera's newspaper *The Irish Press*, O'Malley journeyed across the states and eventually lived among artists in Taos, New Mexico, where he spent time lecturing on Irish literature, before crossing the border into Mexico in December 1930.[67] He lived there for a year, working in rural teacher-training schools and returning to the US in August 1931. It seems likely that Sáenz introduced O'Malley and Crane, since as an education advocate Sáenz helped O'Malley arrange his teaching tours of the country.[68]

The pair met in spring 1931: 'I have the most pleasant literary moments with an Irish revolutionary, red haired friend of Liam O'Flaherty, shot (and not missed) seventeen times', Crane wrote to Cowley. In July Crane's father died, calling him back to the US to deal with the estate. O'Malley looked after Crane's house in Mixcoac while the poet settled his father's affairs and met with Henry Allen Moe. Crane needed to plead his case to ensure that the Guggenheim Foundation did not terminate his fellowship, after reports of his imprisonment for public intoxication in Mexico City had reached Moe's office. Crane returned to Mexico on 29 August, just after O'Malley's departure.[69]

---

[65] Susanne Hall, 'Hart Crane in Mexico: The End of a New World Poetics', *Mosaic: a journal for the interdisciplinary study of literature* 46.1 (2013), pp. 135–49 (p. 144).
[66] Crane to Lorna Dietz, 12 April 1932, *O My Land*, p. 521.
[67] Richard English, *Ernie O'Malley: IRA Intellectual* (Oxford: Oxford University Press, 1998).
[68] Unterecker, *Voyager*, pp. 662, 10; Cormac K. H. O'Malley, 'Ernie O'Malley and the Arts', *Whytes in Association with Christies: The Ernie O'Malley Collection* (Dublin: Whytes, 2019), pp. 8–14. My thanks to Cormac O'Malley for the discussion of this point and, more generally, for shedding light on Ernie O'Malley and Hart Crane's friendship; for a biography, see Harry F. Martin with Cormac O'Malley, *Ernie O'Malley: A Life* (Newbridge: Merrion Press, 2021).
[69] Unterecker, *Voyager*, pp. 669–77; Crane to O'Malley, 19 July 1931, box 3, folder 42, O'Malley papers.

Crane was delighted with the new friendship, describing O'Malley as 'the most quietly sincere and appreciative person, in many ways, whom I've ever met . . . we drink a lot, look at frescos – and aggree! [sic]'[70] As Orla Fitzpatrick has sensitively explored, O'Malley befriended modernist photographers Paul Strand and Edward Weston while travelling through California. Weston's work, along with Tina Modotti's, illustrated Brenner's *Idols Behind Altars*. When O'Malley wasn't teaching in rural villages, his spare time was devoted to archaeological research in the Academy of Fine Arts, which resulted a decade later in his producing a broadcast 'Traditions of Mexican Painting' for the BBC's Third Programme.[71] He had acute insights into the art of the muralists Diego Rivera and Clemente Orozco, admiring Rivera's 'colour, a grand sense of design' and the 'steel-like quality' of Orozco's treatment of indigenous subjects.[72] Crane shared this interest with O'Malley, having explored ways to translate visual art forms into his poetry throughout his career. In 1932 Crane wrote a 'Note on the Paintings of David Siqueiros' for a brochure advertising a talk given by Siqueiros to close his show at the Casino Español in Mexico City. Siqueiros painted a large portrait of Crane, which the sitter slashed during an alcoholic relapse shortly before his death.[73]

Three years after Crane's much-elegised death, O'Malley wrote to Monroe with a vivid portrait of his friend:

> We became friends and remained friends to the end despite my sense of personal discipline and his utter lack of it. Inspired by our memories of poetry and stimulated by rum toddies we wrote long letters to many people, amongst them E.E. Cummings, Wallace Stephens [sic] and yourself whom Hart always referred to as 'Aunt' Harriet. Unfortunately we burnt the letters later on. Hart at the time had books from you to review. We each wrote reviews but I don't know what happened to them. I liked him a great deal. He was generous, enthusiastic and spoke the most amazing rhetoric, good rhetoric. He believed in America, in its creative ability and had a dislike for the nostalgia of induced foreign culture as standard. He was kind to his friends, irritable and pugnacious, but Mexico with its criss cross racial clashes and its general effect on unrest of mind was no place for a stranger to solve personal or creative problems [. . .] I did not like

---

[70] Crane to Cowley, 2 June 1931, *O My Land*, pp. 465–7.
[71] Orla Fitzpatrick, 'From Mexico to Mayo: Ernie O'Malley, Paul Strand and Photographic Modernism', in *Modern Ireland and Revolution: Ernie O'Malley in Context*, ed. Cormac O'Malley (Newbridge: Irish Academic Press, 2016), pp. 28–41; Nicholas Allen, 'Introduction', *Broken Landscapes: Selected Letters of Ernie O'Malley*, ed. Cormac K. H. O'Malley and Nicholas Allen (Dublin: Lilliput Press, 2012), p. xix.
[72] Ernie O'Malley, 'Traditions of Mexican Art', *The Listener*, 23 January 1947, pp. 146–7.
[73] Crane, 'Note on the Paintings of David Siqueiros', in *La Exposición Siqueiros* (Mexico City: Casino Español, 1932); Unterecker, *Voyager*, p. 745.

some of the articles that appeared after his death and I meant to write of him as I had known him, but I did not.[74]

The letter expresses O'Malley's irritation at the reductive portraits of the poet that emerged after his death, revealing a kind, vibrant, difficult and creative friend – an idiosyncratic patriot, hostile to imported Europeanism and US imperialism. O'Malley beguilingly mentions a sheaf of unpublished poems that Crane entrusted him with before his return to Dublin in August 1931, which complicates the idea of the poet's Mexican period as blighted in uncreative self-destruction: 'He said they were for myself as I had stood by him in trouble. I sent them back to Ireland with some books but since I have heard that they have been lost.'[75] In 'Nopal', which could be one of a clutch of lost poems, Crane is likely to have had in mind the legend of the founding of the Aztec capital Tenochtitlan, latterly Mexico City, an image that is depicted in the coat of arms of Mexico. The god Huitzilopochtli commanded the nomadic Aztec people to seek an eagle eating a snake, perched on a prickly pear growing out of a rock in a lake – this sacred spot was to be the location for the capital. The Nahuatl name Tenochtitlan derives from *tetl* (rock) and *nochtli* (prickly pear), an etymology that Crane perhaps picks up on in 'The Circumstance': 'stronger than death smiles in flowering stone'.[76] The city fell after Cortés laid siege to it in 1521.

Among O'Malley's documents is a scribbled note in Crane's hand which repeats a fragment he jotted down elsewhere, 'Cortez: <u>the Enactment</u> – and he put The Cross upon that <u>people</u>'.[77] In 'Nopal', presumably one of the sequence of 'dramatic cantos', the cactus thrusts out of the ground:

> Outfaced and in, a mirror, section-burnt,
> Distorting images recessed in angled green.
> Edge stabbed and pricked, bayoneted by sun.
> Upthrust and out; in rage, despair or what?
> Sucking cool sweetness from the heat [?] shed sand,
> Dribbing weak blood from out of bird pecked tunas
> And armed with desert disregard.[78]

---

[74] O'Malley to Monroe, c. January 1925, box 23, folder 25, O'Malley papers.
[75] Ibid.
[76] Kay Almere Read, *Time and Sacrifice in the Aztec Cosmos* (Bloomington, IN: Indiana University Press, 1998), p. 256, n. 114; Crane, 'The Circumstance', *Complete Poems*, p. 203.
[77] Crane, note on an envelope addressed to Crane c/o Anglo-South American Bank, Ltd: 'Cortez: The Enactment – and he put the Cross upon the <u>people</u>', box 23, folder 25, O'Malley papers. This clutch of poems might explain the title page among Crane's manuscripts, 'Cortez: The Enactment', on Hotel Panuco stationery, with the epigraph 'And he put the Cross / upon that People'. Crane, 'Cortez: The Enactment', box 9, Crane papers.
[78] Crane, 'Nopal'.

'Nopal' shows Crane thinking through the political and cultural contours of his new project. The interest in Mexican visual arts that Crane shared with O'Malley seems to inform the poem. The queasy *mise en abyme* of the cactus's 'Distorting images recessed in angled green' perhaps broaches aspects of the Mexican Churrigueresque: 'Line was broken at every possible angle to form recessions', as O'Malley put it in his 1947 broadcast.[79] This hall of mirrors is placed in a vast field of vision among the 'heat lashed sand', an image forever manipulated and distorted through infinitesimal reflections. The cactus, refracted here, is the anti-symbol to the imposition of the colonial religion 'put upon that people'. The cactus and cross form a chiastic image of rebellion and defiance against oppression and imposition, a dichotomy that seeded Crane's new epic.

'Nopal' appears to work palimpsestically, in line with Brenner's assessment of the coexistence of past and present in contemporary Mexican plastic arts, with 'beautiful things made collectively, by one hand reliving the work of a preceding hand'.[80] As she writes of Rivera: 'To clarify and instruct he will resort to knowledge ancestral and current as proverbs; to convince he will appeal to A.B.C. emotions . . . with frescoes pressing and lucid as posters.'[81] There is a layering of proverb, Churriguresque and ongoing political conflict in 'Nopal' that seems to reflect on the tradition of the muralists. The bloody imagery of transgressed boundaries ('Edge stabbed and pricked') could gesture towards perennial tensions at the US–Mexican border, as well as Mexico's colonial history (in 'The Circumstance', Crane ties both together in the image of 'a bloody foreign clown'). The period saw mass deportations of Mexican Americans between 1929 and 1936. In May 1931 the Mexican president's nephew, Salvador Cortés Rubio, was shot by two plainclothes policemen near Ardmore, Oklahoma, an incident that Crane refers to in his letters.[82]

Prior to the Mexico poems Crane's 'poetry and letters show no interest in the actual ongoing political battles around the status of contemporary Native Americans', as Hall writes. Hall usefully explains Crane's increasing deference to works such as *Idols Behind Altars* in his letters; he 'consistently evaded doing writing that could be conceived of as ethnographic', writes Hall.[83] Hall locates this shift in 'The Broken Tower', as Crane appeared to be growing into a somewhat postcolonial poetic voice.[84] Crane's 'Nopal' reinforces this idea of a significant departure from the cultural appropriation of Native American

---

[79] O'Malley, 'Traditions of Mexican Art', pp. 146–7.
[80] Brenner, *Idols Behind Altars*, p. 32.
[81] Ibid., p. 281.
[82] Crane to Lorna Dietz, 15 July 1931, *Letters*, p. 378.
[83] Hall, 'Hart Crane in Mexico', p. 144.
[84] Ibid., p. 148.

history and themes in *The Bridge*, particularly in the poem 'Powhatan's Daughter'. O'Malley was highly critical of the 'usual type of wealthy person who goes out [. . .] to escape humanity or to become interested in ceremonies, dance or legend of the Indians and who does not care a damn for the actual spoliation of Indians or Mexicans there'.[85] Both Lesley Simpson, who Hall notes gave Crane a 'long reading list' and dismissed his 'naïve' view of Mexico, and O'Malley appear to have challenged how Crane would view his poetic subject and, as Hall puts it, his 'approach to [colonial] history'.[86] Crane appeared to develop an awareness of the naivety (even cultural arrogance) of the project: 'the more I see the more I realize how intricate the subject is', he wrote late in 1931.[87]

Crane's subtle celebration in 'Nopal' of the cactus as a symbol of resistance, 'desert disregard', seems to speak to the influence the Irish republican had on his dislike of 'induced foreign culture'. Helen Delpar detects traces of these concerns in 'The Broken Tower', submerged beneath 'an expression of personal concerns'. Delpar finds Crane acknowledging that 'the native is still a victim of "the lash, lost vantage, and the prison / His fathers took for granted ages since—"'.[88] 'Nopal', then, develops ideas first suggested in 'Bacardi Spreads the Eagle's Wing', as, guided by conversations with O'Malley, Crane began to register his own ideas for an inchoate pan-American, postcolonial poetry.

'Bacardi Spreads the Eagle's Wing': Memorial Issues of *Poetry*, *Contempo* and *The New Republic*

Memorial issues dedicated to Crane of *Poetry*, *The New Republic* and *Contempo* shaped his posthumous reception. Reports and essays entrenched the myth of the self-destructive, 'decadent' and undisciplined poet, with its attendant anti-queer resonances. Underlying the standard narrative of Crane's death are colonial stereotypes of Mexico that trade in crude understandings of the 'ancient Mexican concern with death', as Brenner puts it. Death as 'a motif in art springs from before the Conquest, cuts through the colonial period and appears over and over today', writes Brenner, noting that the symbol of the skull operates as much as a symbol of life and artistic struggle: that which is 'controlled, and made into lasting visible life'.[89]

---

[85] O'Malley to Eithene Golden, 28 March 1935, *Broken Landscapes*, p. 110.
[86] Ibid., p. 142.
[87] Crane to Underwood, 30 November 1931, *O My Land*, p. 494.
[88] Helen Delpar, *The Enormous Vogue of Things Mexican: Cultural Relations between the United States and Mexico, 1920–1935* (Tuscaloosa, AL: University of Alabama Press, 1992), p. 182.
[89] Crane on Brenner: Crane to Frank, 13 June 1931, *O My Land*, p. 469; Brenner, *Idols Behind Altars*, pp. 21–6.

The conventional story, then, has Crane embarking on a doomed voyage, his death inevitable as, frustrated by creative drought as the 'Muse he'd waited for daily had still not come' and impending financial ruin, he succumbed to his darkest self-destructive impulses.[90] Even Waldo Frank, a Hispanist, fell into this narrative. In an interview with Unterecker for *Voyager* Frank explained that he had been 'afraid' for Crane. Like his friends, Munson, Jean Toomer and – briefly – Crane, Frank was interested in the occult philosophers George Gurdjieff and P. D. Ouspensky. His private interest in esoteric religious ideas seems to intersect with orientalism as he recounted Crane's departure in 1931:

> I knew Mexico pretty well, and I knew how strong the death wish was in Mexico. I knew there was a dark side to all that had come out of the Aztec civilization. And I also knew what the climate did to Americans that weren't used to it.[91]

Just a fortnight after Crane's disappearance from the deck of the *Orizaba*, *The New Republic* published an unsigned editorial in which the writer made the disturbing claim that his death was 'a poem of a different sort, a poem of action which the world could interpret in its own fashion'.[92] While this is perhaps one of the most egregious, such romanticising claims were common among the obituaries that emerged in the spring of 1932, alongside intricate and sensitive readings of Crane's poetry and – in print – the elegiac recitation of favourite lines and stanzas.

While some journals proceeded with caution – Michael Roberts's obituary in *The New English Weekly* recorded that Crane had been 'accidentally drowned in the Gulf of Mexico' – the 'myth of Hart Crane' was firmly established in these early reports. Although some were circumspect ('Hart Crane, Poet, Vanishes from Ship New York Bound'), the majority of the immediate newspaper reports took up similar themes to *The New Republic*. Crane was presented as the archetypal tortured, poetic genius. Headlines announced variously that 'Crane Was Despondent Over Money and Poesy, Companion Says',

---

[90] Mariani, *Broken Tower*, p. 391; Tate on Crane as a 'Horrible example of the hostility of capitalist society to the arts', Allen Tate, 'A Poet, and his Life', *Poetry*, 50.4 (1937), pp. 219–24 (p. 221).

[91] Crane to Tate, 15 February 1923, *O My Land*, p. 130. Munson comments on the group's brief interest in Ouspensky in his interview with John Unterecker, in *In Search of Hart Crane*, dir. Leo Hurwitz (1966), available at <https://leohurwitz.com/movie/in-search-of-hart-crane/> (accessed 2 February 2021). Frank interviewed by Unterecker, *Voyager*, p. 650.

[92] Unsigned, 'Death of a Poet', p. 342. This was likely penned by Cowley. The Dadaist idea of the 'significant gesture' and artistic 'action' might go some way to explaining this odd pronouncement.

'Friends Tell of Clevelander's Suicide, "No Place for Poetry," His Lament' and 'Quits a Prosaic World'. His mother, Grace, was left to discover her son's death through one such headline, learning the news from the daily newspaper while working at the Carleton Hotel in Oak Park, Illinois.[93]

Longer obituaries in *The New Republic*, *Contempo*, *Hound & Horn* and *The New English Weekly* sought to establish some kind of meaning in Crane's death through romanticisation – many were, naturally, written by his friends and literary acquaintances. As Tate wrote – despite warning against 'excessive interpretation' of Crane's death – these articles sought 'not only to define his poetry but to connect with the manner of his death'.[94] Munson, showing the immense difficulty of his position, puzzles over the end of their friendship, tenderly recording their period of 'youthful expectancy', which ended as a result of increasingly bad-tempered exchanges between *Broom* and *Secession*. With this wound not healed at the time of Crane's death, Munson's article is, with a coldness that can accompany grief and trauma, preoccupied with recording the details of his last moments. Munson repeats two violent, unsubstantiated rumours: that Crane was 'killed by the churning propeller' and that 'a shark devoured the poet'. Munson ascribes the source of the latter to the ship's captain, Blackadder. The shark theory was bizarrely popular in elegies to the poet, appearing in Forrest Anderson's 'For Hart Crane' (June 1932), John Wheelwright's 'To Hart Crane' (June 1932) and David Wolff's 'Remembering Hart Crane' (November 1934).[95] Munson's trading in gossip was unpalatable for Frank, who wrote to Grace, fearing she might seek it out: 'do not look it up', he wrote, assuring her that he and Cowley had written to the editors to challenge the 'absurd' piece.[96]

While still showing the contested nature of accounts of Crane's final hours and struggles with alcoholism and psychological illness, these articles nonetheless fixed an impression of his final year as entirely doomed, plagued by writer's block, alcoholic relapse and depression. Seeking to ascribe a speculative narrative to the events of that morning in April 1932, Munson makes much of the fact that Crane 'had been almost completely unproductive as a poet for the last

---

[93] *Letters of Hart Crane and his Family*, ed. Thomas S. W. Lewis (New York: Columbia University Press, 1973), p. 656.
[94] Allen Tate, 'In Memoriam Hart Crane', *Hound & Horn*, 5 (July–September, 1932), pp. 612–19 (p. 614).
[95] Gorham Munson, 'A Poet's Suicide and Some Reflections', *The New English Weekly*, 23 June 1932, pp. 237–9 (p. 237); Forrest Anderson, 'For Hart Crane', *Contempo*, 2.4 (5 July 1932), p. 1; Wheelwright, 'To Hart Crane', p. 91; David Wolff, 'Remembering Hart Crane', *The New Republic*, 104.15 (28 November 1934), p. 76.
[96] Frank to Grace Hart Crane, 9 July 1932, box 25, Crane papers.

two years'.[97] Similarly, Allen Tate ends his piece in *Hound & Horn* (notable for the way it lets Crane's poetry breathe, mostly comprised of his favourite of Crane's lines and stanzas) with the speculation that Crane was broken by a sense of his failure. The final sentence of the essay reads: 'A year ago just as he was leaving New York for Mexico, Crane asked Slater Brown if he thought that his poetry would be remembered.'[98] Crane's final year was, in fact, surprisingly productive, despite the fact that what survives of the Mexico poems and fragments does not reveal a coherent plan. What we know from *The Bridge*, however, is that much of his planning emerged in letters. The same is true of the Mexico poem, of which outlines began to take shape in correspondence with Otto Kahn and Caresse Crosby.

Munson's obituary, alongside Tate's in *Hound & Horn*, staked out the ground for critical interpretations of Crane's work, asserting a fixed lineage between Crane, Whitman, the English Romantic poets and the French Symbolists. Surprisingly for the *Secession* editor, Munson downplays the importance of the contemporary literary circles in which Crane wrote and lived as he makes a case for his importance by slotting him into an existing patrilineage. Most egregious, however, is his inauguration of a frustrating pattern of reading Crane's brilliance when writing about the sea into the nature of his death, as in *The New Republic*: 'Did he carry some secret with him into the ocean – into that "great wink of eternity," that "superscription of bent foam and wave" which he celebrated so often in his poems?'[99] William Carlos Williams's remarks in *The Kenyon Review* offer a neat summary of this troubling view: 'Crane had got the end of his method.'[100] The dangers of this retrospective narrative for critics of Crane's poetry are expressed most fully by Joseph Ridell in 'Hart Crane's Poetics of Failure' which, as Warner Berthoff usefully notes, erroneously reads 'death and betrayal into every figured detail of ['The Broken Tower's] argument'.[101]

Frank is relatively sensitive to the complexities of Crane's life, resisting a tendency among his friends – perhaps seeking the comfort of a clear narrative – to see his death in mythological terms. Rather, he notes that the right intervention might have saved his friend. In an interview for Leo Hurwitz's 1966 documentary *In Search of Hart Crane*, and stalling occasionally as he sought the right words, Frank told John Unterecker that:

> there isn't any doubt, for instance, that he was deeply humiliated by the fiasco that he had made of his trip to Mexico. That he had spent his

---

[97] Munson, 'A Poet's Suicide', p. 237.
[98] Tate, 'In Memoriam Hart Crane', pp. 612–19.
[99] Unsigned, 'Death of a Poet', p. 341.
[100] Williams as quoted in Mariani, *Broken Tower*, p. 424.
[101] Riddel, 'Hart Crane's Poetics of Failure', pp. 473–96; see Berthoff's useful notes on Riddel's argument in *Hart Crane: A Reintroduction*, p. 120.

money and not done what he was supposed to do. What he had promised to do. But he was also troubled about the world situation. This had been growing on him. Uhm. He'd lost his hope. I think for a while he was attracted to the communists, and then he soured on that. Right or wrong. But I do also think, as I said to Leo [Hurwitz, producer and director], that these are diseases which have crises and if he had luck he could have gotten over it and he would have become a writer. He would have continued to be a poet, but he would have also perhaps have written prose. Written excellent prose, which he did. So that's . . . But I think he just lost heart and lost faith in himself and the dismal prospect of New York [Unterecker: in 1932?] in 1932 that had a great effect on him [Unterecker: so that all these factors pulled together?] Yes.[102]

As Frank suggests, it is important to resist seeing this year – or indeed Crane's life and works more generally – as edging towards an inevitable precipice.

Dedicated issues of literary and cultural magazines memorialised Crane through new publications, editorials and poetic responses. In July 1932, three months after his death, *Contempo* (based at the University of North Carolina, Chapel Hill) heralded Crane as a guiding influence for the younger contributors to the journal. *Contempo* printed 'Bacardi Spreads the Eagle's Wing' (submitted in March) alongside two of Crane's last letters, penned just days before his journey to Vera Cruz.[103] Milton Avant Abernethy and Anthony J. Buttitta, the magazine's editors, fashioned their journal after *Secession* and *Broom*, airing further arguments between Munson, Cowley and Josephson in the winter of 1931–32, noted in Crane's letters.[104] The two had been reverential in their approach to Crane for a contribution.

Written in 1926, Crane's submission of 'Bacardi Spreads the Eagle's Wing' to *Contempo* in 1932 shows his wish to present a new, more geopolitically engaged aspect of his poetry. Hall reads Crane's own domestic arrangements in Mixcoac as forming a 'contact zone', 'witness to the daily negotiation and evolution of cultures in contact'. 'In a home with two servants of indigenous descent', writes Hall, '[h]e now inhabited a contact zone between a rapidly growing cosmopolitan centre, newly emerging suburbs, and nearby rural villages.'[105] As Crane wrote in his accompanying letter to *Contempo*, 'Bacardi

---

[102] Waldo Frank as quoted by John Unterecker in *In Search of Hart Crane*, 1:23:36.
[103] Crane, 'Dear *Contempo*, 11 March 1932', *Contempo*, 2.4 (5 July 1932), p. 1; 'Dear *Contempo*, 20 April 1932', *Contempo*, 2.4 (5 July 1932), p. 1.
[104] Gorham Munson, 'Questions for Cowley', *Contempo*, 1.14 (15 December 1931), p. 1; Malcolm Cowley, 'Munsonia', *Contempo*, 1.15 (1 January 1932), p. 1; Crane to Cowley, 9 January 1932, *O My Land*, pp. 500–1.
[105] Hall, 'Hart Crane in Mexico', p. 142.

Spreads the Eagle's Wing represents the rather typical "colonial" attitude of two Americans in Cuba employing native labor'.[106] The poem was written during his time on the Isla de la Juventud (until 1978 named the Isle of Pines), working on *The Bridge* and attempting to rebuild Villa Casas, his mother's estate on the island – before the October storm thoroughly destroyed the property (an event preserved in 'The Hurricane', which appeared in *transition* and *The New Republic*).[107] In adopting this 'colonial' voice, the poem creates a 'contact zone', intersecting class and colonial power dynamics.[108] Crane attempts to differentiate himself from other landowning US citizens on the island after the 1925 ratification by the US Senate of the Hay–Quesada Treaty, twenty-one years after it was drawn up. The treaty recognised Cuban sovereignty over the island, and US landowners were eager to sell their properties.[109] The Hart family even considered giving their property to charity, but Crane needed somewhere to work on *The Bridge*, and liked the idea of owning 'a grass plot', even if the Harts let the land and buildings 'rot'.[110] Crane adopts an ironic stance in the poem, which satirises the majority of US landowners (including himself and his own family) who mocked the labourers' boats that 'might as well / Have been made of – yes, say paraffin, – / That thin and blistered . . . just a rotten shell.'[111] Like the Hart estate, the other colonial properties that surrounded it had come to represent the legacy of the US annexation of the island.

The front page of the number displayed a short obituary by William Carlos Williams. Williams's commission to write *Contempo*'s obituary of Crane is surprising (his private correspondence derides Crane as a 'crude homo').[112] While he praises the 'continual surf' of 'Voyages', Williams used the moment to launch an attack on what he, somewhat bizarrely, categorised as Crane's simultaneously commercially minded and obscure poetry: 'he wrote sometimes, really, as though he were seeking to please [. . .] someone who had charge of a New York Sunday Book Supplement . . . he could be at times as bad as that – the gently bubbling putridity of the saleable –'.[113] Mimicking reviews that noted Crane's post-Decadent streak, Williams finds Crane – at his worst – 'a direct step backward to the bad poets of any age', 'vague' and 'blurred'. Most brutally, Williams

---

[106] Crane, 'Dear *Contempo*, 11 March 1932', p. 1.
[107] Unterecker, *Voyager*, pp. 440–56; Crane, 'The Hurricane', *The New Republic*, 67.869 (29 July 1931), p. 277; Crane, 'The Hour' [early version of 'The Hurricane'], *transition*, 9 (December 1927), p. 136.
[108] Mary Louise Pratt, 'Arts of the Contact Zone', *Profession* (1991), pp. 33–40.
[109] See Neagle, *America's Forgotten Colony*.
[110] Unterecker, *Voyager*, p. 392.
[111] Crane, 'Bacardi Spreads the Eagle's Wing', p. 1.
[112] Williams to Ezra Pound, box 55, folder 2518, Pound papers.
[113] William Carlos Williams, 'Hart Crane, 1899–1932', *Contempo*, 2.4 (5 July 1932), pp. 1, 4 (p. 1).

conjures implied knowledge of Crane's psychological instability among the readers of *Contempo*, and castigates the recently dead poet: 'Crane didn't write as low as he knew, or should have known, his life to be.' He should have made better use of his 'agony, which was real and which raised him to distinction'.[114]

While almost entirely wooden to the ear, Forrest Anderson's 'For Hart Crane', published next to the obituary on *Contempo*'s front page, is nonetheless more sensitive in its reading of Crane than Williams. While Williams acknowledges little of Crane's self in his work – and castigates him for it – Anderson writes:

> truth is in the mouths of sailors
> that is why they have no certain place
> in the street which is the first line to a poem
> i heard what was the last line for a poet[115]

Anderson, significantly, plays with the erotic imagery of Crane's poems (as Malcolm Cowley did in his 1926 poem to Crane), gently considering their lack of 'certain place' in the poem (surely a comment on codification). The street and poem alluded to must, presumably, have been 'Cutty Sark' which opens (the only poem of Crane's to mention a street in the first line) 'I met a man in South Street, tall–', and leads into Crane's portrait of the South Street man's fragmented psyche, in which the sailor's sense of reality slips away like 'running sands'.[116] While the poem might be weak, Anderson nonetheless inaugurated a rich tradition of elegies to Crane.

Poetry published a significant memorial sub-section for Crane in 'The Urn'. With help from Grace Hart Crane and Sam Loveman, who advised on the editing of the 1933 *Collected Poems*, Frank arranged for a number of publications to mark both Crane's death and the 1933 publication of the volume. In January 1933 *Poetry* published the 'Urn' arrangement of unpublished poems: 'By Nilus Once I knew', 'The Circumstance', 'Enrich My Resignation', 'Havana Rose', 'Imperator Victus' (the unpublished *Key West* poem), 'Phantom Bark', 'A Postscript', 'Purgatorio', 'Reliquary', 'Reply', 'The Sad Indian' and 'The Visible the Untrue'. The following month, *The New Republic* published Frank's introduction to the new edition alongside four poems: 'And Bees of Paradise', 'Eternity', 'The Return' and 'A Traveller Born'.[117] Aware of Crane's international

---

[114] Ibid.
[115] Anderson, 'For Hart Crane', p. 1.
[116] Crane, 'Cutty Sark', from *The Bridge, Complete Poems*, pp. 71–4 (p. 72).
[117] Waldo Frank, 'An Introduction to Hart Crane', *The New Republic*, 74.950 (15 February 1933), pp. 11–15; Crane, 'Four Poems by Hart Crane' ['Eternity', 'The Return', 'And Bees of Paradise', 'A Traveller Born'], *The New Republic*, 74.950 (15 February 1933), pp. 15–16.

community of writers, Frank sent out copies of the *Collected Poems* to Anita Brenner, Valery Larbaud, André Gide and T. S. Eliot, among others. News of the book soon made its way to Buenos Aires, through Frank's friend Victoria Ocampo, the writer and founding editor of *SUR*. In September Ocampo published Frank's introduction with fragments of Crane's poetry translated by Jorge Luis Borges.[118]

The maudlin title 'The Urn' announces the poems as a monument to the dead poet, and in doing so retrospectively imbues them with an elegiac quality. While subtle, these framing gestures form part of the Crane myth. The 'urn' suggests the containment of the poet's ashes: the remaining fragments of his last works. In reality, what we have here is a mixture of Crane's creative energies, showing new directions emerging. Significantly, included in the sheaf was a love poem to Emil Opffer (with his initials preserved in the dedication in the *Poetry* version), 'The Visible the Untrue', which Simon dates between 1927 and 1929.[119] Alongside is 'The Circumstance', a fragment from Mexico intended for his new epic. The final stanza of the poem, in which Crane wonders 'If you could die, then starve, who live / Thereafter, stronger than death',[120] has been crudely read as a prefiguration of his death, a view that not only rests on a retrospective reading of the poem after the fact, but that elides the distinctions the poem makes between poet, voice and subject ('To Xochipilli').[121] While such lines might appear eerie in the light of Crane's last moments, it is reductive (crass, even) to search through his last poems as if looking for a suicide note.

Forming part of the Crane myth, the framing of these last works as an 'urn' should be resisted: Crane's late poems, including 'Nopal' and the Mexico fragments, pulse with lively, experimental energy. Crane was thoroughly absorbed by his new environment, exploring murals with O'Malley, learning about archaeological digs with Rourke, discussing local and national politics with Siqueiros, anthropology with Simpson and criticism and writing with Brenner and Porter. Composed in early May 1931, shortly after the events it describes, the surreal prose poem 'Havana Rose' is startling in its humour and formal movements – not least because this is Crane's first known prose poem. Essentially an experiment in life writing, the poem narrates Crane's encounters on the *Orizaba* with Dr Hans Zinsser, Harvard bacteriologist. Zinsser had stowed a dozen typhus-infected rats in the cabin of his assistant, Maximiliano Ruiz Castañeda.[122] The

---

[118] Frank to Grace Hart Crane, c. January 1933, box 25, Crane papers; Waldo Frank, 'Un gran poeta Americano: Introducción a Hart Crane', *SUR*, 3.8 (1933), pp. 27–59.

[119] Simon, 'Notes', in Crane, *Complete Poems*, p. 252.

[120] Crane, 'The Circumstance', *Poetry*, p. 179.

[121] See the troubling idea of Crane and the 'sacrificed young man' in Pire's 'Hart Crane's "Accursed Share" in Mexico'.

[122] Unterecker, *Voyager*, pp. 653–5; Hans Zinsser, *As I Remember Him: A Portrait of R.S.* (Boston: Little, Brown, 1940), p. 335.

poem describes the incredible moment when Crane – drunk – spied the two doctors tipping the rats overboard. According to Zinsser's 1935 experimental biography of typhus, *Rats, Lice and History*, Crane began crafting the poem on the deck of the ship, as he watched the rats disappear into the water.[123] 'Havana Rose' is unique in the way that Crane works through an experience, as he mulls over his attempts to find a new poetic theme for his epic, which he sees mirrored in Zinsser's search for a reliable typhus vaccine. The poem closes with a comment on the impossible-seeming scope of his new poetic project, and the fate awaiting Zinsser and Castañeda in Mexico City. In what purports to be a transcription of Zinsser's advice to the poet, offered over 'dinner at La Diana', a restaurant in Havana where the *Orizaba* docked en route to Vera Cruz, Crane writes: 'loose yourself within a pattern's mastery that you can conceive, that you can yield to'.[124]

---

[123] Zinsser, *As I Remember Him*, p. 337; Unterecker, *Voyager*, p. 654.
[124] Zinsser, *As I Remember Him*, p. 335; Crane, 'Havana Rose', from 'The Urn', *Poetry*, 41.4 (1933), pp. 177–96.

EPILOGUE

'THE SHELLEY OF MY AGE': HART CRANE'S AFTERLIVES

> The truth may lie in imagining a connection
> With him or with you; with anyone able to overlook
> Distance, shrug off time, on the right occasion . . .
>
> Alfred Corn, 'The Bridge, Palm Sunday, 1973

'I don't think you were supposed to become as steeped in your material as I did with Hart Crane', writes Eileen Myles in 'hart!'. They continue: 'I attached my homosexual poet to him and took a ride. Planes overhead, a train hurtling along its tracks. They had so much time back then and they were meanwhile very interested in speed. They thought the future would be amazing and it is, don't you think.'[1] As in Myles's 'hart!', Crane is a frequently conjured presence in contemporary poetry, and the recipient of an unusual number of elegies. Periodicals can offer a latitudinal view of literary history, sweeping away retrospectively imposed hierarchies and allowing for a reading of Crane unencumbered by dominant interpretations of his work. The complex matrices of influence and exchange explored in this book trouble attempts to assert the dominance of one particular poet or clique within a literary culture, while showing the complex, emerging processes of canon formation that laid the groundwork for the rise of New Critical approaches to literary studies. As detailed studies have shown, Crane's poetry is attentive to the language and

---

[1] Myles, 'hart!', n.p.

formal movements of his antecedents. But his poems urgently work through the ideas and aesthetic questions that animated contemporary periodical culture. However much Crane might have disliked 'assumptions' of his 'literary ambitions in relation to one group, faction, "opportunity," or another', his poetry suggests a shifting coterie poetics as he moved between communities.[2] As I have explored, this emerged variously: from his adoption of Wildean masks in his early poems in *The Pagan* and *Bruno's Weekly* to his engagement with arguments between *Broom* and *Secession* in 'For the Marriage of Faustus and Helen' to his poems to William Sommer and Gaston Lachaise in *1924*.

Poems to and after Crane, intriguingly, offer a parallel literary history of his work. Poems such as 'hart!' form a body of creative criticism, simultaneously offering independent interpretations of his poetry and teasing at the critical shibboleths that surround his work. More than this, to claim Crane as an interlocutor appears to be a rejection of popular accounts of modernism that emerged in the 1970s and 1980s that place a single poet (*The Pound Era*) or binary ('Pound/Stevens: Whose Era?') at the centre of creative influence.[3] By contrast, poems to Crane offer entreaties to a kind of writerly friendship, a 'connection' that can 'shrug off time', as Alfred Corn puts it in 'The Bridge, Palm Sunday, 1973'.[4] While at its worst, the Crane elegy reinforces the destructive mythologies that surround his death, some of the most generous and incisive criticism of Crane is poetic. Indeed, as discussed in Chapter 2, the first queer reading of his poetry can be found in Malcolm Cowley's simultaneously adoring and teasing 1926 poem 'To Hart Crane', which revels in his friend's coded imagery.[5] Other poems to Crane (or so saturated in his writing that they appear as poems 'after' him) offer examinations of the minutiae of his poetics (John Berryman, Alfred Corn, Melanie Challenger), tease at the critical narratives that surround his work (Denis Devlin, Geoffrey Hill), affirm his queer legacy (Allen Ginsberg, Frank O'Hara, Eileen Myles, Rob Halpern, Colette Labouff Atkinson), question the colonial impulses of his work (Orlando Ricardo Menes) or reimagine the poet within communities, fantastical and otherwise (Adrienne Rich, Robert Creeley, Mark Ford). Institutions have had curious stakes in the Crane elegy: *Poetry* has, to date, published six poems dedicated to Crane (most recently in October 2020), with numerous other contributions to the magazine alluding to the poet.[6] The student magazine

---

[2] Crane to Munson, 8 December 1924, *Letters*, p. 187.
[3] Hugh Kenner, *The Pound Era* (Berkeley, CA: University of California Press, 1973); Marjorie Perloff, 'Pound/Stevens: Whose Era?', *New Literary History*, 13.3 (1982), pp. 485–514.
[4] Alfred Corn, 'The Bridge, Palm Sunday 1973', in *Stake: Selected Poems, 1972–1992* (Washington, DC: Counterpoint, 1999), pp. 15–16 (p. 16).
[5] Cowley, 'Hart Crane', p. 35.
[6] Orlando Ricardo Menes, 'Hear Me, Hart Crane', *Poetry*, 217.9 (2020), p. 15.

Columbia Poetry, meanwhile, published significant elegies by two promising undergraduates, John Berryman and Allen Ginsberg. The two elegies, published just over a decade apart, show the development of the apprentice poets as they resist and imitate Crane's voice.[7]

Shrugging off the urge to break down literary history into a sequence of patrilineages or traditionally masculine, adversarial narratives of literary dominance, in 'The Night Has a Thousand Eyes' Adrienne Rich places Crane among a cast of New York poets and musicians, summoned in the final stanza to help her shape this poem to 'the city gathering / itself for darkness'. 'Hart Miles Muriel Julia Paul / you will meet the eyes you were searching for', writes Rich, remembering Crane's lines from 'For the Marriage of Faustus and Helen': 'There I might find your eyes across an aisle'.[8] As Rich wrote in her 1972 essay 'When We Dead Awaken: Writing as Re-Vision' (the title playing on revision as reviewing and as seeing), a 'radical critique of literature, feminist in its impulse, would take the work first of all as a clue to how we live [. . .] how we can begin to see – and therefore live – afresh'.[9] For Rich, understanding is found in seeing, witnessing – the intimate meeting of gazes. As Crane wrote in 'Reply': 'Thou canst read nothing except through appetite / And here we join eyes in that sanctity.'[10] The vulnerability of this image of 'Re-Vision' as interpretation gestures towards Crane's own process. He teaches a form of radically uncertain, vulnerable reading through his associative metaphors; his poems require radically flexible interpretation.

Myles places Crane in company; the intimate final question of 'hart!' is a conversational opening, 'don't you think'. Crane's poetry was forged through dialogue with his peers, and poems after Crane have continued these distant writerly friendships. As Jacques Khalip discusses in his brilliant article 'Cruising Among Ghosts: Hart Crane's Friends', the Crane elegy not only 'refuse[s] elegiac summary', but the use of 'apostrophe pushes the elegy's turn to the dead into an address of friendship'.[11] In this vein, Myles's Crane is thoroughly embedded in his immediate community. Myles reinforces this through the grammar of the poem; the pronouns place him within a group: 'they were meanwhile very interested in speed. They thought the future would be amazing.' To write 'after Crane', Myles

---

[7] John Berryman, 'Elegy: Hart Crane', *Columbia Review*, 17.1 (1935), pp. 1–2; Allen Ginsberg, 'Hart Crane', *Columbia Review*, 27.2 (1946), pp. 17–18.

[8] The people referred to are Hart Crane, Miles Davis, Muriel Rukeyser, Julia de Burgos and Paul Desmond. Other appearances include saxophonist Charlie Parker and civil engineer John Roebling. Rich, 'The Night has a Thousand Eyes', pp. 43–4.

[9] Adrienne Rich, 'When We Dead Awaken: Writing as Re-Vision', *College English*, 34.1 (1972), pp. 18–30 (p. 18).

[10] Crane, 'Reply' (title given in 'The Urn', also known as 'Thou Canst Read Nothing . . .'), *Complete Poems*, p. 193.

[11] Khalip, 'Cruising Among Ghosts: Hart Crane's Friends', pp. 67, 87.

implies, demands a similar immersion (a version of Rich's 'liv[ing] – afresh'). This requires not so much inhabiting Crane's voice or style, but his process of immersion and association.[12] As Myles explains in 'How I wrote certain of my poems' (the essay that concludes *Not Me*), 'I wandered around Manhattan that year in flowing coats, being mournfully Crane'.[13] Myles's Crane, then, is the figure 'thumbing the midnight on the piers', or threading through 'the hiving swarms' in Times Square:[14] complex, but lively and embodied – a world away from the abstracted, Shelleyan versions of Crane that exist in the worst of the elegies, where he is seen to 'jump [. . .] To trace the visionary company of love', chasing a 'vision' that 'he could never attain'.[15]

Myles's conversations with Crane are remarkable in their insistence on the flexibility and mutability of his writing, which Myles relates to his queer poetic. Discussing an early version of Crane's talismanic lines in 'For the Marriage of Faustus and Helen', 'twisted with the love of things irreconcilable', which would of course become:

> *There is a world dimensional for*
> *those untwisted by the love of things*
> *irreconcilable . . .*[16]

Myles writes: 'That was being gay for me – the slant moon with the slanting hill. The line just never undid itself for me – it's unbelievable – and every time it ripples in the exact same light.'[17]

Eve Kosofsky Sedgwick offers a usefully fugitive definition of queer form as 'the open mesh of possibilities, gaps, overlaps, dissonances and resonances, lapses and excesses of meaning when the constituent elements of anyone's gender, of anyone's sexuality aren't made (or *can't be* made) to signify monolithically'.[18] Myles uses these lines from 'Faustus and Helen' to suggest that Crane's poetry works precisely through a 'rippling' of meaning – shifting, changeable

---

[12] Bringing to mind John Wieners' call in 'Hart Crane, Harry Crosby': 'Let me carry what you threw away. / Come on men, give me the insides of your souls.' Wieners, 'Hart Crane, Harry Crosby, I see you going over the edge' (Detroit Artists' Workshop Press: Free Poems Among Friends, c. 1966–67).

[13] Eileen Myles, 'How I wrote certain of my poems', in *Not Me* (New York: Semiotext(e), 1991), p. 199. Myles also includes Crane's supposed last words in 'Hot Night': 'My / dear – I've simply / disgraced myself', *Not Me*, pp. 51–7 (pp. 54–5).

[14] Crane, 'The Tunnel', *Complete Poems*, pp. 97–101.

[15] Julian Symons, 'Hart Crane', *Poetry*, 54.5 (1942), p. 248.

[16] Crane, 'For the Marriage of Faustus and Helen', *Complete Poems*, pp. 26–32 (p. 26).

[17] Myles, 'hart!', n.p.

[18] Eve Kosofsky Sedgwick, *Tendencies* (Durham, NC: Duke University Press, 1993), p. 8.

associations that just about seem to catch the light with each 're-vision'. Mark Ford's 'The Death of Hart Crane' offers a similarly ephemeral reading of Crane's 'world dimensional'. Ford's surreal letter poem ('*Name and address withheld*') assembles details from Crane's life alongside apocryphal speculations about his death, such as his being 'devoured by a shark' which, as I discussed in Chapter 5, was a common theme in the elegies published immediately after his death. Marsden Hartley's painting *Eight Bells Folly: Memorial to Hart Crane* (1933) has a shark leaping through turquoise waves into the centre of the composition, its teeth bared with what might be lips or what might be blood streaking from mouth to flank.[19] In the imaginary universe of Ford's letter writer, Crane survives. Recalling irritating statements such as William Logan's ('If he had lived a lot longer and written a lot more, we might think much less of him'), the letter writer enters a crowded apartment full of Harts and Harolds in their seventies, 'the galloping strains of Ravel's *Boléro* turned up loud'. 'It dawned on me then that Hart Crane had not only somehow survived his supposed death by water, but that his vision of an America of the likeminded was being fulfilled that very night, as it was perhaps every night, in this apartment on MacDougal Street.'[20]

Allen Ginsberg's 1946 elegy also takes Crane's lines from 'For the Marriage of Faustus and Helen' as a point of departure, but forecloses their possibilities. The poem opens:

> He cringes, beholding their great dignity,
> The sane prophetic ghosts of future seasons.
> Sick lover, like degraded Oedipus,
> He ripped clairvoyant eyes out of his soul,[21]

The poem appears, by contrast, relatively conservative. In 'Hart Crane', the poet foresees a queer future with such clarity and specificity that, like Oedipus, he maims himself. Robert Lowell's famous 'Words for Hart Crane' from *Life Studies* contains a similarly violent undercurrent. As Langdon Hammer has explored, in 'Words for Hart Crane' Lowell is grappling with his mentor, Allen Tate's, view of his late friend's life and work. The result is a fraught reading of Crane's sexuality that begins with sexual violence (Crane as '*Catullus redivivus*', 'wolfing the stray lambs') but ends with a tender resolution in which, I think, Lowell can be seen to depart from Tate's reading:

---

[19] Marsden Hartley, *Eight Bells Folly: Memorial to Hart Crane* (1933), oil on canvas, 31 5/8 x 39½ in., Frederick R. Weisman Art Museum, University of Minnesota. Gift of Ione and Hudson D. Walker (1961).
[20] Ford, 'The Death of Hart Crane', pp. 18–19.
[21] Ginsberg, 'Hart Crane', p. 17.

> Who asks for me, the Shelley of my age,
> must lay his heart out for my bed and board.²²

As Crane did, here Lowell puns on Hart/heart, forging an intimate relationship between poets that is loaned to this dual image of surrender, both physical and erotically possessive ('lay his Hart out') and emotional ('lay his heart out'). This is disarming, interrupting the homophobic narrative drawn from Tate (who described Crane as 'an extreme example of the unwilling homosexual' and deplored his 'monstrous egotism', 'grievously aggravated by homosexuality'),²³ in which Crane's sexuality is presented at first by Lowell as an adopted mask as he is seen to 'play my role of homosexual'.²⁴ Lowell's poem, then, seems to work through Tate's reading of Crane. The poem is discursive, with the young Lowell using the problem of the Crane myth as a way of reckoning with and moving away from his mentor's judgements.

Geoffrey Hill's and Denis Devlin's poems to Crane, like Lowell's, pay careful attention to his interlocutors. Devlin's poem (which, I believe, is discussed here for the first time) considers charges of illogic aimed at the poet, stemming from his 1926 'Discussion' with Harriet Monroe, and popularised in Eastman's articles and later reviews by Tate and Winters. Devlin writes:

> It is intolerable to be taken to task
> On the basis of a proverbial fear whose springs you have taken apart
> and thrown away and forgotten [. . .]²⁵

In essence: Crane's associative mode itself dispatches the logical fallacy presented by Monroe (which would go on to plague discussions of his work). For Devlin, Monroe took Crane 'to task' over a category mistake: logic is not the concern of metaphor and is not, by extension, a reasonable way of assessing poetry.

Hill takes this argument as read, and mocks Crane's detractors by reducing stereotypes of the poet to their absurd conclusions. Hill's poem, like Ford's, offers a useful retort to articles such as Logan's 'On Reviewing Hart Crane', published in *Poetry* in 2008.²⁶ Indebted to Tate's arguments, and written in

---

[22] Robert Lowell, 'Words for Hart Crane', in *Collected Poems*, ed. Frank Bidart and David Gewanter (New York: Farrar, Straus and Giroux, 2003), p. 159.
[23] Brown (ed.), *Robber Rocks*, p. 15; see Hammer on Allen Tate's 'The Poet as Hero', *The New Republic*, 127 (16 November 1952), p. 25, in *Janus-Faced Modernism*, p. 64; Tate, 'A Poet, and his Life', p. 221.
[24] Lowell, 'Words for Hart Crane', p. 159.
[25] Denis Devlin, 'HC', MS33, 790/9 (1–3), Devlin papers. My thanks to Karl O'Hanlon for passing on this manuscript.
[26] William Logan, 'On Reviewing Hart Crane' [retitled 'The Hart Crane Controversy' on the *Poetry Foundation* website], *Poetry*, 193.1 (2008), pp. 53–9.

reply to a flurry of responses to his *New York Times* review of the Library of America edition of Crane's poems, Logan's essay is useful in that it manifests each of the dominant clichés of Crane criticism in a single document.[27] Less an essay than a collection of odd claims, Logan discusses Mariani's corrections to his article, comments on 'the failure of *The Bridge*', complains of Crane's self-regard, offers a gay panic defence for Crane's experience of homophobic violence, and brands his poetry as 'gassy' and 'obscure' (which is, apparently, unappealing to women). Logan offers some unpalatable speculations as to the relationship between suicide and poetic reception – to which he cannot help but add Sylvia Plath. Intentional or not, the essay is an important artefact when considering Crane's reception history. Taken together, Logan's original *New York Times* article, 'Hart Crane's Bridge to Nowhere', and 'On Reviewing Hart Crane' show dominant themes in criticism of the poet and the ease with which these ideas can be reactivated in the pages of a journal such as *Poetry*.[28]

In part 1 of 'Improvisations for Hart Crane', Hill inhabits the voice of a critic who, if one had not come across Logan's article, would seem implausible:

> Super-ego crash-meshed idiot-savant.
> And what have you.
> This has to be the show-stopper. Stay put.
> Slumming for rum and rumba, dumb Rimbaud,
> he the sortilegist, visionary on parole,
> floor-walker watching space, the candy man,
> artiste of neon, traffic's orator [. . .][29]

By appealing to extremes, Hill lambasts reductive portraits of Crane – the caricatures of his poetry as illogical or lacking intellectual rigour. 'Stay put', he writes. That is to say, stay in your place as the 'dumb Rimbaud': the useful exception to high modernism that proves the rule (for example, *The Bridge* as *The Waste Land*'s antagonist). Doing so, Hill suggests, closes off the engaging mutability of Crane's work with its 'possibilities, gaps' and 'slant', swapping nuance for the ease of encapsulating the poet in a memorable gobbet.[30]

---

[27] William Logan, 'Hart Crane's Bridge to Nowhere', *The New York Times*, 28 January 2007, available at <https://www.nytimes.com/2007/01/28/books/review/Logan.t.html> (accessed 29 July 2021); Paul Mariani, letter to the editor, *The New York Times*, 25 February 2007, available at <https://www.nytimes.com/2007/02/25/books/review/Letters.t-1.html> (accessed 29 July 2021).

[28] Logan, 'On Reviewing Hart Crane', pp. 53–9.

[29] Hill, 'Improvisations for Hart Crane', p. 99.

[30] Calvin Bedient, 'Grand Failure', review of Hart Crane's *Complete Poems and Selected Letters* (2006), *Boston Review*, 32.2, available at <http://bostonreview.net/BR32.2/bedient.php> (accessed 12 April 2021).

The poem closes with an adaptation of Crane's opening line from 'Reply'. Hill's 'Thou canst grasp nothing except through appetite' mirrors Crane's 'Thou canst read nothing except through appetite'. As well as working to form a Shakespearean pun, 'read nothing' to 'grasp nothing' is a movement to an interrogative mode: an invitation to reconsider, to hungrily grasp at Crane's complex writing.

Orlando Ricardo Menes's 'Hear Me, Hart Crane' (*Poetry*, October 2020) reads Crane with a refreshing critical attentiveness, showing the possibilities that emerge when his poetry is approached with a different set of questions. Menes plays with the elegy's ability to merge introspective and political questions, the poet's way of 'mediating between private mourning and public commemoration'.[31] Putting pressure on the colonial tenor that emerges in sections of *The Bridge* and, in *Key West*, his 'tendency to tropicalize', Menes places Crane at work on *The Bridge* during his stay on his mother's estate on the Isla de la Juventud in 1926. 'Your mind smelted our mangrove nurseries', Menes writes, holding Crane's lived and imaginary environments in tension. Menes's poem juxtaposes Crane's anxious attempts to demarcate himself from other plantation owners on the island in his letters against unpalatable images that are presented in *The Bridge* and *Key West* poems. Menes finds an uncomfortable source of creativity – an unchallenged whiteness of vision – in Crane's inability to recognise his prejudices: 'I cannot blame you, dear Hart, for don't we all / Make art from paradox?'[32]

The purpose of this book has not been to make a case for asserting Crane's position at the top of an ever-shifting pile of modernist writers, or even to make a claim for his importance as a dominant presence in contemporary poetry. Rather, via Hart Crane, I wished to explore modernism through the latitudinal view offered by periodicals, where now canonical works coexist alongside equally intriguing forgotten poetry and prose. By analysing these networks in detail, the processes by which certain works find their way to posterity and others are forgotten or thoroughly reframed begin to emerge. I hope to have cleared the ground for new studies of Crane uncoupled from the charges of illogic, unintelligibility and failure that emerged in his own lifetime. To read Crane is to embrace not quite knowing. I think here of curiously apt lines from Vahni Capildeo's *Skin Can Hold*, where the provisionality of meaning is fortifying: 'language, commonly accused of failure, / thrown like rope'.[33] There is

---

[31] Stephen Regan, 'The Irish Elegy after Yeats', in *The Oxford Handbook of Modern Irish Poetry*, ed. Fran Brearton and Alan Gillis (Oxford: Oxford University Press, 2012), online edition [unpaginated].

[32] Menes, 'Hear Me, Hart Crane', p. 15.

[33] Vahni Capildeo, *Skin Can Hold* (Manchester: Carcanet, 2019), pp. 105–7 (p. 105).

celebration in the capaciousness of language, to grasp 'the bell-rope' and swing in any number of directions.[34] Crane's poetry teaches us to be vulnerable, fallible, playful readers. As he wrote: 'To trace the visionary company of love, its voice / An instant in the wind (I know not whither hurled).'[35] I hope, ultimately, that this book has reclaimed this mutability as a virtue.

---

[34] Crane, 'The Broken Tower', *Complete Poems*, pp. 160–1 (p. 160).
[35] Ibid., p. 160.

APPENDICES

APPENDIX 1: AN OVERVIEW OF CRANE'S PERIODICAL PUBLISHERS, 1916–32

Title	Dates	Editors	Location	Type	Price	Print run[1]	Publications	Rejections
1924	July–December 1924	E. Seaver, A. Vera Bass	Woodstock, NY	monthly (irregular)	35¢	unknown	4	0
Aesthete, 1925	February 1925	M. Josephson, M. Cowley, K. Burke, H. Crane [as 'Walter S. Hankel']	Greenwich Village, New York	monthly (single issue)	35¢	600	0	0
The American Caravan	1927–28	P. Rosenfeld (I), L. Mumford (I), V. W. Brooks (I), A. Kreymborg (I and II)	New York	annual	$3.50–$5.00	unknown	2	0
Broom	November 1921–January 1923	H. Loeb, A. Kreymborg, G. Prezzolini, E. Storer, L. Ridge, M. Josephson, L. Medgyes, W. Slater Brown, M. Cowley	Rome, Berlin, New York	monthly (irregular)	35–50¢	2,500–4,000	1	1
Bruno's Bohemia	March 1918	G. Bruno	Greenwich Village, New York	monthly (single issue)	10¢	unknown	1	0
Bruno's Weekly	July 1915–December 1916	G. Bruno	Greenwich Village, New York	weekly	5¢	unknown	1	0
The Calendar of Modern Letters	March 1925–July 1927	E. Rickword, B. Higgins, D. Garman	London	monthly; quarterly	1s. 6d.	1,000	6	3
Contempo	May 1931–February 1934	M. A. Abernethy, A. Buttitta	Chapel Hill, NC	fortnightly; monthly	10¢	unknown	2	0
The Criterion	October 1922–January 1939	T. S. Eliot	London	monthly; quarterly	3s. 6d.	800–1,000	1	4

[1] Sources for print run figures given in relevant chapters.

Title	Dates	Editors	Location	Type	Price	Print run[1]	Publications	Rejections
The Dial	January 1920–July 1929	S. Thayer, J. S Watson, A. Gregory, G. Seldes, M. Moore, K. Burke, E. Pound [foreign editor]	New York	monthly	35–50¢	9,500	13	29
The Double Dealer	January 1921–May 1926	J. W. Friend, B. Thompson, J. McClure, A. Goldstein, P. L. Godchaux Jr	New Orleans	monthly (irregular)	25¢	1,500	4	2
The Fugitive	April 1922–December 1925	J. C. Ransom, W. C. Curry, D. Davidson, J. M. Frank, S. H. Hirsch, S. Johnson, Merrill Moore, A. B. Stevenson, A. Tate, L. Riding, W. Y. Elliot, W. Frierson, J. Willis, R. P. Warren	Nashville	monthly; quarterly	25¢	500	4	0
Gargoyle	July 1921–October 1922	A. Moss, G. Munson	Paris	monthly (irregular)	5f./1s. 6d.	unknown	3	2
larus	February 1927–June 1928	J. S. Mangan, V. Thomas, O. Jenkins	Paris/Lynn, MA	monthly (irregular)	35¢	unknown	1	0
The Little Review	March 1914–May 1929	M. Anderson, J. Heap	Chicago, New York	monthly; quarterly (irregular)	15¢–$1.00	3,100	12	7
The Measure	March 1921–July 1926	M. Anderson, K. S. Alling, J. Auslander, L. Bogan, P. Colum, A. K. Gray, C. Hall, R. Hillyer, F. E. Hill, D. Morton, L. Townsend Nicholl, G. O'Neil, P. Sanborn, G. Taggard, W. Welles, E. Wylie, H. Allen	New York	monthly	25¢	unknown	1	0
The Modernist	November 1919	J. W. Fawcett	Greenwich Village, New York	monthly (one-off)	unknown	unknown	3	0
The Modern School	February 1912–spring 1921	H. Kelly, L. Ridge, L. D. Abbott, S. Kerr, W. Thurston Brown, F. D. Anderson, M. Komroff, A. Wolff, C. Zigrosser	Stelton, NJ	monthly	10–25¢	unknown	1	0

Title	Dates	Editors	Location	Type	Price	Print run[1]	Publications	Rejections
The Nation	July 1865–	O. Garrison Villard	New York	weekly	15¢	100,000	1	1
The New Republic	November 1914–	H. Croly, W. Lippman, E. Wilson, B. Bliven, Malcolm Cowley [literary editor 1929–34]	New York	weekly	15¢	30,000–43,000	3	3
The Pagan	May 1916–January 1922	J. Kling, W. Y. Vale, E. O'Neill, M. Endicoff, C. S. Zerner, E. Endicoff, H. Diamond, I. H. Daemon, H. Crane, G. B. Munson, B. Kadish, C. Kunen, M. W. Solomon, W. Holbrook, O. Williams, A. A. Rosenthal, C. P. Neri, L. Cohen	Greenwich Village, New York	monthly	10–25¢	500	18	1
Poetry	October 1912–	H. Monroe, A. C. Henderson, H. B. Fuller, E. Wyatt, H. C. Chatfield Taylor, E. Pound [foreign correspondent], E. Tietjens, H. Hoyt, E. Carnevali, M. Strobel, J. Nelson North, M. D. Zabel	Chicago	monthly	15–25¢	1,600	7	1
S4N	November 1919–July 1925	N. Fitts	Northampton, MA	circular; monthly; quarterly	25¢	9 (as circular); 110–2,000	3	0
The Saturday Review of Literature	August 1924–June 1986	H. S. Canby, W. Rose Benét, A. Loveman, C. Morley	New York	weekly	10¢	20,000	1	0
Secession	April 1922–winter 1924	G. B. Munson, M. Josephson, M. Cowley, K. Burke	Paris, Vienna, Reutte, New York	quarterly; monthly (irregular)	20¢	500	3	1
transition	April 1927–spring 1938	E. Jolas, E. Paul, R. Sage, M. Josephson, S. Gilbert	Paris	monthly; quarterly (irregular)	50¢/10f.	4,000	13	0

APPENDIX 2: TIMELINE OF CRANE'S PERIODICAL PUBLICATIONS, 1916–32

Journal	Date	Title	Volume	Page(s)	Notes
Bruno's Weekly	23 September 1916	C33	3.15	1008	as Harold Hart Crone [sic]
The Pagan	October 1916	To The Pagan	1.6	43	signed H—H— C—
The Pagan	November–December 1916	October–November	1.7–8	33	as Harold H. Crane
The Pagan	March 1917	The Hive	1.11	36	as Harold Crane
The Pagan	April–May 1917	Fear	1.12/2.1	11	as Harold Crane
		Annunciations		11	
The Pagan	October–November 1917	Echoes	2.6–7	39	
The Pagan	December 1917	The Bathers	2.8	19	
The Little Review	December 1917	In Shadow	4.8	50	
The Pagan	January 1918	Modern Craft	2.9	37	
Bruno's Bohemia	March 1918	Carmen de Boheme	1.1	2	as Harold Hart Crane
The Pagan	April–May 1918	Carrier Letter	2.12/3.1	20	
		Postscript		20	
		Editorial Note to a Patriotic Poem		28	
		The Case Against Nietzsche		34–5	
		Tragi-Comique		54–6	
The Little Review	July 1918	Joyce and Ethics	5.3	65	
The Pagan	August–September 1918	Forgetfulness	3.4–5	15	
The Pagan	January 1919	The Ghetto and Other Poems, review of Lola Ridge, *The Ghetto and Other Poems*	3.9	55–6	
The Pagan	February 1919	Minna and Myself, review of Maxwell Bodenheim, *Minna and Myself*	3.10	59–60	

Journal	Date	Title	Volume	Page(s)	Notes
The Modern School	March 1919	To Potapovitch [sic] (de la Ballet Russe)	6.3	80	misprint: title should read 'To Portapovitch'. Later 'To Portapovitch (du Ballet Russe)'.
The Pagan	September 1919	Book review *Sherwood Anderson*, review of Sherwood Anderson, *Winesburg Ohio*	4.5	60–1	
The Modernist	November 1919	Legende Interior North Labrador	1.1	28 28 28	
The Dial	April 1920	My Grandmother's Love Letters	68.4	457	
The Little Review	September–December 1920	A Note on H. W. Mimms [sic] Garden Abstract	7.3	60 78	Misprint for H. W. Minns
The Double Dealer	June 1921	Black Tambourine	1.6	232	
The Double Dealer	July 1921	Sherwood Anderson	2.7	42–5	
The Double Dealer	August–September 1921	Porphyro in Akron	2.8–9	53	
The Dial	October 1921	Pastorale	71.4	422	
The Measure	October 1921	A Persuasion	1.8	14	
Gargoyle	December 1921	Chaplinesque	1.6	24	
The Double Dealer	May 1922	Locutions des Pierrots, trans Jules Laforgue	3.17	261–2	
The Dial	June 1922	Praise for an Urn: To E.N	72.6	606	
Gargoyle	August 1922	The Great Western Plains	3.2	unpaginated	
Gargoyle	September 1922	The Fernery	3.3	unpaginated	
The Little Review	autumn 1922	To J.H.	9.1	39	misprint: masthead states 9.3

Journal	Date	Title	Volume	Page(s)	Notes
The Little Review	winter 1922	Anointment of our Well Dressed Critic or Why Waste the Eggs? Three-Dimensional Vista, by Hart Crane	9.2	23	drawing
Secession	January 1923	Poster	4	20	'Voyages I'
S4N	March–April 1923	Eight More Harvard Poets	4.25	unpaginated	
S4N	May–August 1923	America's Plutonic Ecstasies [with homage to E. E. Cummings]	4.26–9	unpaginated	
The Fugitive	August–September 1923	Stark Major	2.8	120	shortlisted: Poems for the Nashville Prize
S4N	September 1923–January 1924	Waldo Frank	5.30–1	unpaginated	drawing
Broom	January 1923	The Springs of Guilty Song	4.2	131–2	'Faustus and Helen' Part II
Secession	September 1923	For the Marriage of Faustus and Helen	6	1–4	missing Part II
Secession	winter 1923–24	For the Marriage of Faustus and Helen	7	1–4	Parts I, II and III.
The Dial	March 1924	Briefer Mention: review of Romer Wilson, *The Grand Tour*	76.3	198	unsigned
		Briefer Mention: review of Thomas Moult, *The Best Poems of 1922*		200	unsigned
The Little Review	spring–summer 1924	Possessions Recitative	10.1	18 19	
1924	July 1924	Sunday Morning Apples *To William Sommer*	1	1	
		Interludium To "*La Montagne,*" by Lachaise		2	

Journal	Date	Title	Volume	Page(s)	Notes
1924	December 1924	Voyages	4	119	'Voyages IV' as "Religious Gunman"
		Knitting Needles and Poppycock		136–9	
Aesthete, 1925	February 1925	Chanson	1.1	27	contested authorship; excluded from publication tallies
The Fugitive	September 1925	Legend	4.3	77	
		Paraphrase		78	
The Fugitive	December 1925	Lachrymae Christi	4.4	102–3	
The Little Review	spring–summer 1926	Voyages II	12.1	13–15	
		Voyages III			
		Voyages V			
		Voyages VI			
The Dial	May 1926	Again	80.5	370	'The Wine Menagerie' variant, ed. M. Moore
The Calendar of Modern Letters	July 1926	At Melville's Tomb	3.2	105	
		Passage		106–7	
		Praise for an Urn		108	
The Dial	September 1926	Repose of Rivers	81.3	204	
Poetry	October 1926	At Melville's Tomb	29.1	25	
		A Discussion with Hart Crane		34–41	
larus: the celestial visitor	March 1927	March	1.2	14	
The Calendar of Modern Letters	April–July 1927	Southern Cross	4.1	107–8	As 'Three Songs from The Bridge'
		National Winter Garden		109	
		Virginia		110	
transition	April 1927	O Carib Isle	1	101–2	
transition	June 1927	Cutty Sark	3	116–19	
		The Harbor Dawn: Brooklyn Heights		120–1	
The Dial	June 1927	To Brooklyn Bridge	82.6	489–90	

Journal	Date	Title	Volume	Page(s)	Notes
The Nation	29 June 1927	To Emily Dickinson	124.3234	718	
The New Republic	10 August 1927	Old Song	51.662	309	
The American Caravan	September 1927	Ave Maria	1	804–6	
Poetry	October 1927	Cutty Sark	31.1	27–30	
		O Carib Isle		30–1	
The Dial	October 1927	Powhatan's Daughter	83.4	329–32	'The Dance'
transition	October 1927	Van Winkle	7	128–9	
The Criterion	November 1927	The Tunnel	6.5	398–402	
transition	December 1927	East of Yucatan I: Island Quarry	9	132	
		East of Yucatan II: Royal Palm		133	
		East of Yucatan III: Overheard		134	
		East of Yucatan IV: El Idiota		135	
		East of Yucatan V: The Hour		136	'The Hurricane'
The Dial	February 1928	The Air Plant	84.2	140	
The Dial	September 1928	The Mermen	85.3	230	
Second American Caravan	1929	The River	2	113–18	
transition	February 1929	Moment Fugue	15	102	
The Dial	February 1929	Caricature of Slater Brown	86.2	122	
The Dial	April 1929	A Name for All	86.4	297	
transition	June 1929	Proclamation	16–17	back pages	
transition	November 1929	The Mango Tree	18	95	
The Saturday Review	15 March 1930	Cape Hatteras	6.34	821–2	
Poetry	April 1930	Eldorado	36.1	13–15	'Indiana'

Journal	Date	Title	Volume	Page(s)	Notes
transition	June 1930	To the Cloud Juggler: In Memoriam Harry Crosby	19–20	223	
Poetry	November 1930	To Brooklyn Bridge	37.2	108–9	Helen Haire Levinson Prize: $200 for *The Bridge*
The New Republic	29 July 1931	The Hurricane	67.869	277	
Poetry	April 1932	From Haunts of Prosperine, review of James Whaler, *Green River: A Poem for Rafinesque*	40.1	44–7	
The New Republic	8 June 1932	The Broken Tower	71.914	91	published posthumously but sent to Cowley before Crane's death
Contempo	5 July 1932	Dear Contempo Bacardi Spreads the Eagle's Wing	2.4	1 1	published posthumously but submitted before Crane's death

APPENDIX 3: TIMELINE OF CRANE'S KNOWN REJECTIONS, 1916–32

Journal	Title	Date	Source
1924	no known rejections	N/A	N/A
Aesthete, 1925	no known rejections	N/A	N/A
The American Caravan	no known rejections	N/A	N/A
Broom	Chaplinesque	3 November 1921	Crane to Kreymborg, 3 November 1921, box 1, folder 13, Loeb/Broom papers
Bruno's Bohemia	no known rejections	N/A	N/A
Bruno's Weekly	no known rejections	N/A	N/A
The Calendar of Modern Letters	Cutty Sark	19 March 1927	Rickword to Crane, 19 March 1926, box 7, Crane papers
	The Harbor Dawn	19 March 1927	Rickword to Crane, 19 March 1926, box 7, Crane papers
	O Carib Isle	13 April 1927	Rickword to Crane, 13 April 1927, box 7, Crane papers
Contempo	no known rejections	N/A	N/A
The Criterion	The Air Plant	16 July [1923?]	Crane, 'The Air Plant' MS, box 10, Crane papers
	Passage	21 October 1925	Crane to William Slater Brown, *O My Land*, pp. 206–7
	The Wine Menagerie	21 October 1925	Crane to William Slater Brown, *O My Land*, pp. 206–7, noted in Schwartz and Schweik, *Hart Crane: A Descriptive Bibliography* [hereafter S&S]
	To Brooklyn Bridge	12 August 1926	Crane to Frank, *O My Land*, p. 268

Journal	Title	Date	Source
The Dial	Garden Abstract	25 May 1920	Crane to Munson, *Letters*, pp. 38–9
	Porphyro in Akron	24 September 1920	Crane to Munson, *O My Land*, pp. 41–2
	Black Tambourine	24 February 1921	Crane to Munson, *Letters*, p. 55; noted in S&S
	The Bridge of Estador	20 April 1921	Crane to Munson, *O My Land*, pp. 60–1; noted in S&S
	Two Watercolours	16 May 1921	Crane to Munson, *O My Land*, pp. 61–2
	Chaplinesque	c. November 1921	noted in S&S, p. 93 [date inferred from *The Little Review* rejection]
	Poster ['Voyages I']	19 July 1922	Crane to Tate, *O My Land*, pp. 95–6; noted in S&S.
	Faustus and Helen	6 February 1923	Crane to Munson, *O My Land*, pp. 122–4; noted in S&S
	Stark Major	15 February 1923	Crane to Tate, *O My Land*, pp. 129–30; noted in S&S
	Low Hung Whang	21 November 1923	Crane to Gilbert Seldes, box 2, folder 49, *Dial*/Thayer papers [insincere submission]
	Recitative	18 March 1924	Alyse Gregory to Crane, box 2, folder 49, *Dial*/Thayer papers
	Belle Isle	18 March 1924	Alyse Gregory to Crane, box 2, folder 49, *Dial*/Thayer papers
	Possessions	18 March 1924	Alyse Gregory to Crane, box 2, folder 49, *Dial*/Thayer papers
	In a Court	18 March 1924	Alyse Gregory to Crane, box 2, folder 49, *Dial*/Thayer papers
	Lachrimae Christi	18 March 1924	Alyse Gregory to Crane, box 2, folder 49, *Dial*/Thayer papers
	Sunday Morning Apples	13 August 1925	Alyse Gregory to Crane, box 2, folder 49, *Dial*/Thayer papers
	Passage	10 December 1925	Moore to Crane, box 2, folder 49, *Dial*/Thayer papers
	At Melville's Tomb	14 January 1926	Moore to Crane, box 2, folders 50, *Dial*/Thayer papers
	Trough of Moon	28 October 1926	Moore to Crane, box 2, folder 50, *Dial*/Thayer papers
	Cutty Sark	27 November 1926	Moore to Crane, box 2, folder 49, *Dial*/Thayer papers
	San Cristobal [Ave Maria]	17 December 1926	Moore to Crane, box 2, folder 49, *Dial*/Thayer papers
	The Harbor Dawn	17 December 1926	Moore to Crane, box 2, folder 49, *Dial*/Thayer papers
	To Emily Dickinson	15 June 1927	Moore to Crane, box 2, folder 49, *Dial*/Thayer papers
	Van Winkle	14 July 1927	Gratia Sharpe to Crane, folder 49, *Dial*/Thayer papers
	The River	10 August 1927	Burke to Crane, box 2, folder 49, *Dial*/Thayer papers
	The Air Plant	18 October 1927	Moore to Crane, box 2, folder 49, *Dial*/Thayer papers
	The Tunnel		Moore to Crane, box 2, folder 49, *Dial*/Thayer papers
The Double Dealer	Chaplinesque	c. November 1921	noted in S&S, p. 93 [date inferred from *The Little Review* rejection]
	Review of G. B. Shaw *Methuselah* (title unknown)	1 October 1921	Crane to Munson, *O My Land*, p. 108.

Journal	Title	Date	Source
Fortune	Profile of Standard Oil's Walter Teagle; Article on George Washington Bridge	c. winter 1930–31	Russel Davenport commissioned and subsequently rejected the two articles after their completion; noted in Brown (ed.), *Robber Rocks*, p. 121, and Crane to Wright, *O My Land*, pp. 438–9
The Freeman	Garden Abstract	8 June 1920	Crane to Munson, *Letters*, p. 41.
The Fugitive	no known rejections	N/A	N/A
Gargoyle	Garden Abstract	c. June 1920	Crane to Munson, *Letters*, p. 40.
	Black Tambourine	21 November 1921	Crane to Munson, *Letters*, pp. 70–1.
Hound & Horn	The Tunnel	c. 1927.	Lincoln Kirstein, *Mosaic: Memoirs* (New York: Farrar, Straus & Giroux, 1994), p. 187
larus: the celestial visitor	no known rejections	N/A	N/A
The Liberator	To Portapovitch	12 February 1919	Crane to Zigrosser, box 9, folder 346, Zigrosser papers
The Little Review	North Labrador	c. autumn 1919	noted in S&S, p. 101
	My Grandmother's Love Letters	13 December 1919	Crane to Munson, *O My Land*, pp. 24–5; noted in S&S
	Porphyro in Akron		
	The River	c. September 1920	noted in S&S, pp. 103–4
	Voyages I	c. summer 1927	noted in S&S, p. 105
	Chaplinesque	c. summer 1922	noted in S&S, p. 110
		21 November 1921	Crane to Munson, *Letters*, p. 70; noted in S&S
The Masses	Voyages 2, 3, 5, 6	17 March 1926	Crane to Munson, *O My Land*, pp. 231–5
The Measure	no known rejections	N/A	N/A
The Modernist	no known rejections	N/A	N/A
The Modern School	no known rejections	N/A	N/A
The Nation	The River	18 July 1927	Crane to Winters, *O My Land*, pp. 343–4
The New Republic	Garden Abstract	8 June 1920	Crane to Munson, *Letters*, p. 41
	Van Winkle	14 March 1927	Crane to Tate, *O My Land*, pp. 325–6
	The Harbor Dawn	14 March 1927	Crane to Tate, *O My Land*, pp. 325–

Journal	Title	Date	Source
New York Post Literary Review	Chaplinesque	c. November 1921	noted in S&S, p. 93 [date inferred from *The Little Review* rejection]
The Pagan	To Portapovitch	12 February 1919	Crane to Zigrosser, box 9, folder 346, Zigrosser papers
Poetry	Moment Fugue	18 July 1928	Monroe to Crane, 18 July 1928, box 7, Crane papers
S4N	no known rejections	N/A	N/A
The Saturday Review	no known rejections	N/A	N/A
Secession	Belle Isle	c. January 1923	Crane to Munson, n.d. [c. January 1923], box 22, Crane/Munson correspondence
transition	no known rejections	N/A	N/A
The Virginia Quarterly	The River	September 1927	Editors to Crane, 10 September 1927, box 11, folder 24, *Virginia Quarterly* papers
	Southern Cross		Editors to Crane, 10 September 1927, box 11, folder 24, *Virginia Quarterly* papers
	National Winter Garden		Editors to Crane, 10 September 1927, box 11, folder 24, *Virginia Quarterly* papers
	Virginia		Editors to Crane, 10 September 1927, box 11, folder 24, *Virginia Quarterly* papers

BIBLIOGRAPHY

Unpublished Material

Brenner, Anita, 'Give to Caesar', box 13, Crane papers.
'Los Combates de Celaya', unsigned broadside, c. 1931, box 10, Crane papers.
'Corrido de Los Temblores..!', unsigned broadside, c. 1931, box 10, Crane papers.
Crane, Hart, 'Belle Isle', enclosed in a letter to Munson, n.d. [c. January 1923], box 22, Crane/Munson correspondence.
— *The Bridge* [galley proofs], box 1, folder 2, both in Crane Collection, Austin.
— *The Bridge* [MS], box 9, Crane papers.
— 'Cortez: The Enactment – and he put the Cross upon the people', box 23, folder 25, O'Malley papers.
— 'Cortez: The Enactment', box 9, Crane papers.
— *Key West: An Island Sheaf* [Lohf C1], box 9, Crane papers.
— *Key West* [Banner Note Book: 'Hart Crane's Poems, Original MS, GHC'], box 9, Crane papers.
— 'Nopal', box 2, folder 59, O'Malley papers.
— 'The Wine Menagerie', box 1, folder 1, Crane Collection, Austin.
Devlin, Denis, 'HC', MS33, 790/9 (1–3) Devlin papers.
Josephson, Matthew, 'Dada', box 13, folder 332, Josephson papers.
Munson, Gorham, '*Secession* Announcement', c. spring 1922, box 1, folder 1, Crane family papers.
'La Persecusion de Villa', unsigned broadside, c. 1931, box 10, Crane papers.

Thayer, Scofield, and James Sibley Watson, 'Statement of Intent', box 9, folder 309, *Dial*/Thayer papers.
— 'General Instructions for Editorial Department', box 9, folder 318, *Dial*/Thayer papers.
Wieners, John, 'Hart Crane, Harry Crosby, I see you going over the edge' (Detroit Artists' Workshop Press: Free Poems Among Friends, c. 1966–67).

Published Works

'1930 Honor Roll' [unsigned], *The Nation*, 132.3419 (17 January 1931), p. 8.
'About Us', *Poetry Foundation* [unsigned], <https://www.poetryfoundation.org/foundation/about> (accessed 10 December 2021).
Adjusto-Lite advertisement, 'The Lamp with a Clamp', *Popular Mechanics Advertising Section*, 5.38 (1922), p. 163.
'Advance in Price' [unsigned], *The Little Review*, 7.3 (1920), unpaginated.
Advertisement [unsigned], *The Pagan*, 2.12–3.1 (1918), back pages.
Ahmed, Sara, 'Slammed Doors', *Feminist Killjoys*, 17 March 2020, <https://feministkilljoys.com/2020/03/17/slammed-doors/> (accessed 27 May 2021).
Aiken, Conrad, 'Briefer Mention: *White Buildings*', review of Crane, *White Buildings* (1926), *The Dial*, 82.4 (1927), p. 432.
— 'The Function of Criticism', *Broom*, 1.1 (1921), pp. 33–8.
Aldington, Richard, 'The Imagists', *Greenwich Village*, 2.2 (15 July 1915), pp. 54–7.
— *The Imagists* (New York: Bruno's Chapbooks Special Series, 1915).
Alighieri, Dante, *The Divine Comedy: Purgatory*, ed. and trans. Mark Musa (London: Penguin, 1985).
Amin, Kadji, Amber Jamilla Musser and Roy Pérez, 'Queer Form: Aesthetics, Race, and the Violences of the Social', *ASAP/Journal*, 2.2 (2017), pp. 227–39.
Anderson, Forrest, 'For Hart Crane', *Contempo*, 2.4 (5 July 1932), p. 1.
Anderson, Margaret, *My Thirty Years War* (New York: Greenwood, 1930).
'Announcement No. 1' [unsigned], *The Pagan*, 2.10 (1918), back pages.
A.N.P., 'They Say Now That Jazz Beat the Kaiser', *The Dallas Express*, 21 May 1921, p. 1.
Antliff, Allan, 'Carl Zigrosser and *The Modern School*: Nietzsche, Art, and Anarchism', *Archives of American Art Journal*, 34.4 (1994), pp. 16–23.
Apollinaire, Guillaume, *Calligrammes*, trans. Anne Hyde Greet (Berkeley, CA: University of California Press, 1980).
Aragon, Louis, 'Bottle Found at Sea', trans. Matthew Josephson, *Secession*, 1 (spring 1922), pp. 4–7.
— 'Madame a sa Tour Monte . . .' *The Dial*, 72.1 (1922), pp. 20–8.
Arckens, Elien, '"In This Told-Backward Biography": Marianne Moore Against Survival in Her Queer Archival Poetry', *Women's Studies Quarterly*, 44.1/2 (2016), pp. 111–27.

Arens, Egmont, *Little Book of Greenwich Village* (New York: Washington Square Book Shop, 1918).
Assman, Aleida, 'T.S. Eliot's Reinvention of Tradition', in *T.S. Eliot and the Concept of Tradition*, ed. Giovanni Cianci and Jason Harding (Cambridge: Cambridge University Press, 2007), pp. 13–24.
Avrich, Paul, *The Modern School Movement: Anarchism and Education in the United States* (Oakland, CA: AK Press).
Baker, John, 'Commercial Sources for Hart Crane's "The River"', *Wisconsin Studies in Contemporary Literature*, 6.1 (1965), pp. 45–55.
Barnes, Djuna, *The Book of Repulsive Women: 8 Rhythms and 5 Drawings* (New York: Bruno's Chapbooks. 1915).
— *Nightwood* (New Directions: New York, 2006).
Baudelaire, Charles, *Artificial Paradises*, trans. Patricia Roseberry (Harrogate: Broadwater, 1999).
— *Baudelaire: His Prose and Poetry*, ed. T. R. Smith (New York: Boni and Liveright, 1919).
— *Les Paradis artificiels: Petits Poëmes en prose* (Paris: Editions Baudinière, 1900).
— *Le Spleen de Paris: Petits Poèmes en prose, with Fanfarlo*, trans. Francis Scarfe (London: Anvil, 2012).
— 'The Stranger', *Bruno's Weekly*, 1.13 (14 October 1915), p. 115.
— 'The Windows', *Bruno's Weekly*, 1.13 (14 October 1915), p. 26.
Bazin, Victoria, *Modernism Edited: Marianne Moore and* The Dial *Magazine* (Edinburgh: Edinburgh University Press, 2019).
Beals, Carleton, *Mexican Maze* (Philadelphia: J.B. Lippincott, 1931).
Beardsley, Aubrey, 'The Mysterious Rose Garden', *The Yellow Book*, 4 (1895), p. 14.
Beasley, Rebecca, 'Pound's New Criticism', *Textual Practice*, 24.4 (2010), pp. 649–68.
Beckett, Angela, 'The (Ill)ogic of Metaphor in Crane's *The Bridge*', *Textual Practice*, 21.1 (2011), pp. 57–80.
Bedient, Calvin, 'Grand Failure', review of Hart Crane's *Complete Poems and Selected Letters*, *Boston Review*, 32.2 (2006), <https://bostonreview.net/articles/bedient-on-hart-crane-langdon-hammer/> (accessed 12 April 2021).
Benét, William Rose, 'The Phoenix Nest', *The Saturday Review of Literature*, 3.36 (2 April 1927), p. 708.
— [as 'The Phoenician'], 'The Phoenix Nest', *The Saturday Review*, 4.23 (31 December 1927), p. 496
— 'Round About Parnassus', *Saturday Review of Literature* 6.50 (5 July 1930), p. 1176.
Benjamin, Walter, *Illuminations*, ed. Hannah Arendt, trans Harry Zohn (London: Pimlico, 1999).

Berlant, Lauren, 'Intimacy: A Special Issue', *Critical Inquiry*, 24.2 (1998), pp. 281–8.
Berryman, John, 'Elegy: Hart Crane', *Columbia Review*, 17.1 (1935), pp. 1–2.
Berthoff, Warner, *Hart Crane: A Reintroduction* (Minneapolis, MN: University of Minnesota Press, 1989).
Blake, William, *Selected Poems*, ed. G. E. Bentley (London: Penguin Classics, 2006).
Bloom, Harold, *The Anatomy of Influence: Literature as a Way of Life* (New Haven, CT: Yale University Press, 2011).
Boillet, F., 'The Methodological Study of Literature', *transition*, 1 (April 1927), pp. 57–8.
Bornstein, George, *Material Modernism: The Politics of the Page* (Cambridge: Cambridge University Press, 2001).
Boughn, Michael, *H. D.: A Bibliography, 1905–1990* (Charlottesville, VA: University of Virginia Press, 1993).
Bourdieu, Pierre, *The Field of Cultural Production* (Cambridge: Polity, 1996).
Bourgeois, Louise, 'Gaston Lachaise's Obsession', *Art Forum*, 30.8 (1922), pp. 85–7.
Bourne, Randolph S., 'Our Cultural Humility', *The Atlantic Monthly*, 114.3 (1914), pp. 503–7.
— 'Trans-national America', *The Atlantic Monthly*, 118.1 (1916), pp. 86–97.
Boyd, Ernest, 'Aesthete: Model 1924', *The American Mercury*, 1.1 (1924), pp. 51–6.
Bradshaw, Michael, 'Hedgehog Theory: How to Read a Romantic Fragment Poem', *Literature Compass*, 5 (2008), pp. 73–89.
Bratton, Francesca, 'Hart Crane "from this side": Edgell Rickword and *The Calendar of Modern Letters*', *PN Review*, 46.4 (2020), pp. 52–4.
— '"An Imagist in Amber": Hart Crane's Early Publications in Greenwich Village', *English*, 68.261 (2019), pp. 1–34.
— '"Knitting Needles and Poppycock": Hitherto Unknown Prose Pieces by Hart Crane and Bibliographic Clarifications', *Notes & Queries*, 66.2 (2019), pp. 313–14.
Bray, Stephen Guy, *Loving Verse: Poetic Influence as Erotic* (Toronto: University of Toronto Press, 2006).
Brenner, Anita, *Idols Behind Altars* (New York: Harcourt, Brace, 1929).
Breton, André, *Manifeste du surréalisme; Poisson soluble* (Paris: Editions du sagittaire chez Simon Kra, 1924).
Britzolakis, Christina, 'Making Modernism Safe for Democracy: *The Dial*', in *The Oxford Critical and Cultural History of Modernist Magazines, Volume II: North America 1894–1960*, ed. Peter Brooker and Andrew Thacker (Oxford: Oxford University Press, 2012), pp. 85–103.

Brogan, Jacqueline Vaught, *Part of the Climate: American Cubist Poetry* (Berkeley, CA: University of California Press, 1991).
Brooker, Peter, 'Harmony, Discord and Difference', in *The Oxford Critical and Cultural History of Modernist Magazines, Volume I: Britain and Ireland, 1880–1955*, ed. Peter Brooker and Andrew Thacker (Oxford: Oxford University Press, 2009), pp. 314–38.
Brooker, Peter, and Andrew Thacker (eds), *The Oxford Critical and Cultural History of Modernist Magazines, Volumes I–III* (Oxford: Oxford University Press, 2009–16).
Brooks, Charles S., *Hints to Pilgrims* (New Haven, CT: Yale University Press, 1921).
Brown, Susan Jenkins (ed.), *Robber Rocks: Letters and Memories of Hart Crane, 1923–1932* (Middletown, CT: Wesleyan University Press, 1969).
Brunner, Edward, *Splendid Failure: Hart Crane and the Making of "The Bridge"* (Chicago: University of Illinois Press, 1985).
Bruno, Guido, *Adventures in American Bookshops, Antique Stores and Auction Rooms* (Detroit: The Douglas Book Shop, 1922).
— advertisement for poetry reading, *Greenwich Village*, 2.1 (23 June 1915), p. 41.
— advertisement for *Bruno's Bohemia*, 1.1 (1918), back pages.
— 'Bohemia Everywhere', *Bruno's Bohemia*, 1.1 (1918), p. 3.
— 'Bohemia Over Here', *Bruno's Bohemia*, 1.1 (1918), p. 2.
— 'Bohemia Over There', *Bruno's Bohemia*, 1.1 (1918), p. 1.
— 'Books and Magazines of the Week', *Greenwich Village*, 2.2 (15 July 1915), p. 66.
— 'Books and Magazines of the Week', *Bruno's Weekly*, 1.15 (30 October 1915), p. 162.
— 'Books and Magazines of the Week', *Bruno's Weekly*, 1.22 (18 December 1915), pp. 298–9.
— *Fragments from Greenwich Village* (New York: Guido Bruno, 1921).
— 'Frontispiece to Greenwich Village', *Greenwich Village*, 2.1 (23 June 1915).
— 'Greenwich Village in Modern Fiction', *Bruno's Weekly*, 1.16 (6 November 1915), p. 169.
— 'Greenwich Village: The Romance of One Night', *Bruno's Weekly*, 1.13 (14 October 1915), p. 127
— 'In Our Village: Djuna's Exhibit', *Bruno's Weekly*, 1.14 (21 October 1915), pp. 142–3
— 'In Our Village: Spring and Poets', *Bruno's Weekly*, 2.14 (1 April 1916), pp. 593–4.
— 'Les Confidences: Being the Confessions of a Self-Made American', *Bruno's Weekly*, 2.18 (29 April 1916), pp. 647–53.
Bullough, Vern L. (ed.), *Before Stonewall: Activists for Gay and Lesbian Rights in Context* (Abingdon: Routledge, 2008).

Bulson, Eric, *Little Magazine, World Form* (New York: Columbia University Press, 2016).
Butterfield, R. W., *The Broken Arc: A Study of Hart Crane* (Edinburgh: Oliver and Boyd, 1969).
Bynner, Witter, 'Poems and Translations', translations of Charles Vildrac, 'An Inn' and 'A Castle in Spain', *The Dial*, 68.4 (1920), pp. 473–8.
Cahill, Daniel, *Harriet Monroe* (New York: Twayne, 1973).
Cann, Louise G., 'Lachrimae Christi', *The Pagan*, 4.6 (1919), pp. 36–7.
Capildeo, Vahni, *Skin Can Hold* (Manchester: Carcanet, 2019).
Carr, Helen, *The Verse Revolutionaries: Ezra Pound, H. D., and the Imagists* (London: Jonathan Cape, 2009).
Carroll, Robert, and Stephen Prickett (eds), *The Bible: Authorized King James Version* (Oxford: Oxford University Press, 1997).
Caws, Mary Ann (ed.), *Manifesto: A Century of Isms* (Lincoln, NE: University of Nebraska Press, 2000).
Chase, Stuart, *Mexico: A Study of Two Americas* (New York: Macmillan, 1931).
Chauncey, George, *Gay New York: Gender, Urban Culture, and the Makings of the Gay Male World, 1890–1940* (New York: Basic Books, 1994).
Chekhov, Anton, 'Dushitka', *The Pagan*, 2.5 (1917), pp. 3–11.
Chesterton, G. K., 'A Song of Gifts to God', *Bruno's Weekly*, 2.9 (26 February 1916), p. 503.
Childe, Stark, 'Tale of a Wooden Leg', *1924*, 1 (July 1924), pp. 25–9.
Chinitz, David E., *T. S. Eliot and the Cultural Divide* (Chicago: University of Chicago Press, 2005).
Cianci, Giovanni, and Jason Harding, *T.S. Eliot and the Concept of Tradition* (Cambridge: Cambridge University Press, 2007).
Clearfield, Andrew Mark, *These Fragments I Have Shored: Collage and Montage in Early Modernist Poetry* (Ann Arbor, MI: UMI Research Press, 1984).
Cocks, H. G., *Classified: The Secret History of the Personal Column* (London: Random House, 2009).
Cocteau, Jean, 'Cock and Harlequin', *The Dial*, 71.1 (1921), pp. 52–62.
'Contributor's Notes' [unsigned], *S4N*, 4.26–29 (1923), pp. 50–1.
'Contributors' Notes' [unsigned], *The Little Review*, 12.1 (spring–summer 1926), p. 2.
Corn, Alfred, *Stake: Selected Poems, 1972–1992* (Washington, DC: Counterpoint, 1999).
Costello, Bonnie, 'Editing *The Dial*', in *Selected Letters of Marianne Moore*, ed. Bonnie Costello (London: Penguin, 1997).
— *Marianne Moore: Imaginary Possessions* (Cambridge, MA: Harvard University Press, 1981).
Cowley, Malcolm, 'Anthology', *The Little Review*, 12.1 (1926), pp. 33–6.

— *Blue Juniata: Poems 1919–1929* (New York: Jonathan Cape and Harrison Smith, 1929).
— *Conversations with Malcolm Cowley*, ed. Thomas Daniel Young (Jackson, MS: University of Mississippi Press, 1986).
— 'Day Coach', *Secession*, 1 (spring 1922), pp. 1–5.
— *Exile's Return: A Literary Odyssey of the 1920s* (London: Penguin, 1994).
— 'Munsonia', *Contempo*, 1.15 (1 January 1932), p. 1.
— 'Poem', *Secession*, 3 (August 1922), p. 13.
— 'A Preface to Hart Crane', review of *The Bridge*, *New Republic*, 62.803 (23 April 1930), pp. 276–7.
Cowley, Malcolm, and Waldo Frank, 'Communications on Seriousness and Dada', *1924*, 4 (December 1924), pp. 140–2.
Crane, Hart [as Harold Hart Crane], 'Annunciations', *The Pagan*, 1.12–2.1 (1917), p. 11.
— 'The Air Plant', *The Dial*, 84.2 (1928), p. 140.
— 'The Air Plant', in *Modern American Poetry: A Critical Anthology*, ed. Louis Untermeyer (New York: Harcourt, Brace and World, 1930), p. 533.
— 'America's Plutonic Ecstasies [with homage to e. e. cummings]', *S4N*, 4.26–29 (1923), pp. 50–1.
— 'Anointment of Our Well Dressed Critic or Why Waste the Eggs? Three-Dimensional Vista, by Hart Crane', *The Little Review*, 9.2 (1922), p. 23.
— 'At Melville's Tomb', *The Calendar of Modern Letters*, 3.2 (1926), p. 105.
— 'At Melville's Tomb', *Poetry*, 29.1 (1926), p. 25.
— 'At Melville's Tomb', in *Modern American Poetry: A Critical Anthology*, ed. Louis Untermeyer (New York: Harcourt, Brace and World, 1930), p. 534.
— 'Ave Maria', *The American Caravan: A Yearbook of American Literature*, 1 (September 1927), pp. 804–6.
— 'Bacardi Spreads the Eagle's Wing', *Contempo*, 2.4 (5 July 1832), p. 1.
— 'The Bathers', *The Pagan*, 2.8 (1917), p. 19.
— 'Black Tambourine', *The Double Dealer*, 1.6 (1921), p. 232.
— *The Bridge* (New York: Horace Liveright, 1930).
— *The Bridge* (Paris: Black Sun, 1930).
— *The Bridge: Annotated*, ed. Lawrence Kramer (New York: Fordham, 2011).
— *The Bridge: Uncollected*, ed. Ben Mazer (Asheville: Madhat, 2015).
— 'Briefer Mention: Romer Wilson, *The Grand Tour*', review of Romer Wilson, *The Grand Tour of Alphonse Marichaud* (1923), *The Dial*, 76.3 (1924), p. 198.
— 'Briefer Mention: Thomas Moult, *The Best Poems of 1922*', review of Thomas Moult, *The Best Poems of 1922* (1923), *The Dial*, 76.3 (1924), p. 200.
— 'The Broken Tower', *The New Republic,* 71.914 (8 June 1932), p. 91.
— [as 'Harold Hart Crone'], 'C33', *Bruno's Weekly*, 3.15 (23 September 1916), p. 1008.

— 'Cape Hatteras', *The Saturday Review*, 6.34 (15 March 1930), p. 821.
— 'Caricature of Slater Brown', illustration, portrait of William Slater Brown, *The Dial*, 86.2 (1929), p. 123.
— [as Harold Hart Crane], 'Carmen de Boheme', *Bruno's Bohemia*, 1.1 (1918), p. 2.
— 'Carrier Letter', *The Pagan*, 2.12–3.1 (1918), pp. 34–5.
— 'The Case Against Nietzsche', *The Pagan*, 2.12–3.1 (1918), pp. 34–5.
— 'Chaplinesque', *Gargoyle*, 1.6 (1921), p. 24.
— *Collected Poems*, ed. Waldo Frank (New York: Horace Liveright, 1933).
— *Collected Poems*, ed. Waldo Frank (London: Boriswood, 1938).
— *Complete Poems*, ed. Marc Simon (New York: Liveright, 2001).
— *Complete Poems and Selected Letters*, ed. Langdon Hammer (New York: Library of America, 2006).
— 'Cutty Sark', *transition*, 3 (June 1927), pp. 116–19.
— 'Cutty Sark', *Poetry*, 31.1 (1927), pp. 27–30.
— 'Cutty Sark', in *The New Poetry: An Anthology of Twentieth-Century Verse in English*, ed. Harriet Monroe and Alice Corbin Henderson (New York: Harcourt, 1930), p. 106.
— 'Dear Contempo', *Contempo*, 2.4 (5 July 1932), p. 1.
— 'East of Yucatan' ['Island Quarry', 'Royal Palm', 'Overheard', El Idiota', 'The Hour'], *transition*, 9 (December 1927), pp. 132–6.
— 'Echoes', *The Pagan*, 2.6–7 (1917), p. 39.
— 'Editorial Note to a Patriotic Poem', *The Pagan*, 2.12–3.1 (1918), p. 28.
— 'Eight More Harvard Poets', *S4N*, 4.25 (1923), pp. 12–14.
— 'El Idiota', *transition*, 9 (December 1927), p. 135.
— 'Eldorado', *Poetry*, 36.1 (1930), pp. 13–15.
— [as Harold Hart Crane] 'Fear', *The Pagan*, 1.12–2.1 (1917), p. 11.
— [as Harold Hart Crane] 'Fear', in *A Pagan Anthology* (New York: Pagan Publishing Company, 1918), p. 18.
— 'The Fernery', *Gargoyle*, 1.4 (1922), p. 19.
— 'For the Marriage of Faustus and Helen', *Secession*, 6 (September 1923), pp. 1–4.
— 'For the Marriage of Faustus and Helen', *Secession*, 7 (winter 1923–24), pp. 1–4.
— 'For the Springs of Guilty Song', *Broom*, 4.2 (1923), pp. 131–2.
— 'Forgetfulness', *The Pagan*, 3.4–5 (1918), p. 15.
— 'Forgetfulness', in *A Second Pagan Anthology*, ed. Joseph Kling (New York: Pagan Publishing Company, 1919), p. 17.
— 'From Haunts of Proserpine', review of James Whaler, *Green River: A Poem for Rafinesque* (1931), *Poetry*, 40.1 (1932), pp. 44–7.
— 'Four Poems by Hart Crane' ['Eternity', 'The Return', 'And Bees of Paradise', 'A Traveller Born'], *The New Republic*, 74.950 (15 February 1933), pp. 11–15.
— 'Garden Abstract', *The Little Review*, 7.3 (1920), p. 78.

— 'General Aims and Theories', in *The Complete Poems and Selected Letters of Hart Crane*, ed. Langdon Hammer (New York: Library of America, 2006), pp. 160–4.
— 'The Ghetto and Other Poems', review of Lola Ridge, *The Ghetto and Other Poems* (1918), *The Pagan*, 3.9 (1919), pp. 54–6.
— 'The Great Western Plains', *Gargoyle*, 1.3 (1922), p. 7.
— 'The Harbor Dawn: Brooklyn Heights', *transition*, 3 (June 1927), pp. 120–1.
— 'The Harbor Dawn', in *An Anthology of Younger Poets*, ed. Oliver Wells (Philadelphia: Centaur, 1932), pp. 1–2.
— 'Sr. Hart Crane, distinguido literato norteamericano, que se encuentra en México en viaje de estudio', unsigned anonymous interview, *El Universal*, 18 April 1931.
— 'The Hive', *The Pagan*, 1.11 (1917), p. 36.
— 'The Hour', *transition*, 9 (December 1927), p. 136.
— 'The Hurricane', *The New Republic*, 67.869 (29 July 1931), p. 277.
— 'In Shadow', *The Little Review*, 4.8 (1917), p. 50.
— 'Interior', *The Modernist*, 1.1 (1919), p. 28.
— 'Interludium (to "La Montagne" by Lachaise)', *1924*, 1 (July 1924), p. 2.
— 'Island Quarry', *transition*, 9 (December 1927), p. 132.
— 'Joyce and Ethics', *The Little Review*, 5.3 (1918), p. 65.
— [as 'Religious Gunman'], 'Knitting Needles and Poppycock', *1924*, 4 (December 1924), pp. 136–9.
— 'Lachrymae Christi', *The Fugitive*, 4.4 (1925), pp. 102–3.
— 'Legend', *The Fugitive*, 4.3 (1925), p. 77.
— 'Legende', *The Modernist*, 1.1 (1919), p. 28.
— *The Letters of Hart Crane 1916–1932*, ed. Brom Weber (New York: Hermitage House, 1952).
— *The Literary Manuscripts of Hart Crane*, ed. Kenneth Lohf (Columbus, OH: Ohio State University Press, 1967).
— 'Locutions des Pierrots', *The Double Dealer*, 1.3 (1921), p. 82.
— 'The Mango Tree', *transition*, 18 (November 1929), p. 95.
— 'March', *larus: the celestial visitor*, 1.2 (1927), p. 14.
— 'The Mermen', *The Dial*. 85.3 (1928), p. 230.
— 'The Mermen', in *Anthology of Magazine Verse for 1929 and Yearbook of American Poetry*, ed. William Stanley Braithwaite (New York: George Scully, 1929), p. 75.
— 'Minna and Myself', review of Maxwell Bodenheim, *Minna and Myself* (1918), *The Pagan*, 3.10 (1919), p. 59.
— 'Modern Craft', *The Pagan*, 2.9 (1918), p. 37.
— 'Modern Poetry', in *Revolt in the Arts: A Survey of the Creation, Distribution and Appreciation of Art in America*, ed. Oliver Martin Sayler (New York: Brentano's, 1930), pp. 294–8.

- 'Moment Fugue', *transition*, 15 (February 1929), p. 102.
- 'My Grandmother's Love Letters', *The Dial*, 68.4 (1920), p. 457.
- 'A Name for All', *The Dial*, 86.4 (1929), p. 297.
- 'A Name for All', in *Anthology of Magazine Verse for 1929 and Yearbook of American Poetry*, ed. William Stanley Braithwaite (New York: George Scully, 1929), pp. 74–5.
- 'National Winter Garden', *The Calendar of Modern Letters*, 4.1 (1927), p. 109.
- 'North Labrador', *The Modernist*, 1.1 (1919), p. 28.
- 'A Note on H.W. Mimms [sic]', *The Little Review*, 7.3 (1920), p. 60.
- 'Note on the Paintings of David Siqueiros', *La Exposición Siqueiros* (Mexico City: Casino Español, 1932).
- 'O Carib Isle', *transition*, 1 (April 1927), pp. 101–2.
- 'O Carib Isle', *Poetry*, 31.1 (1927), pp. 30–1.
- 'O Carib Isle', in *Anthologie de la nouvelle poésie américaine*, ed. and trans. Eugene Jolas (Paris: Simon Kra, 1928), pp. 46–7.
- *O My Land, My Friends: The Selected Letters of Hart Crane*, ed. Langdon Hammer and Brom Weber (New York: Four Walls Eight Windows, 1997).
- 'October–November', *The Pagan*, 1.7–8 (1916), p. 33.
- 'October–November', in *A Pagan Anthology* (New York: Pagan Publishing Company, 1918), p. 18.
- 'Old Song', *The New Republic*, 51.662 (10 August 1927), p. 309.
- 'Overheard', *transition*, 9 (December 1927), p. 134.
- 'Paraphrase', *The Fugitive*, 4.3 (1925), p. 78.
- 'Passage', *The Calendar of Modern Letters* 3.2 (July 1926), pp. 106–07.
- 'Pastorale', *The Dial*, 71.4 (1921), p. 422.
- 'A Persuasion', *The Measure*, 1.7 (1921), p. 14.
- 'Poem' ['O Carib Isle'], in *In transition: A Paris Anthology*, ed. Noel Riley Fitch (London: Anchor, 1990), p. 82.
- 'Porphyro in Akron', *The Double Dealer*, 2.8–9 (1921), p. 53.
- 'Possessions', *The Little Review*, 10.1 (1924), p. 18.
- 'Poster' ['Voyages I'], *Secession*, 4 (January 1923), p. 20
- 'Postscript', *The Pagan*, 2.12–3.1 (1918), p. 20.
- 'Power: Cape Hatteras', in *Modern American Poetry: A Critical Anthology*, ed. Louis Untermeyer (New York: Harcourt, Brace and World, 1958), p. 528.
- 'Powhatan's Daughter' ['The Dance'], *The Dial*, 83.4 (1927), pp. 329–32.
- 'Powhatan's Daughter' ['The Dance'], in *Anthology of Magazine Verse for 1928 and Yearbook of American Poetry*, ed. William Stanley Braithwaite (New York: Harold Vinal, 1928), pp. 84–7.
- '"Powhatan's Daughter" from *The Dance*', in *Great Poems of the English Language: An Anthology*, ed. W. A. Briggs and William Rose Benét (New York: Tudor Publishing, 1928), pp. 1444–6.

— 'Praise for an Urn: to E.N', *The Dial*, 72.6 (1922), p. 606.
— 'Praise for an Urn: to E.N', *The Calendar of Modern Letters*, 3.2 (1926), p. 108.
— 'Praise for an Urn: In Memoriam Ernest Nelson', in *An Anthology of Younger Poets*, ed. Oliver Wells (Philadelphia: Centaur, 1932), p. 7.
— *The Prose Manuscripts*, ed. Joseph Katz, *The Yearbook of American Bibliographical and Textual Studies*, 2 (Columbia, SC: University of South Carolina Press, 1972).
— 'Recitative', *The Little Review*, 10.1 (1924), p. 19.
— 'Repose of Rivers', *The Dial*, 81.3 (1926), p. 204.
— 'Repose of Rivers', in *The New Poetry: An Anthology of the Twentieth-Century Verse in English*, ed. Harriet Monroe and Alice Corbin Henderson (New York: Harcourt, 1930), p. 104.
— 'The River', *American Caravan: A Yearbook of American Literature*, 2 (1928), pp. 804–6.
— 'Royal Palm', *transition*, 9 (December 1927), p. 133.
— 'Royal Palm', in *Modern American Poetry and Modern British Poetry*, ed. Louis Untermeyer (New York: Harcourt, 1930), p. 533.
— 'Sherwood Anderson', review of Sherwood Anderson, *Winesburg, Ohio* (1919), *The Pagan*, 4.5 (1919), pp. 60–1.
— 'Sherwood Anderson', *The Double Dealer*, 2.7 (1921), pp. 42–5.
— 'Southern Cross', *The Calendar of Modern Letters*, 4.1 (1927), pp. 107–8.
— 'Southern Cross', in *An Anthology of Younger Poets*, ed. Oliver Wells (Philadelphia: Centaur, 1932), p. 5.
— 'Stark Major', *The Fugitive*, 2.8 (1923), p. 120.
— 'Sunday Morning Apples *To William Sommer*', *1924*, 1 (July 1924), p. 1.
— 'Three Songs from *The Bridge*', *The Calendar*, 4.1 (1927), pp. 107–10.
— 'To Brooklyn Bridge', *The Dial*, 82.6 (1927), pp. 489–90.
— 'To Brooklyn Bridge', *Poetry*, 37.2 (1930), pp. 108–9.
— 'To Brooklyn Bridge', in *The New Poetry: An Anthology of the Twentieth-Century Verse in English*, ed. Harriet Monroe and Alice Corbin Henderson (New York: Harcourt, 1930), pp. 103–4.
— 'To the Cloud Juggler', *transition*, 19–20 (June 1930), p. 223.
— 'To Emily Dickinson', *The Nation*, 124.3234 (29 June 1927), p. 718.
— 'To Emily Dickinson', in *Anthology of Magazine Verse for 1927 and Yearbook of American Poetry*, ed. William Stanley Braithwaite (Boston: B. J. Brimmer, 1927), p. 78.
— 'To J. H.', *The Little Review*, 9.1 (1922), p. 39.
— 'To Potapovitch [*sic*] (de la Ballet Russe)', *The Modern School*, 6.3 (1919), p. 80.
— 'To *The Pagan*', *The Pagan*, 1.6 (1916), p. 43.
— 'Tragi-Comique', *The Pagan*, 2.12–3.1 (1918), pp. 54–6.

— 'The Tunnel', *The Criterion*, 6.5 (1927), pp. 398–404.
— 'The Tunnel', in *Modern American Poetry and Modern British Poetry*, ed. Louis Untermeyer (New York: Harcourt, 1930), p. 529.
— 'The Tunnel', in *Twentieth Century Poetry*, ed. John Drinkwater, Henry Seidel Canby and William Rose Benét (New York: Houghton Mifflin, 1929), pp. 573–7.
— 'The Urn' ['By Nilus Once I Knew', 'The Circumstance', 'Enrich My Resignation', 'Havana Rose', 'Imperator Victus', 'Phantom Bark', 'A Postscript', 'Purgatorio', 'Reliquary', 'Reply', The Sad Indian', 'The Visible the Untrue'], *Poetry*, 41.4 (1933), pp. 177–96.
— 'Van Winkle', *transition*, 7 (October 1927), pp. 128–9.
— 'Van Winkle', in *Modern American Poetry: A Critical Anthology*, ed. Louis Untermeyer (New York: Harcourt, Brace and World, 1930), p. 521.
— 'Virginia', *The Calendar of Modern Letters*, 4.1 (1927), p. 110.
— 'Voyages' ['Voyages IV'], *1924*, 4 (December 1924), p. 119.
— 'Voyages' ['Voyages II'], in *An Anthology of Younger Poets*, ed. Oliver Wells (Philadelphia: Centaur, 1932), p. 4.
— 'Voyages' ['Voyages II', 'III', 'V', 'VI'], *The Little Review*, 12.1 (1926), pp. 13–15.
— 'Voyages' ['Voyages V'], in *An Anthology of Younger Poets*, ed. Oliver Wells (Philadelphia: Centaur, 1932), p. 4.
— 'Voyages II', in *Modern American Poetry: A Critical Anthology*, ed. Louis Untermeyer (New York: Harcourt, Brace and World, 1930), p. 519.
— 'Voyages II', in *The New Poetry: An Anthology of Twentieth-Century Verse in English*, ed. Harriet Monroe and Alice Corbin Henderson (New York: Harcourt, 1930), p. 105.
— 'Voyages II', in *The Book of Living Verse: English and American Poetry from the Thirteenth Century to the Present Day*, ed. Louis Untermeyer (New York: Harcourt, Brace, 1932), pp. 610–11.
— 'Voyages VI', in *Modern American Poetry: A Critical Anthology*, ed. Louis Untermeyer (New York: Harcourt, Brace and World, 1930), p. 520.
— 'Voyages VI', in *The Third Book of Modern Verse*, ed. Jessie B. Rittenhouse (New York: Houghton, 1927), pp. 30–1.
— 'Waldo Frank' [sketch], *S4N*, 5.30–31 (1923–24), p. 4.
— *White Buildings* (New York: Boni and Liveright, 1926).
Crane, Hart, Grace Hart Crane, C. A. Crane et al., *Letters of Hart Crane and his Family*, ed. Thomas S. W. Lewis (New York: Columbia University Press, 1973).
Crane, Hart, and Harriet Monroe, 'A Discussion with Hart Crane', *Poetry*, 29.1 (1926), pp. 34–41.
Crane, Hart, and Marianne Moore, 'Again', *The Dial*, 80.5 (1926), p. 370.

— 'Again', in *An Anthology of Magazine Verse for 1926 and Yearbook of American Poetry*, ed. William Stanley Braithwaite (Boston: B. J. Brimmer, 1926), p. 102.
Crane, Hart, William Salisbury, John W. Draper, Jubal Agmenon and Allan Norton, 'Oscar Wilde: Poems in His Praise', *Bruno's Weekly*, 3.15 (23 September 1916), p. 1008.
Crosby, Harry, 'Observation Post', *transition*, 16–17 (June 1929), pp. 197–205.
Curry, Routledge, 'Veni, Vidi, Vici', *The Pagan*, 1.11 (1917), p. 37.
D'Annunzio, Gabriele, 'Francesca da Rimini', *The Pagan*, 1.7–8 (1916), pp. 3–30.
— 'The Hero', *The Pagan*, 3.2 (1919), pp. 12–15.
Davies, Arthur B., 'The Statement', in *Documents of the 1913 Armory Show: The Electrifying Moment of Modern Art's American Debut* (Tuscon, AZ: Hol Art Books, 2009), pp. 1–2.
Davies, Catherine A., *Whitman's Queer Children* (London: Bloomsbury Academic, 2012).
De Quincey, Thomas, *Confessions of an English Opium Eater and Other Writings* (Oxford: Oxford University Press, 2013).
'Death of a Poet' [unsigned], *The New Republic*, 70.910 (11 May 1932), pp. 340–2.
Delpar, Helen, *The Enormous Vogue of Things Mexican: Cultural Relations between the United States and Mexico, 1920–1935* (Tuscaloosa, AL: University of Alabama Press, 1992).
'Dernière Heure' [unsigned], *Le Coeur à Barbe*, 1.1 (1922), back cover.
di Prima, Diane, *Revolutionary Letters* (San Francisco: City Lights, 2021).
Dickinson, Emily, *Complete Poems*, ed. Thomas H. Johnson (London: Faber and Faber, 1975).
Dijkstra, Bram, *Cubism, Stieglitz and the Early Poetry of William Carlos Williams* (Princeton, NJ: Princeton University Press, 1978).
Dismorr, Jessie, 'London Notes', *Blast*, 2 [War Number] (1915), p. 66.
Douglas, Alfred, 'To Oscar Wilde', *Bruno's Weekly*, 3.15 (23 September 1916), p. 1009.
Drinkwater, John, and William Rose Benét (eds), *Twentieth Century Poetry* (New York: Houghton Mifflin, 1929).
Eastman, Max, 'The Cult of Unintelligibility', *Harper's Magazine*, 158.947 (1929), pp. 632–9.
— 'Poets Talking to Themselves', *Harper's Magazine*, 163.977 (1931), pp. 563–74.
Edelman, John, 'Ferrer School Entertainments', *The Modern School*, 6.5 (1919), pp. 81–2.
Edelman, Lee, *Transmemberment of Song: Hart Crane's Anatomies* (Stanford, CA: Stanford University Press, 1987).

Edwards, Robert, 'Greenwich Village Today', in Kelsey McKinney, 'In the Galleries: A Map of Greenwich Village from the *Greenwich Village Quill*', *Ransom Center Magazine*, <https://sites.utexas.edu/ransomcentermagazine/2012/01/05/in-the-galleries-a-map-of-greenwich-village-from-the-greenwich-village-quill/> (accessed 14 May 2018).
Eliot, T. S., *Complete Poems and Plays* (London: Faber and Faber, 1969).
— *The Letters of T. S. Eliot, Volume 3: 1926–1927*. ed. Valerie Eliot, John Haffenden and Hugh Haughton (New Haven, CT: Yale University Press, 2012),
— 'The Love Song of J. Alfred Prufrock', *Poetry*, 6.3 (1915), pp. 130–5.
— 'The Possibility of a Poetic Drama', *The Dial*, 69.5 (1920), pp. 441–7.
— *The Waste Land* (New York: Boni and Liveright, 1922).
— *The Waste Land* (London: Hogarth Press, 1923).
English, Richard, *Ernie O'Malley: IRA Intellectual* (Oxford: Oxford University Press, 1998).
Fawcett, James Waldo, 'Poems and Other Things', *Bruno's Weekly*, 3.6 (22 July 1916), p. 860.
Field, Andrew, *Djuna: The Life and Times of Djuna Barnes* (New York: G. P. Putnam's Sons, 1983).
Field, Mike, 'Reclaiming Hart Crane's "Splendid Failure"', *Arts and Sciences* (fall 2011) <http://krieger.jhu.edu/magazine/2011/10/reclaiming-hart-cranes-splendid-failure/> (accessed 5 December 2015).
Fitzpatrick, Orla, 'From Mexico to Mayo: Ernie O'Malley, Paul Strand and Photographic Modernism', in *Modern Ireland and Revolution: Ernie O'Malley in Context*, ed. Cormac O'Malley (Newbridge: Irish Academic Press, 2016), pp. 28–41.
Flint, F. S., 'Imagisme', *Poetry*, 1.6 (1913), pp. 198–200.
— 'Springs', *Greenwich Village*, 2.2 (15 July 1915), p. 59.
Ford, Mark, *Six Children* (London: Faber and Faber, 2011).
— *This Dialogue of One: Essays on Poets from John Donne to Joan Murray* (London: Eyewear, 2014).
Frank, Waldo, *America Hispana, a Portrait and a Prospect* (New York: Charles Scribner and Sons, 1931).
— 'For the Declaration of War', *Secession*, 7 (winter 1923–24), pp. 5–14.
— 'Un gran poeta Americano: Introducción a Hart Crane', *SUR*, 3.8 (1933), pp. 27–59.
— 'An Introduction to Hart Crane', *The New Republic*, 74.950 (15 February 1933), pp. 11–15.
— 'The Poetry of Hart Crane', *The New Republic*, 50.641 (16 March 1927), pp. 116–17.
— 'Seriousness and Dada', *1924*, 3 (September 1924), pp. 70–3.
Front matter [unsigned], *The Measure*, 1.1 (1921).

Front matter [unsigned], *Iarus: the celestial visitor*, 1.2 (1927).
Front matter [unsigned], *Broom*, 1.1 (1921).
Front cover [unsigned], *The Masses*, 1.1 (1911).
Gabriel, Daniel, *Hart Crane and the Modernist Epic: Canon and Genre Formation in Crane, Pound, Eliot and Williams* (Basingstoke: Palgrave, 2007).
Gallup, Donald, *T.S. Eliot: A Bibliography* (London: Faber and Faber, 1969).
Giles, Paul, *Hart Crane: The Contexts of 'The Bridge'* (Cambridge: Cambridge University Press, 1986).
Ginsberg, Allen, 'Hart Crane', *Columbia Review*, 27.2 (1946), pp. 17–18.
Golding, Alan, '*The Dial*, *The Little Review* and the Dialogics of Modernism', *Little Magazines and Modernism*, 15.1 (2005), pp. 42–55.
Gorman, Herbert, 'Tradition and Experiment in Modern Poetry', review of Crane, *White Buildings* (1926), *New York Times*, 27 March 1927, p. 2.
Group Mu, 'Collages', *Revue d'aesthetique*, 1.3–4 (Paris, 1978).
Guttenplan, D. D., *"The Nation": A Biography* (New York: Nation Publishing, 2015).
Hall, Susanne, 'Hart Crane in Mexico: The End of a New World Poetics', *Mosaic: a journal for the interdisciplinary study of literature*, 461.1 (2013), pp. 135–49.
Hammer, Langdon, *Hart Crane and Allen Tate: Janus-Faced Modernism* (Princeton, NJ: Princeton University Press, 1993).
Hamsun, Knut, 'The Conqueror', *The Pagan*, 1.3 (1916), pp. 3–10.
Hankel, Walter S. [*nom de plume*], 'Chanson', *Aesthete, 1925*, 1.1 (1925), p. 27.
Harding, Jason, *The Criterion: Cultural Politics and Periodical Networks in Interwar Britain* (Oxford: Oxford University Press, 2002).
— 'T. S. Eliot's Shakespeare', *Essays in Criticism*, 62.2 (2012), pp. 160–77.
— (ed.), *T. S. Eliot in Context* (Cambridge: Cambridge University Press, 2011).
Harris, Frank, 'Oscar Wilde', *Bruno's Weekly*, 3.1 (17 June 1916), pp. 780–1.
'Hart Crane: Author of *The Bridge*' [unsigned], *Wilson Bulletin for Librarians*, 5 (October 1930), p. 104.
Haughton, Hugh, 'Allusion: The Case of Shakespeare', in *T. S. Eliot in Context*, ed. Jason Harding (Cambridge: Cambridge University Press, 2011), pp. 157–68.
Haviland, Paul L., 'We are Living in the Age of the Machine', *291*, 1.7–8 (1915), p. 1.
Haw, Richard, *Brooklyn Bridge: A Cultural History* (New Brunswick, NJ: Rutgers University Press, 2005).
H.D. 'Huntress', *Greenwich Village*, 2.2 (15 July 1915), p. 57.
Heaney, Seamus, *Preoccupations: Selected Prose 1968–1978* (London: Faber and Faber, 1985).
Heap, Jane, 'Exposé', *The Little Review*, 8.2 (1922), pp. 46–7.

— 'Ulysses', *The Little Review*, 9.1 (1922), pp. 34–5.

Henderson, Alice Corbin, 'Poetry of the North American Indian', review of *The Path on the Rainbow: An Anthology of Songs and Chants from the Indians of North America*, ed. George W. Cronyn (1918), *Poetry*, 12.1 (1919), pp. 41–7.

Hill, Geoffrey, 'Improvisations for Hart Crane', *Daedalus*, 133.4 (2004), pp. 99–101.

Hobday, Charles, *Edgell Rickword: A Poet at War* (Manchester: Carcanet, 1989).

Hoffman, F. J., C. F. Ulrich and C. Allen, *The Little Magazine: A History and Bibliography* (Princeton, NJ: Princeton University Press, 1947).

Holley, Margaret, 'The Model Stanza: The Organic Origin of Moore's Syllabic Verse', *Twentieth Century Literature*, 30.2–3 (1984), pp. 181–91.

Homer, William Innes, *Avant-Garde Painting and Sculpture in America: Exhibition Catalogue* (Newark, DE: University of Delaware Press, 1975).

Hooley, Charles [as Charles Vale], 'A Brilliant Failure', review of Oscar Wilde, *The Portrait of Mr W. H.* (1921), *The Dial*, 71.3 (1921), pp. 359–64.

Hopkins, David, *Dada's Boys: Masculinity After Duchamp* (New Haven, CT: Yale University Press, 2007).

Hueffer, Ford Madox, *Antwerp* (London: The Poetry Bookshop, 1915).

Hutchinson, Percy, 'Hart Crane's Cubistic Poetry in *The Bridge*', *The New York Times*, 27 April 1930, p. 2.

'Indian Poems from the Sioux' [unsigned], trans. Mary Katherine Reely, *The Pagan*, 2.11 (1918), pp. 21–2.

Irwin, John T., *Appollinaire [sic] Lived in Paris, I Live in Cleveland, Ohio: Hart Crane's Poetry* (Baltimore, MD: Johns Hopkins Universityy Press, 2011).

Jolas, Eugene, 'The Idiot', *The Pagan*, 4.1 (1919), p. 53.

— *The Man from Babel*, ed. Andreas Kramer and Rainer Rumold (New Haven, CT: Yale University Press, 1998).

— [as Theo Rutra], 'Poems', *transition*, 7 (October 1927), pp. 144–5.

— 'Proclamation', *transition*, 17 (June 1929), unpaginated.

— 'The Revolution of Language and James Joyce', *transition*, 11 (February 1928), pp. 109–12.

— 'Super Occident', *transition*, 15 (February 1929), pp. 11–18.

Jolas, Eugene, and Elliot Paul, 'Introduction', *transition*, 1 (April 1927), p. 137.

— 'Suggestions for a New Magic', *transition*, 3 (June 1927), pp. 178–9.

Jones, Gavin, *Strange Talk: The Politics of Dialect Literature in Gilded Age America* (Berkeley, CA: University of California Press, 1999).

Joost, Nicholas, *Scofield Thayer and "The Dial"* (Carbondale, IL: Southern Illinois University Press, 1964).

Joost, Nicholas, and Alvin Sullivan, *'The Dial': Two Author Indexes: Anonymous and Pseudonymous Contributors; Contributors in Clipsheets* (Carbondale, IL: Southern Illinois University Press, 1971).
Josephson, Matthew, 'Apollinaire: Or Let Us Be Troubadours', *Secession*, 1 (spring 1922), pp. 9–13
— 'Beware of Editors', *Le Coeur à Barbe*, 1.1 (1922), p. 6.
— 'Do You Fear the Dark?', *Broom*, 5.2 (1923), pp. 95–6.
— *Galimathias* (Broom: New York, 1923).
— *Life Among the Surrealists* (New York: Holt, Rhinehart and Winston, 1962).
— 'Made in America', *Broom*, 2.3 (1922), pp. 226–70.
— 'A Modern Joan of Arc', review of Joseph Delteil, *Joan of Arc* (1925), *The Saturday Review*, 47.2 (19 June 1926), p. 869.
— 'The Oblate', *Secession*, 3 (August 1922), p. 14.
— 'Peep Peep Parrish', *Secession*, 3 (August 1922), pp. 6–11.
— 'Pursuit', *Broom*, 4.2 (1923), pp. 164–7.
Joyce, James, 'Work in Progress', *transition*, 1 (April 1927), pp. 9–30.
Keats, John, *The Complete Poems*, ed. John Barnard (Oxford: Oxford University Press, 1988).
Kenner, Hugh, *The Pound Era* (Berkeley, CA: University of California Press, 1973).
Kerfoot, J. B., 'A Bunch of Keys', *291*, 1.3 (1915), back cover.
— 'The Cloak Room Mystery', *Camera Work*, 19 (July 1907), pp. 28–31.
Khalip, Jacques, 'Cruising Among Ghosts: Hart Crane's Friends', *Arizona Quarterly: A Journal of American Literature, Culture, and Theory*, 64.2 (2008), pp. 65–93.
Killingsworth, M. Jimmie, *Whitman's Poetry of the Body: Sexuality, Politics, and the Text* (Chapel Hill, NC: University of North Carolina Press, 1989).
Kindley, Evan, *Poet-Critics and the Administration of Culture* (Cambridge, MA: Harvard University Press, 2017).
Kingham, Victoria, 'Audacious Modernity', in *The Oxford Critical and Cultural History of Modernist Magazines, Volume II: North America 1894–1960*, ed. Peter Brooker and Andrew Thacker (Oxford: Oxford University Press, 2012), pp. 398–419.
— 'Commerce, Little Magazines and Modernity', PhD thesis, De Montfort University, 2009.
Kirstein, Lincoln, *Mosaic: Memoirs* (New York: Farrar, Straus and Giroux, 1994).
Kisch, Arnold I., *The Romantic Ghost of Greenwich Village: Guido Bruno in His Garret* (Oxford: Peter Lang, 1976).
Kling, Joseph, 'As It Seems', *The Pagan*, 3.3 (1918), p. 35.
— 'Ave Maria', *The Pagan*, 6.4–5 (1921), p. 30.
— 'In Answer to Numerous Questions', *The Pagan*, 2.5 (1917), front pages.

— 'In Re Judea et al', *The Pagan*, 1.3 (1916), pp. 43–4.
— 'Paroles d'un Blesse', *The Pagan*, 1.7–8 (1916), p. 44.
— 'The Theatre', *The Pagan*, 1.1 (1916), p. 3.
— [as 'Ben S'], 'To My Brother Connoisseurs', *The Pagan*, 1.2 (1916), pp. 32–5.
— [as 'Ben S'], 'Twenty', *The Pagan*, 1.5 (1916), p. 37.
— 'Une Vie', *The Pagan*, 1.5 (1916), pp. 7–18.
— 'Why Complain', *The Pagan*, 1.10 (1917), p. 42.
Knox, George, 'Crane and Stella: Conjunction of Painterly and Poetic Worlds', *Texas Studies in Literature and Language*, 12.4 (1971), pp. 689–707.
Kreymborg, Alfred, *Mushrooms: 16 Rhythms* (New York: Bruno's Chapbooks, 1915).
— *To My Mother: Ten Rhythms* (New York: Bruno's Chapbooks, 1915).
— *Troubadour* (New York: Sagamore Press, 1957).
Lacoue-Labarthe, Philippe, and Jean-Luc Nancy, *The Literary Absolute: The Theory of Literature in German Romanticism* (Albany, NY: SUNY Press, 1978).
Laforgue, Jules, *The Complete Poems*, trans. Peter Dale (London: Anvil Press Poetry, 2004).
Laib, Monnie, 'Twilight', *The Pagan*, 2.6 (1917), p. 11.
Latham, Sean, and Robert Scoles, 'The Changing Profession: The Rise of Periodical Studies', *PMLA*, 121.2 (2006), pp. 517–31.
Le Blanc, H., *The Art of Tying the Cravat: Demonstrated in Sixteen Lessons Including Thirty Two Different Styles Forming A Pocket Manual* (New York: D. A. Forbes, 1829).
— 'The Importance of Neckties: The History of the Cravat', *Bruno's Weekly*, 2.11 (11 March 1916), p. 3.
Leavell, Linda, Cristianne Miller and Robin G. Shulze (eds), *Critics and Poets on Marianne Moore* (Lewisburg, PA: Bucknell University Press, 2005).
Levey, David W., *Herbert Croly and "The New Republic"* (Princeton, NJ: Princeton University Press, 2014).
Levine, Caroline, *Forms: Whole, Rhythm, Hierarchy, Network* (Princeton, NJ: Princeton University Press, 2015).
Loeb, Harold, 'The Mysticism of Money', *Broom*, 3.2 (1922), pp. 115–30.
— *The Way It Was* (New York: Criterion Books, 1959).
Logan, William, 'Hart Crane's Bridge to Nowhere', *The New York Times*, 28 January 2007, <https://www.nytimes.com/2007/01/28/books/review/Logan.t.html> (accessed 29 July 2021).
— 'On Reviewing Hart Crane', *Poetry*, 193.1 (2008), pp. 53–9.
Lohf, Kenneth, *The Literary Manuscripts of Hart Crane* (Columbus, OH: Ohio State University Press, 1967).
Long, Hoyt, and Richard Jean So, 'Turbulent Flow: A Computational Model of World Literature', *Modern Language Quarterly*, 77.3 (2016), pp. 345–67.

Longworth, Deborah, 'The Avant-Garde in the Village: *Rogue*', in *The Oxford Critical and Cultural History of Modernist Magazines, Volume II: North America 1894–1960*, ed. Peter Brooker and Andrew Thacker (Oxford: Oxford University Press, 2012), pp. 465–82.
Lowell, Amy, 'Two Generations in American Poetry', *The New Republic*, 37.470 (5 December 1923), pp. 1–3.
Lowell, Robert, *Collected Poems*, ed. Frank Bidart and David Gewanter (New York: Farrar, Straus and Giroux, 2003).
Lyons, Paddy, Willy Maley and John Miller (eds), *Romantic Ireland from Tone to Gonne: Fresh Perspectives on Nineteenth Century Ireland* (Cambridge: Cambridge Scholars, 2013).
Mallarmé, Stéphane, *Collected Poems and Other Verse*, trans. E. H. and A. M. Blackmore (Oxford: Oxford University Press, 2008).
Marek, Jayne, *Women Editing Modernism: "Little" Magazines and Literary History* (Lexington, KY: University Press of Kentucky, 1995).
Mariani, Paul, *The Broken Tower: A Life of Hart Crane* (New York: Norton, 2000).
— letter to the editor, *The New York Times*, 25 February 2007, <https://www.nytimes.com/2007/02/25/books/review/Letters.t-1.html> (accessed 29 July 2021).
Marichalar, Antonio, 'La estética de retroceso y la poesía de Hart Crane', review of Crane, *White Buildings* (1926), *Revista de Occidente*, 5.47 (1927), pp. 260–3.
Martin, Harry F., with Cormac O'Malley, *Ernie O'Malley: A Life* (Newbridge: Merrion Press, 2021).
Matson, Norman H., 'Expatriate', *Gargoyle*, 2.1–2 (1922), pp. 18–22.
McCarthy, John R., 'Flimagism III', *The Pagan,* 5.3/4/5 (1920), p. 20.
McGann, Jerome, *Edgar Allan Poe: Alien Angel* (Cambridge, MA: Harvard University Press, 2014).
— *The Textual Condition* (Princeton, NJ: Princeton University Press, 1991).
McHugh, Vincent, 'Crane's *Bridge*: Mighty Symbol of the Nation', *New York Evening Post*, 19 April 1930, p. 11.
McKenzie, D. F., *Bibliography and the Sociology of Texts* (Cambridge: Cambridge University Press, 1999).
McMillan, Dougald, *Transition 1927–1938: The History of a Literary Era* (London: Calder and Boyars, 1975).
Mellby, Julie L., 'William Sommer. "The apples, Bill, the Apples"', Princeton Graphic Arts Collection Blog, <https://www.princeton.edu/~graphicarts/2012/06/sommer.html> (accessed 23 July 2021).
Menes, Orlando Ricardo, 'Hear Me, Hart Crane', *Poetry*, 217.9 (2020), p. 15.
Messinger, Lisa Mintz (ed.), *Stieglitz and his Artists: Matisse to O'Keeffe* (New York: Metropolitan Museum of Art, 2011).

Meyer, Agnes Ernst, 'Mental Reactions', *291*, 2 (April 1915), p. 3.
Milford, Nancy, *Savage Beauty: The Life of Edna St. Vincent Millay* (New York: Random House, 2001).
Miller, Cristianne. 'Tongues "loosened in the melting pot"', *Modernism/modernity*, 14.1 (2007), pp. 455–76.
Mirbeau, Octave, 'The Pocketbook', *The Pagan*, 1.4 (1916), pp. 10–31.
Mircir, Melanie, *The Passion Projects: Modernist Women, Intimate Archives, Unfinished Lives* (Princeton, NJ: Princeton University Press, 2019).
Monroe, Harriet, 'A Discussion with Hart Crane', *Poetry*, 29.1 (1926), pp. 34–41.
— 'Looking Backward', *Poetry*, 33.1 (1928), pp. 32–8.
— 'The Motive of the Magazine', *Poetry* 1.1 (1912), pp. 26–8.
— 'Why Not Laugh?', *Poetry*, 33.4 (1929), pp. 206–9.
Moore, Marianne, *The Absentee* (New York: House of Books, 1962).
— 'The Art of Poetry No. 4', interview by Donald Hall, *The Paris Review*, 26 (summer–fall 1961), pp. 41–66.
— 'Bowls', *Secession*, 5 (July 1923), pp. 12–13.
— *The Complete Poems* (London: Faber and Faber, 1967).
— *The Complete Prose of Marianne Moore*, ed. Patricia C. Willis (London: Faber and Faber, 1987).
— '*Harmonium*', review of Wallace Stevens, *Harmonium* (1923), *The Dial*, 76.1 (1924), pp. 84–91.
— 'Holes Bored in a Workbag by the Scissors', *Bruno's Weekly*, 3.17 (7 October 1916), p. 1137.
— '*Hymen*', review of H.D., *Hymen* (1921), *Broom*, 4.2 (1923), pp. 133–5.
— '*Kora in Hell*', review of William Carlos Williams, *Kora in Hell: Improvisations* (1920), *Contact*, 1.4 (1921), pp. 5–8.
— '*Natives of Rock*', review of Glenway Westcott, *Natives of Rock: Poems 1921–1922* (1925), *The Dial*, 81.1 (1926), pp. 69–72.
— 'Picking and Choosing', *The Dial*, 68.4 (1920), pp. 421–2
— 'Poet of the Quattrocento', *The Dial*, 82.3 (1927), pp. 213–15.
— '*The Sacred Wood*', review of T. S. Eliot, *The Sacred Wood* (1920), *The Dial*, 70.3 (1921), pp. 336–9.
— *Selected Letters of Marianne Moore*, ed. Bonnie Costello (London: Penguin, 1997).
Morand, Paul, 'Paris Letter', *The Dial*, 78.3 (1924), pp. 239–43.
Moretti, Franco, *Distant Reading* (London: Verso, 2013).
Mori, Masaki, *Epic Grandeur: Toward a Comparative Poetics of the Epic* (Albany, NY: SUNY Press, 1997).
Morrison, Mark, *The Public Face of Modernism: Little Magazines, Audiences and Reception, 1905–1920* (Madison, WI: University of Wisconsin Press, 2001).

Moss, Howard, 'Disorder as Myth: Hart Crane's *The Bridge*', *Poetry*, 62.1 (1945), pp. 32–45.
Motherwell, Robert (ed.), *The Dada Painters and Poets: An Anthology* (Boston, MA: G. K. Hall, 1981).
Mott, Frank Luther, *A History of American Magazines, Volume V: 1905–1930* (Cambridge, MA: Harvard University Press, 1968).
Mouffe, Chantal, *For a Left Populism* (London: Verso, 2019).
Moult, Thomas (ed.), *The Best Poems of 1922* (Nendeln: Kraus Reprint, 1969).
Mourant, Chris, *Katherine Mansfield and Periodical Culture* (Edinburgh: Edinburgh University Press, 2019).
Munro, Niall, *Hart Crane's Queer Modernist Aesthetic* (Basingstoke: Palgrave, 2015).
Munson, Gorham, *The Awakening Twenties: A Memory-History of a Literary Period* (Baton Rouge, LA: Louisiana State University Press, 1985).
— 'A Bow to the Adventurous', *Secession*, 1 (spring 1922), pp. 15–19.
— 'Explanatory', *Secession*, 7 (winter 1923–24), back pages.
— 'Exposé No. 1', *Secession*, 1 (spring 1922), pp. 22–4.
— 'How to Run a Little Magazine', *The Saturday Review*, 15.22 (26 March 1937), pp. 3–4, 14.
— 'Interstice Between Scylla and Charybdis', *Secession*, 2 (July 1922), pp. 30–2.
— 'The Mechanics for a Literary *Secession*', *S4N*, 3.21 (1922), pp. 1–9.
— 'Notes', *Secession*, 7 (winter 1923–24), front matter.
— 'A Poet's Suicide and Some Reflections', *The New English Weekly*, 23 June 1932, pp. 237–9.
— 'Questions for Cowley', *Contempo*, 1.14 (15 December 1931), p. 1.
— 'Skyscraper Primitives', *The Guardian*, 1.5 (1925), pp. 164–78.
— 'Tinkering with Words', review of Matthew Josephson, *Galimathias* (1923), *Secession*, 7 (winter 1923–24), pp. 30–1.
Munson, Gorham, et al. [the editors], 'Peculiar Arithmetic', *Secession*, 2 (July 1922), p. 53.
Myles, Eileen, 'hart!', *Harp and Altar*, 6 (spring 2009), <http://www.harpandaltar.com/interior.php?t=s&i=6&p=39&e=68> (accessed 17 March 2021).
— *Not Me* (New York: Semiotext(e), 1991).
Nancy, Jean-Luc, and Philippe Lacoue-Labarthe, *The Literary Absolute: The Theory of Literature in German Romanticism* (New York: SUNY Press, 1978).
Neagle, Michael E., *America's Forgotten Colony: Cuba's Isle of Pines* (New York: Cambridge University Press, 2016).
Nicholl, Louise Townsend, 'Spring Poetry', *The Outlook and Independent*, 155.4 (1930), pp. 146–7.
Norton, Peter D., *Fighting Traffic: The Dawn of the Motor Age in the American City* (Cambridge, MA: MIT Press, 2008).

'Notes on Contributors' [unsigned], *The Fugitive*, 2.8 (1923), p. 127.

Office of the Commissioner of Internal Revenue, *Statistics of Income from Returns of Net Income for 1926 Including Statistics of from Estate Tax Returns* (Washington DC: United States Government Printing Office, 1928).

O'Hara, Frank, *Selected Poems*, ed. Mark Ford (New York:Knopf, 2008).

O'Malley, Cormac K. H., 'Ernie O'Malley and the Arts', *Whytes in Association with Christies: The Ernie O'Malley Collection* (Dublin: Whytes, 2019), pp. 8–14.

— (ed.), *Modern Ireland and Revolution: Ernie O'Malley in Context* (Newbridge: Irish Academic Press, 2016).

O'Malley, Ernie, *Broken Landscapes: Selected Letters*, ed. Cormac K. H. O'Malley and Nicholas Allen (Dublin:Lilliput Press, 2012).

— 'Traditions of Mexican Art', *The Listener*, 23 January 1947, pp. 146–7.

Oppenheim, James, Waldo Frank and Van Wyck Brooks, 'Editorial', *The Seven Arts*, 1.1 (1916), pp. 52–7.

Pace, Eric, 'Norman Cousins', obituary, *The New York Times*, 1 December 1990, <http://www.nytimes.com/1990/12/01/obituaries/norman-cousins-75-dies-edited-the-saturday-review.html> (accessed 27 August 2018).

Parker, Robert Dale, 'Modernist Literary Studies and the Aesthetics of American Indian Literatures', *Modernism/modernity*, 5.4, https://doi.org/10.26597/mod.0189 (accessed 18 March 2021).

Parker, R. A., 'Paris, Madly Jazzing, Sees Jazz as the Music of the Future', *New York Tribune*, 20 March 1921, p. 7.

Parkhurst, Winthrop, 'Vers Libre', *The Pagan*, 4.6 (1919), p. 11.

Parkinson, Thomas Francis, *Hart Crane and Yvor Winters: Their Literary Correspondence* (Berkeley, CA: University of California, 1978).

Parisi, Joseph, and Stephen Young (eds), *Dear Editor: A History of Poetry in Letters* (New York: W. W. Norton, 2002).

Perloff, Marjorie, 'Collage and Poetry', in *Encyclopaedia of Aesthetics*, ed. Michael Kelly (New York: Oxford University Press, 1998), vol. 1, pp. 384–7 .

— 'Pound/Stevens: Whose Era?', *New Literary History*, 13.3 (1982), pp. 485–514.

Perzynski, W., 'The Murder', *The Pagan*, 1.6 (1916), pp. 3–6.

Pierce, Frederick E., 'Four Poets', *The Yale Review*, 1.17 (2 October 1927), pp. 166–9.

Pire, Beatrice '"If you could die": Hart Crane's "Accursed Share"', *European Journal of American Studies*, 13.2 (2018), pp. 1–11.

'Platform' [unsigned], *The Modernist*, 1.1 (1919), unpaginated.

Pound, Ezra, *The Cantos* (New York: New Directions, 1999).

— 'A Communication from Ezra Pound', *1924*, 3 (September 1924), pp. 97–8.

— 'Ferrex on Petulance', *The Egoist*, 1.1 (1 January 1914), pp. 9–10.

— 'A Few Don'ts by an Imagiste', *Poetry*, 1.6 (1913), pp. 200–6.
— (ed.), *The Glebe: Des Imagistes-An Anthology* (New York: Albert and Charles Boni, 1914).
— '*Odes et Prières*', review of Jules Romains, *Odes et Prières* (1913), *Poetry*, 2.5 (1913), pp. 187–9.
— *Pound/The Little Review: The Letters of Ezra Pound to Margaret Anderson*, ed. Thomas L. Scott and Melvin J. Friedman (New York: New Directions, 1989).
— *The Selected Letters of Ezra Pound 1907–1941*, ed. D. D. Paige (New York: New Directions, 1971).
Powel, Gretchen, and Peter Powel, 'Manhattan: 1929', photograph: reproductions, *transition*, 16–17 (June 1929), pp. 72–3.
Pratt, Mary Louise, 'Arts of the Contact Zone', *Profession* (1991), pp. 33–40.
Rainey, Lawrence, *Institutions of Modernism: Literary Elites and Public Culture* (New Haven, CT: Yale University Press, 1998).
— *Revisiting "The Waste Land"* (New Haven, CT: Yale University Press, 2005).
Raisin, Ovro'om, 'Silent Footsteps', *The Pagan*, 1.6 (1916), pp. 25–7.
— 'Tamud-Student's Monody', *The Pagan*, 1.3 (1916), p. 41.
Raleigh, Sir Walter, *Discoverie of Guiana*, ed. Joyce Lorimer (London: Ashgate, 2006).
Ramazani, Jahan, *A Transnational Poetics* (Chicago: University of Chicago Press, 2009).
Read, Herbert, 'Foreign Reviews', *The Criterion*, 2.6 (1926), p. 226.
Read, Kay Almere, *Time and Sacrifice in the Aztec Cosmos* (Bloomington, IN: Indiana University Press, 1998).
Reed, Brian, *Hart Crane: After his Lights* (Tuscaloosa, AL: University of Alabama Press, 2006).
— 'Hart Crane's Victrola', *Modernism/Modernity*, 7.1 (2000), pp. 99–125.
Reverdy, Pierre, 'L'image', *Nord-Sud*, 2.13 (1918), pp. 3–8.
Rich, Adrienne, *Midnight Salvage* (New York: Norton, 1999), pp. 43–50.
— 'When We Dead Awaken: Writing as Re-Vision', *College English*, 34.1 (1972), pp. 18–30.
Richards, I. A., 'A Background for Contemporary Poetry', *The Criterion*, 3.12 (1925), pp. 511–28.
Rickword, Edgell, *Behind the Eyes: Collected Poems and Translations* (Manchester: Carcanet, 1976).
— 'A Conversation with Edgell Rickword', interview by Michael Schmidt and Alan Young, *Poetry Nation*, 1 (1973), pp. 73–89.
Riddel, Joseph, 'Hart Crane's Poetics of Failure', *ELH*, 33.4 (1966), pp. 473–96.
Riding, Laura, and Madeleine Vara, 'The Cult of Failure', *Epilogue*, 1.1 (1935), pp. 60–6.
Riley, Peter, *Against Vocation: Whitman, Melville, Crane and the Labors of American Poetry* (Oxford: Oxford University Press, 2019).

Rilke, Rainer Maria, *Die Sonette an Orpheus* (Munich: Insel-Verlag, 1923).
Roberts, Michael, *The Faber Book of Modern Verse* (London: Faber and Faber, 1936).
Robertson, John Dill, 'They Say Now That Jazz Beat the Kaiser', *The Dallas Express*, 21 May 1921, p. 1.
Rodensky, Lisa (ed.), *Decadent Poetry from Wilde to Naidu* (London: Penguin, 2006).
Rogers, Stephen, 'Village Voices', in *The Oxford Critical and Cultural History of Modernist Magazines, Volume II: North America 1894–1960*, ed. Peter Brooker and Andrew Thacker (Oxford: Oxford University Press, 2012), pp. 445–64.
Rosenwaike, Ira, *Population History of New York* (Syracuse, NY: Syracuse University Press, 1972).
Rowe, H. D., 'Hart Crane: A Bibliography', *Twentieth Century Literature*, 1.2 (1955), pp. 94–113.
Rust, Brian A. L., and Sandy Forbes, *British Dance Bands on Record: 1911–1945* (London: General Gramophone Publications, 1987).
Sanders, Emmy Veronica, 'America Invades Europe', *Broom*, 1.1 (1921), pp. 89–93.
Schwartz, Joseph, and Robert C. Schweik, *Hart Crane: A Descriptive Bibliography* (Pittsburgh, PA: University of Pittsburgh Press, 1972).
Schultz, Susan M., 'The Success of Failure: Hart Crane's Revisions of Whitman and Eliot in *The Bridge*', *South Atlantic Review*, 54.1 (1989), pp. 55–70.
Schulze, Robin G., 'Textual Darwinism: Marianne Moore, the Text of Evolution, and the Evolving Text', *Text*, 11 (1998), pp. 270–305.
Scott, C. Kay, 'Imagists', in 'Amazon Forests', *The Pagan*, 4.6 (1919), pp. 12–17.
Seaver, Edwin, 'For the Paintings of Judson Smith', *1924*, 4 (December 1924), p. 127.
— *So Far So Good: Recollections of a Life in Publishing* (Westport, CT: Lawrence Hill, 1986).
Sedgwick, Eve Kosofsky, *Between Men* (New York: Columbia University Press, 1985).
— *Tendencies* (Durham, NC: Duke University Press, 1993).
Selzer, Jack, *Kenneth Burke in Greenwich Village: Conversing with the Moderns, 1915–1931* (Madison, WI: University of Wisconsin Press, 1996).
Sharp, William (ed.), *The Pagan Review*, 1.1 (1892).
Shaw, Lytle, *Frank O'Hara: the Poetics of Coterie* (Iowa City, IA: University of Iowa Press, 2006).
Shelley, Percy Bysshe, *The Complete Poetical Works*, ed. Thomas Hutchinson (Oxford: Clarendon Press, 1904).
Shepard, Odell, 'Hart Crane', *The Bookman*, 72.1 (1930), pp. 86–7.

Sherry, Vincent, *Modernism and the Reinvention of Decadence* (Cambridge: Cambridge University Press, 2014).
Simon, Marc, *Samuel Greenberg, Hart Crane and the Lost Manuscripts* (Herndon, VA: Humanities Press, 1978).
'Singers of the New Age: A Group of Distinguished Poets Who Have Found Fresh Material in the American Scene' [unsigned], *Vanity Fair*, 33.1 (1929), p. 89.
Smith, Jessie Carney (ed.), *Encyclopaedia of African American Popular Culture* (Denver, CO: Greenwood, 2011).
Sologub, Fyodor, 'The White Dog', *The Pagan*, 1.2 (1916), pp. 3–9.
Sonin, Max Light, 'To the Author of Lustra', *The Pagan*, 3.6 (1918), p. 22.
Spence, Lewis, *Atlantis in America* (London: E. Benn, 1925).
Spratling, William, *Little Mexico* (New York: Cape and Smith, 1932).
Stansell, Christine, *American Moderns: Bohemian New York and the Creation of a New Century* (Princeton, NJ: Princeton University Press, 2009).
Stella, Joseph, *Brooklyn Bridge*, painting: photographic reproduction, *Broom*, 1.1 (1921), p. 2.
— '*Brooklyn Bridge* (A Page from My Life)', *transition*, 16–17 (June 1929), pp. 86–8.
Stevens, Wallace, 'Earthy Anecdote', ill. Rockwell Kent, *The Modern School*, 5.7 (1918), p. 1.
— 'Thirteen Ways of Looking at a Blackbird', *Others*, 4.2 (1917), pp. 25–7.
Stewart, John L., *The Burden of Time: The Fugitives and Agrarians* (Princeton, NJ: Princeton University Press, 1965).
'The Story of Oscar Wilde's Life and Experience in Reading Gaol' [unsigned], *Bruno's Weekly*, 2.4 (22 January 1916), pp. 400–1.
Sumner, John S., 'Adult or Infantile Censorship?', *The Dial*, 68.4 (1920), p. 381.
Sutherland, Camilla, '"El pájaro de cuatro notas": The Reception of Argentine Women Writers and Artists' Work in Avant-garde Magazines (1920–1930)', *Journal of Iberian and Latin American Studies*, 23.3 (2017), pp. 399–416.
Taggard, Genevieve, 'An Imagist in Amber: *White Buildings*', *The New York Herald Tribune*, 29 May 1927, p. 4.
Tapper, Gordon, *The Machine that Sings: Modernism, Hart Crane, and the Culture of the Body* (Abingdon: Routledge, 2006).
Tashjian, Dickran, *Skyscraper Primitives: Dada and the American Avant-Garde, 1910–1925* (Middletown, CT: Wesleyan University Press, 1975).
Tate, Allen, *Collected Poems 1919–1976* (New York: Farrar, Straus and Giroux, 2007).
— 'A Distinguished Poet: *The Bridge*', *Hound & Horn*, 1.3 (1930), pp. 580–5.
— 'Euthanasia', *The Double Dealer*, 3.17 (1922), p. 262.
— 'Hart Crane and the American Mind', *Poetry*, 40.4 (1932), pp. 210–16.

— 'In Memoriam Hart Crane', *Hound & Horn*, 5 (July–September 1932), pp. 612–19.
— 'A Poet, and his Life', *Poetry*, 50.4 (1937), pp. 219–24.
— 'The Poet as Hero', *The New Republic*, 127 (16 November 1952), p. 25.
Thayer, Scofield, 'Comment', *The Dial*, 68.3 (1920), p. 408.
Tóibín, Colm, *New Ways to Kill Your Mother* (London: Viking, 2012).
Trabowitz, Lara, 'Djuna Barnes's *Nightwood*: Jewishness, Antisemitism, Structure, and Style', *Modern Fiction Studies*, 51.2 (2005), pp. 311–34.
Tryphonopoulos, Demetres P., and Stephen J. Adams (eds), *The Ezra Pound Encyclopaedia* (Westport, CT: Greenwood Press, 2005).
Tzara, Tristan, 'How to Make a Dadaist Poem', in *The Dada Painters and Poets: An Anthology*, ed. Robert Motherwell (Boston, MA: G. K. Hall, 1981), p. 92.
Tzara, Tristan, et al., 'Pour Faire Pousser le Coeur', *Le Coeur à Barbe*, 1.1 (1922), p. 1.
Unterecker, John, *Voyager: A Life of Hart Crane* (New York: Farrar, Straus and Giroux, 1969).
Untermeyer, Louis, 'Einstein and the Poets', *Broom*, 1.1 (1921), pp. 84–6.
Vildrac, Charles, *A Book of Love*, trans. Witter Bynner (New York: E. P. Dutton, 1923).
Vincent, John Emil, *Queer Lyrics: Difficulty and Closure in American Poetry* (Basingstoke: Palgrave, 2002).
Vizenor, Gerald, *Manifest Manners: Postindian Warriors of Survivance* (Hanover, NH: Wesleyan University Press, 1994).
Wachtel, Andrew (ed.), *Petrushka: Sources and Contexts* (Evanston, IL: Northwestern University Press, 1998).
Weber, Brom, *Hart Crane: A Biographical and Critical Study* (New York: Russell and Russell, 1970).
Weir, David, *Decadence and the Making of Modernism* (Amherst, MA: University of Massachusetts Press, 1995).
Wheeler, Belinda, and Lola Ridge, 'Lola Ridge's Pivotal Editorial Role at *Broom*', *PMLA*, 127.2 (2012), pp. 283–91.
Wheelwright, John Brooks, 'Note to "For the Marriage of Faustus and Helen"', *Secession*, 6 (September 1923), p. 4.
— 'To Hart Crane', *The New Republic*, 71.914 (8 June 1932), p. 91.
'*White Buildings*', review of Crane, *White Buildings* (1926) [unsigned], *Times Literary Supplement*, 24 February 1927, p. 130.
White, Eric B., *Transatlantic Avant-Gardes: Little Magazines and Localist Modernism* (Edinburgh: Edinburgh University Press, 2013).
Whitman, Walt, *Leaves of Grass*, ed. Jerome Loving (Oxford: Oxford University Press, 2009).
Wilde, Oscar [as 'C.3.3.'], *The Ballad of Reading Gaol* (London: Leonard Smithers, 1898).

— 'Hitherto Unpublished Letters by Oscar Wilde', *Bruno's Weekly*, 2.11 (11 March 1916), pp. 543–4.
— 'Impressions of America', *Bruno's Weekly*, 2.21 (20 May 1916), pp. 724–6.
— 'La Mer', *Bruno's Weekly*, 2.14 (1 April 1916), p. 3.
— 'Quantum Mutata', *Bruno's Weekly*, 2.18 (29 April 1916), p. 655.
— *Salomé* (London: John Lane, 1907).
Williams, William Carlos, 'Hart Crane, 1899–1932', *Contempo*, 2.4 (5 July 1932), pp. 1, 4.
— *Selected Letters*, ed. John C. Thirwell (New York: New Directions, 1984).
— 'To a Solitary Disciple', *Others*, 2.2 (1916), pp. 145–7.
Wilson, Edmund, *Classics and Commercials: A Literary Chronicle of the 1940s* (New York: Farrar, Straus and Giroux, 1951).
Wilson, Romer, *The Grand Tour* (London: Methuen, 1923).
Winters, Yvor, 'Hart Crane's Poems', review of Crane, *White Buildings* (1926), *Poetry*, 30.1 (1927), pp. 47–51.
— *In Defense of Reason: Primitivism and Decadence, a Study of American Experimental Poetry* (Denver, CO: Alan Swallow, 1947).
— 'The Progress of Hart Crane', review of Crane, *The Bridge* (1930), *Poetry*, 36.3 (1930), pp. 153–65.
Wolff, David, 'Remembering Hart Crane', *The New Republic*, 104.15 (28 November 1934), p. 76.
Wordsworth, William, *The Poetical Works of William Wordsworth*, vol. I (London: Edward Moxton, 1837).
Yingling, Thomas E., *Hart Crane and the Homosexual Text* (Chicago: University of Chicago Press, 1990).
Young, Alan, *Dada and After: Extremist Modernism and English Literature* (Manchester: Manchester University Press, 1983).
Zinsser, Hans, *As I Remember Him: A Portrait of R.S.* (Boston: Little, Brown, 1940).
Zorach, Marguerite, *Others*, 5.3 (1919), front cover.
Zukofsky, Louis, 'A: 9', *Poetry*, 58.3 (1941), pp. 128–30.
— 'A: 29', *Poetry*, 46.2 (1933), p. 312.
— 'A: Second Movement', *Poetry*, 40.1 (1932), pp. 26–9.

INDEX

1924, 7, 9, 12, 47, 58, 74, 66, 69, 80–5, 88, 92, 102, 119, 123, 146, 192; *see also* Seaver, Edwin
291, 11n43, 47–8, 120n138, 143; *see also* Stieglitz, Arthur

Abernethy, Milton Avant, 186; *see also Contempo*
Academy of Fine Arts (Mexico City), 179
Adams, Henry, 13
Advertisements, 24, 68–9, 72–3, 81, 153
Aesthete, 1925, 58, 80–1; *see also* Walter S. Hankel
Aguglia, Mimi, 35
Ahmed, Sara, 6
Aiken, Conrad, 10, 61, 67, 68, 103, 107, 116, 125–6, 162
Aldington, Richard, 24, 26, 36, 38–40, 39n112, 54, 102
Alighieri, Dante, 151
Allen, Nicholas, 179n71
The American Caravan, 34n84, 134, 144, 152; *see also The Second American Caravan*; Rosenfeld, Paul; Kreymborg, Alfred
American Civil Liberties Union, 18
The American Mercury, 64, 81n128
Amin, Kadji, Amber Jamilla Musser, and Roy Pérez, 9
anarchism, 18, 51–2
Anderson, Forrest
'For Hart Crane', 184, 188
Anderson, Margaret, 17, 55, 61, 82, 85–6
My Thirty Years War, 86
see also The Little Review
Anderson, Maxwell, 61; *see also The Measure*
Anderson, Sherwood, 58, 64, 67, 73
anthologies, 20, 24, 35–6, 87, 102, 114, 135
antisemitism, 20, 26, 26n46, 57
Apollinaire, Guillaume, 48, 65, 66, 68, 71, 152, 156, 158
Aragon, Louis, 56, 58–9, 65, 70, 75–6, 157
Arens, Egmont, 24

242

Armory Show, 33
Arnold, Matthew, 13
Arp, Hans, 155
Atkinson, Colette Labouff, 192
The Atlantic Monthly, 49, 67

Baker, John, 69
Ballets Russes, 52, 113
Barnes, Djuna
   The Book of Repulsive Women, 24
   Nightwood, 26
Baron, Jacques, 70
Barrett, Alfred, 9
Baudelaire, Charles, 23, 27, 31–2, 46, 84, 110–11, 113, 115
   Les Fleurs du mal, 100, 115
   Les Paradis artificiels, 27, 32, 103, 109–12, 115
Bazin, Victoria, 5, 13, 94, 107
BBC Third Programme, 179
Beals, Carleton, 176
Beardsley, Aubrey, 19, 22, 28, 30, 31, 35
Beasley, Rebecca, 5
Benét, William Rose, 114, 162–3, 173–4
Benjamin, Walter, 21
Bergson, Henri, 34
Berlant, Lauren, 3, 60
Berryman, John
   'Elegy: Hart Crane', 192–3
Berthoff, Warner, 185
Bizet, Georges
   Carmen, 29, 31
Blackadder, Captain J. E., 184
Blackmur, R. P., 119, 144, 162
Black Sun Press, 129, 133, 135, 156, 159
Blake, William, 56, 123–4, 126
Blast, 142
Bloom, Harold, 8, 140
Bodenheim, Maxwell, 35, 52
Bogan, Louise, 96
Boni, Alfred and Charles, 39
Boni and Liveright, 39, 111, 129, 133, 135–6, 143, 156, 170
The Bookman, 162–3

Borges, Jorge Luis, 189
Bornstein, George, 4, 12, 21
Bourdieu, Pierre, 7, 97
Bourgeois, Louise, 83
Bourne, Randolph, 6, 49, 67, 103, 51
Boyle, Kay, 156
Bradshaw, Michael, 131
Braque, Georges, 62
Brenner, Anita, 174–6
   Idols Behind Altars, 168, 176
Breton, André, 1, 56–7, 65, 69, 75, 79, 155, 157
   Manifeste du surréalisme, 93
Britztolakis, Christina, 97
Brooker, Peter and Andrew Thacker, 5n12, 98n21
Brooks, Charles S., 17–18
Brooks, Van Wyck, 50, 155
Broom, 1–3, 10, 12–13, 47–8, 53, 56–93, 98, 106, 120, 123, 146, 153–6, 184, 186, 192; *see also* Aesthete, 1925; Cowley, Malcolm; Dada; Josephson, Matthew; Munson, Gorham; Surrealism; Wheelwright, John Brooks
Brown, Susan Jenkins, 81, 135, 150n104
Brown, William Slater, 65, 68, 80–1, 84, 185
Brum, Blanca Luz, 177
Bruno, Guido, 11, 22, 24, 18–19, 21–33, 35, 39, 115, 143; *see also* Bruno's Bohemia; Bruno's Weekly
Bruno's Bohemia, 11, 21–33; *see also* Bruno, Guido; Decadence; Imagism
Bruno's Weekly, 11, 21–33, 36, 101, 192; *see also* Bruno, Guido; Decadence; Imagism
Bryn Mawr, 104, 114
Bulson, Eric, 5–6, 10
Burke, Kenneth, 58, 65, 80, 87, 90, 103, 110
Butterfield, R. W., 8, 81n130
Buttitta, Anthony J., 186
Bynner, Witter, 100

243

The Calendar of Modern Letters, 32, 116n116, 134–5, 144–7, 154; *see also* Rickword, Edgell
Calles, Plutarco Elías, 177
calligrammes, 47–8, 70, 99, 152, 158, 170
Camera Work, 142; *see also* Stieglitz, Arthur
Canby, Henry Seidel, 114
Cann, Louise G., 34
Capildeo, Vahni, 198
Carr, Helen, 36
Castañeda, Maximiliano Ruiz, 189–90
censorship, 8–9, 22, 24, 46, 57–8, 86, 98, 104, 118n128, 146
   trials and imprisonment, 8–9, 22, 24, 86
Challenger, Melanie, 192
Chase, Stuart, 176
Chaucer, Geoffrey, 66
Chauncey, George, 25
Chesterton, G. K., 23
Clark, Donald B., 65
Clearfield, Andrew, 113
Cleveland Plain Dealer, 12n48
Coates, Robert, 62
Cocks, H. G., 9n33
Cocteau, Jean, 68, 98n22
Le Cœur à Barbe, 57, 69; *see also* Tzara, Tristan
Coleridge, Samuel Taylor, 131
collage (poetic form), 10, 14–15, 19, 31–2, 60, 77, 105–6, 100–10, 113, 122, 128–32, 140, 143, 157
   and Cubism, 69, 131–2
   and Dada, 69–70, 72–3, 87
   and Surrealism, 69, 157, 160, 170
Colum, Mary, 52, 119
Colum, Padraic, 35, 52, 61, 119; *see also The Measure*
Columbia Poetry, 193
Columbus, Christopher, 152, 154, 159
Conrad, Joseph, 24
Contact, 106

Contempo, 170, 182, 184, 186–8; *see also* Abernethy, Milton Avant; Buttitta, Anthony J.
Contemporary Verse, 24
Corday and Gross, 73, 85
Corn, Alfred
   'The Bridge, Palm Sunday 1973', 191–2
corridos, 177
Cortés, Hernán, 167, 180
Costello, Bonnie, 94, 107
coterie poetics, 3, 7, 60, 80–93, 119, 174, 192
Cowley, Peggy Baird, 2n4, 103, 177
Cowley, Malcolm, 1–2, 9, 26, 35, 56–8, 62, 65–8, 70, 76, 80–2, 84–5, 103, 118n126, 129, 163, 167, 172, 173, 178, 183n91, 184, 186, 188, 192
   'Anthology: Hart Crane', 87–9, 91, 97, 192
   Exile's Return, 1, 18–19, 24, 34, 56, 58, 98n24, 155
   'A Preface to Hart Crane', 118n126, 129, 154, 161–3
   see also Broom; *Secession*; *Aesthete, 1925*; *The New Republic*
Crane, Clarence Arthur
   confectionary business, 82–3
   death, 178
   marriage to Grace Hart Crane, 26, 144
   relationship with Hart Crane, 90–1, 139
Crane, Grace Hart, 22, 145, 184
   as editor of Hart Crane's poetry, 170n23, 188–9
   Isla de la Juventud estate, 187, 198
   marriage to C. A. Crane, 26, 114
   relationship with Hart Crane, 101, 114, 139
   as subject of Hart Crane's poetry, 99, 101, 139

Crane, Hart
  alcoholism and drinking episodes, 54, 103, 112, 157, 178–9, 184
  antisemitism, 20, 20n12
  arrests, 6, 156, 178
  and Christian Science, 118
  death, 118, 139, 145, 163, 167, 168–9, 173, 179–80, 182–3, 184–6, 188–9, 192, 195
  as editor, 20, 48, 52, 53n179
  education, 26, 114
  employment, 73, 82–3, 85, 114, 153
  finances, 90, 133, 135, 176–7, 183–4, 186: blackmail, 90–1; contributors fees, 63, 134–5; living costs, 176; poetry prizes, 62, 169; publisher's advances, 134; support from Otto Kahn, 133–4
  Guggenheim Fellowship, 6, 15, 166–7, 169, 176–8: application, 166–7
  homosexuality, 25, 27n53, 44–6, 85, 88–92, 111, 177, 189, 194–5
  interviews, 21–2, 129, 176
  'logic of metaphor', 3, 9, 11, 13, 20, 31–2, 46, 54, 60, 78, 93, 95, 102, 114, 117, 122–3, 157, 160, 164, 170, 172: associational principle, 32, 37, 43–4, 73–4, 76, 90, 93, 94, 112, 122, 127, 158, 164, 165, 171, 175, 194–5;and the body, 13–14, 90–1, 93, 112–13; and collage, 32, 54, 73, 110, 113, 122; and juxtaposition, 32–3, 50, 54, 75–6, 110, 157; and metonymy, 31–2, 76, 91, 101–2; and queer poetics, 3, 8–9, 12, 18, 21, 29, 33, 46–7, 85, 107, 111, 113, 127, 130, 148, 164–5, 182, 192, 194–5; and Surrealism, 73–7, 170
  'machine age' poetry, 11, 19, 36, 48, 53–4, 57, 59–60, 64–5, 68–9, 70–6, 77–80
  name variants and pseudonyms, 2n4, 12, 22, 27, 66, 82, 196
  notebooks, 88n172, 157
  prose poetry, 189
  reception history, 9, 10–12, 14–16, 37, 41, 55, 91, 95–6, 101, 107–8, 114–116, 116–27, 129–31, 160, 161–5, 182–90, 191–9: association with failure, 9–10, 15–16, 118, 124, 129–30, 160, 161–5, 185, 197–8
  as reviewer, 13, 20, 33, 99, 102, 186, 117n119, 179
  romantic relationships, 89, 91–2, 146–7, 177, 189
  translations, 38n106, 61, 111
  and visual arts, 15, 33, 80, 82–3, 102, 141, 181, 192; *see also* Cubism; Walker Evans; Gaston Lachaise; William Sommer; Joseph Stella
  works by: 'Again', 11, 94–5, 103–16, 117, 127;'Annunciations', 41; 'At Melville's Tomb', 14, 31, 95, 107, 112, 116–17, 121, 123, 124, 130, 146, 164, 170–1; 'Ave Maria', 34, 133–4, 152, 159; 'Bacardi Spreads the Eagle's Wing', 182, 186–7; 'The Bathers', 45; 'Belle Isle' ('Voyages VI'), 84–5, 99; 'Black Tambourine', 61–3; *The Bridge*, 2, 10, 14, 36, 44, 59, 60, 72–3, 74–6, 78, 91, 97, 102, 110, 117–18, 125–7, 128–65, 167, 169–70, 182, 185, 187–8, 197–8; 'Briefer Mentions', 13, 99, 102; 'The Broken Tower', 19, 168, 173, 181–2, 185, 199; 'C33', 22, 25–9, 31–2, 38, 53, 88, 146;'Cape Hatteras', 36, 135, 137–38, 152, 173; 'Carmen de Boheme', 22, 26–7, 29–33, 38, 41, 53, 92; 'Chaplinesque', 44, 48, 50, 63; *Collected Poems* (1933), 2n5, 170, 188–89; 'Cortez: The Enactment', 180; 'Cutty Sark', 93, 132–34, 144, 148, 152, 158–9, 188; 'Dear Contempo', 186–7; 'The Circumstance', 168, 176, 180–1, 188–9; 'The Dance', 135, 160; 'A

Crane, Hart (*cont.*)
  Discussion with Hart Crane', 4, 10–11, 14, 31–2, 47, 91, 95, 116–27, 172, 196; 'East of Yucatan', 168–9, 189; 'Echoes', 20, 28, 42–3, 45, 75; 'El Idiota', 34, 169; 'Eldorado', 134–35, 138; 'Fear', 20; 'The Fernery', 63; 'For the Marriage of Faustus and Helen', 10, 12, 13, 46–7, 53–4, 60, 66, 68, 71–3, 73–4, 76, 77–80, 82, 84, 88–9, 91, 100, 111, 127, 131, 137, 148, 153, 170, 192–5; 'Forgetfulness', 20, 38–9; 'Four Poems by Hart Crane', 188; 'Garden Abstract', 62; 'General Aims and Theories', 31, 37, 72, 74–5, 77, 110; 'The Great Western Plains', 63; 'The Harbor Dawn', 133–4, 144, 159; 'Havana Rose', 168, 176, 188, 189–90; 'The Hive', 20, 41, 43–4, 47; 'The Hour', 169n20, 187; 'The Hurricane', 169n20; 'In Shadow', 41; 'Interior', 53; 'Interludium to "La Montagne") by Lachaise', 80, 83; 'Island Quarry', 169n20; *Key West*, 2, 15, 119, 167, 169–72, 188, 198; 'Knitting Needles and Poppycock', 12, 59, 66; 'Lachrymae Christi', 34; 'Legende', 38, 53; 'Locutions des Pierrots', 38n106, 61, 100, 111; 'The Mango Tree', 63, 170, 172; 'March', 62n33; 'The Mermen', 107; 'Modern Craft', 38, 41, 44–7, 88; 'Moment Fugue', 124, 158, 169n22; 'My Grandmother's Love Letters', 13, 63, 96–101, 105, 170; 'A Name for All', 172; 'National Winter Garden', 146–7, 160; 'Nopal', 2, 15, 167–8, 179–82, 189; 'North Labrador', 53; 'A Note on H. W. Minns', 153; 'Note on the Paintings of David Siqueiros', 15, 179; 'O Carib Isle', 138, 169–72;'October-November', 37–8, 41–2, 92; 'Old Song', 172–3; 'Passage', 32, 106, 135–6, 146; 'Pastorale', 99, 101–2; 'A Persuasion', 61; 'Porphyro in Akron', 48, 53–4, 61, 72–3; 'Possessions', 99n27; 'Poster', ('Voyages I') 80, 84, 88–90, 92; 'Postscript', 39, 41, 46; 'Powhatan's Daughter' ('The Dance'), 49, 134–5, 138, 159, 182; 'Praise for an Urn: to E.N.', 96, 99–100, 136, 146; 'Recitative', 99n27, 103; 'The River', 69, 152, 159–60; 'Royal Palm', 172; 'The Springs of Guilty Song', 60n22, 76, 77–80; 'Southern Cross', 146–7; 'Stark Major', 62; 'Sunday Morning Apples: To William Sommer', 80, 83, 99n27, 102; 'Three Songs from *The Bridge*', 133, 135, 137, 146–7, 154; 'To Brooklyn Bridge', 44, 75–6, 108, 132, 134–5, 136, 145, 147–8; 'To the Cloud Juggler', 155n128; 'To Emily Dickinson', 169n22, 173; 'To J.H.', 86n159; 'To Portapovitch', 20, 41, 51–2; 'To *The Pagan*', 35; 'Tragi-Comique', 12, 20; 'The Tunnel', 135, 139–40, 144–6, 148–55, 159, 173, 194; 'The Urn', 188–90, 193n10; 'Van Winkle', 135, 144, 148, 155, 159–60; 'Virginia', 144, 146, 150; 'Voyages', 12n52, 13, 60, 80–93, 100, 111, 125, 127, 131, 137, 146–8, 170, 187; 'Well/Well/Not-At-All', 50; *White Buildings*, 2, 10n 37 and 39, 17n1, 21, 37, 41, 52, 79, 89, 91, 101, 116–17, 125–7, 134, 145–6, 162, 171, 173; 'The Wine Menagerie', 11, 13, 27, 31–2, 54, 79, 90, 100, 127, 135, 136n33
writer's block, 53, 61, 184
creative-critical practices, 10–11, 13, 16, 39, 87–9, 91, 94, 97, 103, 105, 108, 191–9; *see also* editing

Creeley, Robert, 192
The Criterion, 4, 5, 32, 134–6, 144–54; see also Eliot, T. S.
Crosby, Caresse, 145, 155–6
　publication of *The Bridge*, 129, 132–3, 139, 156, 159, 185
Crosby, Harry, 154, 155–6, 157, 194n12
　elegy by Hart Crane, 155n128
Cubism, 14–15, 28, 78, 120, 131–2, 141–3, 158, 160, 165, 167
　and collage, 132
Cullen, Countee, 119
cummings, e. e., 65, 83, 174, 179
Curry, Routledge, 44

Dada, 1–4, 7, 48, 57, 63, 65–6, 69, 71–5, 81, 98, 100, 130, 132, 183n92
　and masculinity, 58–9
　significant gesture, 58–9, 183n92
D'Annunzio, Gabriele, 35
Davies, Arthur B., 33n83
Davies, Catherine A., 8
Decadence, 10–12, 18, 21–33, 35–7, 54, 95, 103, 106, 115, 126
　post-Decadence, 4, 9, 12–13, 17–55, 92, 95, 115, 187
Dell, Floyd, 58
Delpar, Helen, 182
Dempsey, James, 98
De Quincey, Thomas, 18, 112
de Sade, Marquis, 146
de Valera, Éamon, 178
Devlin, Denis, 192, 196
The Dial, 3, 4, 5, 7–8, 11, 13, 47, 53–4, 64, 65–7, 77, 79, 82, 90, 93, 94–6, 96–103, 103–16, 117, 123, 125, 127, 132, 134–6, 144, 162, 172–3; see also Gregory, Alyse; Moore, Marianne; Seldes, Gilbert; Thayer, Scofield; Watson, James Sibley
Dickinson, Emily, 8, 94n4
di Prima, Diane
　Revolutionary Letters, 131

Dodge, Mabel, 19
The Double Dealer, 12n50, 38n106, 47, 48, 61, 63, 72, 100, 111, 161
Douglas, Lord Alfred, 23
Drayton, Michael, 66
Dreiser, Theodore, 35
Drinkwater, John, 114

Eastman, Max, 4n9, 9, 10n36, 91, 123, 124, 157, 174–5, 196
　'The Cult of Unintelligibility', 4n9, 10, 91, 123, 157, 174
　'Poets Talking to Themselves', 10, 154, 174
École des Beaux-Arts, 83
Edelman, Lee, 4n9, 8, 12, 114, 130
Edgeworth, Maria, 107
editing (periodicals), 3, 23, 29, 33–4, 39, 47–8, 96, 120, 124–5, 156–7, 162–3, 172
　as adversarial, 10–11, 56–93
　as creative, 10–11, 13, 94–6, 103–16
　interventions, 11, 14, 66, 77–80, 94–127, 117
The Egoist, 24, 115
elegy, 146, 155n128, 198
　elegies to Hart Crane, 15, 173, 184, 188, 191–9
Eliot, T. S., 46, 59, 73, 79–80, 97, 106, 115, 123–4, 135–6, 139, 144–6, 148, 189
　Four Quartets, 145
　'The Love Song of J. Alfred Prufrock', 31, 119
　The Sacred Wood, 104
　The Waste Land, 140, 148–54, 160, 167, 197
　see also *The Criterion*
Elliot, Paul, 154, 158; see also *transition*
Ellis, Vivien Locke, 34
Eluard, Paul, 65, 69
Evans, Walker
　photographs of Brooklyn Bridge, 133
The Exile, 154

INDEX

exile journals, 1, 8, 10, 13, 18, 34, 47–8, 54, 56–93, 95, 100, 102–3, 121, 127, 155, 171, 174

Faber and Faber, 144
Fargue, Leon-Paul, 158
Fawcett, James Waldo, 52–3; *see also* *The Modernist*
Ferrer, Francisco, 52; *see also* *The Modern School*
fin-de-siècle, 19–20, 26, 31–3, 35–6, 39, 56, 53–4, 92, 124
First World War, 57, 71, 145, 156
Fitzgerald, F. Scott, 144
Fitzpatrick, Orla, 179
Fletcher, John Gould, 119
Flint, F. S., 24, 39, 41, 100
Ford, Ford Madox, 119
  Antwerp, 135
Ford, Mark, 84
  'The Death of Hart Crane', 16, 195
fragment forms, 14, 69, 78, 84, 91, 105, 113, 118, 122, 128–44, 148, 151–5, 160, 162, 164–5, 168, 176, 180, 185, 189; *see also* publishing as form
Frank, Waldo, 50, 72, 84, 89, 98, 106, 109, 126, 132, 135, 140, 146–7, 164, 167–8, 183–6
  America Hispana, 167
French Line Pier, 57
Friendship and Freedom, 8, 22
Frost, Robert, 119, 153
The Fugitive, 34n84, 47, 61–2, 82n135, 121
  Nashville Prize, 62
  see also Ransom, John Crowe; Riding, Laura; Tate, Allen
Futurism, 4, 59, 62, 68, 72, 74, 120
  American Futurism, 57, 62–73, 74

Gabriel, Daniel, 14n58
Gargoyle, 12, 44, 47–8, 57, 62–3, 120, 132, 154; *see also* Moss, Arthur; Munson, Gorham

Geddes, Virgil, 35
Georgian poetry, 102
Gerber, Henry, 8–9
Gide, André, 189
Giles, Paul, 8, 59, 75, 130, 157
Ginsberg, Allen
  'Hart Crane', 192–3, 195
The Glebe, 39
Goldman, Emma, 51
Gold Rush (1849), 138–9
Graves, Robert, 155–6
Green, Fiona, 107
Greenberg, Samuel, 83–4
Greenwich Village, 24–5, 40
Gregory, Alyse, 96, 98
Grito, 177, 191n59
Group Mu, 128, 132
Guardian (Philadelphia), 47n151, 85
Guggenheim Foundation, 6, 15, 166–7, 169, 176–8
Guggenheim, Rose, 67
Gurdjieff, George, 183

Hall, Donald, 54, 103, 106–7
  interview with Marianne Moore, 95
Hall, Susanne, 178–9n65, 181–2, 186
Halpern, Rob, 192
Hammer, Langdon, 9, 12, 18, 73, 114, 129–30, 163, 169n21, 170, 195
Hamsun, Knut, 35
Hankel, Walter S. (group pseudonym), 80–1; *see also Aesthete, 1925*
Harding, Jason, 5, 144
Hardy, Thomas, 105
Harper's, 157, 174–5
Harris, Frank, 22
Hart, Elizabeth Belden, 101
  as a subject of Hart Crane's poetry, 99–101
Hartley, Marsden
  Eight Bells Folly: Memorial to Hart Crane, 195
Hay-Quesada Treaty, 187
H. D., 24, 62, 97, 102, 106
Heaney, Seamus, 126

248

Heap, Jane, 17, 61, 65, 85–6, 96;
  see also *The Little Review*
Hemingway, Ernest, 56–7, 155
Henderson, Alice Corbin, 49n156, 120;
  see also *Poetry*
Herrick, Robert, 72
Hill, Geoffrey
  'Improvisations for Hart Crane', 16, 106, 197
Hillyer, Robert, 107
Hobday, Charles, 145
Hoffman, F. J., C. F Ulrich and C. Allen, 68
USS Homeric, 156
homophobia, 8–9, 10, 21, 47, 54, 89, 95, 103, 115, 126, 162n159, 182, 187, 195–7; see also Crane, Hart, reception history
Hound & Horn, 128–9, 144, 161, 163, 184, 185
Hue & Cry, 80
Hughes, Langston, 119
Huitzilopochtli, 180
Hurwitz, Leo
  In Search of Hart Crane, 183n91, 185–6
Hutchinson, Percy, 143

Imagism, 4, 12, 21, 24, 32–47, 73, 75, 100, 111, 113, 115, 119–20, 174
  Des Imagistes, 39
Industrial Workers of the World (Wobblies), 33
International News Service, 56
In Which, 24
Irish Civil War, 178; see also O'Malley, Ernie
The Irish Press, 178; see also de Valera, Éamon; O'Malley, Ernie
Irving, Washington, 154
Irwin, John T., 8, 13, 60, 86, 101, 113, 147, 152

James, Henry, 105
jazz, 48, 68, 72, 148–51

Jefferson, Mary, 154
Jefferson, Thomas, 154
Jolas, Eugene, 34, 35, 50, 154–6, 170–1
  The Man From Babel, 155
  'The Revolution of the Word', 156–8, 171
  see also *transition*
Jones, Gavin, 50
Jonson, Ben, 66, 106
Josephson, Hannah, 58
Josephson, Matthew, 2, 50, 56–8, 63–74, 76–8, 80–2, 85–7, 89, 109, 120n138, 121, 154, 172, 186
  and Dada, 70–2
  Galimathias, 70–1
  Life Among the Surrealists, 81, 64n45
  'Pursuit', 76–7
  see also *Broom*; *Secession*; *Aesthete, 1925*
Joyce, James, 56, 119, 124, 157, 174
  Finnegans Wake, 130, 170–1
  Ulysses, 86, 98, 118n128

Kahn, Otto, 66, 87, 129–30, 133, 138–9, 160, 167, 185
Keats, John, 63, 73
  'The Eve of St. Agnes', 72–3
  negative capability, 73
  'Ode on a Grecian Urn', 46
Kenner, Hugh, 192
Kent, Rockwell, 51, 52
Kerfoot, J. B., 47–8
Khalip, Jacques, 15n65, 193
Kingham, Victoria, 22, 33, 35, 53n178
Kling, Joseph, 11, 18–20, 22n26, 23, 33–5, 39–42, 44, 47–53, 73;
  see also *The Pagan*
Knox, George, 141
Kreymborg, Alfred, 21, 24, 52, 57, 67–8, 99, 116
  Edna, The Girl of the Street, 22, 24
  Mushrooms, 24
  To My Mother, 24

249

Lachaise, Gaston, 80, 82–3, 98, 141, 192
Laforgue, Jules, 38, 46, 61, 100, 111, 115
Laib, Monnie, 42
Larbaud, Valery, 156, 189
larus: the celestial visitor, 62
Latham, Sean, and Robert Scoles, 16
Laukhuff, Richard, 26
Lawrence, D. H., 13
Léger, Fernand, 62
Levine, Caroline, 3n7
Lewis, Wyndham, 62
The Liberator, 51
The Link: A Monthly Social Medium for Lonely People, 9, 22
The Listener, 179n72
Littérature, 69, 155; see also Breton, André; Soupault, Philippe, Aragon, Louis
The Little Review, 24, 39, 41, 47, 51–3, 60–1, 63–6, 80, 82, 84–93, 97, 98, 118, 120–1, 141, 142; see also Anderson, Margaret; Heap, Jane
Loeb, Harold, 2, 57, 63–4, 67–8, 70, 77–9
Logan, William, 15, 195–7
Lohf, Kenneth, 109n84, 132
The London Mercury, 145
Longworth, Deborah, 27
Loveman, Sam, 156, 168, 188
Lowell, Amy, 40, 61, 66, 67–9, 102, 119
Lowell, Robert
   and Allen Tate, 195–6
   'Words for Hart Crane', 195–6
Loy, Mina
   Love Songs, 135
Lynd, Robert, 105

McCarthy, John R., 40
McGann, Jerome, 4, 138
McKenzie, D. F., 4, 8, 15
MacLeish, Archibald, 103, 107
'machine age', 11, 19, 36, 48, 53–4, 57, 59–60, 64–5, 68–9, 70–4, 76, 78, 93
Mallarmé, Stéphane, 8, 19, 37–8

Marek, Jayne, 5, 96, 104, 107–8
Mariani, Paul, 27n53, 61, 96n10, 162, 197
Marinetti, Filippo, 157
The Masses, 34, 85
   see also *The New Masses*
Matisse, Henri, 62
The Measure, 61, 161; see Anderson, Maxwell; Colum, Padraic; Nicholl, Louise Townsend
Melville, Herman, 8, 138, 152
Menes, Orlando Ricardo, 192
   'Hear Me, Hart Crane', 198
Mew, Charlotte, 115
Mexican muralism, 2, 4, 167, 179, 181, 189
   Churrigueresque, 167, 181
   see also Orozco, Clemente; Rivera, Diego; Siqueiros, David Alfaro
Meyer, Agnes Ernst, 143
Millay, Edna St. Vincent, 119
Miller, Cristiane, 49–50
The Minaret, 24
Minns, H. W., 15
Mirbeau, Octave, 35
Mircir, Melanie, 5
The Modernist, 38, 47, 52–3, 61; see also Fawcett, James Waldo
The Modern School, 20n12, 21, 39, 47, 51–3; see also Zigrosser, Carl; Ferrer, Francisco
Modotti, Tina, 176, 179
Moe, Henry Allen, 167, 178
Monro, Harold, 67, 135
Monroe, Harriet, 2n6, 4n9, 9, 10, 11, 13–14, 31–2, 40, 74, 91, 95–6, 157, 164, 168, 172, 173–4, 175, 179, 196
   'A Discussion with Hart Crane', 116–27
   see also Crane, Hart, reception history
Moore, Marianne, 5, 26, 54, 65–6, 79, 94–6, 100, 117, 119, 127, 173
   creative-critical practice, 10, 13, 103–5

editing 'The Wine Menagerie', 10–11, 13–14, 54–5, 79, 103–16, 123, 124, 126
'Holes bored in a workbag by the scissors', 24
'Picking and Choosing', 94, 105
'Pym', 104–6, 111n94
see also The Dial; Hall, Donald; Crane, Hart, reception history; works by Hart Crane, 'Again'
Morand, Paul, 98
Moréas, Jean, 37–8, 75
'Symbolist Manifesto', 37
Moretti, Franco, 6
Moss, Arthur, 62–3; *see also* Gargoyle
Moss, Howard, 161n153
Mouffe, Chantal, 11, 13, 59
Moult, Thomas, 102
Mourant, Chris, 5
Munro, Niall, 8, 12, 14, 18, 24, 28, 36, 130
Munson, Gorham B., 1–2, 7, 20, 23, 26, 31, 33, 35–6, 47–8, 50, 51, 52, 53n179, 56–77, 77–80, 80–5, 87, 90, 99, 120n138, 121, 146n82, 183, 184–6
Awakening Twenties, 47, 67
see also Secession; Broom; Gargoyle
Murry, John Middleton, 34
Myles, Eileen
'hart!', 16, 191–4
Not Me, 194

Nagle, Edward, 35, 83, 141
Nagle, Isabel Dutaud, 83, 141
The Nation, 4, 96, 127, 168–73
New Criticism, 8, 75, 129, 191
The New English Weekly, 183–4
The New Masses, 85
The New Republic, 3, 4, 68, 96, 97, 118, 126, 127, 161, 168, 170–3, 177, 182–8, 196; *see also* Cowley, Malcolm
New York Herald Tribune, 107, 156, 162, 174

New York Socialist Party, 23
The New York Society for the Suppression of Vice (Comstock), 24, 98, 146
The New York Times, 62, 105, 125, 143, 197
The New York Tribune, 150
Nicholl, Louise Townsend, 61, 161; *see also* The Measure

Ocampo, Victoria, 189; *see also* SUR
O'Flaherty, Liam, 178
O'Hara, Frank, 83, 192
O'Keeffe, Georgia, 141
O'Malley, Cormac, 167, 178n68
O'Malley, Ernie, 2, 15, 166–8, 176–82
O'Neill, Eugene, 52
The Open Window, 34
Opffer, Emil, 89, 91–2, 146–7, 189
Oppenheim, James, 50
SS *Orizaba*, 2, 183, 189–90
Orozco, Clemente, 179; *see also* Mexican muralism
Others, 24, 39, 50, 67, 119, 120, 135, 143
Otis Lithography Company of Cleveland, 82
Ouspensky, P. D., 183
The Outlook and Independent, 161

The Pagan, 7, 11–12, 18–24, 33–47, 47–51, 52–3, 61–3, 67, 73, 92, 101, 115, 143, 192
The Pagan Anthology, 20, 35n94
see also Decadence; Imagism; Kling, Joseph
The Pagan Review, 34
The Paris Review, 95, 103, 107
Parkhurst, Winthrop, 39–40
parody, 27, 29, 39–40, 47–8, 88–9, 127
Pearse, Padraic, 52
pedagogy, 51–2
see also Ferrer, Francisco; *The Modern School*

Perloff, Marjorie, 69, 132, 192n3
The Phoenix, 24
Picabia, Francis, 86
Picasso, Pablo, 62
Plath, Sylvia, 197
Pocahontas, 139, 154, 159
Poe, Edgar Allan, 8, 84, 138
Poetry, 3, 11, 13, 15, 24, 31, 39, 65, 67, 91, 93, 95–6, 102, 107, 111, 114, 116–27, 129, 131n15, 132, 134–5, 144, 145, 162–3, 167, 169, 170, 172–5, 182, 188–90
   Helen Haire Levinson Prize, 166n3, 169
   Poetry Foundation, 119
   see also Monroe, Harriet; Henderson, Alice Corbin; Zabel, Morton Dauwen
polyglot modernism, 7, 19, 34–5, 48–51, 155, 157
Portapovitch, Anna, 52
Portapovitch, Stanislav, 52
Porter, Katherine Anne, 176, 189
Pound, Ezra, 24, 26, 32, 39–42, 46, 52, 81, 86, 97, 100, 106, 107, 114–15, 119, 120, 121, 124, 126, 131, 154, 192
   The Cantos, 97, 121, 131
Powel, Gretchen and Peter, 142
Prampolini, Ernesto, 67
Pratt, Mary Louise, 187
publishing (periodicals)
   costs and finances, 34, 57, 64–6, 67, 118–19
   print runs and circulation, 7, 15, 33, 65, 86, 97–9, 127, 167, 170, 172–73
publishing as form, 10, 12, 14, 78, 91–2, 130, 132–44
Puccini, Giacomo
   La Bohème, 26, 29–30

The Quill, 18, 22, 62; *see also* Moss, Arthur

ragtime, 48, 150

Rainey, Lawrence, 4, 98n21, 156
Raisin, Ovro'om, 43
Raleigh, Sir Walter, 138, 154
Ramazani, Jahan, 4–5, 7, 19
Ransom, John Crowe, 144
Ravel, Maurice
   Boléro, 195
Ray, Man, 52, 56, 62
Read, Herbert, 145
Reed, Brian, 8, 60, 154
Regan, Stephen, 198n31
Reverdy, Pierre, 75
Revista de Occidente, 32, 41, 126
Ribemont-Dessaignes, Georges, 69
Rich, Adrienne, 192–4
   'The Night Has a Thousand Eyes', 16, 193–4
Richards, I. A., 32
Rickword, Edgell, 126, 144, 145–7, 152, 156
   'The Handmaid of Religion', 146
   see also The Calendar of Modern Letters
Ridge, Lola, 52, 57, 67
Riding, Laura, 62, 121, 144, 146, 156, 161n153; *see also The Fugitive*
Rilke, Rainer Maria
   Die Sonette an Orpheus, 135
Rimbaud, Arthur, 8, 16, 115, 197
Rivera, Diego, 176, 179, 181; *see also* Mexican muralism
Roberts, Michael, 154, 183
Robertson, Dr John Dill, 150
Robinson, Edwin Arlington, 97
Rodensky, Lisa, 35
Rogers, Stephen, 18, 22, 23
Rogue, 21, 22
Rorty, James, 85
Rosenfeld, Paul, 58, 64
Rourke, Milton, 177, 189
Rowe, H. D., 2n6
Rubio, Salvador Cortés, 181
Rychtarik, Charlotte, 50, 109
Rychtarik, Richard, 109

S4N, 12, 47, 58, 92, 119
Sáenz, Moisés, 177–8
Sage, Robert, 154; *see also transition*
St Augustine of Hippo, 151
Sandburg, Carl, 48, 102, 119
Sanger, Margaret, 53n178
La Santé, 156
The Saturday Review of Literature, 3, 96, 127, 134–5, 137, 144, 162, 168–74; *see also* Benét, William Rose; Canby, Henry Seidel
Schlegel, Friedrich, 141
Schmidt, Michael and Alan Young, 145
Schmidt, Michael, and Alan Young, 145
Schmitt, Carl, 52, 141
Schnitzler, Arthur, 35
Schneider, Isidor, 58
Schoonmaker, Frank, 80
Schwartz, Joseph, and Robert C. Schweik, 2n6
Seaver, Edwin, 9, 80–2, 84, 84n149, 87
Secession, 1–2, 3, 7, 10, 12–13, 33, 47–8, 53, 56–60, 74–7, 77–80, 80–93, 119–21, 123, 146, 153–4, 156, 173, 184–5, 186, 192
  conflict with *Broom*, 1–2, 56–9, 62–73
  see also Broom; Cowley, Malcolm; Dada; Josephson, Matthew; Munson, Gorham; Surrealism; Wheelwright, John Brooks
The Second American Caravan, 134; *see also The American Caravan*
Sedgwick, Eve Kosofsky, 25, 95n9, 113, 194
Seldes, Gilbert, 96, 98–9, 106, 127
The Seven Arts, 50, 67
Shaw, Lytle, 60n21
Shakespeare, William, 172, 198
  Romeo and Juliet, 88
Sharp, William, 34
Shaw, George Bernard, 24, 105
Shelley, Percy Bysshe, 196
  fragment poems, 160
  'Ode to the West Wind', 160n150

Shepard, Odell, 162–3
Sherry, Vincent, 114–15
Simon, Marc, 83, 167n8, 169–70, 189
Siqueiros, David Alfaro, 15, 177, 179, 189
  guest of Hart Crane, 177
  portrait of Hart Crane, 179
  see also Mexican muralism
Simpson, Lesley, 166, 182, 189
Sitwell, Edith, 174
Smith, Judson, 81
So, Richard Jean, and Hoyt Long, 6
Society for Human Rights (Chicago), 8
Sologub, Fyodor, 35
Sommer, William, 80, 82–3, 102, 192
Soupault, Philippe, 65, 68, 155, 156–7
Southern Agrarians, 61–2; *see also The Fugitive*
Spence, Lewis, 140
Spratling, William, 176–7
Stein, Gertrude, 56, 57, 68, 70, 103, 107, 124, 141, 143, 144, 145, 146, 158, 172, 174
Stella, Joseph, 141–2, 144
  Brooklyn Bridge, 67, 142
Stevens, Wallace, 52, 65, 67, 110, 119, 192
  'Earthy Anecdote', 51
  'Thirteen Ways of Looking at a Blackbird, 143
Stieglitz, Arthur, 47, 120n138, 141–2; *see also 291; Camera Work*
Stramm, August, 158
Stravinsky, Igor, 113
Stubbs, Tara, 107
Der Sturm, 24
Sumner, John M., 98
Sunwise Bookshop, 67
SUR, 189; *see also* Ocampo, Victoria
Surrealism, 1–3, 4, 7, 59, 69, 120, 130
  proto-surrealism, 13, 19, 59, 73–7, 92, 171
  metaphor, 13, 20, 54, 73–7, 75–6, 92, 98, 141, 157–8, 160, 171
  see also Crane, Hart, 'logic of metaphor'

Sutherland, Camilla, 174n45
Swinburne, Algernon Charles, 8, 18
Symbolism, 3, 13, 33–47, 60, 73, 75
    115, 120
    post-Symbolism, 20, 47–8
Symons, Julian, 194n15
Symons, Arthur, 23

Taggard, Genevieve, 17, 37, 41, 61, 101,
    117, 125, 162, 174
Tagore, Rabindranath, 52, 119
Tapper, Gordon, 13–14, 60, 93n195, 113
Tashjian, Dickran, 48, 65
Tate, Allen, 9, 14, 52, 61, 80, 85, 121,
    128, 144, 161–2, 164, 172, 183n90
    'A Distinguished Poet', 129, 166
    'Euthanasia', 61
    'Hart Crane and the American Mind',
        118, 163
    and Lowell, Robert, 195–6
    'In Memoriam Hart Crane', 184–5
    'Retroduction to American History', 154
Telling Tales, 135
Tepoztécatl, 177
Thayer, Scofield, 7, 64, 96–8, 100,
    108, 118n128; see also *The Dial*;
    Watson, James Sibley
This Quarter, 154
Times Literary Supplement, 126
Tipyn o'Bob, 104
Tóibín, Colm, 4n9
Toklas, Alice B., 156
transition, 3, 34n84, 47, 50, 62,
    75n101, 120, 121, 132, 134, 138,
    142, 144, 154–9, 169–71, 187
    'Proclamation', 157
    see also Jolas, Eugene; Paul, Elliot;
        Sage, Robert; Surrealism
transnationalism, 3–7, 10, 12, 19, 21,
    23, 30, 47–50, 54, 59–60, 62, 63,
    87, 98, 102, 103, 120, 140
Tree, Iris, 115
RMS Tuscania, 156
Tzara, Tristan, 1, 56–7, 65, 69–70, 72;
    see also *Le Coeur à Barbe*

UEPOC (Pro-worker and Peasant Student
    Union, Mexico), 189; see also *Grito*
United States Postal Service, 98; see also
    censorship
El Universal, 176; see also Crane, Hart,
    interviews
University of North Carolina (Chapel
    Hill), 137, 186; see also *Contempo*
Unterecker, John, 2n4, 22n19, 48,
    170n24, 183, 185–6
Untermeyer, Louis, 61, 64, 67–8, 85, 102

Vail, Laurence, 62
Vanderbilt University, 47, 61; see also
    The Fugitive
Vanity Fair, 15, 97–8, 167, 169
    'Singers of the New Age', 15
Vildrac, Charles, 99, 100, 115
    rhythmic constant, 100–1
The Virginia Quarterly, 137
Vorticism, 62

Wall Street Crash, 118
Walsh, Ernest, 154
Walton, Eda Lou, 167
Watson, James Sibley, 7, 98, 108
Watts, Isaac, 113
Weber, Brom, 8, 22n20, 26, 32, 81,
    99, 169
Weir, David, 36–7
Westcott, Glenway, 58
Weston, Edward, 176, 179
Wheelwright, John Brooks, 80
    edit of 'For the Marriage of Faustus
        and Helen', 66, 77, 79
    'To Hart Crane', 173, 184
    see also *Secession*
White, Eric B., 7, 25, 81n131
Whitman, Walt, 8, 9, 80, 88, 113, 126,
    137–8, 140, 147, 152, 185
    Leaves of Grass, 113, 137–8, 161
    'Passage to India', 137
    'The Sleepers', 113
    'Song of Exposition', 137
    'Song of Myself', 137

Wiegand, Charmion von, 66, 142
Wieners, John, 194n12
Wilde, Oscar, 8, 19, 22–5, 29, 35–6, 42–3, 146
  The Ballad of Reading Gaol, 25
  'Impressions of America', 22
  Incarceration, 27–8
  'La Mer', 31
  The Portrait of Mr. W.H., 115
  'Quantum Mutata', 22
  Salomé, 28–9, 31, 35, 43, 49
Williams, Tennessee, 139
Williams, William Carlos, 80, 82, 89n177, 106, 119, 121, 143, 144, 185, 187–8
  Kora in Hell, 106
  'Hart Crane', 187
The Wilson Bulletin, 129; *see also* Crane, Hart, interviews
Winters, Yvor, 9, 14, 54, 68, 109, 116–17, 119, 120, 121, 124–5, 162–4, 196
  advocacy for Hart Crane's poetry, 116–17, 124–5
  'Hart Crane's Poems', 91
  Primitivism and Decadence, 54, 89n176, 126, 162

'The Progress of Hart Crane', 10, 117–18, 162
  see also Crane, Hart, reception history
Wishart & Company, 146
Wolff, David
  'Remembering Hart Crane', 184
Woolf, Virginia, 68
Wordsworth, William, 136
  The Prelude, 136

The Yale Review, 125
Yeats, William Butler, 119, 126
The Yellow Book, 23, 28
Yingling, Thomas, 8, 12, 18, 25, 45, 46, 60, 110–11, 130, 148, 162n159, 164

Zabel, Morton Dauwen, 117–18, 172, 175; *see also Poetry*
Zigrosser, Carl, 20n12, 21, 51–3;
  see also The Modern School
Zinsser, Hans, 189
  As I Remember Him, 189–90
  Rats, Lice and History, 190
Zorach, Marguerite, 143
Zukofsky, Louis, 35
  A, 131n15